D1544845

THE EUROPEAN UNDERSTANDING OF INDIA

General Editors of the Series

K. A. BALLHATCHET

P. J. MARSHALL

D. F. POCOCK

European attempts to understand India have been pursued in a variety of fields. Many of the books and articles that resulted are still of great historical importance. Not only do they provide valuable information about the India of the time; they are also of significance in the intellectual history of Europe. Each volume in the present series has been edited by a scholar who is concerned to elucidate both its Indian and its European relevance.

The Economic Development of India
under the East India Company
1814-58

The Economic Development of India under the East India Company 1814–58

A Selection of Contemporary Writings

Edited by

K. N. CHAUDHURI

Lecturer in Economic History
School of Oriental and African Studies
University of London

CAMBRIDGE

AT THE UNIVERSITY PRESS

1971

Published by the Syndics of the Cambridge University Press
Bentley House, 200 Euston Road, London N.W.1
American Branch: 32 East 57th Street, New York, N.Y.10022

© Cambridge University Press 1971

Library of Congress Catalogue Card Number: 78-129932

ISBN: 0 521 07933 0

Made and printed in Great Britain
by William Clowes and Sons, Limited
London, Beccles and Colchester

Contents

Note on Indian Currency and Weights

CURRENCY

100 sicca rupees = 116 current rupees
100 Arcot rupees = 108 current rupees
100 Bombay rupees = 110 current rupees

(A current rupee was an imaginary coin, being money of account.)

1 sicca rupee = 16 annas = 64 pice
1 Bombay rupee = 4 quarters = 400 reas
1 Arcot rupee = 16 annas = 64 pice

In India sums larger than a thousand are always written in multiples of 100 and the punctuation after the first three digits from the right is every two digits instead of three.

1 lakh = 1,000 × 100 = 1,00,000 = 100,000 rupees
1 crore = 1,00,000 × 100 = 1,00,00,000 = 10,000,000 rupees

WEIGHTS

1 bazar maund = 40 seers = 640 chattaks = 82 lb. 2 oz. 2·1 dr.
1 factory maund = 40 seers = 640 chattaks = 74 lb. 10 oz. 10·6 dr.
1 Bombay maund = 40 seers = 28 lb.

Introduction[1]

I

This book brings together a number of tracts on Indian economic problems,[2] including the evidence given by Horsley Palmer before the Select Committee of the House of Commons in 1831. The problems discussed here are primarily concerned with Indian trade during the period from 1814 to 1858, as the regulation and management of India's external trade and finance was one of the most urgent of the many economic problems facing British policy-makers in the Indian empire. During the three decades following the Charter Act of 1813, which partially ended the East India Company's exclusive commercial monopoly, India's foreign trade underwent some fundamental changes, after having retained its undisturbed character for many centuries. Some of these were structural changes, others quantitative. Between 1814 and 1858 the value and volume of Indian exports and imports more than quadrupled. But at the same time the commodity composition and direction of trade also changed. The most important change, however, concerned India's balance of payments and owed its origin to the military conquest of India by the East India Company, and to the fact that Britain was fast becoming the world's leading industrial nation and her capital city the dominant centre of international trade and finance.[3] Thus British influence, both political and economic, appears to have played a vital part in the transition of India's

[1] I am indebted to the Editors of the *Economic History Review* for permission to use material published in my article 'India's Foreign Trade and the Cessation of the East India Company's Trading Activities, 1828–40', *Econ. Hist. Rev.* XIX (2nd series, 1966), 345–63.

[2] In these reprints the substance of the texts is exactly as in the originals, except where editor's remarks have been added. Capitalization and punctuation have been modernized, however, and italics used more sparingly. The printing of numbers has also been made more consistent with current practice.

[3] Cf. L. H. Jenks, *The Migration of British Capital to 1875* (London, 2nd ed., 1963), pp. 193–208.

external trade from a traditional to a modern pattern, and to have introduced features which it was to retain for more than a hundred years.

Apart from questions arising out of commercial problems, the works reprinted in this volume are also concerned with the general economic development of India and with an analysis of the effects of British rule on the sub-continent. It is generally agreed that the first half of the nineteenth century was a crucial period of transition for India's domestic economy.[1] For it was during these years, it has been said, that the political association with Great Britain transformed India into a primary producing country with her economy controlled and directed from outside.[2] The economic potential of the colonies provided Britain with a convenient means of meeting the rising needs of her industries for raw materials and of securing food supplies for an expanding population. Also 'economic imperialism', in the sense of a conscious attempt on the part of Britain to exploit her overseas dependencies for economic purposes, was already becoming a reality.[3] Foreign trade, assisted by the fiscal policy of the British Government in India, was taken to be one of the main instruments of this change. When the Government commuted the traditional Indian land-revenue payments into cash sums and fixed them rigorously, the effect of such a policy, it has been alleged, was to force the Indian cultivators to produce commercial crops for the export market at the expense of food crops and subsistence agriculture.[4]

If the British land policy was one aspect of the alleged transformation of India into a colonial type of economy, its commercial counterpart was the absence of protection which exposed India to the full competition of British manufacturing industries, many of which, because of the shift in the production functions

[1] Cf. A. Tripathi, *Trade and Finance in the Bengal Presidency 1793–1833* (Calcutta, 1956), pp. 137–8; D. Thorner, *Land and Labour in India* (London, 1962), p. 25; W. C. Neale, *Economic Change in Rural India* (New Haven and London, 1962), pp. 6–8.

[2] Cf. *Minutes of Evidence taken before the Select Committee of the House of Lords appointed to consider the Petition of the East India Company for Relief 1840*, Parliamentary Papers, 1840, vol. 7, Q. 191.

[3] Jenks, *Migration of British Capital*, p. 197.

[4] Thorner, *Land and Labour*, p. 108.

brought about by the Industrial Revolution, were in a position to undersell Indian domestic products. This was a process that caused from quite early on considerable contemporary disquiet. Charles Grant, for example, in his evidence before the Parliamentary Committee of 1821 questioned the justice of allowing an expansion of imports into India of British goods which could compete on favourable terms with the domestic product, while Indian manufactures were shut out from the British market by high protective duties.[1] But by and large the decline of the Indian textile and to a certain extent other manufacturing industries and the accompanying re-allocation of resources to the production of commercial crops for export not only provided the advocates of the newly developing theory of comparative costs in international trade with a near-perfect example, but by the same token were later used by nationalist historians of India as the lynch-pin in their arguments against what they considered to be the exploitation of the country by the economic system of the imperial power.[2]

It should perhaps be noted that the British policy in regard to the changing productive system of India did not stand in isolation. Other colonial powers were faced with very similar problems which were the outcome of economic changes in Europe itself. For example, the Dutch administration in the East Indies found itself, upon the collapse of the Dutch East India Company, confronted with the almost identical problem of devising a system that would lead to the production of export crops needed in the home country. The essential difference was that whereas after various experiments the Dutch were compelled to adopt a method of forced cultivation, the so-called 'culture system', in India the working of market capitalism succeeded in a large measure in bringing about the desired objective.[3] The origin and role of the market mechanism as it

[1] *Third Report before the Select Committee of the House of Commons*, 1821, p. 304; Parliamentary Papers, 1821, vol. 6 [paper 746].

[2] See Crawfurd in the text; for the nationalist viewpoint see R. C. Dutt, *Economic History of British India* (London, 1904), pp. vii–viii.

[3] Cf. J. S. Furnivall, *Netherlands India: A Study in Plural Economy* (Cambridge, 1944); A. de Kat Angelino, *Colonial Policy* (The Hague, 1931); Neale, *Economic Change*.

developed in India in the nineteenth century have caused considerable controversy. It has been widely assumed that the penetration of the Indian economy by a capitalist system was a British responsibility, the expression 'capitalism' being interpreted in its classic Marxist sense as a system which not only leads to the creation of a final product market but also to one in which the factors of production themselves are saleable commodities.[1] In India the evidence of this process is generally found in the emergence of a market in land, wage labour, and the whole changing character of economic relationships in agriculture. This was no doubt partly true, but the intensification of the market forces within the Indian economy in the early nineteenth century cannot be treated as a new and revolutionary situation. A comparison of Indian financial institutions and the actual operation of the market mechanism in the seventeenth and eighteenth centuries with those in the nineteenth reveals a continuity pointing to the existence of a well-developed commercial sector dependent on both a capital and labour market.[2] It is well known that the structure and organization of the textile industry, for example, were such as to make the position of the weavers practically indistinguishable from that of wage labour. Even more striking is the fact that a very large number of people were engaged in services of various kinds and paid in money wages. Again, the operation of the capital market, amply documented in both contemporary Indian and European sources, was not confined to the needs of trade and commerce but also served the handicraft industries and agriculture. In this respect, the analysis of the Indian situation by John Crawfurd in his *Sketch of the Commercial Resources . . . of British India* offers some interesting corroborative evidence. While extremely critical of what he considered to be India's economic backwardness, Crawfurd was impressed not so much by any fundamental structural dissimilarity between the European and Indian econo-

---

[1] For a recent statement of this view see S. N. Mukherjee's Introduction to *St Anthony's Papers, Number 18, South Asian Affairs Number Two* (Oxford, 1966), p. 16. For this interpretation of capitalism see M. Dobb, *Studies in the Development of Capitalism* (London, 1963), p. 7.

[2] Cf. Irfan Habib, 'Potentialities of Capitalistic Development in the Economy of Mughal India', *Journal of Economic History*, xxix (1969), 32–78.

mies, as by the apparent weakness of Indian financial institutions and industrial techniques.

A second distinctive feature of the relationship between India and Britain was the important role performed by India in the British international payments system in this period, which is well illustrated by the tracts printed here. Although in relation to India's total economic activity, the proportion of her foreign trade and its contribution to the total national income were not likely to be very substantial, nevertheless an element of instability was introduced through trade largely as a result of its connexion with national finance. In the eighteenth century British trade with Asia was mainly bilateral and it was carried on with the help of a massive export of precious metals from Europe. The rise of the China trade, however, with the rapid increase in the consumption of Chinese tea and silk in the European markets and the growth of Britain's cotton trade with America opened the way for greater diversification which reached its definitive form in the early nineteenth century on the basis of a series of triangular trading arrangements. The main nexus in this multilateral system was provided on the one hand by the triangular trading relations between India, China, and Britain, and on the other by Britain, China, and the United States. The reciprocal international payment arrangements between these trading partners were naturally determined by the balance of indebtedness among them. Since Britain occupied a large creditor position *vis-à-vis* India, who herself had a similar position in relation with the rest of the world, Britain was able to increase her imports from these areas while at the same time she increased her exports to India.[1] Thus apart from being a source of raw materials and a potential market for Britain's industrial products, India was of vital significance to Britain in a strictly financial sense. It was this aspect of their relationship that gave rise to the endless discussions in our period on how to remit home the 'Indian

[1] For Britain's multilateral trade structure and India's role in it see S. B. Saul, *Studies in British Overseas Trade 1870–1914* (Liverpool, 1960), chapter VIII; M. Greenberg, *British Trade and Opening of China, 1800–42* (Cambridge, 1951); R. C. O. Matthews, *A Study in Trade-Cycle History: Economic Fluctuations in Britain 1833–1842* (Cambridge, 1954), p. 79.

tribute', and the effect of an economic drain later provided the nationalist historians of India with a ready point of controversy.[1] However, as we shall see, India's strong position in regard to her export trade relieved her of much of the burden of acting as a clearing-house in an imperial system.

II

It is somewhat surprising that the period which, from the point of view of India's foreign trade, saw such radical and far-reaching changes should also have been the one to elude any modern historical analysis. Thus our basic source material still consists of nineteenth-century writings. The rationale behind the selection of the works presented in this volume was determined by two considerations: the need to illustrate the quantitative aspects of Indian trade, and to cast light on its institutional and policy features. The tract by Prinsep, and Tooke's Appendix come under the first category, and between them provide a full description of the dynamics of trade both at the beginning and the end of the period. Tooke's work is particularly valuable in this respect as it deals with the problem of capital inflow into India as a result of the railway construction, which was one complication absent during the earlier decades of the century. J. H. Palmer's parliamentary evidence and Crawfurd's *Sketch* on the other hand describe the mechanism of India's foreign commerce and its institutional history. These works are arranged in accordance with their content rather than in chronological order of writing.

Prinsep's tract was one of the earliest attempts to estimate India's balance of payments position and point out the close relationship between the unilateral transfer of funds from India – described by contemporaries as the 'remittance problem' – the volume of exports and imports, and the fluctuations in the foreign exchange market. It was also a systematic attempt

---

[1] The word 'drain' was used throughout the period to describe the problem of a unilateral transfer of capital from India, though it was widely popularized by the nationalists later. For the use of the expression in the eighteenth century, see K. A. Ballhatchet, 'European Relations with Asia', in *New Cambridge Modern History*, VIII (Cambridge, 1965), 231.

to correct the official undervaluation implicit in the methods followed by the Indian customs house in calculating India's foreign trade figures. Both in his analysis and presentation of factual material, it is apparent that Prinsep was considerably influenced by his commercial experience as a merchant engaged in Indian trade.

Of all the authors presented in this volume, Prinsep offers the smallest amount of biographical information. It is, however, certain that he was a member of the famous Prinsep family which was connected with India as merchants and high Government officials from 1770 to 1904. Sir Henry Thoby Prinsep in his unpublished account of the Prinsep family in India writes that the founder of the family, John Prinsep, had nine sons, 'my father Henry Thoby Prinsep . . . was followed by his next brother, William, in 1817, and by his elder brother, George (the third son) in 1825. They both became merchants, and both eventually joined the house of Palmer and Co. in Calcutta.'[1] The George Prinsep mentioned here is obviously the author of the *External Commerce of Bengal* which was published in 1823. Thus the information given in the above account would appear to be slightly inaccurate, since in his preface George Alexander Prinsep states that he visited Calcutta in 1822 from Bombay for three months in order to collect material for his book. His firm is listed in the *East India Register* among the British merchants trading in Bombay in 1823 and it continues to be listed until 1828. In the following year, his name disappears from the Bombay firms and reappears in the Bengal register which mentions his being in the service of Palmer & Co. since 1825.[2] This was apparently the source of confusion in Sir Henry Thoby's account, for it is likely that he became an agent of the Palmer Company in 1825, although his firm continued to operate in Bombay under his own name. In the bankruptcy proceedings connected with the failure of the Palmers in 1830 his name is mentioned among the list of partners.[3] Prinsep died in Calcutta in 1838.

The printed version of the *External Commerce of Bengal* deals

[1] Sir Henry Thoby Prinsep, Three Generations in India 1770–1904, India Office Library, MSS Eur. C. 97, Part II, p. 44.

[2] India Office Library, *East India Registers*, 1820–32.

[3] *Calcutta Government Gazette*, 16 May 1831.

with India's foreign trade between 1813–14 and 1820–21. But at some later date, Prinsep added a MS appendix which revised the figures to 1823–24. The version presented here follows the copy in the Goldsmiths' Library of Economic Literature, University of London, which contains the author's subsequent annotations together with the MS appendix bound into the volume. Since much of the material presented in his book was quantitative and his main objective was to re-compute the real value of Indian exports and imports, it may be useful, before we turn our attention to his conclusion, to describe the sources from which the statistics were collected and indicate briefly the methods followed in their presentation. The main body of information about the annual external trade of British India for this period is to be found in the Commercial Reports of the three Presidencies concerned. These Reports, which exist only in manuscript form, were compiled from the detailed customs house records in the Financial Departments of the provincial governments and sent over annually to the Court of Directors and the Board of Control in England. The data contained in these Reports relate to the total exports and imports of merchandise and treasure and to the trade of the main and subordinate ports. The re-exports were recorded separately in the case of Bengal but included in the general accounts for Bombay and Madras. The imports and exports were generally credited to the countries in which the port of shipment for imports and the port of discharge for exports were situated. Consequently, the countries which did not possess a sea-borne trade did not appear in the official Indian records even if they had a commercial connexion with India. There was also a certain amount of switching of goods from one market to another after shipment, carried on particularly by the American traders. This practice, however, was not likely to affect the balance of payment account, though it had obvious relevancy to the state of international demand.

The usefulness which can be attached to the figures given in the Commercial Reports is naturally dependent on the methods of their compilation and the system of computing their values. So far as the exports are concerned, the system of valuation was such as to undervalue seriously all the commodities. As pointed out by Prinsep, the customs-house authorities usually rated certain staple articles at a fixed valuation, some they took at the supposed market price, while others again were taken at the contracted price of the goods.[1] By comparing the total official figures for exports and imports, Prinsep showed that the latter was nearly equal in value to the former, when it was well known that the exports considerably exceeded the imports. Thus, in order to arrive at a close approximation to the actual values, he re-calculated the export values by using the quantities of commodities exported from Bengal and the current prices.[2] With regard to the imports, the position was easier. The value of these as they arrived at the ports was entered into the books according to their original invoice value. The correction carried out by Prinsep for imports was in the method of official rate of conversion from foreign currencies (in which they were originally valued) into Bengal sicca rupees, rates which, he considered, did not reflect the true market rates of exchange. Though the import figures, according to this method of computation, are likely to be fairly dependable, it was pointed out that they did not include freight charges, commission, or insurance.

The most important contribution made by Prinsep at a theoretical level was to draw attention to the invisible service items in India's balance of payments, of which no records ever appeared in official estimates. By separating the external account of India into its three principal components, merchandise, service, and capital, he was able to demonstrate the interdependence of Government finance, particularly its loan operations, the rates of exchange, bullion movements, and finally the volume of merchandise exports and imports. During this period the main pressure in the national finance arose through the movements in the capital account of India's balance of payments, since the East India Company alone had to make an annual remittance of about £3 million to Britain in order to meets its

---

[1] Prinsep, see text, and Appendix C, No. 1.

[2] The Commercial Reports generally contain a brief summary of the prices of the most important export and import commodities. But the most comprehensive source of Indian prices during this period is the *Bengal Exchange Price-Current* (1820–58), a weekly publication now preserved in West Bengal Records Office, Calcutta.

financial obligations, a sum which was further increased by private remittance in the form of profits on European investments in India and the savings of the Company's servants. In order to maintain the capital export at this level, it was of course necessary to create a permanent export surplus. Any shortfall in India's foreign exchange earnings through exports, in the face of the pressure generated in the capital account, was likely to be immediately reflected in adverse rates of exchange, leading possibly to an outflow of bullion. The lesson which Prinsep drew from his estimates of the various items in the Indian balance of payments was that, in order to avoid any deflationary consequences and to increase India's capacity to import British manufactures, it was necessary to follow a policy of active export promotion, including perhaps a policy of free trade.

The next work in our series, Appendix xxiii from the sixth volume of Tooke's *A History of Prices*, continues the theme pursued by Prinsep and contains what was perhaps the most detailed contemporary analysis in quantitative terms of the dynamics of Indian trade in the 1840s and 1850s. As an economic theorist Thomas Tooke (1774–1858) was perhaps the most important of the four authors in the volume. A co-founder along with Malthus, Ricardo, and James Mill of the Political Economy Club in 1821, Tooke was at the centre of contemporary discussions on monetary and financial matters, and his early views followed the lines laid down in the report of the bullion committee of 1810 and were based on 'classical' or Ricardian monetary theories, which postulated a close relationship between the level of prices and the quantity of money in circulation. This standpoint, however, he gradually changed and in the later volumes of his *A History of Prices*, on which he began work in the 1830s, he practically dissociated himself from the supporters of the 'currency school' and came to place far less emphasis on the quantity theory of money.[1] For students of Indian trade history his Appendix is valuable chiefly as indicating the influence of a new factor which had appeared, the effect of railway investments and the transfer of real resources from Britain to

---

[1] For the biographical details see *The Dictionary of National Biography*, hereinafter referred to as *D.N.B.*

India in the form of capital export in the 1850s. It als
detailed tables of both Indian trade and bullion mov
and from India, which cannot be easily found outside
rally inaccessible official trade statistics.

The mechanism of Indian trade and the operatio
foreign exchange market touched upon by both Prir
Tooke was described in full depth and detail by J. H.
(1779–1858) in his evidence before the Select Comm
1831. A Governor of the Bank of England since 1830
partner in the East India House of Palmers, Mackillop ar
Palmer belonged to an important London merchant f
and was in a position to be intimately acquainted with the
cacies of the foreign exchange dealings between India, C
and Britain. Palmer's contributions to the theoretical fina
and banking problems of the time were important and
pamphlet 'The Causes and Consequences of the Pressure u
the Money Market' (London, 1837) did much to establish
reputation as an economist.[1] He was also partly responsible
the introduction of what has come to be known as 'Palmer
Rule' in the Bank of England, by which the Bank attempted
reduce the disturbances in the English currency, arising fro
external sources, to a type which would occur under a purel
metallic currency by keeping its security holding, including dis
counted bills, at a constant level.[2] The Indian issues on which
Palmer was asked to give his views by the parliamentary committee were threefold. First of all there was the question of the
exact operation of the exchange mechanism under a metallic
currency system, and the effects of external fluctuations on the
level of internal prices and economic activity. Secondly, much
more important from the Company's point of view, was the
question whether, if it was to relinquish its Indian trade, the
Company would be able to rely on the existing bill market to
transfer its annual remittance of £3 million to Britain. Finally,
a wider problem was also raised. What was the effect on India
of this continuous drain of capital?

---

[1] *D.N.B.*
[2] For a discussion of this point see Jacob Viner, *Studies in the Theory of International Trade* (New York and London, 1937), p. 224.

In an age of active economic thinking, it was perhaps natural that the whole question of the Indian remittances and the theoretical reasoning behind the process of unilateral payments should have received thorough investigation from the Select Committee and from businessmen connected with eastern trade. The Indian situation provided a close parallel to the experience of the Napoleonic Wars when England had to make large payments on the Continent. There was also the example of the Irish remittances to the absentee landlords in England.[1] The contemporary economists approached the question both in terms of adjustments to a disequilibrium in a country's balance of payments, and with the specific factors that created an export surplus through which the transfer of funds could be effected. The answer given by Palmer to the two theoretical problems implied in the questions put to him was essentially the same as those of the classical economists, particularly Ricardo and John Stuart Mill, who used price discrepancies between the paying and receiving countries to explain the mechanism of the transfer process. Since the currency of the three trading partners, Britain, India, and China, involved in the triangular trading system was metallic, albeit of different standard, the rates of exchange between sterling, rupee and tale were simply fixed by mint par, i.e. the intrinsic value of the coins. The prevailing rate, at mint par, between London and Calcutta in 1831 was calculated by Palmer at 1s. 11d. per rupee taking into account the bullion price of silver in London, which was the basis of the Indian standard. It is obvious that under this arrangement the specie 'export and import points' – the rate at mint par plus the cost of transporting bullion to and from India – would determine the limits within which the rates of exchange would be allowed to fluctuate. In fact, Palmer pointed out that in view of the commercial depression in India the rate had fallen to 1s. 10¼d. which had caused the bullion to flow out from India to Britain during the past year or so.[2]

Although Palmer was of the opinion that the East India Com-

---

[1] Cf. *S. C. on Affairs of the East India Company*, Parliamentary Papers, 1831–32, vol. 10 (735 II), QQ. 1369, 1419.

[2] Palmer, see text, QQ. 1291, 1318.

pany would not experience any great difficulty in purchasing the necessary quantities of bills in view of the total value of Indian exports to both Britain and China, the recent efflux of silver from India and the disturbances to trade raised the awkward question of how equilibrium was restored in such a situation. Palmer's response was that the East India Company could in a crisis of this kind always fall back on bullion remittance which, according to him, would lead to a contraction of the currency and the resultant fall in the domestic prices in India would probably lead to a rise in the international demand for her exports and a fall in her imports which would automatically restore the balance.[1]

This was identical with the theoretical reasoning later developed by Mill. If the currencies of two countries with each other were on a metallic standard – gold or silver – and bullion moved freely between them, then the mechanism of adjustment of the balance of indebtedness of one country to its foreign obligations will be, according to Mill, as follows:

Commerce being supposed to be in a state of equilibrium when the obligatory remittances begin, the first remittance is necessarily made in money. This lowers prices in the remitting country, and raises them in the receiving. The natural effect is that more commodities are exported than before and fewer imported, and that, on the score of commerce alone, a balance of money will be constantly due from the receiving to the paying country. When the debt thus annually due to the tributary country becomes equal to the annual tribute or other regular payment due from it, no further transmission of money takes place; the equilibrium of exports and imports will no longer exist, but that of payments will; the exchange will be at par, the two debts will be set off against one another, and the tribute or remittance will be virtually paid in goods.[2]

The main weakness of the classical theory of the transfer process was of course the unawareness that adjustments can take place to a balance of payments disequilibrium through upward or downward shifts in the income of the countries concerned brought about by the foreign trade multiplier, provided that the marginal propensity to import is high enough. In the voluminous Minutes of Evidence before the Select Committee of 1831–32, and 1840,

[1] Palmer, see text, QQ. 1327, 1369, 1373, 1406.
[2] J. S. Mill, *Principles of Political Economy*, Book III, chapter XXI, para. 4.

while the quantity theory of money and its relationship with international trade were repeatedly stated, only one person noted the connexion between the levels of income and foreign trade. This was George Larpent, Chairman of the East India and China Association, who stated that the varying factor in the volume of British exports to India was the level of general purchasing power which in its turn depended on the state of the harvest in the case of an agricultural country like India. He further pointed out that in the years of bad harvests or famines India's imports from Britain perceptibly fell off.[1] Although the classical economic thinking, including that of Horsley Palmer, generally ignored the process of adjustment due to fluctuations in national income (the Keynesian foreign trade multiplier) of which exports were a component, Palmer did make an extremely important point in regard to the question whether the annual 'tribute' which India had to pay did not gradually impoverish the country. His reply was that as long as Government taxes levied on the people of India were re-expended in the form of financing the exports for which there was an international demand, the degree of impoverishment or drain was actually small, since the cost of producing the export goods remained in the country. In modern terms the point which Palmer was making was essentially the effect of public expenditure on the levels of employment and income, since the result of a policy of financing exports through taxation was to divert resources to the export industries and thus increase the income of the factors engaged in the production of export goods. If there is some spare capacity in the economy it allows the existing level of employment to be maintained, even if it does not lead to actual growth which might have followed an autonomous increase in exports.[2]

If the main emphasis in the works of Prinsep and Palmer was on the technical and theoretical aspects of Indian trade, the pamphlet by John Crawfurd (1783–1868) reflected a wider

[1] *S. C. on the Petition of the East India Company for Relief*, Parliamentary Papers, 1840, vol. 7, Q. 200.
[2] On this point see my article 'India's International Economy in the Nineteenth Century: An Historical Survey', *Modern Asian Studies*, II (1968), 44–5.

interest and was intended to draw attention to the general problems of economic development in India and the institutional features of her foreign trade. Crawfurd's own connexion with the east was a distinguished one. His detailed personal knowledge of Upper India was acquired presumably during the period of his service in the Indian army from 1803 to 1808 in a medical post.[1] Later he was transferred to Penang and took part in the administration of Java under Sir Stamford Raffles during the period of the British occupation of the island. Although the best known works of Crawfurd were on South East Asia, he wrote a number of tracts on British India, of which the *Sketch of the Commercial Resources . . . of British India* (1837) was perhaps the most important. It was published anonymously but the authorship can be definitely attributed to Crawfurd. The evidence for this comes from two sources. In the first place, the copy of the tract in the Goldsmiths' Library, University of London, is inscribed ' by John Crawfurd' in what appears to be his own handwriting.[2] Secondly, in the India Office Library there is a manuscript by Crawfurd entitled 'Description of India' written in 1832–33 which contains the rough draft of many of the passages found in the *Sketch*.[3]

Crawfurd's general purpose in writing the *Sketch* was not only to present a description of the existing economic conditions of British India but also to suggest ways of improving them. In many ways his observations reflected the growing disparity between the levels of technology in a traditional economy such as that of India and those in a much more developed system such as was emerging in Western Europe. Until about the middle of the eighteenth century, European observers in India showed little awareness of the superiority of their own economic methods and organization as compared to those in India. But by the early nineteenth century, such views had become commonplace.

---

[1] For his biographical details see *D.N.B.* and also *A History of the Indian Medical Service 1600–1913*, II (London, 1914), 129.

[2] A comparison between Crawfurd's signature dating from 1815 and that appearing on the title page of the *Sketch* shows certain discrepancies between the two, though the general shape is similar. The writing is much closer to that of the MS in the India Office Library dating from 1832–33.

[3] India Office Library, MSS Eur. D. 457.

According to Crawfurd, India's basic economic institutions were in such a state of backwardness as to depress materially the levels of income and consumption. Indian agriculture was primitive, and painfully dependent for its prosperity on the vagaries of a tropical climate, with a negligible rate of capital formation. The undeveloped state of internal transport was a serious hindrance to the flow of goods and services within the country and to its regional economic integration. In industrial skills and manufactures, the situation was no better, though it was admitted that at one time India had certain advantages over other nations, particularly in the textile industry.[1] It was only the Indian merchant class which could claim anything approaching equality to its counterpart in Europe, an admission which probably reflects Crawfurd's predilection for merchants and mercantile pursuits in general.[2] Crawfurd's solution for the economic improvement of India was based on a plan for monetary and currency reforms, matched by moderation in the State's taxation demands, and the gradual introduction of the surplus capital of Britain and British entrepreneurial skills. Crawfurd's unshakeable belief in the elevating role of British capital is perhaps best seen in his statement that most of the export commodities from India 'have been rendered available to the consumption of civilized nations solely through the agency of the capital and ingenuity of British subjects'.[3] Of the commodities listed, i.e. indigo, raw silk, opium, cotton, saltpetre, and sugar, Crawfurd was able to show that only indigo was not substantially the result of peasant production.

III

Any examination of India's trade and finance in the nineteenth century must deal with two major themes: the institutional background and the organization of trade, and the actual mechanism and quantities involved. In this section we shall deal with the

[1] Crawfurd, see text.
[2] *Ibid.* Crawfurd is described by E. T. Stokes as being the paid Parliamentary Agent of Calcutta's European merchants in England; see *The English Utilitarians and India* (Cambridge, 1959), p. 62, n. 4.
[3] *Ibid.*

first theme. The following two sections will describe the changes in the commodity composition and direction of trade, and the balance of payments position. For at least half of the period under review, the nature of India's foreign trade was considerably influenced by the curious organizational structure which had developed over the fifty years since the last quarter of the eighteenth century. The main characteristic of this was the division of trade between private commercial firms, the so-called Agency Houses, and the East India Company which also functioned as the Government of the country. By 1828, the central theme of all public discussions on the organization of India's external trade was the question whether the East India Company should be allowed to continue its commercial activities when its Charter came up for renewal in 1833. In June 1827, Holt Mackenzie, the Financial Secretary to the Government of Bengal, strongly warned the Court of Directors at home against the consequences of adopting any financial measures which might start off an economic crisis in India. The effect of such a crisis, he stressed, would be to give an opportunity to the enemies of the Company to accuse it of having sacrificed the true interests of India for mere commercial exploitation.[1] The whole question derived its edge from the fact that the manner in which the Company conducted its trading operations had certain peculiar features. From as early as 1765, when the Company had assumed the office of Revenue Collector in Bengal, and particularly since the Charter Act of 1813, the normal considerations of strict profitability did not apply to the Company's trade. This was primarily due to the fact that it was carried on mostly with the public revenues of India in settlement of the Company's financial obligations to its shareholders, to the British Government, and in settlement of the administrative

---

[1] Consider the following passage: 'The common and popular cry would be raised that we had looked merely to the commercial dividend and sacrificed the interests of the country to the commercial profits of the Company. Even those who might allow the claims of the Commercial Department in account, would still argue that under a National Government no such event could have ever occurred; that the division of interests between the Indian and Home Treasury is to be solely traced to the present system which vests the Government of the country in a commercial body.' Financial Letters and Enclosures Received from Bengal, 7 June 1827, vol. 19, 1827–28, p. 57.

charges incurred on its behalf at home. When the revenue surpluses fell short of the requisitions, the exports were financed by floating rupee loans in India, which were largely subscribed by the Company's European servants, though a certain amount was held by Indian business interests as well.[1] Until 1813, the East India Company had of course possessed the legal monopoly of the Indian trade. However, in this year the trade of India was finally thrown open, although the Company still kept its exclusive rights in the China trade. By the early 1830s the economic basis of the Company's East India trade had become wholly unreal and the Company had accumulated heavy losses, at least on paper. The serious position combined with the uncertainties over its commercial privileges in the impending renewal of its Charter caused the Court of Directors in 1831–32 to reduce drastically the scale of their trading operations. When the new Charter was granted by Parliament in 1833, the Company's trade ceased altogether. Henceforth, the East India Company was concerned solely with the territorial government of India and had no longer any part in the trading affairs of either China or India.

The end of the Company's trade was accompanied by virtually a complete failure of all the old Agency Houses in Calcutta which was shaken by an unparalleled credit crisis and economic depression during 1830–33. At least part of the reason for this can be ascribed to the fact that the activities of the Agency Houses had become closely connected with and complementary to those of the Company.[2] Indeed, long before the Company had officially lost its monopoly, the greater part of India's foreign trade had fallen into the hands of the private traders represented by the Agency Houses. According to Crawfurd, before the great failure of 1830–33, Calcutta had fifty firms, Bombay seventeen, and Madras ten. These firms also had subsidiary branches at Canton, Penang, Singapore, and of course

---

[1] In 1836, the total amount of the Registered Debt was computed at Rs. 276 million (£27·6 m); of this the Europeans held Rs.204 m (£20·4 m), and the Indians Rs.72 m (£7·2 m); India Financial Proceedings, 5, 20 Jan. 1836.

Unless otherwise stated the MS references are to the Company's records available at the India Office Library.

[2] A. Tripathi, *Trade and Finance in the Bengal Presidency*, p. 144.

London. The term 'Agency House' had by our period become something of a misnomer. For although when originally founded they had acted (and of course still did) as mere agents for merchants and manufacturers trading with India, they now operated largely on their own. One of the best descriptions of the wide variety of business conducted by the Agency Houses is to be found in Crawfurd's *Sketch*. The effect of the East India Company's monopoly in Asian trade and the system by which the Company granted licences to a few chosen private traders to carry on business which the Company itself could not handle, was to secure a kind of sub-monopoly to the big Houses in India. Most of the European and American business with India fell into their hands. But much more important for India's domestic economy was the fact that the business transacted by the Agency Houses included deposit banking, issuing paper money, financing the indigo producers, shipping and insurance, and investments in urban properties. Greenberg has ascribed the economic orgin of the Agency Houses to the need for widening the market for the British industrial manufacturers, and has thus linked them with the growth of the 'consignment' system in overseas trade.[1] The argument is that if the domestic market in Britain during the early phase of the Industrial Revolution was not expanding fast enough for the new industrialists to run their plant at maximum capacity and since the opportunity cost of machinery was zero, it paid them to export the surplus quantities even below the cost of production, because it helped to reduce the cost per unit of output. As a result the manufacturers were prepared to consign their products to overseas markets on speculation. The Agency Houses in India and various Asian trading ports handled such 'consignment business' and charged a commission on each transaction.

Apart from acting as entrepreneurs, it is clear that the Agency Houses were the main instruments through which Western capitalism and business institutions were being introduced in India in response to the requirements of the world market. Thus between the peasant producers in the Indian villages on the one hand and the new external tie, the world

[1] M. Greenberg, *British Trade and the Opening of China*, p. 144.

market, on the other, the European commercial houses stood as a vital link. To some extent this was merely a modification and greater refinement of the existing Indian system which can be described as a 'Dual Economy' with a fairly well developed commercial sector which not only actively organized production in the industrial handicrafts sector but also distributed the surplus product of the more backward and traditional agriculture.[1] The innovation which the European business firms introduced was primarily in the ownership, management, and mobilization of capital for productive purposes. That the Agency Houses themselves were aware of their role is evident from a memorial which they presented to Lord William Bentinck, the Governor General, in 1833 while seeking financial aid from the Government. In defence of their system of operations, which had lately come under public criticism, they asserted,

Long as we have occupied your Lordship's attention upon this general question we cannot help remarking that the existing system be it good or bad is in principle essentially the same as prevails in all commercial countries, to which our own owes her commercial position. It draws capital into commercial channels, adds daily to the National Wealth, diffuses it again through innumerable ramifications, promoting enterprise, spreading industry and activity through the land, sustaining the national resources, securing national greatness. It is not merely merchant lending to merchant, trader to trader, but from every source capital is invited into the channels of agriculture, manufacture, and commerce. It is the wealth of every class freely devoted to promote common prosperity, confidence and credit diffusing their vivifying influence through the whole of this wonderful fabric of modern civilization.[2]

The necessity of making these eloquent assertions arose from the fact that the Agency Houses, then on the brink of suspension, threatened ruin to a large number of people who had invested their savings through them and hence felt morally reprehensible. Their financial position had gradually become shaken with the increasing competition in the export trade after the opening of the Indian trade in 1814 and by the continued commercial de-

[1] The term 'Dual Economy' was first used by J. H. Boeke in his *Economics and Economic policy of Dual Societies as exemplified by Indonesia* (New York, 1955). He used it in a somewhat technical sense which is not followed here.

[2] Bengal Financial Consultation 1, 26 April 1833; the memorial was signed by the following firms: Cruttenden Mackillop & Co., Colvin & Co., Fergusson & Co.

pression in Great Britain since 1825.[1] The credit of the Houses was further impaired by large withdrawals of capital to Europe by retiring partners and by unsound business practices in general.[2] The crisis finally came with the severe trade depression in 1830 when Palmer & Co., one of the largest and oldest of the Agency Houses, stopped payment. This event was the signal for widespread and general failures among other Houses during the ensuing years. No satisfactory explanation has ever been offered for the crisis which was clearly of major importance to the business history of India during this period. The magnitude of the problem can be gauged from the fact that the total liability of the bankrupt European Houses came to about £15 million, an amount of debt which, it was remarked, 'a century ago would have shaken the Government of this country with fear of bankruptcy'.[3]

It seems that the Calcutta failures began at first out of a commercial crisis caused by the depression in the export trade. Crawfurd, who made some attempt to trace the origin of the crisis, was inclined to attribute it to overspeculation in the indigo trade, and the way in which the Agency Houses, who were large-scale owners of produce, financed their exports. The confidence of the depositors was shaken in the first place by the protestation of bills of exchange which the Agency Houses had drawn on their principals in London against the value of their export consignments from Bengal. When the proceeds from the sale of the latter failed to cover the amount of the bills, the London Houses, already the largest creditors of the Calcutta firms, became nervous and returned the bills to Bengal. When the facts became known, the result was a general run on all the major Houses. The case of Alexander & Co. can be taken as typical. At the time of the failure of the Palmers in January 1830, they had a total banknote circulation of about Rs.2 million, being

[1] Cf. S. G. Checkland, 'John Gladstone, As Trader and Planter', *Economic History Review*, vii (2nd series, 1954–55), 217–22.

[2] The detailed history of the Agency Houses in this period will be found in Tripathi, *Trade and Finance*; Benoy Chowdhury, *Growth of Commercial Agriculture in Bengal (1757–1900)* (Calcutta, 1964); S. B. Singh, *European Agency Houses in Bengal (1783–1833)* (Calcutta, 1966); and Greenberg, *British Trade*.

[3] Extract from *The Times* in Canton Register, 13 May 1834, quoted by Greenberg, *British Trade*, p. 165.

both an issuing house as well as a bank of deposit. The first consequence of the panic was a run on Alexanders to the extent of almost its entire circulation. The second was a rapid withdrawal of deposits from the House. Since it was not the practice of establishments such as Alexanders to keep large amounts of liquid funds at call, they extensively borrowed from the Bank of Bengal, which fulfilled many of the functions of a central bank, depositing Government securities and mortgaging their other assets. When this was found to be insufficient they again applied to the Bank for accommodation on simple personal security, and up until June 1831 nearly Rs.1 million had been advanced to them by the Bank. But in December 'from some unaccountable and unfounded rumour' the notes of Alexander & Co. were suddenly returned. With this fresh crisis, three other Agency Houses, Fergusson & Co., Cruttenden & Co., and Mackintosh & Co., came forward and lent the credit of their names to obtain further discount accommodation at the Bank of Bengal in support of Alexanders. In this way, the Bank was induced to continue acceptances for another Rs.1·7 million until the former failed in December 1832.[1] Since the Bank of Bengal was a semi-Government concern, the whole operation illustrates in a remarkable manner the close connexion between official and private financial affairs in Bengal at this time.

It is evident that in its later phase the crisis had quite clearly assumed the character of a liquidity crisis. The recoverable assets of the Agency Houses were locked up in innumerable indigo factories, in advances to other export producers, and in landed properties, none of which could be realized at short notice. Furthermore, the stringency in the money market was aggravated by a contraction in the actual quantity of money in circulation owing to an unfavourable movement in the balance of trade.[2] When in 1833 the three of the principal remaining

[1] The Bank of Bengal's Reply to some observations of the Governor General, dated 4 October 1833, India Financial Proceedings 3, 7 March 1835; West Bengal Records Office, Board of Trade, Commercial Consultation No. 20, 18 January 1831, in Proceedings vol. 496, pp. 366–7.

[2] This was due to the fact that the greater part of the currency was metallic and in silver. In 1833, it was said that 'but for the issues of the Bank of Bengal Calcutta itself would be without a circulating medium', Bengal Financial Consultation 1, 26 April 1833.

Agency Houses petitioned the Government for relief, it was stated in the memorial that out of the extensive properties belonging to the late firm of Palmer & Co. scarcely Rs.900,000 were realized from sales conducted by the receivers, and that 'this state of things can only be attributed to the actual want of available capital or to its being withheld from the circulation in consequence of the want of confidence occasioned by late event'. The memorial went on to say that gold had long since disappeared, and silver was now rapidly vanishing from country circulation, while the copper coinage of the Government had actually appreciated by 25% or more.[1]

It was ironical that the private traders who had been the strongest advocates of free trade principles and were against all forms of restriction and monopoly, particularly that of the East India Company, should have been reduced to applauding the virtues of Government intervention. Their *laissez-faire* doctrines were overthrown as early as 1826 when they first sought financial help from the authorities.[2] In 1830, their renewed claims for assistance were justified on the ground that

the Government of a country in the slowly rising and colonial position of British India has a nearer interest in these matters than the Government of the Mother Country or any older State where production and commerce are widely and generally diffused and hence adjusted themselves in the course of ages to the amount and nature of capital and of individual enterprise.[3]

In 1833 in their desperation they even turned to the example of recent economic events in Britain[4] in order to sustain their arguments for Government intervention and stated that

the commercial prosperity of England has more than once been shaken to its foundation, and has only been saved from utter destruction by the

[1] *Ibid.*
[2] Financial Letters and Enclosures Received, vol. 17, 1826, pp. 482–3.
[3] Bengal Financial Consultation 1, 18 May 1830.
[4] The reference is obviously to the crisis of 1825 when the Bank of England was obliged to assist a large number of London banks; see Gayer, Rostow, and Schwartz, *The Growth and Fluctuations of the British Economy, 1790–1850*, i (Oxford, 1953), 205; T. S. Ashton and R. S. Sayers (ed.), *Papers in English Monetary History* (Oxford, 1953), pp. 96–108.

interference of Government itself or those of great national Establishments . . . When appalling commercial calamities occur it has not been
the practice, either of the British Government or the Bank of England to
shut their eyes and fold their arms and untouched by public misery to
permit ruin and desolation to overspread the country.[1]

It must be pointed out that the failure of the older Agency
Houses did not lead to a radical alteration in the structure of
business in India. For new establishments on the pattern of the
old ones were immediately formed, mainly on the initiative of
the London firms connected with Indian trade. It was the operation of these trading houses which, later in the nineteenth
century, became famous as constituting the managing-agency
system of India, the organizational foundation of India's industrial growth. The new European firms handled the bulk of
India's exports and imports with Europe and also participated
in the 'Country Trade' which, however, they shared with a
large number of Indian traders.[2] The prosperity of these
business firms was now inextricably bound up with fluctuations
in India's foreign trade and the repercussions of any sizeable
depression originating outside India were immediately felt in
the Indian money markets. Thus the periodic monetary and
commercial crisis which was such a marked feature of British
financial history in the nineteenth century was also present in the
case of India though on a smaller scale. After the dramatic
upheavals of the early 1830s, the second crisis in India came in
1847–48, which was largely the associated effect of the severe
depression in England in those years, and, apart from numerous
failures of native Indian business firms and banks, it led to the
closure of the important and powerful Union Bank of Calcutta
in 1847. The Bank had been the main financial support of the
indigo factories in Bengal in the 1840s and the greater part of its
resources were tied up in loans to the indigo planters. The
demand for indigo had been depressed for some years and when
the price finally broke in London in the wake of the financial
crisis of 1847, the chain-reaction brought down the Bank in

---

[1] Bengal Financial Consultation 1, 26 April 1833.

[2] Greenberg, *British Trade*, p. 145; Wong Lin Ken, 'The Trade of Singapore
1819–69', *Journal of the Malayan Branch of the Royal Asiatic Society*, XXXIII,
part 4 (1960), 162–3.

Introduction

Calcutta and in a lesser way repeated the experience of 1830–33.[1]

IV

A quantitative analysis of India's foreign trade in this period reveals a remarkably high rate of growth, as can be seen from Table 1. The exports expanded in value from just over Rs.68

Table 1 (Values in million rupees).

Year	Merchandise		Treasure	
	Exports	Imports	Exports	Imports
1814–15	68·3	11·9	0·96	11·14
1821–22	109·4	59·2	4·17	5·76
1828–29	111·29	53·63	4·6	20·4
1839–40	119·5	56·5	2·8	19·6
1845–46	170·0	91·0	8·0	25·0
1850–51	181·0	115·0	5·0	38·0
1854–55	183·0	124·0	19·0	20·0

Source: 1814–15 and 1821–22 figures are taken from Prinsep's estimates. 1828–29 and 1839–40 figures are from my own calculations given in the Statistical Appendix to the Introduction. The subsequent years are taken from Tooke.

million in 1814–15 to Rs.183 million in 1854–55. The expansion in imports was even more impressive, from about Rs.11·9 million in 1814–15 to Rs.124 million in 1854–55. The rate of increase in exports was just under three times the value of the base year, while imports expanded by over ten times. The other significant conclusion to be drawn from this table is the large imports of treasure and the size of the balance which remained after deducting the value of the imports of goods and treasure from that of the exports. It should be noted, however, that the trends indicated by the value figures should not be taken as evidence of the state of the international demand for exports and the Indian domestic demand for imports. The value figures possess an obvious relevancy in the context of the balance of payments position. But in order to understand the true significance of their fluctuations it is necessary to correlate them with

[1] For a description of the crisis of 1847–48 and the circumstances leading to the failure of the Union Bank, see B. Chowdhury, *Growth of Commercial Agriculture in Bengal*, pp. 112–20.

the volume figures, since price fluctuations might seriously disguise the actual expansion in the volume of trade. It is difficult to construct a price index for the whole period on the basis of the existing data, but we know that the first half of the nineteenth century was a period of falling prices in India; and the general import prices of European goods were also falling as a result of the growth of factory production and the reduction in marine freight charges.[1]

Turning to the exports first, in 1814 the export items were indigo (an industrial dye), piece goods, raw silk, raw cotton, opium, sugar, spices, oil seeds, and various other miscellaneous goods. The actual percentage share of the important items in the total value can be studied for a selected number of years in Table 2. This broad structure of the commodity composition of

Table 2 *India's exports: commodity composition, percentage shares of selected items in total value.*

Year	Indigo	Piece goods	Raw silk	Cotton	Opium	Sugar
1814–15	20·0	14·3	13·3	8·0	not available	3·0
1828–29	27·0	11·0	10·0	15·0	17·0	4·0
1834–35	15·0	7·0	8·0	21·0	25·0	2·0
1839–40	26·0	5·0	7·0	20·0	10·0	7·0
1850–51	10·0	4·0	4·0	12·7	34·1	10·1
1857–58	6·1	2·9	2·9	15·6	32·7	4·3

Source: See note to Table 1.

India's export trade confirms the widely-held opinion that the most striking change in the character of her international trade in the first half of the nineteenth century lay in the almost entire transformation of her exports into the category of primary commodities with a corresponding concentration on manufactured goods in her imports. The manufacturing and commercial interests in England were beginning to be aware of India's position as a potential supplier of raw material and the advantages which accrued from it to the home industries. In 1840 the

[1] For a weighted index of India's export and import prices between 1828 and 1840 see my article 'India's Foreign trade and the cessation of the East India Company's Trading Activities', *Econ. Hist. Rev.* XIX (2nd series, 1966), figure 3, p. 351.

East India Company itself petitioned Parliament for certain reforms of the tariff regulations as they applied to India. In the course of the hearing held by the Select Committee, it was stated that

this Company has in various ways, encouraged and assisted by our great manufacturing ingenuity and skill, succeeded in converting India from a manufacturing country into a country exporting raw produce. . . . The peculiar state of the relation between this country and India and the necessity of extracting from the latter three millions of money for Home Charges . . . and the altered state of Indian industry in its being converted from a manufacturing country into a country exporting raw produce, are circumstances which . . . ought to influence the Legislature to afford every possible protection to its agricultural produce.[1]

Apart from the structural change involving the commodity composition, another feature of Indian trade was the short-period changes which were very marked and often quite violent. The type of instability which we find today associated with the primary commodities in world trade seems to have operated in the nineteenth century as well. The main characteristic of this instability is violent fluctuations in demand for raw material often exhibited in cyclical movements which of course leave a corresponding effect on the prices of the export commodities. In India's case, Prinsep's tables (Appendix C, No. 1) setting out the value of individual export items clearly point to the existence of fluctuations of this type. Indeed, the entire business history of British India from 1814 to 1858 can be divided into seven unequal periods alternating between prosperity and depression, the generally upward trend being sharply punctuated by years of slump. The opening of trade in 1814, coinciding with the conclusion of a general peace in Europe, and the reduction in freight rates, led to a boom in Indian exports which, according to Prinsep's calculations, reached a peak in 1817–18. The value of exports from Bengal in this year stood at Rs.84·5 million compared to Rs.60 million 1813–14. But this rate of increase could not be sustained and the last year in Prinsep's original estimate, 1820–21, ended with figures much below the peak

---

[1] *S. C. on the Petition of the East India Company for Relief*, Parliamentary Papers, 1840, vol. 7, Q. 191.

year. George Larpent stated in 1821 that in the years 1814–15 the prices of many of the Indian articles had risen by 100–200% which attracted a great deal of speculative capital. But the intense competition had led to a lowering in the rate of profits, and in fact during the previous year or so many items had shown a loss.[1] Larpent's evidence is supported by the much more positive statement made by Charles Grant, who had been a prominent member of the East India Directorate for many years and was generally hostile to the proliferation of private trading firms in India. When the Committee put the following question to him: 'Do you not consider it to be an injury to the interests of India, to have occasional inducements held out, under temporary circumstances, to go into a cultivation, which, when those circumstances cease, must be dropped?' Grant replied 'I believe India has several times suffered, from causes of that sort; and I think that is one of the evils of the whole of the trade, between India and Europe, that it is liable to very great fluctuations, and within my memory, has never been reduced to a regular steady trade.'[2]

That the position had not changed substantially at a later period is confirmed by the detailed statistics available for the years 1828 to 1840.[3] The main problem in this respect arose from the difficulty of adjusting the total levels of output according to the state of world demand, particularly in the production of the three staple commodities, indigo, opium, and raw cotton, the first two of which were heavily dependent on foreign trade. The wide physical separation of the markets and the slow state of transport and communications made it difficult to relate foreign prices to domestic ones, a difficulty that was strengthened by the low short-term elasticities of supplies for these export commodities owing to their agricultural nature. Consequently, any sudden and violent fluctuation in demand tended to produce a corresponding effect on their prices in the domestic market. Moreover, business predictions

---

[1] Larpent was at this time a member of the house of Paxton, Cockerell, Trail & Co, East India agents; *Third Report, Minutes of Evidence before the Select Committee on Foreign Trade*, Parliamentary Papers, 1821, vol. 6, p. 218.

[2] *Ibid.* p. 306.

[3] See my article, *Econ. Hist. Rev.* XIX (2nd series, 1966).

about the long-term trend of world demand for India's exports were not likely to be unanimous. Prinsep's prediction in 1823 about the future expansion of India's exports was distinctly pessimistic. Again, in 1836, a proposal was made in London for setting up a joint-stock bank in India with its capital subscribed in England the purpose of which was to be the encouragement of the Indian export industries by advances of loans, and Crawfurd's pamphlet was partly written in its support.[1] The supporters of the proposed bank stated that in the existing state of trade the demand for Indian exports far exceeded the supply, and the high rate of interest in India was taken to be an indication of the scarcity of capital which retarded their production. Coming immediately after the great depression of 1830–33 this statement might cause some surprise, and Horsley Palmer who wrote an objection against the scheme argued that far from there being a shortage it was ill-judged increases in the past in the investments on Indian export commodities that led to an over-expansion followed by ruinous consequences.[2]

If we look at the indices of the major articles of export to Britain during the period 1828 to 1840, it would appear that Palmer was at least partly right in thinking that one of the principal sources of instability in the exporting industries could be assigned to the state of the supplies. For an explanation of the movements in the prices and volumes of the various items, it is obviously necessary to take into consideration two factors likely to affect them: first, the demand conditions prevailing in the countries for which the exports were destined, and secondly, the state of the supplies in the exporting industries. In the case of India's exports in the early nineteenth century, the economic fluctuations in her two principal markets, Great Britain and China, largely account for the proportional fluctuations in the commodity composition of her trade, although the variations in demand affected the prices of the different export articles according to their respective position in the domestic economy. Articles heavily dependent on foreign demand were much more susceptible to price fluctuations than those for which there was a

---

[1] Crawfurd, see text, chapter VII.
[2] J. H. Palmer, *Reasons Against an Indian Joint-Stock Bank* (London, 1837).

domestic market. Throughout our period Great Britain undoubtedly remained India's most important market for exports. This coupled with the fact that she stood in a special financial relationship with India, which was independent of trade, exerted a marked influence on the latter's economy and was responsible for associated changes in the volume of India's trade with other trading partners. Thus a recession or boom in Britain was of obvious moment to India, since the amplitude of fluctuations in the Indian exports to the former, which was severe during the period 1828–40 (see editor's Appendix on p. 46) was the most important single factor determining the movements in the total exports. The relative shares of the various countries in the

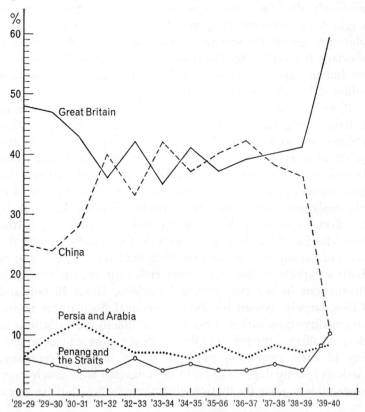

Figure 1 *Percentage share of selected countries in India's total export value.*

Introduction

export total are set out in the accompanying chart (Figure 1).
In 1828 48% of the exports went to Britain. Next in order of
importance came China which took 25% followed a long way
down by the Persian Gulf regions (7%), France (6%),
Penang and the Straits Settlements (6%), and the United
States (3%), the remaining 2% being shared by Mauritius,
Burma, Indonesia, New South Wales, Sweden, and Portugal.
The shift as India's leading trade partner between Britain and
China is significant. In 1829, although the total value of exports
to Britain rose in absolute terms (see editor's Appendix), her
percentage share showed a slight decline, which became marked
during the next two years. By 1831–32 it had fallen to 36%. At
the same time, the share of China had been steadily rising and in
the latter year exceeded that of Britain. Thereafter, a curious
alternating pattern set in until 1835–36, in which the share of
China recorded an increase when that of Britain exhibited a
decline. It is conceivable that the reason for this is to be found in
the pressure created by capital movement from India to Britain.
The problem of effecting remittances to England and the position
of China in the triangular trade of India, Britain and herself had
possibly the tendency to swell her imports from India in those
years in which there was a relative fall in the Indian exports to
Britain.

The relative changes in the direction of export trade, particularly the pattern described above, were the natural consequence of similar fluctuations in the commodity composition
of the exports, since for certain items such as indigo, raw silk, or
sugar Britain was the largest importer, while other articles such
as opium and cotton mostly went to China. The market for
indigo was a highly unstable one, since it was an industrial
raw material for which the elasticity of demand was probably
very low. However, the expansion of the textile industry in
England in the eighteenth and early nineteenth century also led
to a secular growth in the demand for the Indian dye. In
the seventeenth century indigo had been extensively exported to
Europe from India, but competition from West Indian producers
later drove it out of the European markets, and indigo, which
was still cultivated in Northern India, was chiefly sent to the

Middle East.[1] The revival of the indigo trade of India dates from the 1780s when French wars and the slave revolt in the West Indies began to reduce supplies from this source.[2] The production of indigo in Bengal was given a tremendous stimulus through the purchases of the East India Company when the Company decided to use indigo as a means of remitting home its surplus revenue. Thus the rapid increase in the number of indigo factories (establishments which processed the dye from plants grown by Indian peasants) under European management was a direct outcome of the remittance problem and it provided a convenient outlet for the investment of surplus European capital.[3] But the effect of the Government purchases had been to force up prices in the internal market, while prices in the foreign markets fell in direct proportion to the accumulation of stocks. The London price of indigo, for instance, declined from £90 per chest in 1825 to £45 in 1831.[4] During 1830–31 the East India Company limited its purchases, thus causing a catastrophic drop in the price in Calcutta.[5] The failure of the Agency Houses further accentuated this fall, and the indigo market in Bengal did not finally begin to recover until 1835–36. The dye, however, continued to occupy an important place in the Indian exports, though by the 1850s its share in the total value had considerably declined.

The two other major articles of export, opium and cotton, were largely dependent on the demand from China. The greater part of the opium grown in India, both Bihar and Malwa, eventually found its way to the Chinese market, and the total exports during the early nineteenth century expanded at a phenomenal rate. The sale of Bengal opium was a Government monopoly. It was grown by peasants in Bihar and in the country around Benares, the extent of cultivation being controlled by a

[1] English Factory Records from Surat contain many references to the Persian market for Indian indigo.

[2] Chowdhury, *Growth of Commercial Agriculture in Bengal*, p. 74.

[3] *S. C. on Affairs of the East India Company*, Parliamentary Papers, 1831–32, vol. 10 (735 II), p. 167. Bengal Financial Consultation 1, 26 April 1833.

[4] *S. C. on Affairs of the East India Company*, 1831–32, vol. 10 (725 II), Appendix 4, p. 536.

[5] West Bengal Records Office, Board of Trade, Proceedings vol. 494, 579.

system of Government price-fixing and cash advances to the producers. When the crop was ready for sale, it was taken over by the Government agents, and auctioned to private traders in Calcutta. Since opium was a contraband in China, the East India Company was unwilling to export it directly on its own account, and left the active development of this trade in the hands of country traders. The reason why the Company encouraged the cultivation and export of opium to China in the face of official Chinese opposition was twofold. Opium provided a substantial part of Government revenue, and secondly, it was an ideal solution to the problem of financing the Company's purchases of tea and raw silk in China. In the eighteenth century the East India Company had been forced to export from Europe large quantities of silver to China in order to balance its trade. After the political acquisition of Bengal, this need was largely eliminated, at first by shipping bullion from India and later by supplying opium for which a growing demand appeared in the Far East. The balance of China's trade with Europe and India which had been for so long in her favour finally turned and China was now in the position of having to pay for the Indian opium and cotton in silver. Although opium exports were a most lucrative item of India's foreign trade, its history was not entirely without the kind of fluctuations observable in the case of indigo. In fact the price of opium declined continuously as cultivation expanded in India in response to the Chinese demand, and the rise in total value was brought about by increasing the volume of shipment.

The export of Indian cotton was much more susceptible to changes in foreign demand. A considerable impetus was given to its export to England by the brief war with America in 1812, and it was used by the East India Company as a means of remittance, though largely to the China market. By the early 1820s, however, the trade in Indian raw cotton was severely depressed, and the volume of exports did not begin to rise until 1834. The relationship between the movements in the volume of cotton exported and the course of domestic prices was a complicated one, since the latter were influenced by the state of both domestic and foreign demand and the expected out-turn of the crop in India as well as in China. Thus cotton was perhaps the only article of export which occasionally exhibited an increase in price which was proportionately greater than the rise in the volume exported.[1] There were two other export items for which there was a considerable demand in our period. The first was raw silk which was a traditional export commodity from Bengal, and until the end of the Company's trade in the 1830s the bulk of the best quality silk came from the Company's own silk winding-stations and was shipped abroad on its own account. The other was Bengal sugar which showed a phenomenal increase from 1836–37 onwards as a result of the equalization of duties on the East India products with those on the West Indian.[2]

In contrast to the exports, both the commodity structure of the imports and the regional distribution of trade showed much greater stability. Great Britain supplied the greater proportion of the total imports, and was followed by China, and the Persian Gulf areas. The British imports consisted of cotton yarn, cotton piece goods, wearing apparel, metal goods, various other miscellaneous manufactures, and at least half of the total imports of wines and spirits. The rate of increase in the cotton goods was indeed remarkable. From Rs.90,000 in 1813–14, the imports of cotton goods into Calcutta expanded to Rs.2·6 million in 1819–20.[3] In 1828–29 the total value of imported cotton piece goods and yarn stood at Rs.16 million. By 1839–40 this had increased to Rs.26 million. It is well known that the substitution of the foreign machine-produced textiles – mainly British – for the Indian domestic manufactures was due to the relative cheapness of the former, and the competitive position of the Indian textiles was further restricted by the commercial policy of the Government. The tremendous increase in the value of the cotton imports during this period must be viewed against the back-

---

[1] Greenberg, *British Trade*, p. 90; West Bengal Records Office, Board of Trade, Commercial Consultation No. 16, 18 August 1829, Proceedings vol. 478, pp. 226–30; Bombay Records Office, Commercial Department, vol. 3/5, 1831, pp. 173–6; vol. 3/66, 1833, pp. 182–3; vol. 3/66, 1833, pp. 1–28.

[2] See my article, *Econ. Hist. Rev.* xix (2nd series, 1966), table 1, p. 347.

[3] *Minutes of Evidence, S. C. on Foreign Trade*, Parliamentary Papers, 1821, vol. 6, p. 209.

ground of declining costs and prices in Britain, which indicates that not only was there a net expansion in the volume but that the price elasticity of the demand for British textiles in India was very high.[1] That this was a revolutionary development in India's foreign trade there is no doubt. For the first time perhaps in the history of her trading relations with the West, India stood in the position of a buyer whose traditionally low-cost products were being pushed out of both the domestic and foreign markets by European products.

V

The extent to which the mechanism of Indian foreign trade was influenced and determined by the problem of capital transfers was shown in detail by both Prinsep and Palmer. The main components in the Indian balance of payments account can be seen in Table 3. The East India Company's Home Charges were naturally the largest element in the capital account. The various breakdowns of the Home Charges are given by Crawfurd,[2] and

Table 3 *The components of India's balance of payments in the nineteenth century.*

Merchandise		Service	
Credit	Debit	Credit	Debit

1. Exports	2. Imports	3. Freight
		5. Commercial and
		   banking commission
		7. Insurance
			4. Freight
			6. Commercial and
			   banking commission
			8. Insurance

Treasure		Capital	
Credit	Debit	Credit	Debit

9. Imports	10. Exports	11. Loans raised in
		   London
			12. The East India Com-
			   pany's Home Charges
			13. Interest on foreign loans
			14. Repatriation of profits on
			   foreign investments
			15. Remittance of private
			   European savings

[1] Cf. Matthews, *Trade-Cycle History*, p. 129; A. H. Imlah, *Economic Elements in Pax Brittanica* (Cambridge, Mass., 1958), p. 103–4.
[2] See Crawfurd, text.

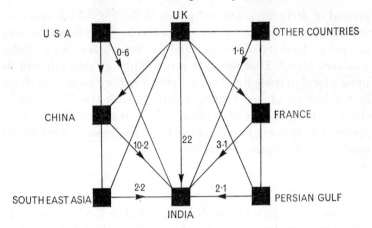

Figure 2   *India's balance of trade in 1828–29: merchandise and treasure. Figures are in million Rs. Arrows indicate favourable balances.*

between 1814 and 1858 these amounted on an average to £3·5 million. The private export of capital was estimated by Prinsep to be about £1 million in 1822. In addition, the Government of India was frequently asked by the Court of Directors at home to remit further sums in order to liquidate part of the public debt incurred on behalf of the Indian Government. Thus in all, it would seem that India had to meet an annual capital export of £5–6 million. India's very large export surplus on merchandise balance of trade throughout the period was clearly the result of this unilateral transfer of funds, and it is also evident that she effected the transfer by a multilateral payment system. The figures of net balance given in column 7 of my Appendix indicate both the geographical pattern of the payments arrangement as well as the total size of the outflow between 1828 and 1840. These figures do not include invisible service items such as insurance, shipping charges, and commissions, but the calculations made by Prinsep did, since he estimated the exports and imports on a c.i.f. basis. The structure of multilateral trade and the exact relationship between India and her various trading partners can be best understood with the help of a diagram, the form of which was devised by S. B. Saul.[1] For the period 1813 to

[1] Saul, *Studies in British Overseas Trade*, p. 58; his estimates were for the period 1870 to 1914.

1820 Prinsep's Appendix E gives the approximate size of the outflow for the trade as a whole.[1] It will be seen from the diagram (Figure 2) that in 1828–29 India had a positive trade balance with all the important countries trading with her. The export surplus with Great Britain came to Rs.22 million, while her balance with China stood at Rs.10·2 million, after imports of treasure have been taken into account. Since Britain, India's chief creditor, had a considerable negative balance with China in this period on account of her imports of tea and silk from China, the trade with the latter provided India with the largest means of settling her obligation to the former. But it is also clear from the treasure account in our table that the reciprocal obligations between the three countries were not evenly balanced so as to prevent a movement of bullion. For example, in this year, there was a net *outflow* of Rs.3·1 million to Britain while Rs.10·8 million was *imported* in silver from China. The movement of bullion was naturally determined by the state of the exchanges between India and Britain on the one hand and Britain, China, and India on the other. The fluctuations in the rates of exchange in their turn were governed by the demand for foreign exchange and the balance of payments position. A third factor in the relative movement of treasure in these areas was the price and the supply of American bills in Canton. If these bills were offered in large quantities and at a favourable rate, it tended to raise the exchange rate to India, and vice versa. The total demand made on India in 1828–29 for remittances could not have been excessive since there was a total net import of bullion worth Rs.15.8 million, and except for two extraordinarily bad years, India always had an excess of bullion imports. How India's positive balances with countries other than Britain and China were liquidated is uncertain. The Americans were beginning to reduce their imports of treasure into India and Canton, substituting bills on banking houses both in America and Britain, and their rapidly expanding cotton trade with the latter facilitated this operation. Thus the volume of American exports to Britain and imports from China and

---

[1] Prinsep, see text, p. 110; the figures for 1850–55 will be found in Tooke's *Appendix*, p. 714.

India was an important factor in the Indian remittance problem since the sale of American bills in these countries provided an additional supply of sterling.[1] The French merchants also went to London for credit. But the two Asian trading regions, the Persian Gulf and the Malayan Archipelago, remain puzzling, as it is not known how the fairly substantial balances remaining in these areas were disposed of.[2]

Until 1833 the East India Company remitted part of its annual Home Charges through its investment on export goods. The rest was transferred by means of bills of exchange on London and by buying silver in Canton (which was used to pay for its purchases in China) in exchange for bills on London and the Government treasury in Bengal. The method followed by the East India Company in transferring its funds since the cessation of its trade was twofold: first, by selling rupee bills in London for sterling to the importers of the Indian produce and secondly, by buying sterling bills in India from the exporters, the bills being secured by the 'hypothecation' of the goods to the Company. The question which of these two methods was to be followed in raising the necessary funds was determined by the money market in London and in India and by the immediate trade prospects. The company regulated the supply of funds or bills by raising or lowering the rates of exchange.[3]

There was some criticism of this system from business circles, as by introducing an element of uncertainty due to the timing of the operations, it encouraged unnecessary speculation. It was, for example, pointed out by George Larpent that when the Company threw a large amount of funds into the Calcutta money market, the immediate effect was to depreciate the exchange below the prevailing commercial rates and this had the tendency to encourage speculation in exports by cheapening them in terms of foreign currency irrespective of the normal

---

[1] Cf. Letter from H. H. Lindsey, Secretary to the Select Committee of Supracargoes at Canton, Bengal Financial Consultation 1, 28 February 1832; Matthews, *Trade-Cycle History*, p. 79; *Minutes of Evidence S. C. on the Petition of the East India Company for Relief*, Parliamentary Papers, 1840, vol. 7, QQ. 175, 176, 188.

[2] On this point see the remarks of Prinsep, text.

[3] For a description of the exchange operations of the Company see Tooke, *History of Prices*, vi (1857), 677.

business calculations. His advice to the Government was that they should not look to rates beyond the specie export point and should not expect to make a profit from direct exchange operations. To this it was objected that as the Company's external obligations were fixed in terms of a foreign currency, the Company owed it to the people of India who paid these charges to make the remittances at as favourable a rate as possible.[1] In fact, in 1838 H. J. Prinsep, the Secretary to the Supreme Government and the brother of George Alexander Prinsep, stated quite categorically in a minute that 'the Government as a remitter of funds for its home expenditure should consider itself in the same light as an individual would and should seek only to do the best for itself and for the Home Treasury that it can'.[2] However, in the early 1850s under strong pressure from the Calcutta commercial firms the Company stopped buying sterling bills in India and simply sold their own bills in London in return for drafts on their India treasury.[3]

The economic analysis implicit in the reasoning outlined above was of course the classical theory of the effect of exchange rate depreciation on exports. In practical terms, the usefulness of the classical theory or its modern counterpart, the Keynesian income analysis, is limited in several ways. In establishing a causal relation between India's foreign obligations and the substantive course of her trade, it is necessary to ask how far India's active balance of trade was 'spontaneous' and to what extent it was the 'induced' effect of the transfer problem. In other words, the question is whether India's export surplus would have remained at the level it did on the grounds of world demand for her exports alone had there not been pressure from the unilateral transfer of funds. It is of course evident from most empirical studies on balance of payments problems that a strict separation of the two factors is not always possible. In India's case, as we have seen, there had been a fairly sustained growth in the private sector of her foreign trade since 1814, but

---

[1] *Minutes of Evidence, S. C. on the Petition of the East India Company for Relief,* Parliamentary Papers, 1840 vol. 8, QQ. 160–94.

[2] India Financial Proceedings 5, 5 February 1838.

[3] *Returns relative to the Hypothecation of Goods in India,* Parliamentary Papers, 1850, vol. 41, [657].

imports rose faster than exports. Both in Prinsep's estimates and in the evidence given before the Parliamentary Committees of 1831–32 doubts were frequently expressed about the chances of increasing the level of exports from India which alone, it was felt, could lead to the increased ability of India to import goods from Britain after meeting her external liabilities. In 1830, Mackillop, partner in Palmers, Mackillop & Co., pointed out in reply to a question that in the present state of India's foreign trade, she could not afford or supply sufficient means for the remittance of the proceeds of goods sent home annually from England, in addition to the amount transferred by the East India Company and private individuals.[1] Such was also the opinion of Horsley Palmer who was much more categorical in his statement that the levels of imports into India could not rise in the given state of the exports as long as the export of capital also continued at the present level.[2] It turned out that such fears were very much exaggerated and the gloomy predictions were shown to be wrong by the continued importation of bullion into India, a sure sign that the balance of payments remained on the whole in India's favour. It is obvious that while the transfer problem had a marked influence on the rates of exchange and the movements of bullion over short periods, its effect on the total size of exports and imports were both complex and obscure. This was due to the fact that a number of different factors were at work. The character and nature of India's various foreign markets was one. A recession or boom in Britain affecting the size of Indian exports was an 'autonomous' factor which, owing to the presence of the transfer problem, could lead to movements in the rates of exchange that could in their turn influence the course of India's exports to other markets. Again, the influence of capital movements on the rates of exchange and consequently on short-term fluctuations in exports and imports was dependent on where the exchange operations originated and whether the risk-bearer was the Indian exporter or the foreign merchant.[3]

---

[1] *S. C. on the Affairs of the East India Company*, Parliamentary Papers, 1831–32, vol. 10 (735 ii), p. 545.
[2] Palmer, see text, Q. 1339.   [3] *Ibid*. QQ. 1341–44.

There was one fact, however, which stands out quite clearly. The simple 'gold standard' mechanism did work to restore equilibrium in the foreign exchange market. This can be seen by looking at the two major years of crisis in this period, 1821–22 and 1831–32. As George Prinsep pointed out, India's very strong position in regard to her exports between 1815 and 1818 was reflected in unusually large imports of treasure and very high exchange rates. But with the depression in trade beginning in 1819, the situation began to deteriorate and the exchanges were given some artificial support by the Government in 1820–21 by allowing the Company's interest bills to be paid in England by drafts on the Court of Directors. But the Company itself was forced to export bullion in 1821–22, in which year the exchange rate on London stood at only 2s. per rupee as against 2·7d. in 1818.[1] The events of 1831–32 were very similar, when there was a net export of treasure from India amounting to Rs.6·7 million, the result of a combination of trade depression and a sharp increase in the remittances made by the East India Company. In January 1831, the exchange rate in Calcutta fell to 1·9d. or below the specie export point and caused the British exporters of goods to India to remit their funds in bullion.[2] The effect of the fall in the level of exports and the consequent outflow of the precious metals was a general deflation of both prices and incomes which was felt in all the three Presidencies. But its effects were particularly severe in Bengal which bore the greater part of the burden of taxation and which suffered the greatest efflux of silver.

Although the total amount of bullion exported was not large compared to the annual importations in good years, nevertheless an actual contraction in the currency seemed to have taken place. It was, for example, stated by Charles Trevelyan that

about the year 1832 such quantities of silver had been remitted to England, to supply the great remittances which the Company was making at that time, that there really was no silver left in Bengal to pay the Land Tax; and in several districts the zamindars told us that they should be very happy to pay it in copper or produce . . . money became much scarcer and more valuable; the price of grain and other articles for home consumption

[1] Prinsep, see text.
[2] Palmer, see text, Q. 1318.

fell in an extraordinary degree; and the Land Tax, which is payable in
fixed sums of money was felt for a time as a most oppressive burden. . . .[1]

The Select Committee's report analysing the causes of the
deflation in Bengal commented,

The causes of these results are to be found principally in the great consumption of the precious metals which takes place in India. . . . It is to be
remembered too, that in India a temporary deficiency of metallic currency
is not supplied, as in this country by an issue of paper. An export of
treasure is a net diminution of the circulating medium; and while the
habits of the people remain what they are, and the monetary system what
it is, any considerable export of treasure must produce embarrassments
similar to those which have been described by Mr. Trevelyan.[2]

The connexion between an exclusively metallic currency system
in India and the very large annual importation of treasure was
also pointed out by Tooke who estimated the annual loss by
wear and tear at 1% out of a total stock of £400 million.[3] But by
1850 a new factor had appeared in India's external balance-sheet:
the railway construction in India and the export of capital by the
railway companies. Most of the earlier British investments in
India were made from the savings of the Company's European
servants and by re-investing the retained profits by European
business houses. Thus there does not seem to have been any
transfer of actual resources from Britain to India. But the magnitude of the railway investments not only absorbed the pressure
of capital transfer from India but also led to an increase in the
imports of merchandise and treasure into India in the 1850s.[4]
The high income effect of these investments and the renewed
stimulus to India's foreign trade with the outbreak of the
Crimean war can perhaps be seen in the upward trend of Indian
prices which began to show itself from 1855.

In conclusion, it may be pointed out again that a review of
India's foreign trade between 1814 and 1858 demonstrates the
close interrelation between the ordinary course of trade and
capital movements. The magnitude of the transfer problem

---

[1] *S. C. on the East India Company's Petition for Relief*, Parliamentary Papers,
1840, vol. 7, p.v. QQ. 804, 812.
[2] *Ibid.*
[3] Tooke, see text.
[4] Tooke, see text.

which can be seen by comparing India's export earnings and the total outflow of capital also explains why foreign trade occupied such a crucial position in her finances. For the same reason, it acquired a political importance which it would not probably have merited had the circumstances been different. Although the dependence of India's economy as a whole on foreign trade and export specialization does not appear to have been great, the presence of the transfer problem nevertheless introduced an element of instability that was both short-term and long-term. As long as the level of world demand for India's exports remained high, the transfer problem solved itself. But any downward trend in this demand was likely to produce the type of short-term dislocation described above. What the long-term effect of the transfer problem on the Indian economy was is a speculative question. But as it encouraged the exporting industries at the expense of the other sectors, the result was probably a basic imbalance in the structure of the economy as a whole.

Contemporary economists looking at Indian problems, including the authors in this volume, were, however, concerned to an overwhelming degree with the much more urgent task of the economic modernization of India. From the point of view of European intellectual history, and in particular European economic thinking, the main contribution of the tracts lies in an extension of the methods of economic analysis and discussion to Asia and Asian problems. During the late eighteenth and early nineteenth centuries the rapid development in industrial technology and the corresponding progress in the refinement of existing financial and economic institutions in Europe were accompanied by an intense theoretical examination of the factors that make for economic development and growth. Beginning with Adam Smith, this was the main theme running through the writings of classical English economists such as Malthus, Ricardo, and J. S. Mill. But in Europe the two major tasks outlined by the classical economists—the need to increase the physical output of labour through capital accumulation, and free trade which would intensify the division of labour and bring fresh resources into the productive framework—were largely achieved by a combination of the revolution in technology and a new outlook in Government policy.[1] In the case of Asia, the problem, then as now, remained one of transforming a static and long-established traditional economy into a new structure to bring it into line with the rate of progress achieved in more advanced countries. This was recognized by Mill and stated clearly in his *Principles of Political Economy*, as the following quotation will show:

In countries where the principle of accumulation is as weak as it is in the various nations of Asia; where people will neither save, nor work to obtain the means of saving, unless under the inducement of enormously high profits, nor even then if it is necessary to wait for a considerable time for them; where either productions remain scanty, or drudgery great, because there is neither capital forthcoming nor forethought sufficient for the adoption of the contrivances by which natural agents are made to do work of human labour; the desideratum for such a country, economically considered, is an increase of industry, and of the effective desire of accumulation. The means are, first, a better government: more complete security of property; moderate taxes, and freedom from arbitrary exaction under the name of taxes; a more permanent and more advantageous tenure of land, securing to the cultivator as far as possible the undivided benefits of the industry, skill, and economy he may exert. Secondly, improvement of the public intelligence; the decay of usages or superstitions which interfere with the effective employment of industry; and the growth of mental activity, making the people alive to new objects of desire. Thirdly, the introduction of foreign arts, which raise the returns derivable from additional capital to a rate corresponding to the low strength of the desire of accumulation: and the importation of foreign capital, which renders the increase of production no longer exclusively dependent on the thrift or providence of the inhabitants themselves, while it places before them a stimulating example, and by instilling new ideas and breaking the chains of habit, if not by improving the actual condition of the population, tends to create in them new wants, increased ambition, and greater thought for the future.[2]

The strength of these ideas and the prevailing faith in the efficacy of the suggested means of improvement can be measured from the fact that from Prinsep to Crawfurd, most of the writings in the volume very closely echo the views set out by Mill. Although a critic might point out that the contemporary economic discussions on India were concerned to a large extent

---

[1] On classical economists see H. Myint, *Theories of Welfare Economics* (London, 1948) pp. 6–13.

[2] J. S. Mill, *Principles of Political Economy*, Book I, Chapter XIII, para. 1.

with the question how Indian resources can best be developed to suit purely British needs, nevertheless it was clearly recognized that even this limited purpose could not be fully realized without real internal progress and change. On such technical points as methods of international accounting, the mechanism of foreign exchange, capital flows, and balance of payments disequilibrium, Prinsep, Palmer, and Tooke, as we have already seen, followed purely classical economic reasoning. For Indian economic and intellectual history, the phenomenon of a deliberate analysis of her economic problems, initiated by these early British writers, was responsible for giving rise to an entirely new tradition that was later taken over vigorously by Indians themselves.

Statistical Appendix

Balance of trade and treasure account

In million Rs. (calculated in Company's rupees)

Source: India Office Library, Commercial Reports, Bengal, Bombay, and Madras, 1828–40.

Methods of calculation: These figures are based on the above Custom house reports which have been reworked to exclude coastal trade, to correct undervaluation of exports and to convert the sicca, Madras, and Bombay rupees into Company's rupees.

1828–29

	Merchandise			Treasure			Total balance
	1	2	3	4	5	6	7
	Export	Import	Balance	Export	Import	Balance	
United Kingdom	53·7	34·8	+ 18·9	3·4	0·3	+ 3·1	+ 22·0
France	6·5	2·9	+ 3·6	—	0·5	− 0·5	+ 3·1
Sweden	0·3	0·1	+ 0·2	—	—	—	+ 0·2
Hamburg	—	0·5	− 0·5	—	—	—	− 0·5
Lisbon	0·1	—	+ 0·1	—	—	—	+ 0·1
United States	3·3	0·8	+ 2·5	—	1·9	− 1·9	+ 0·6
New South Wales	0·09	0·03	+ 0·06	—	—	—	+ 0·06
Persian Gulf	8·1	3·3	+ 4·8	0·2	2·9	− 2·7	+ 2·1
China	28·4	7·4	+ 21·0	—	10·8	− 10·8	+ 10·2
Penang and Straits	6·7	2·2	+ 4·5	0·6	1·5	− 0·9	+ 3·6
Indonesian Archipelago	0·6	0·3	+ 0·3	—	0·2	− 0·2	+ 0·1
Manila	—	—	—	—	0·1	− 0·1	− 0·1
Pegu	1·2	0·6	+ 0·6	—	2·0	− 2·0	− 1·4
Africa	2·3	0·7	+ 1·6	0·4	0·2	+ 0·2	+ 1·8
Total	111·29	53·63	57·66	4·6	20·4	− 15·8	+ 41·86

1829–30

United Kingdom	59·9	29·6	+ 30·3	8·2	0·1	+ 8·1	+ 38·4
France	7·0	2·3	+ 4·7	—	0·1	− 0·1	+ 4·6
United States	3·9	1·4	+ 2·5	—	1·3	− 1·3	+ 1·2
New South Wales	0·2	—	+ 0·2	—	—	—	+ 0·2
Persian Gulf	12·8	3·8	+ 9·0	0·1	3·2	− 3·1	+ 5·9
China	30·4	8·3	+ 22·1	—	13·7	− 13·7	+ 8·4
Penang and Straits	6·5	3·0	+ 3·5	—	1·6	− 1·6	+ 1·9
Indonesia	0·4	0·3	+ 0·1	—	0·1	− 0·1	0·0
Manila	0·7	—	+ 0·7	—	0·2	− 0·2	+ 0·5
Pegu	1·2	0·4	+ 0·8	—	1·3	− 1·3	− 0·5
Africa	2·3	1·0	+ 1·3	0·6	0·3	+ 0·3	+ 1·6
Total	125·3	50·1	+ 75·2	8·9	21·9	− 13·0	+ 62·2

1830–31

| | Merchandise | | | Treasure | | | Total balance |
	1 Export	2 Import	3 Balance	4 Export	5 Import	6 Balance	7
United Kingdom	45·8	34·4	+11·4	5·3	—	+ 5·3	+16·7
France	5·7	1·3	+ 4·4	—	—	—	+ 4·4
Sweden	0·3	0·2	+ 0·1	—	—	—	+ 0·1
United States	3·5	1·8	+ 1·7	—	1·0	− 1·0	+ 0·7
Persian Gulf	13·1	5·8	+ 7·3	—	2·2	− 2·2	+ 5·1
China	29·4	8·2	+21·2	—	9·6	− 9·6	+11·6
Penang and Straits	4·3	3·2	+ 1·1	0·1	2·5	− 2·4	− 1·3
Indonesia	0·4	0·2	+ 0·2	—	0·1	− 0·1	+ 0·1
Manila	0·2	—	+ 0·2	—	—	—	+ 0·2
Pegu	1·7	0·6	+ 1·1	—	1·2	− 1·2	− 0·1
Africa	1·3	0·8	+ 0·5	0·3	0·1	+ 0·2	+ 0·7
Total	105·7	56·5	+49·2	5·7	16·7	−11·0	+38·2

1831–32

| | Merchandise | | | Treasure | | | Total balance |
	1 Export	2 Import	3 Balance	4 Export	5 Import	6 Balance	7
United Kingdom	35·3	29·7	+ 5·6	16·9	—	+16·9	+22·5
France	2·6	0·6	+ 2·0	—	—	—	+ 2·0
Hamburg	0·1	—	+ 0·1	—	—	—	+ 0·1
United States	4·8	1·3	+ 3·5	—	1·0	− 1·0	+ 2·5
Persian Gulf	9·7	4·1	+ 5·6	—	2·2	− 2·2	+ 3·4
China	38·7	4·9	+33·8	—	5·6	− 5·6	+28·2
Penang and Straits	4·1	2·4	+ 1·7	0·1	1·8	− 1·7	0·0
Indonesia	0·2	0·1	+ 0·1	—	0·1	− 0·1	0·0
Pegu	1·1	0·6	+ 0·5	0·4	0·4	0·0	+ 0·5
Africa	1·2	1·0	+ 0·2	0·5	—	+ 0·5	+ 0·7
Total	97·8	44·7	+53·1	17·9	11·1	+ 6·8	+59·9

1832–33

| | Merchandise | | | Treasure | | | Total balance |
	1 Export	2 Import	3 Balance	4 Export	5 Import	6 Balance	7
United Kingdom	43·0	29·0	+14·0	11·6	—	+11·6	+25·6
France	5·3	1·6	+ 3·7	—	—	—	+ 3·7
Portugal	0·3	—	+ 0·3	—	—	—	+ 0·3
United States	3·2	0·7	+ 2·5	—	0·5	− 0·5	+ 2·0
Persian Gulf	6·7	1·9	+ 4·8	0·1	1·2	− 1·1	+ 3·7
China	33·6	4·6	+29·0	—	5·9	− 5·9	+23·1
Penang and Straits	6·3	2·1	+ 4·2	0·6	3·1	− 2·5	+ 1·7
Indonesia	0·3	0·1	+ 0·2	—	0·1	− 0·1	+ 0·1
Pegu	1·2	0·9	+ 0·3	—	1·3	− 1·3	− 1·0
Africa	1·4	0·8	+ 0·6	0·8	4·4	+ 0·8	+ 1·4
Total	101·3	41·7	+59·6	13·1	12·1	+ 1·0	+60·6

1833–34

	Merchandise			Treasure			Total balance
	1	2	3	4	5	6	7
	Export	Import	Balance	Export	Import	Balance	
United Kingdom	38·5	26·0	+12·5	4·7	—	+ 4·7	+17·2
France	6·7	1·7	+ 5·0	—	—	—	+ 5·0
Sweden	0·2	0·1	+ 0·1	—	—	—	+ 0·1
United States	4·3	0·5	+ 3·8	—	0·4	− 0·4	+ 3·4
New South Wales	—	—	—	—	—	—	—
Persian Gulf	7·7	2·9	+ 4·8	0·1	2·3	− 2·2	+ 2·6
China	47·5	5·5	+42·0	—	13·1	−13·1	+28·9
Penang and Straits	5·1	1·6	+ 3·5	—	2·6	− 2·6	+ 0·9
Indonesia	0·3	—	+ 0·3	—	0·1	− 0·1	+ 0·2
Manila	—	0·3	− 0·3	—	—	—	− 0·3
Pegu	1·3	1·2	+ 0·1	0·2	0·3	− 0·1	0·0
Africa	2·1	0·8	+ 1·3	0·5	0·1	+ 0·4	+ 1·7
Total	113·7	40·6	+73·1	5·5	18·9	−13·4	+59·7

1834–35

	1	2	3	4	5	6	7
United Kingdom	41·7	27·8	+13·9	0·6	0·1	+ 0·5	+14·4
France	5·2	1·4	+ 3·8	—	0·2	− 0·2	+ 3·6
United States	2·4	0·5	+ 1·9	—	0·6	− 0·6	+ 1·3
New South Wales	0·4	—	+ 0·4	—	—	—	+ 0·4
Persian Gulf	5·7	2·5	+ 3·2	0·1	2·4	− 2·3	+ 0·9
China	37·1	5·7	+31·4	—	12·1	−12·1	+19·3
Penang and Straits	5·4	2·7	+ 2·7	—	2·7	− 2·7	0·0
Indonesia	0·2	—	+ 0·2	0·1	0·1	0·0	+ 0·2
Manila	—	6·3	− 0·3	—	—	—	− 0·3
Pegu	1·3	1·0	+ 0·3	0·4	0·8	− 0·4	− 0·1
Africa	2·1	0·8	+ 1·3	0·2	1·0	− 0·8	+ 0·5
Total	101·5	42·7	+58·8	1·4	20·0	−18·6	+40·2

1835–36

	1	2	3	4	5	6	7
United Kingdom	51·9	30·7	+21·2	0·1	—	+ 0·1	+21·3
France	6·3	1·5	+ 4·8	—	—	—	+ 4·8
United States	5·7	0·8	+ 4·9	—	1·4	− 1·4	+ 3·5
New South Wales	0·5	—	+ 0·5	—	—	—	+ 0·5
Persian Gulf	10·4	2·3	+ 8·1	0·1	3·8	− 3·7	+ 4·4
China	55·8	5·4	+50·4	—	13·9	13·9	+36·5
Penang and Straits	4·9	2·5	+ 2·4	—	2·1	− 2·1	+ 0·3
Indonesia	0·2	0·1	+ 0·1	—	—	—	+ 0·1
Manila	—	0·1	− 0·1	—	—	—	− 0·1
Pegu	1·5	1·6	− 0·1	0·1	0·8	− 0·7	− 0·8
Africa	1·4	1·0	+ 0·4	0·1	0·4	− 0·3	+ 0·1
Total	138·6	46·0	+92·6	0·4	22·4	−22·0	+70·6

1836–37

	Merchandise			Treasure			Total balance
	1	2	3	4	5	6	7
	Export	Import	Balance	Export	Import	Balance	
United Kingdom	62·2	38·3	+23·9	—	—	—	+23·9
France	4·9	2·1	+ 2·8	—	—	—	+ 2·8
United States	4·7	0·6	+ 4·1	—	0·7	− 0·7	+ 3·4
New South Wales	0·3	—	+ 0·3	—	—	—	+ 0·3
Persian Gulf	9·0	3·0	+ 6·0	0·1	3·6	− 3·5	+ 2·5
China	67·2	5·3	+61·9	0·1	12·4	−12·3	+49·6
Penang and Straits	5·6	2·2	+ 3·4	—	1·9	− 1·9	+ 1·5
Indonesia	0·3	0·1	+ 0·2	—	0·1	− 0·1	+ 0·1
Pegu	1·8	1·9	− 0·1	0·7	0·9	− 0·2	− 0·3
Africa	2·7	0·7	+ 2·0	0·2	0·5	− 0·3	+ 1·7
Total	158·7	54·2	+104·5	1·1	20·1	−19·0	+85·5

1837–38

United Kingdom	47·2	32·1	+15·1	0·7	0·2	+ 0·5	+15·6
France	3·7	1·4	+ 2·3	0·2	0·2	0·0	+ 2·3
United States	1·4	0·7	+ 0·7	—	0·6	− 0·6	+ 0·1
New South Wales	0·4	—	+ 0·4	—	—	—	+ 0·4
Persian Gulf	10·0	2·8	+ 7·2	0·2	3·1	− 2·9	+ 4·3
China	45·0	4·4	+40·6	—	17·4	−17·4	+23·2
Penang and Straits	6·1	3·1	+ 3·0		3·1	− 3·1	− 0·1
Indonesia	0·3	—	+ 0·3	—	0·1	− 0·1	+ 0·2
Manila	—	0·2	− 0·2	—	—	—	− 0·2
Pegu	1·8	2·6	− 0·8	1·4	0·8	+ 0·6	− 0·2
Africa	3·2	1·0	+ 2·2	0·1	0·8	− 0·7	+ 1·5
Total	119·1	48·3	+70·8	2·6	26·3	−23·7	+47·1

1838–39

United Kingdom	50·8	35·1	+15·7	—	0·3	− 0·3	+15·4
France	7·5	1·1	+ 6·4	—	0·2	− 0·2	+ 6·2
United States	3·6	0·7	+ 2·9	—	0·8	− 0·8	+ 2·1
New South Wales	0·5	—	+ 0·5	0·1	—	+ 0·1	+ 0·6
Persian Gulf	9·3	3·2	+ 6·1	0·2	3·2	− 3·0	+ 3·1
China	45·3	4·6	+40·7	0·1	21·4	−21·3	+19·4
Penang and Straits	5·1	2·8	+ 2·3	—	2·4	− 2·4	− 0·1
Indonesia	0·4	—	+ 0·4	—	0·1	− 0·1	+ 0·3
Manila	—	0·1	− 0·1	—	—	—	− 0·1
Pegu	1·8	2·2	− 0·4	0·6	0·6	0·0	− 0·4
Africa	2·2	0·9	+ 1·3	0·2	0·9	− 0·7	+ 0·6
Total	126·5	50·7	+75·8	1·2	29·9	−28·7	+47·1

	1839–40						
	Merchandise				Treasure		Total balance
	1	2	3	4	5	6	7
	Export	Import	Balance	Export	Import	Balance	
United Kingdom	68·3	42·9	+25·4	—	4·4	− 4·4	+21·0
France	7·6	1·6	+ 6·0	—	2·1	− 2·1	+ 3·9
United States	4·0	0·4	+ 3·6	—	1·2	− 1·2	+ 2·4
New South Wales	0·7	—	+ 0·7	—	0·3	− 0·3	+ 0·4
Persian Gulf	9·0	3·3	+ 5·7	0·2	2·5	− 2·3	+ 3·4
China	12·1	2·0	+10·1	1·0	5·0	− 4·0	+ 6·1
Penang and Straits	11·9	2·9	+ 9·0	0·1	2·7	− 2·6	+ 6·4
Indonesia	0·1	0·1	0·0	—	—	—	0·0
Manila	1·1	0·2	+ 0·9	—	—	—	+ 0·9
Pegu	2·7	2·4	+ 0·3	1·3	0·5	+ 0·8	+ 1·1
Africa	2·0	0·7	+ 1·3	0·2	0·9	− 0·7	+ 0·6
Total	119·5	56·5	+63·0	2·8	19·6	−16·8	+46·2

1

George Alexander Prinsep, Remarks on the External Commerce and Exchanges of Bengal, with Appendix of Accounts and Estimates (1823)

ADVERTISEMENT

The investigation that led to the following remarks has been my occupation during a three months' visit to this Presidency from Bombay. It was suggested by the discordance of opinion, which I found among the best-informed on the subject of the exchange with London.

To the characteristic liberality of the Marquis of Hastings' administration, I am indebted for the facility with which I obtained the data, whereon my estimates are founded. The Calcutta annual trade reports were freely offered me by the Board of Customs; in which, as in every other department, I experienced every disposition to satisfy such inquiries, as were not precluded by pending financial operations.

The results may perhaps be found interesting to the Indian stock-holder at home, as well as to the merchant and manu-facturer: for a clear statement of the actual or probable balance of trade, in the intercourse of Great Britain with Bengal, will afford the best clue to the rate of exchange that may be fairly reckoned upon for the future: which is a matter of less impor-tance to those engaged in the commerce, than to those who derive a net income from Indian resources.

G.A.P.

Calcutta, October 1822

[The handwritten corrections made by Prinsep in 1824 are indicated by deletions being placed within square brackets

N.B. Such errors, as may occur in the voluminous figures of the text and Appendix must be charged upon the utter inexperience of the Editor in Europe, in matters of commerce.

followed by corrections in italics or by putting additions in square brackets in italics. – *Editor*]

External Commerce of Bengal

In the last* annual trade report, drawn up at Calcutta by the Board of Customs Salt and Opium, a statement is inserted, showing the official valuations of the annual imports and exports by sea, from 1813–14 to 1820–21 inclusive, and comprehending the Company's outward† and home investments.‡ The totals of merchandise during those eight years are stated at

	Total	Per ann.
Imports	Rs.16,79,14,286 or	2,09,89,286
Exports	44,58,91,038 or	5,57,36,380
the latter exceeding the former by	27,79,76,752 or	3,47,47,094

But, on adding to the imports

the apparent specie balance of	Rs.21,66,79,214 or	2,70,84,902
and the amount of bills upon the Bengal treasury, remitted as returns to Calcutta	8,14,95,993 or	1,01,86,999
we find a deficit in the declared amount of the exports to the extent of	2,01,98,455 or	25,24,807
which, exclusive of the surplus export on the Company's account, *viz.*	Rs. 3,34,34,406 or	41,79,301
would amount to	5,36,32,861 or	67,04,108

Such a result must very much surprise those who have been wont to estimate at a large sum the annual remittance of private capital accumulated by the savings and industry of Europeans in India; which, by what is perhaps the lowest computation, has been rated at half a million,§ and by some at a million, a million

---

* Of 1820–21: that of 1821–22 is now in preparation. If received in time, it will be added.

† Except military stores.

‡ *Vide* Appendix A.

§ *Vide* Mr Bosanquet's speech at the India House on the question of the renewal of the chapter, 26th January 1813. [Bosanquet was a member of the East India Company's Directorate at this time. He had been twice Chairman of the Company, in 1803 and 1811. A member of an important London merchant family, he had been long active in the political affairs of the East India Company. The speech referred to in the text can be found in *Debates Held on the 19th, 22nd, and 26th January 1813 at the adjoined Courts of East India Proprietors with an Appendix*, by an Impartial Reporter (London, 1813), p. 229. *Editor*]

and a half, two millions,* and even three millions† sterling. Nor is there reason to suppose that, during the same period, there was any considerable transfer of capital from Europe, for the purpose either of investment in the Company's securities here, or of permanent employment in Bengal. A similar anomaly results from the examination of the trade reports of preceding years; and naturally induces the question, 'Why, if such has been the state of the Indian commerce, did the exchange with England so long remain above a bullion-exportation rate? It would seem that a large balance must be owing by the country, or that capital must have been sunk, instead of accumulated, in it by Europeans!'

The anomaly is explained by the discovery that the Calcutta trade reports have the general defect of Custom-house returns in regard to the valuations, which, far from approximating to the truth, are not even formed upon a consistent plan. I will endeavour to fix the general outlines of the method pursued, before I introduce a set of corrected statements; but, as an apology for any misconceptions on my part, it is proper to mention that, notwithstanding an express clause in the Regulations‡ to that effect, it does not appear that any printed 'Book of Rates' exists, although it ought to have been 'revised and republished annually'; and moreover, that, in many cases, the practice can by no means be ascertained by perusal of the various ordinances comprised in the Regulations.

To begin with imports: when a ship arrives, her manifest is

---

* 'It is no extravagant assertion to advance, that the annual remittances to London on account of individuals have been at the rate of nearly two millions per ann. for a series of years past, and from sources within ourselves, independent of the commerce of foreigners', para. 96 of a letter from the Court of Directors to the Governor in Council of Fort William, dated 20 June 1810, in answer to their financial letter of 23 August 1809. *Vide* Papers on East-India Affairs, printed by order of the House of Commons, 10th July 1813. [Parliamentary Paper, House of Commons, 1812–13, vol. 10, p. 324. *Editor*]

† 'I could only give a vague estimate of the amount of this *indirect* or *private* tribute, which very much resembles the rents and profits drawn by British proprietors from the sugar plantations in the West Indies; but it is unquestionably considerable, and I am disposed to think, that it cannot fall short of three millions sterling per annum at the present period.' *Vide* Remarks on the Plans of Finance lately promulgated by the Honourable Court of Directors and by the Supreme Government of India, October 1821, by H. St George Tucker, Esq., p. 3.

‡ Regulation vi, 1814, clause 3.

delivered at the Custom-house, and the several consignees are required to exhibit their original invoices. The goods are then valued at their cost, all packages* and charges deducted (except the casks containing wine and beer); the amount being converted into rupees at rates generally giving an advantage to the Revenue,† of which the most important are those of

The £ sterling fixed at	Sa. Rs.10
– dollar – Spanish or American	2¼
– livre or franc of France	10 per 24
– Madras star pagoda	3¾

Whereas it would seem more natural to value

The £ sterling at the current rate of exchange	
– dollar at the Calcutta mint price of	Sa. Rs.206¼ per 100
– franc ditto	10‡ per 25
– Madras pagoda according to the exchange; or at the mint price of	3·6¾ as.

And further, an augmentation is added of 30 per cent upon China invoices, and 15 per cent upon the produce of Madras. In the year 1814, it was ordered that the Company's goods should be valued and pay duty like those of individuals; and I am not aware of any deviation from this rule in the case of their imports.

With regard to exports, the practice is equally devoid of consistency. Some articles are rated at a fixed valuation; others at the supposed Calcutta market-prices; others at the *aurung* prices. To mention the most important, I include, under:

CLASS 1. Indigo, always valued at Rs.100 per factory maund. Silk, Bengal filature, Rs.7; other sorts, Rs.6 per bazar seer; and grain, Rs.1 per maund. At present it comprehends also: sugar, brown, Rs.5; other sorts, Rs.8 per bazar maund (the average valuations of 1817–18 and 1818–19 were between Rs.8 and 9,

* In some recent instances a duty has been levied on packages whose contents were exempt: this circumstance has, no doubt, been owing to a misinterpretation of orders.

† Regulation IX, 1810, clause 60: and Regulations I, 1812, clause 19: Bombay and Brazil are omitted, together with the currency of some other countries; and the French franc is still termed livre tournois.

‡ The value of the 5 franc piece in the market is now Rs.190 per 100, equal to Rs.9½ per 25 francs.

upon the whole export). Saltpetre, rated at Rs.6 per bazar maund; which is Rs.1 to 1½ above its present value. In:

CLASS 2. Are comprehended a great variety of minor articles, besides the important one of opium, which is registered at the same prices. In:

CLASS 3. Piece-goods, both silk and cotton; raw cotton also, I believe.

Re-exported commodities, which are entered at the valuations assumed on their arrival, may be set down as forming a fourth class.

An order was made that the Company's exports should be placed upon the same footing as the private-trade, and subject to like duties and valuation. This rule, however, does not appear to have been strictly observed, if we may judge merely by the reports themselves. For, during those years in which the Company's trade was excluded from the general annual statements, * the average Custom-house valuation of silk was between Rs.5½ and 6½, per seer; whereas, in the two following years which embrace their interest, the average is Rs.10 12 as. and Rs.12 10 as.: so that, in this article at least, it would seem their goods are taken at the real cost, and those of individuals still at the old rates.†

But, in order to ascertain the amount of capital employed in the external commerce of a nation, it is not sufficient to procure an exact statement of the prime cost and market-prices of the articles of traffic. The trade must be considered as an aggregate of private transactions; and the invoices inwards and outwards as alone indicating their amount. Thus, if a merchant in London sends out an investment of goods, the proceeds thereof (which for general calculation, we may consider as the exact amount of his invoices, i.e. of the prime cost, interest and all charges paid by him) must be reinvested in some specific return – in merchandise, produce, bullion, or bills of exchange, the remittance

---

* I.e. prior to the year 1819–20.
† Since writing this, I understand the distinction to be general with respect to the Company's exports.

of which will be attended with certain definite charges, forming part of the gross amount. For instance, on Manchester goods, whereof

the prime cost is	£100	0	0

he incurs

charges for packages, land-carriage, shipping expenses, freight and insurance, all expressed in the invoice, say 10 per cent	10	0	0
	110	0	0
Carried forward	£110	0	0

ADD

twelve months' interest, if the price of the goods be that of only six months' credit	5	10	0
	£115	10	0

It follows that a system of valuation, which should assume the net, as the real, cost and value of the goods, would in this case rate them $15\frac{1}{2}$ per cent too low. But there are many bulky commodities, whereon the freight and other invoice charges are 20, 30, and even 40 per cent. Probably we may deem them to average full 20 per cent upon the total merchandise imported into Calcutta.

Now, taking up the consignment from London at Calcutta, its place of destination, the consignee has £115 10s. to remit; or say, at the old exchange of 2s. 6d., Sa. Rs.924.

For this purpose he buys, say

a chest of indigo at	Rs.900	0	0

charges

– $2\frac{1}{2}$ per cent commission thereon	22	8	0
– shipping expenses	1	8	0

and closes the transaction by

an invoice of	Rs.924	0	0

Or he procures

saltpetre to the amount of	Rs.870	0	0

charges

– 5 per cent commission	43	8	0
– shipping expenses	10	8	0
Making a total return of	Rs.924	0	0

Thus, supposing the entry in the Custom-house registers to be the real prime cost, we have an actual remittance exceeding their valuation by above $2\frac{1}{2}$ and 6 per cent respectively.

When foreigners come to the Calcutta market, their export invoices bear a further charge for duties, which, in some cases, are also incurred in our own, especially in the country trade. In the last case, and generally where ships owned in Bengal are employed, the freight is an invoice charge, or, if not, a remittance of capital. Moreover, that portion of the trade which is conducted on Calcutta account is mostly insured there; and occasionally even when Bengal houses of business are not interested in the speculation, it is so insured; consequently the premium becomes an invoice charge. The average amount of these expenses, perhaps without including freight, I estimate differently, according to the circumstances of each year, reducing it gradually from 11 per cent in 1813–14 to 7 per cent towards the close of the period under examination.

By these corrections,* the balance is greatly increased on the side of exports; and, upon revising in like manner the reported, or Custom-house valuations of the bullion trade,† which appears almost entirely under the head of imports, there will be found a large excess in the amount stated, which further augments the balance by 32 lakhs. The calculation is made upon a scale of reduction applicable only to the Spanish dollar,‡ which is assumed as worth the mint price of Rs.$206\frac{1}{4}$ per 100, instead of Rs.225, the Custom-house rate. Perhaps it might more properly have been taken at Rs.$205\frac{1}{2}$, its present, and I believe its average, value; the mint delays and custom of declaring the assay causing a discount upon the dollar in the market of from $\frac{1}{2}$ to 1 per cent. The charges are added to the export, and deducted from the import, value; because in the latter it is the net, and in the former, as with merchandise, the invoice

---

* *Vide* Appendix B and C. The official amount of exports from Great Britain to all India in 1820 was £2,421,763 (Quarterly Review, No. 53, p. 535). The Custom-house valuation of imports at Calcutta in 1820–21 is Rs.1,13,20,797; and my corrected valuation at Ex. 2s. 3d. only, Rs.1,00,75,509, exclusive of charges.

† *Vide* Appendix D.

‡ Full nine-tenths of the bullion imported has been in the shape of Spanish dollars.

amount, which is debited and credited in merchants' accounts. Now it appears that about half the bullion import has been effected by the country trade; and the other half by that of Europe and America. Supposing one-third of the whole to have been insured at Calcutta at an average premium of 2 per cent, and stating the commission on the receipt and sale at $\frac{1}{2}$ per cent, we shall find, after making a small allowance for other charges, the net import value of the dollar only Rs.203 per 100: while it is raised to about Rs.212 on export for private account, by the addition of $\frac{1}{2}$ per cent to the mint price for commission, and 2 per cent for insurance premium; being probably in that case wholly insured at Calcutta.

Wherefore, instead of an annual excess of capital introduced into Bengal by its external trade, to amount of $25\frac{1}{4}$ lakhs, or, independent of the Company's operations, of 67 lakhs, we have now an apparent surplus remittance from Calcutta amounting to a

	Per Ann.
total of no less than*	Rs.13,20,43,625 or 1,65,05,453
inclusive of bullion sent out by the company during the last five years, for purposes unconnected with commerce amounting to	1,92,17,970† or 24,02,246

so that it would be more correct to state

the surplus export at	lakhs 1,512$\frac{1}{2}$ or 189
the Company's proportion being about	‡600 or 75
and that of individuals about	912 or 114

There is even some ground to believe the balance still underestimated:§ one-tenth of the export valuation has not been scrutinized; and the percentage allowance for charges probably

* *Vide* Appendix E.

† The amounts given in Appendix A are here reduced to the valuation of Rs.203 per 100 dollars, being at that rate included in the corrected general statement, Appendix E.

‡ This is not shown in any of the tables in the Appendix.

Their reported total export	Rs.7,99,54,485
Do. import (half in bullion)	4,65,20,079
give a total balance of	Rs.3,34,34,406

which, with addition of profit, remittance, and allowance for exchanges and charges, gives nearly 600 lakhs.

§ *Vide* Appendix C, note to the second statement.

falls short of the truth, if the freights of Indian shipping be duly computed. Besides, regard must be had to the general nature of the trade, and to the proportion of Bengal interest therein, which I consider not to exceed one-tenth upon the imports of merchandise, and perhaps (including opium) one-half upon the exports, at least during the period of our inquiry. Now, the former have certainly, on the whole, been more attended with loss upon invoice than the latter, notwithstanding the unfortunate cotton speculations of 1818 and 1819: whence it is fair to conclude that the difference between the *net proceeds* of imported goods and the amount of the property remitted is a few lakhs more than it will appear by the mode of calculation I have adopted. To hazard a conjecture upon the subject, I should name from 1,060 to 1,100 lakhs, or per ann. 135 lakhs,* as the surplus remittance of individuals, with every allowance whatever; and, for the total surplus, about 1,700 lakhs, or per ann. 210 to 214 [*215*] lakhs, inclusive of both private and public account, with the single exception of the Company's home-trade profits, transferred to India for appropriation as a sinking fund, for the gradual extinction of the Indian debt. Such a transfer of capital, so long as it is made in the shape of bullion, can no otherwise affect commerce, than inasmuch as it accelerates the reduction of the burthen of dividends payable to absentees, whereby the Company's remittances to meet their home demands are so considerably inflated.†

We may thus safely assume the existence of a very large remittable private capital, in conformity with the opinions long since entertained. When we look at the rapid progress of the political power of the Company, and at the still more rapid

* *Vide* note to Appendix C:

Supposing a possible under-valuation of exports to the extent of above	lakhs 36
Add only 3 per cent loss on imports	6
and we have	lakhs 42

which is twice as much as I here assume as deficient in the above annual surplus private remittance of 109 [*114*] *lakhs*, and leaves room for abatement in the charges, and for bargains made below the market prices of Calcutta.

† For the effect of a state expenditure of this kind, or international commerce and exchange, *vide* Blake on Expenditure of Government, 1823, Murray. [The reference to Blake's work could not be traced. It probably refers to Sir Francis Blake who wrote a number of books on public finances during this time. *Editor*].

increase of the commercial intercourse between Great Britain and its dependencies in the east, since the relaxation of the old exclusive system, we can hardly doubt that, in every branch, civil, military, and commercial, there has been a great augmentation in the total of savings and profits, compared with those of ten, twenty, thirty, and forty years ago. Yet the large proportion of Company's securities held by absentees in Europe,* and known to be a part only, perhaps not one-fourth† of those savings and profits, and the very considerable sums invested by Europeans remaining in India, ‡ seem to indicate that they have averaged above half a crore of rupees per ann. in the three Presidencies, during the last fifty years;§ before which period the British commerce and establishments in Asia were comparatively insignificant.||

It may be worth while to examine this point more in detail. At present, the salaries of the Bengal civil service amount annually to about 82 lakhs;¶ of which 20 lakhs are paid to men whose average receipts are under Rs.2,000 per month, the rate of salaries corresponding with the average of the thirteenth year of

* Estimated at about 6 crore Rs. It has been ascertained that the remittable loans lately called in were represented nearly as under:

	2,28 lakhs	by the government agents, acting for individuals.
	3,41	by Calcutta agency houses.
	1,80	by natives, including 104 *lakhs* due to the Nuwaub Vizier.
	7,49	
And	4,00	owned in the other presidencies.
Total	11,49 lakhs.	

† I consider most mercantile accumulations to follow the domicile of the proprietors; and that heirs usually withdraw their funds from India.

‡ Probably nothing short of 4 crore: indeed I have heard it estimated at double the interest of absentees. No correct opinion upon this point can be formed from the explanations under note * above because, under the term natives, are not comprehended the Indo-British and Portuguese interests. Besides, the natives are supposed to have a much larger stake in the non-remittable portion of the debt; for it is known they subscribed largely to the loan of 1814–15. Perhaps, if we include temporary purchases by mercantile establishments, we must admit Europeans to hold a complete moiety of the whole.

§ *Vide* the head of finance in the letter of the Court referred to *supra*, p. 2, especially para. 57 to 66.

|| In 1785, the whole Indian debt was under two millions sterling. *Vide* Mr Impey's speech at the India House, 21 July 1813.

¶ By the average of the last six years; but I understand they are now 85 lakhs including extra allowances of every kind.

service. Making allowance for outfit and debts incurred in the
first years of service, I shall assume that no accumulation takes
place until the latter scale of income is obtained; and that the
average savings thereafter may be about one-third; which, with
the remittances of the pension-fund for widows and children at
home, would amount to 21½ lakhs, for the accumulations of the
civil service.

The pay of the King's and Company's officers on the Bengal
Military Establishment, the entire emoluments of the medical
department included, may be computed roundly at 150 lakhs, and
the saving therefrom at 10 per cent; which, added to the regi-
mental allowances of full colonels, and the remittances on account
of the military fund, may render the annual transfer of capital in
this department about 19 lakhs, without including the pay of invalids and retired officers, which I consider as separately provided for by the Company.

European mercantile profits may be classed as follows:

	lakhs
Commission on gross sales of two-thirds of all merchandise imported – say 180 lakhs, at 5 per cent	9
Ditto on 200 lakhs of bullion, at ½ per cent	1
Ditto on two-thirds of exported merchandise, 500 lakhs, at 3* per cent	15
Ditto on drawing and purchasing bills of exchange; on book accounts, where 5 per cent commission has not been charged, on insurance-loss settlements, and other transactions liable to this rate of commission – say [*The manuscript made '1 crore at 1%' amount to '10 lakhs', an error corrected as below, but the assumption of 1 crore came from the knowledge that the commission of account yielded a large sum annually to all the great agency houses: the 10 lakhs ought therefore to be repeated and the principal sum extended to 10 crore – perhaps these sums are too large. I have been expecting particular information upon the subject.*] 1 [*10*] crore, at 1 per cent	1 [*10*]
Commission on sales of indigo for the planters – say 120† lakhs, at 2½ per cent	3
Carried forward lakhs	29 [*38*]

* On all the valuable articles of export, the commission is 2½ per cent; and on
the rest 5 per cent. See 'General Rates of Agency Commission in Calcutta'.

† The amount this year is full 200 lakhs. The regular European houses appear to
have the agency of seven-eighths of the whole crop.

Commission on the management of executors – say 40 lakhs,

at 5 per cent	2
Ditto on freights, insurances, recovery of debts, and various undefined objects of agency – say	5
Total commissions	lakhs 36 [45]
Estimated profits in trade	20
Ditto of insurance and banking companies	11
Total	lakhs 67 [76]

of which probably one-half is saved for remittance, and the other absorbed in personal and other expenditure.

But European industry now finds employment in Bengal in various other ways besides external commerce. To the profession of the law, I cannot allow a remittable saving short of 4 lakhs. A numerous class of considerable tradesmen and auctioneers has gradually sprung up, whose accumulations, exclusive of the proportion assignable to the Indo-British* population, are probably as much as 8 lakhs. The Indigo planters have been subject, at times, to [very][1] heavy losses, while, on the other hand, the present season affords them a very large profit: on the whole, we cannot but suppose an average return for the capital they invest, sufficient to yield a saving beyond their expenses of production and interest of capital advanced; the remittable surplus from this branch of industry will be moderately computed at 5 per cent upon 80 lakhs, which is scarcely the value of the European stake therein.

These indigo works, too, are in some instances partially mortgaged to absentees; who likewise are possessed of considerable property in houses in Calcutta and elsewhere, and have lent money at interest to individuals, or left it in the Bengal agency houses. Whatever accumulations are so invested at present, may be considered as yielding a distinct surplus remittance of perhaps 5 or 6 lakhs, at the least.

Thus, I conceive it possible that the annual amount of private capital remittable from Bengal may be little short of [*full*] a crore of rupees, exclusive of the Company's interest-bills, and of the demands from the other Presidencies for the purpose of like remittance, through the superior facilities presented by the

* Native born, or creole, and not likely to quit the country.

[1] ['Very' was deleted by Prinsep in the corrected version of 1824.—*Editor*]

export of Bengal; exclusive also of the profits made and withdrawn by Armenians, Persians and other Asiatic foreigners, to
an extent probably much exceeding any influx of capital into the
markets of India from the neighbouring countries of Asia.

The Bombay and Madras Military Establishments* jointly
rather exceed that of Bengal; and the aggregate charges of
their joint civil service appear to be about half those of the
superior Presidency: therefore, by a similar computation, we
find a further remittable accumulation of 30 lakhs to be reckoned upon from this quarter. The joint amount of their trade
being nominally in the ratio of one to four in comparison with
that of Bengal, gives a further remittable surplus, that can
scarcely be set down at less than 12 lakhs.[1] Nor is it improbable
that Ceylon, Sumatra, Penang, etc. may contribute to the
amount of 8 lakhs more. So that there will appear a total accumulation of 145½ [150] lakhs,† available for annual remit-

* The ratio of the total establishments is given; but, as the civil expenditure of
Bengal includes various stipends under treaties with the native powers, it may be
concluded that the proportionate amount of the Bombay and Madras civil salaries
is stated too low. Their exact amount could not be obtained when this statement
was drawn up. In the estimates of the Madras civil fund of Dec. 1813, a sub-
scription of 2 per cent is stated to yield 17,000 star pagodas, which, at the par of
Rs.3 6¾as. per star pagoda would make the then principal about 29½ lakhs. But I
doubt whether the emoluments of the whole service were included; as contributions
of the same individual were limited to sixteen years.

† Summary of private accumulations:

			dec.
Bengal	civil	lakhs	21·5
	military		19·0
	commercial		33·5
	law		4·0
	retail-trade		8·0
	indigo works		4·0
	mortgage, houses, etc.		5·5
		Total	95·5
Madras and Bombay	civil		11·0
	military		19·0
	commercial, etc.		12·0
		Total	42·0
Ceylon, etc.			8·0
		Grand total	145·5

[1] [In the corrected version this sentence is changed to '*The joint amount of their
trade being normally as far as Europeans are concerned in the above ratio of one to four,
in comparison with that of Bengal, the remittable surplus from this and other sources
can be scarcely set down at less than twelve lakhs.*' – Editor]

tance from India on individual account. If to this be added the estimated *dividends* due to absentee proprietors of the Company's Bengal securities, i.e. 6 per cent upon 6 crore, and the dividend upon about 4 crore, [*which I have*] computed to belong to Europeans in India, we have a total on private account of 205½ lakhs; equivalent, at the present exchange, to [something less] *more* than two millions sterling, * resulting from our connexion with India – the whole of which is a clear surplus superadded to the wealth of the ruling state. The nature and amount of the surplus public revenue† does not come within the scope of this inquiry; but it were easy to show a total pecuniary benefit of more than four millions sterling per annum, resulting chiefly from our political relations with Hindustan.

Let us now consider the causes which have produced so important an alteration in the rate of exchange as we have witnessed within the last three years. This subject claims our attention, before we survey the future prospects of the external commerce of Bengal, more especially with Europe.

* Mr Cropper, in his late pamphlet on the sugar-trade, has the following passage, page 46: 'It is estimated, that the savings from civil and military employments, and from the gains of commerce remitted home to this country, amount annually to about £3,000,000 sterling; and for the interest of the debt we may add £1,000,000 more.' For these estimates he refers us to Mr H. St George Tucker, 'On the Plans of Finance of the East India Company', whose pamphlet I have already quoted. They are probably taken at the exchange of 2s. 6d. per rupee. [James Cropper, *Letter addressed to William Wilberforce, M.P., recommending the encouragement of the cultivation of sugar in our dominions in the East Indies, as the natural and certain means of effecting the total and general abolition of the slave trade* (London, 1822). – *Editor*]

† Surplus private revenue	£2,000,000
An actual public do. of about 230 lakhs beyond the interest of the Indian debt; leaving a surplus beyond the home charge of about	1,000,000
Value of industry employed at home, in furnishing supplies to the armies and other establishments in India, certainly full	1,000,000
Pay and pensions to officers retired and on furlough: this item in the year ending 1 March 1814, amounted to	266,000

(*Vide* Mr Hume's speech at the India House, 21 July 1813.)

The above sums do not include the Company's remittances to cover the home charges, not referable to territorial expenditure; nor such profits on trade as might exist, were we deprived of territorial possession in Asia. Mr Tucker (p. 2) gives our Asiatic dominion a much higher pecuniary value than I have ventured to assume. His estimate of four-fifths, as the ratio of the European British interest in the territorial debt, is thought greatly to exceed the truth, whatever it might have been in his time, ten years ago.

The demand for remittances on account of private accumulation I have supposed to be regularly progressive; and I have endeavoured to show that, while in all India that accumulation may have exceeded half a crore annually, on the average of the last fifty years, it is at this moment probably three times as much. Now, if the whole remittance be conjectured to have passed to Europe from Bengal,* which is by no means an unlikely circumstance, we shall find it fully covered by the trade up to 1817–18 inclusive; the surplus exports of that and the four preceding years,† taken not according to the highest estimate, having averaged about 157 lakhs, ‡ without reckoning the Company's trade. In fact, there seems to have been no difficulty in obtaining wherewithal to effect this large annual transfer of property: for, although the Bengal consumption of European commodities was daily augmenting, and the accumulation of private capital too in a reduced ratio; such was the increased demand in Europe for Asiatic products, fomented simultaneously by the general peace and by the greater freedom of commerce, whereby the charges of their transport were so considerably diminished, that a most unusually large supply of bullion was required, to balance the excess of exports beyond the amount of capital destined for mere remittance. And that supply seems to have been rather deficient than superabundant; for the exchange was not at all depressed thereby; but continued in 1818 to average 2s. 7d. to 2s. 8d. which rate it rarely

---

* A large portion of the Madras and Bombay remittances, no doubt, is made through Bengal. The surplus imports and bills from the latter, have in the eight years averaged about 30 lakhs per annum, and independent of public drafts from Poonah upon Furruckabad, etc. The Madras trade appears nearly balanced; but I understand very large drafts have occasionally been made in that Presidency and at Hyderabad upon Furruckabad, Benares and Delhi; and that the salt imports are omitted in the trade reports; which renders it probable, that the transfer of capital has fully equalled that of Bombay, whose resources for returns to Europe are greater.

† As per Appendix E, last column, deducting the Company's.

‡   Of 1813–14 about   lakhs 120
                1814–15   155
                1815–16   260
                1816–17   130
                1817–18   120
                         157 × 5 = lakhs 785

exceeded during any part of the five* or of any preceding years. But in 1818–19, a most excessive bullion importation occurred; the [*supply from*] Europe† export alone being double that of 1817–18: and, as the value of the exports declined nearly 70 lakhs,‡ at the same time that the increase in bullion was nearly 140§ lakhs, a great depression in the exchange would certainly have then occurred, had not a new loan absorbed a large amount of European funds, equal in all probability to the total of the customary surplus remittance of the year: for, at this precise time, the high credit of the Company and the falling rate of interest at home rendered this kind of investment peculiarly desirable. However, the large deficit of half a crore, shown by comparing the exports and imports of the private trade, swelled the balance for remittance in 1819–20, notwithstanding the subscriptions to the loan: and, as the private imports of bullion were in that year upon a footing with 1816–17 and 1817–18,‖ it was found difficult to provide saleable commodities to an extent corresponding with the funds available. There was no remedy but to purchase at an apparent loss; or, in other words, to indemnify the merchant for the loss by accepting from him bills at a lower exchange: bullion sent out for purchases of cotton, silk, indigo, sugar and other Asiatic products was either bartered for them at advanced prices, or procured a return, which, on arrival at the place of consumption, found a market already overstocked. The demand for those commodities the following year was consequently more limited; in the instance of cotton indeed, extinguished altogether. Europe sent out less than half the bullion supply of 1819–20; the United States 27 instead of 46 lakhs;¶ but the balance of exportable produce was still short

---

* *Vide* Appendix B, imports from Great Britain.

† The United States also sent bullion to nearly double the amount of the preceding or any other year.

‡ Notwithstanding an export of 8,37,759 maunds of cotton, exceeded only by that of 1817–18, viz. 10,03,363 maunds, for which large returns are said to have been owing long afterwards to Bengal. *Vide* trade reports.

§ Exclusive of the Company's profit transfer from England.

‖ Although there was a falling off in merchandise of 100 lakhs, but that of the two years before was partly on hand, unsold and unremitted for.

¶ Custom-house valuation.

of the funds waiting for remittance:* and the exchange continued to decline; while the resource of Indian loans was entirely closed, and the temptation to buy existing securities removed by the high premium they then began to bear in the market. We may perhaps venture an opinion that the rate of exchange on London would already, in 1819–20, certainly in 1820–21, have fallen below 2s.;† and the bullion would that year have flowed back from India to Europe, as it has done during the year just expired; had not the exchange been artificially supported by some financial arrangements of the Company, which it is in this place necessary to notice.

The Indian loans have usually been contracted on the terms of payment of the dividends, either in India, or by bills upon the home treasury, drawn at twelve months' date, and at the fixed exchange of 2s. 6d. per sicca rupee. While the current exchange was not below this rate, native creditors and all European fund-holders resident in India continued to receive their dividends in cash, as indeed it was their interest to do. For that portion only which belonged to retired servants and others, resident in Europe, drafts on London were required; and those only when the rate of exchange did not offer a more favourable remittance.‡ But no sooner was it perceived that such bills were saleable at a premium, in consequence of the state of the exchange towards the close of the year 1819–20, than a demand was made for bills instead of cash, by every class of security-holders; by which means a quantity of bills was thrown into the market in 1820–21 and the following year, probably exceeding the usual amount of Company's bills by 100 lakhs§ per annum; which bills, if negotiated at premiums corresponding to the

* Private surplus exports 1819–20   about   105 lakhs
                          1820–21   73
                                              178
         deduct surplus imports 1818–19   51
                                      3)127 = 42

† *Vide* Appendix I, first division.

‡ During a great part of the year 1814–15, bills of six month's sight, drawn by the first houses of Calcutta, were negotiated at 2s. 9d., and those of 12 months' sight at 2s. 10d. Until 1819, the exchange was constantly above 2s. 6d. *Vide* Appendix B, 1.

§ Exclusive of 56 lakhs due to the Begum, and about 104 lakhs to the Nuwaub Vizier, the total Indian debt was about 23½ crore, of which perhaps a crore and a

exchange of 2s. 3d. and 2s. 1d., would augment the means of private remittance by 111 and 120 lakhs successively in each of those years. We have thus an addition of 111 lakhs to the surplus private exports of 1820–21, which are thereby increased to about 184 lakhs: and, supposing that remittances were kept back in some measure by those who contemplated the return of a higher exchange, we shall find the average of 1818–19 to 1820–21, when thus augmented,* still much below that of the preceding five years. And there is ground to believe, if 1821–22 could be brought into the account with its extra amount of 120 lakhs in Company's bills, that the average of the last four years† would likewise be much under that of the five preceding.

half was composed of small subscriptions, below Rs.12,000, and therefore not entitled to interest bills on London,

say 22 crore at 6 per cent	132 lakhs
deduct, usual remittance to absentee proprietors of stock, exceeding Rs.12,000, say about	32
	100 lakhs

The dividends to Europeans in India, estimated altogether at 36 *lakhs*, are not noticed above; because, if they previously swelled the remittable *funds* without contributing any *means* of remittance, they form no deduction from the mass of additional *means* afforded by the Company's bills.

The following is an accurate list of the bills drawn on the Court of Directors for interest on the Bengal debt, during the eight years.

	Bengal	Madras	Bombay	Total
1813–14	36,58,898	18,78,862	4,93,742	60,31,502
1814–15	14,83,750	11,07,872	1,91,322	27,82,944
1815–16	11,11,116	6,39,095	2,16,039	19,66,250
1816–17	12,90,543	12,15,285	3,66,572	28,72,400
1817–18	23,26,426	19,00,675	5,17,324	47,44,425
1818–19	13,05,641	9,43,635	3,62,654	26,11,930
1819–20	25,16,018	21,01,540	5,96,774	52,14,332
1820–21	89,00,966	26,21,874	8,67,082	123,89,922

Here there is no very important difference compared with the preceding estimate. I cannot explain the cause of the large amounts drawn in 1813–14 and 1817–18, when the exchange averaged above 2s. 6d. The year 1821–22 being the first in which bills for principal were granted, the amount is kept back until the close of the late loan account.

*	1818–19, deficit in exports	51 lakhs
	1819–20, surplus	105
	1820–21, do.	73
		127 lakhs
	Company's bills,	111
		3)238 = 79⅓
†	1821–22, say	100 lakhs
		120
		4)458 = 114½

It might be said that, excepting the loss incurred by paying at a fixed rate of exchange higher than that of the market, it ought to be the same thing, whether the Company provide the cash for their Indian dividends in Bengal or in London. Granted: provided that the exact amount, which individuals would remit in some other shape were not these bills offered them, be remitted by the Company to answer these bills at home. But we have shown that the private remittances in trade were deficient by more than that amount; and it also appears that the Company's remittances, though larger than usual in 1819–20 and 1820–21,* were by no means calculated to meet the excess of bills, in addition to the regular home demands. Whatever deficit may have existed in this respect, has no doubt been covered by the large bullion export of the Company last year, amounting to 110 lakhs by Custom-house valuation; and by a like further remittance of 70 lakhs† in the beginning of the present: a mode of transfer that has been also adopted in a few instances by individuals, and sufficiently exemplifies the impossibility of balancing the trade by any other means, at the period alluded to. For some months, however, we have seen a change, though perhaps only of a temporary nature, produced apparently by the concurrent operation of two causes. The Bengal government wisely availed itself of its high credit to pay off all the remittable loans, opening at the same time a new loan not remittable,

---

* Company's balance of exports, exclusive of profit imports and receipts from the British Government; but including charges, undervaluations, etc.

1813–14	about	85¼ lakhs
1814–15		38
1815–16		44
1816–17		51¼
1817–18		72
1818–19		75
		6)366 = 61
1819–20		114
		7)480 = 68¼
1820–21		120

† 40 lakhs from Madras, per H.M.S. *Glasgow*, and 30 lakhs from Bombay, per H.M.S. *Ganges*; both in the current year. [For invoice of the bullion shipped see India Office Library, The Accountant General's Department, Range 1, vol. 38, 1822–23, pp. 90–120, 121–3. – *Editor*]

[*So far as concerns the dividend, except only in the case of absentees who are allowed the option of bills at 2s. 1d. This loan of which the capital is eventually redeemable by bills on London at 2s. 6d. is now called remittable to distinguish it from that of 1823 of which both capital and interest are in all cases payable in cash.*] but bearing the same rate of interest; which new loan, as it was expected, has absorbed the greatest part of the amount invested in the old securities, probably to the extent of above 9,* out of 11 crore. Bills at long dates, and bearing interest, were drawn upon the Court of Directors, and delivered to such proprietors as dissented from the transfer; and part of these bills, being negotiated at Calcutta, furnished an unexpected source of remittance. At the same time, the most considerable of agricultural products saleable in Europe, the important article of indigo, became an object of eager demand, in consequence of its augmented consumption and of the diminution of the stock in hand in Europe. Yet, notwithstanding that the indigo crop of this year will occupy double the usual capital with which it is purchased for shipment, a large proportion of it being already sold in anticipation, the exchange, which four months back was at 2s. 2d., can now scarcely be quoted above 2s. for the rupee. I might notice likewise the high prices at which opium has this year been exported; but the increase in the capital it absorbs does not necessarily affect the home trade, except by cutting off all chance of a remittance through Canton: since the Company's home investment from China does not exceed their imports into Canton by a sum larger than the drafts of their agents upon the Bengal treasury, for which they will find a ready negotiation.

In estimating the future external trade of Bengal, I labour under the disadvantage of being without the report of the past year, the statements not being yet complete. I have also had in contemplation the precarious state of two most important branches of commerce – opium and cotton: the one dependent on Chinese caprice and corruption; the other on the power, yet unascertained, of American competition.

* It may be less; for there is known to be a large sum waiting the option of absentee proprietors; but the calculation is formed upon a general view of their apparent interest.

EXPORTS. Confining my view to the next five years, during which I think the continuance of maritime peace may be fairly presumed, I will take the total yearly export of opium at 5,000 chests,* valuing it at Rs.3,000 per chest, and increasing the quantity or the valuation 5 per cent per annum; for it is impossible to reckon upon any interruption in a trade that has hitherto been regularly progressive. The China demand for cotton I consider must revive after the current year; and, as the manufacture of piece-goods in Bengal has very much declined, in consequence of the competition of British fabrics, I conceive there will be a surplus of cotton grown, which by its cheapness may force itself into the European market in a progressive ratio, nearly commensurate with the decline in the production and export of piece-goods.

Indigo has attracted perhaps too much attention; and it is hard to calculate how far the spirit of speculation may push its production. I assume a demand for about 120,000 maunds;† and that land will be instantly applied to the raising of indigo sufficient to yield an average crop, which at the end of two seasons shall exceed that quantity. In that case, the declining market price will gradually reduce the supply to the demand, by throwing the inferior lands out of cultivation; but the effect will hardly be felt until a period beyond the limit of my research. A much larger supply may no doubt be obtained – perhaps as much as 150, or even 200,000 maunds, although its total exchangeable value should not exceed the rate I have allowed.

I take the exports of silk at the average rate of increase in quantity presented by the reports of the eight years included in my statements:‡ and, supposing the present cost prices to be stationary, allow a progressive augmentation of 5 per cent per annum.

On sugar I allow a similar advance, notwithstanding the late imposition of an additional duty at home in favour of the West Indies. Prices are by no means at the lowest here: Spain and

---

* *Vide* Appendix G.

† The average crop of nine years, ending with 1821–22, was89, 200 maunds; that of 1822–23, expected to be between 90 and 100,000 maunds.

‡ *Infra* Appendix A.

Portugal are likely to be consumers, having nearly lost their own sugar colonies, or being apparently on the eve of entire separation from them: and I look generally to the continental demand as one that will admit of extension.

Saltpetre is a very doubtful article: yet I have ventured to give it a small annual augmentation of $2\frac{1}{2}$ per cent, and to fix its export at a much higher amount than mere speculation, without the experience of the last nine years, would seem to justify.

Grain I set down at below the average between 1813 and 1821,* and take it at 14 lakhs only, because I see no prospect of any considerable demand in Europe. Perhaps it is rated too low, with an annual augmentation of half a lakh. Its chief export is to the Mauritius, the coasts of Malabar and Coromandel, Penang and the Persian Gulf.

Lack of all sorts I have valued low, because otherwise I deem it incapable of supporting any competition with cochineal: and I have been rather sanguine in allowing it an annual advance of 4 per cent, on the assumption of a very ample supply. But, until it shall cease to pay charges, it will not cease to be collected and exported.

To ginger I allow also a small progressive increase of 3 or 4 per cent; assuming an export of 60,000 maunds, instead of the excessive exports of 74,143 maunds in 1818–19, and 75,491 maunds in the following year.

Gunnies were in 1819–20 exported to the extent of 4,323,802 bags: this trade has wonderfully increased, being at the same time very unsteady. I take it no higher than 3,000,000 bags; allowing an augmentation of 250,000 bags annually.

Sundries – these are the principal articles of export. There are a great variety of others of comparatively small importance; such as hides, borax, shawls, turmeric, safflower, wax, ivory, castor-oil, gums, tobacco, munjeet, hemp, etc. etc., which I have supposed may amount to 25 lakhs: and, as new articles may possibly be found from time to time, I allow an annual augmentation of 10 per cent on the aggregate amount.

Re-exports – various spices and foreign Asiatic products are

---

* Rupees 11,97,444, exclusive of charges, and the prices lower than the present.

brought to the Calcutta market for re-export; European commodities are likewise re-shipped in certain quantities for the Gulf, the Eastern Islands, etc. etc. I find the amount of both these classes of export about 44 lakhs, which may be liable to some diminution, say of one lakh per annum, from the facility now given of a more direct trade between the several places, whose mutual commerce has heretofore depended upon their intercourse with Calcutta. Thus, Bombay now receives all her European supplies direct, and sends a portion of them to the Gulf; the pepper of Malabar finds shipping and a ready sale at Bombay for England; and Singapore in the Eastern Archipelago is now visited by licensed ships direct from Great Britain, to the prejudice of the particular trade of Bengal.

Let us now see in what proportions the various exports are likely to be distributed over the world, and the probable amount of merchandise which each country will contribute in return.*

IMPORTS. Great Britain supplies half the total value of our imports, whether we estimate the proportion of her own products, or that of the goods introduced direct from her ports. I consider her cotton fabrics as still extending their consumption among the natives, and not yet at the lowest possible manufacturing prices at home, the use of power looms being quite new, and confined to some coarse descriptions of cloth. Assuming 40 lakhs to be the actual amount, I allow an increase of 7 per cent per annum. Woollens, I take at 25 lakhs, with an increase in the ratio of 5 per cent, founded on the increasing consumption of the cloths of low quality in the upper provinces. Spelter has but recently been introduced from Europe as a substitute for tutenague, and already meets it on equal terms, in respect of the quantity imported: being much cheaper than its rival from China, it may probably supersede it altogether: I therefore assume, for the five next years, an annual augmentation of 10 per cent upon its present amount of about 8 lakhs. The other metals, and likewise glassware, hardware, earthenware, clocks and watches, may admit an advance of 5 per cent upon the

---

* The imports *from* each country are here meant, not the total quantity of the products of each imported.

amount of their assumed valuations*: naval stores, paints and linseed-oil, of 4 per cent: supplies purely for the Europeans and their descendants, of 3 per cent – except wines and brandy, which seem to have declined in consumption as well in quantity as in value, through an alteration, which indeed we may call an improvement, in the habits of society within the last ten years. I suppose, therefore, a merely stationary demand for this class of imports. About 4 lakhs must be allowed for sundries; and, as ingenuity is always actively employed in discovering new objects of desire, I give this item a ratio of 10 per cent progressive increase. Thus, we have a total import of 158 lakhs the first, and a probability of more than 200 lakhs at the close of the fifth, year, all charges included.

EXPORTS. On the other hand, I do not calculate upon any extension of the total value of the exports to Great Britain during the five years of our inquiry; because I consider that the price† of indigo will constantly be declining, and that the quantity sent home will not advance, except perhaps for the two next ensuing seasons, to recruit the present reduced stock at home: for the increase of the home consumption of Britain may barely cover the deficit in such part of the total export, as is remitted merely in depot for the continental demand, which will every day be supplied more directly. Assuming the present crop at 100,000 maunds, I allow 70,000 for [British consumption] *export to the United Kingdom.*

On raw-silk, I admit an augmentation of 5 per cent; on sugar and cotton, of 10 per cent, calculating the export of the latter to revive in the second year of the five. I have already explained my motives for believing both these articles capable of bearing the competition of the West Indies and America, to a certain extent, provided that shipping freights continue moderate; and I hope to see the exports of both increase in the full ratio assigned them. The West Indian interest cannot surely be strong enough in the national councils to add a third protecting duty to the last imposition on Asiatic sugars, even if it shall prevail to protract the unjust and impolitic operation of existing

* *Vide* Appendix F.   † *Vide* Appendix F, *in note.*

regulations of finance. Liberal men of all parties, on the principles of humanity, as well as of political economy, warmly protest against a system of legislative partiality, which gives an artificial value to slavery, and cramps the consumption of the parent state, and sacrifices her capital, for the benefit of a class of speculators that have little merit to plead, and little benefit to offer in return.

The present exports of saltpetre can scarcely be maintained, without war in some part of Europe. Taking all chances, however, I value them rather boldly at the fixed rate of 250,000 maunds, which perhaps I have priced too highly at Rs.5, since I understand it may now be bought at 4½, and is likely to be yet cheaper. Silk piece-goods, for re-export to our colonies and other parts, I assume at 150,000 pieces, or 10½ lakhs, without increase, since our own manufactures are interfering with them, though less perhaps than with cotton articles. The latter I suppose to decrease 5 per cent; and I take them at the low valuation in quantity [*of*] 200,000 pieces, because the Company have discontinued their orders. Lack, of all sorts, I suppose to be stationary in the home demand, allowing a small extension to its introduction on the Continent.* Spices, and other Asiatic re-exports from Calcutta, I also take at the fixed amount of about 12 lakhs, allowing for the continually increasing freedom of trade, and of direct intercourse between the places of consumption and production. But upon the item of sundries, valued at 11 lakhs, must be allowed an advance of 10 per cent, on account of the new commodities it may possibly embrace. Thus, adding the invoice charges, computed at only 6 per cent,† instead of 7 (the

---

* *Vide* Appendix G.

				lakhs
† Supposed prime cost				100
Commission on	90	at	2½ per cent	2¼
Ditto	10	at	5 per cent	½
Ditto of account on	50	at	1 per cent	½
Shipping, packages, etc.				1
Invoice, say	50	at	3 per cent ⎱	1¾
Commisions on ditto			½ per cent ⎰	
				6 per cent

Freight payable at home, but a small proportion of it being perhaps a remittance of capital, and therefore entitled to be included.

assumed percentage charge upon the whole export trade), we have, for the total export invoices to Great Britain, 330 lakhs* for the first, and nearly the same for the succeeding four years; which exceeds our first year's import invoices by 172 lakhs, and our last by only 130 lakhs; a sum in both cases unequal to the actual demands of remittance on the Company's and private account.

France, though a small importer of merchandise into Bengal by direct commerce, to amount say of 4 lakhs, which may perhaps admit of an annual augmentation of 5 per cent, seems likely to be an improving customer in point of quantity, at the progressive rate of 7 per cent per ann., or even more rapidly at first; whether through the greater facility of direct intercourse in British bottoms, or the employment of more French capital in distant branches of trade, in lieu of procuring their Asiatic supplies, as at present, from the emporium of London. Her actual exports from Calcutta I assume at about 25 lakhs,† exclusive of charges: i.e. indigo, 16 lakhs; sugar, 4 lakhs; silk, 1 lakh; and other articles, 4 lakhs. Cotton is omitted altogether; because it is conceived that British looms will work up the Bengal cottons at prices too high for the French manufacturer to employ them in competition with those of the French colonies, of Brazil, and of the United States. In value, however, the ratio of increase is much affected by the supposed prices of the various commodities, and especially of indigo.‡

Holland, it is presumed, will confine her Indian trade to her own settlements. Her direct intercourse with Hindustan since the peace has been very limited and irregular.

Copenhagen is at present the only Baltic port which sends a vessel to Calcutta, and in quantity may be expected to augment both import and export 5 per cent every year; the former being now about 1 lakh, and the latter 4 lakhs,§ exclusive of what smuggling trade may be carried on at Serampore. Sweden, by

---

* Exports to Great Britain, inclusive of charges and commission, lakhs 329·9
† Exports to France, with charges, commission, and duties   28·0
‡ Vide Appendix II.
§ Exports to Denmark, with duties and charges   5·0

Carried over   lakhs 362·9

her sumptuary laws, seems, for the present, likely to interdict all Asiatic products: and Russia has but tried the experiment with a single vessel in 1815–16, at the precise time when the falling prices of all colonial produce in the markets of Europe must have occasioned considerable loss by the speculation. The bold, but ill-judged, little adventure to the Kamschadale port of Okhotsk, in 1817–18, scarcely deserves to be brought into the account.

Portugal has little to send out except her wines; and these are chiefly brought by our own shipping from Madeira. I will set down her imports at the fixed rate of 1 lakh. She has usually been a large customer for piece-goods; but as this demand is likely to decline, I assume for her exports an almost constant valuation of 20 lakhs,* deducting 2 lakhs the last year, for depreciation of commodities: upon which, I think, there is some chance of increase, in the event of her drawing hence her home-supply of sugar, upon the occurrence of hostilities, or the suspension of her present relations, with Brazil.

Spain, in political situation, much resembles the other nation of the peninsula: and we are yet to see how long Cuba will remain singular among her late American possessions in attachment to the parent state. I hold her continued allegiance to be very doubtful indeed; and as her large consumption of sugar and coffee, especially of the former, is supplied by that colony, I meet the chances of its loss with an allowance of an additional lakh every successive year of the five, commencing in the first with an export of 1 lakh.† For returns, she has nothing but a little wine, and such supply of mercury as the Bengal market may require, from the mines of Almaden, where it is procured at less cost than in any other part of the world. I take them altogether at 1 lakh for the second, rising to 2 lakhs for the fifth year; and at nothing during that now in progress.

The commerce with the Mediterranean, hitherto classed under the head of Gibraltar and Malta, to which ports it has

Bengal exports brought over	lakhs	362·9
* Ditto Portugal, with duties and charges		22·0
† Exports to Spain, with ditto		1·0
Carried over	lakhs	385·9

been confined, I consider capable of extension by means of British tonnage in the ratio of 20 per cent per annum upon a total of exports valued at 9 lakhs* the first year, and of imports valued at 4 lakhs. Judging from recent advices from Smyrna which have been communicated to me, I should infer the probability of a much more rapid advance within a short period, unless the ill success of former experiments, made under less favourable circumstances, should retard the natural influx of the due proportion of Asiatic products into that channel. I assume, however, an almost stationary value for the fourth and fifth years, because there may be some check produced by over-speculation in the first two or three of the five; and because the chief article, indigo, will certainly decline in price, and possibly sugar, piece-goods and cotton likewise.

The United States furnish an inconsiderable import of merchandise, which I estimate at 2 lakhs, allowing a small yearly augmentation. With their characteristic spirit of adventure, although hostilities continued nearly twelve months longer in America than in Europe, they were the first among foreign traders to renew their commerce with Bengal. The very large quantities of Asiatic produce which they took off for their carrying, as well as for their home trade, were chiefly purchased with bullion. They also brought into this market a portion of those excessive supplies of British manufactured goods which inundated their own markets immediately after the restoration of peace, and thus contributed to injure the sale of those directly imported. It appears certain that the Americans pushed their Indian trade for a while, more especially in 1818–19, beyond its natural bounds. In the year quoted, they introduced a total import of Rs.95,62,809, and exported to the value of Rs.70,26,531; whereas in 1820–21, they brought only Rs.28,88,174, and took a return of Rs.19,25,079, according to the Custom-house valuations, the last item being less by a few thousand rupees than the exports to South America during the same year, exclusive of Brazil. The future exports to be set down

Bengal exports brought over	lakhs 385·9
* Ditto Mediterranean, with duties and charges	10·0
Carried over	lakhs 395·9

to the United States I estimate as follows; bearing in mind that her wealth and power of consumption with respect to foreign articles probably increase in a ratio twice as great as her population.

Indigo: 12 lakhs with 15 per cent annual augmentation in quantity.
Saltpetre: 2 lakhs with 10 per cent do. do.
Piece goods – silk: 6 lakhs with 10 per cent do. do.
Ditto – cotton: 6 lakhs amount stationary. N.B. The experience of the two last years almost justifies the exclusion of this class of goods, which probably are wanted chiefly for the carrying trade.
Sugar: 5 lakhs amount stationary. N.B. The cultivation of sugar is rapidly extending in the Southern States of the Union.
Sundries: 4 lakhs with 10 per cent advance per annum.* N.B. This item may sometimes include a little cotton for the carrying, or circuitous, trade.

Note that the whole item of sundries is estimated at a slowly progressive ratio, considering that it embraces all new articles; because it is imagined that the late relaxation of our exclusive policy will expose American tonnage in foreign ports to far more effectual competition with our own than it has hitherto had to sustain. I have further to remark that, in computing the first year's importation at 2 lakhs and the total net exportation at 35 lakhs in the account of the commerce of this Presidency with the United States, I am attempting to determine the value of a trade which depends upon a great variety of contingencies, and has always been subject to great fluctuation, both in the quantum of value, and in the quantum of commodities; and that, in adjusting the value of exports for the tables in the Appendix, I have deemed it necessary to make a liberal allowance in the second year for an expected large export of indigo, the demand for which from the United States is now checked by the exorbitant prices presented by the demand from Europe, and to assume a subsequent depreciation in commodities commensurate with the advance in the quantity required.

Brazil, if embroiled in hostilities with Portugal, will, during her troubles, require a diminished supply of Asiatic products. As

Bengal exports brought over	lakhs 395·9
* Exports to United States, with charges	38·0
Carried over	lakhs 433·9

her demand has been chiefly for piece-goods, which now scarcely support the competition of British fabrics, and there is great appearance of political confusion in that country, I shall take the total net value at from 5½ to 6 lakhs,* deducting 4 per cent in each successive year. In return, a very small amount of merchandise may be expected, say about Rs.40,000 per annum.

The western ports of South America have furnished a large supply of copper in part payment of the various commodities exported thereto, which, with this exception, she must purchase almost entirely with bullion. The trade of Mexico is now open, and will contribute a certain quantity, perhaps 2 lakhs, of cochineal, for consumption chiefly on the other side of India. I value the whole imports of merchandise from that quarter at 10 lakhs, with a growing annual increase of 5 per cent. To the export trade I attach a higher value: its present amount may be 30 lakhs† since the recent enrolment of Mexico in the list of independent states; and its progressive ratio would scarcely be overrated at 10 per cent per ann. Its natural rate of progression, however, in consequence of the very recent opening of the Mexican ports, seems to be 20 per cent the second, 10 per cent the third, no increase the fourth, and 5 per cent for the succeeding years; which rate of increase has been assumed in the tables annexed. Its demand is principally for Bengal and Madras cotton cloths, which I think will preserve their preference in the Spanish-American markets longer than in any other beyond the Indian seas. On these articles, however, I do not so much rely for an extension of the trade, as on spices, sugar, drugs, grain, wax and a variety of objects, whose utility and relative cheapness here will in time be duly appreciated in this new market, which I am far from deeming susceptible of that vast extension that some theorists appear to anticipate. Its importance to Bengal is enhanced by the prospect of a direct and cheaper supply of bullion to make up the balance of trade: an advantage common to every country supporting an intercourse at the same

	Bengal exports brought over	lakhs 433·9
* Brazil, with duties and commissions, etc.		6·4
† Spanish America, with duties and charges including freight		35·0
	Carried over	lakhs 475·3

time with India and Spanish America, and requiring Asiatic commodities to an amount exceeding the joint value of her own exchangeable products, and of the [circuitous or other returns she may] *remittances she may on other account* be entitled to.

The Cape of Good Hope sends a few articles – wines and re-exported European supplies, say about 1 lakh annually, with little prospect of increase; in return for about $2\frac{1}{2}$ lakhs in piece-goods, $\frac{1}{2}$ lakh in sugar, and 1 or 2 lakhs in sundries*; upon which, in the aggregate, I assume an average advance of 4 per cent per ann. It might be rated higher, but for the chance of increasing competition between the piece-goods of India and those of Great Britain. This trade is balanced partly with bullion, and partly with colonial government bills, and the drafts of invalids resorting to that settlement from Bengal.

The Isle of France furnishes, *in transitu*, French silks and wines, some re-exported British goods, and altogether about 8 lakhs in merchandise; in exchange for piece-goods, about 3 lakhs; grain, 3 lakhs; and sundries, about 2 lakhs.† I will suppose an augmentation of 1 per cent only upon the exports, which, in the item of piece-goods, may probably rather decline.

The Arabian and Persian Gulfs afford, next to China, the most important branch of what is called the country trade. I value their imports into Calcutta at 15 lakhs in merchandise, and their exports at 55 lakhs.‡ The former may be expected to increase in the ratio of 10 per cent, if the average progress be equal to that of the last ten years; but the latter, after the second year,§ I assume to fall off in value about 10 per cent; because, whatever augmentation may occur in the demand for sugar, indigo (which article will be at a lower price), and some minor articles, a corresponding reduction seems likely to be felt in Bengal piece-goods, and in the request for our printed calicoes

	Bengal exports with charges, brought over	lakhs 475·3
*	Cape of Good Hope, with charges	5·0
†	Isle of France, with freight and charges	11·0
‡	Arabian and Persian Gulph, with ditto	60·0
	Carried over	lakhs 551·3

§ The motive for adding 5 lakhs the second year is that the export of indigo and other articles has been checked this season, both by price and by the over-trade of the last.

and other British manufactures now obtained more naturally from Bombay, since that market also is become an emporium for every description of European commodities.

The Maldive Islands maintain a commercial intercourse, which seems to have declined considerably. I assume a fixed valuation of 1 lakh for their imports; and, including charges, a similar sum for their returns.* Nine years ago, they appear to have averaged nearly 2 lakhs each way.

The trade with Ceylon, and the coasts of Malabar, Coromandel, and Sumatra, though much influenced by the relative abundance of the grain crops, I shall take at a permanent valuation; though perhaps a decline might be reckoned upon, because their direct intercourse with Europe respectively renders them every day more independent of the mart of Calcutta for a vent and supply.

Ceylon imports into Calcutta	1 lakh	exports	2† lakhs
Bombay	ditto	11	do.	32‡
Madras	ditto	8	do.	10¼§
Sumatra	ditto	2½	do.	6‖

From Java, an import may be looked for to the extent of 5 lakhs, which for the same reason I take as a stationary amount, being only one third of the importation of 1816–17. Her favourable position for the smuggling of opium into China might very much augment the proportion of the present exports, should its introduction into Canton by the present channels be rendered more difficult by any casualty. I assume 700 chests as about the actual demand for Java, at Rs.3,000 per chest, and allow an augmentation of 5 per cent per annum for advance in price and consumption, which however I cannot admit beyond the fourth year, as there are many circumstances that seem to prescribe a limit to this trade. She requires also about 6½ lakhs in native cotton piece-goods, and ½ lakh in silk

Bengal exports brought over	lakhs 551·3
* Maldive Islands, with charges	1·0
† Ceylon, with ditto and freight	2·4
‡ Bombay, with ditto and freight	37·0
§ Madras, with ditto and sometimes freight	12·0
‖ Sumatra, with ditto and freight	6·6
Carried forward	lakhs 610·3

ditto, both of them perhaps capable of a similar advance; besides
5 lakhs in sundries, which I consider stationary, inasmuch as
British goods are now getting into a course of direct supply.
Thus the first year exhibits an export to Java of 33 lakhs.*

The timber trade of Pegu has naturally been affected by the
ruin of the country shipping interests: the imports from that
coast are reduced to about 2 lakhs, the returns being composed
equally of merchandise and bullion.† Perhaps both may be susceptible of some increase, which at present I will not venture to
estimate.

Penang, Singapore, etc. are now resorted to by ships direct
from England, and would probably fall off in their supplies to
Calcutta, but for the necessity of extending the total amount of
their returns for the articles they receive from Bengal. I therefore assign them a trifling augmentation of 1 per cent upon
8 lakhs, the present estimated value of their import; and I
suppose 4 lakhs to be the amount exported thither in piece-
goods of native fabric; 18 lakhs 600 in chests of opium, and
2 lakhs in sundries; all likely to increase in the ratio of 5 per cent
per annum.‡

The importance of the Manilla trade is lessened very materially by the late events in Mexico, which will no longer effect
the interchange of her commodities with those of India through
the medium of the Philippine Islands. However, as this port
presents a convenient resort for the traders in opium, as well as a
small consumption of the drug, it is not improbable that the
commerce of this Archipelago may absorb a supply from Bengal
far exceeding its own demands, which appear to be about
3 lakhs. Consequently, I estimate them at 4 lakhs,§ with an
annual increase of 6 per cent; and the returns in merchandise
[of] at 1 lakh, with an increase of 10 per cent.¶

Bengal exports, brought over	lakhs 610·3
* Java, with duties and charges	35·0
† Pegu, with ditto, freight, etc.	1·2
‡ Penang, etc. with duties, freight, etc.	26·0
§ Philippine Islands, with ditto, ditto, etc.	4·5
Carried forward	lakhs 677·0

¶ It may be taken as a general rule, that, where there is any prospect of increase,
its ratio will be the larger, the smaller the actual amount, on which it is to be
reckoned.

But, next to the market of Great Britain, there is none which is nearly so important to the commerce of Bengal as that of China. Her supplies in merchandise are nearly one-seventh of the total import, and one-third of the gross import, exclusive of that from Great Britain. They consist of a great variety of articles: tea, tutenague, nankeens, velvets and other silk piece-goods, raw silk, camphor, paper, toys, cassia, rhubarb, etc. etc.; but, as the new settlement at Singapore will draw off a portion of such of them as are destined for re-shipment to Europe, I allow no progressive augmentation of the total amount, which is assumed at 42 lakhs, rather above the average rate, and approaching that of 1818–19. The exports to China bear a still larger proportion to the whole than her supplies; being at present about one-fifth of the gross export of Bengal, without taking into consideration the extraordinary prices of the two last opium sales. These, indeed, might affect the accuracy of my calculations, if any part of the opium entries were made after the close of the Custom-house year 1821–22;* since, in that case, it would be necessary, in the estimate for 1822–23, to substitute the price of Rs.4,500, instead of Rs.3,000 per chest; whereas otherwise, it would not be surprising to find the last year's export to China amount to 200 lakhs. altogether. I have already observed, incidentally, upon the precarious nature of this branch of trade; but, as past experience obliges me to reckon upon its continuance, I will suppose a demand for 3,700† chests of this article, say 111 lakhs, and, in the present season a very moderate shipment of cotton by the Company alone, say 20 lakhs which, with some addition of other articles, will render the whole amount nearly 140 lakhs‡ with a prospect of gradual increase in the ratio of 5 per cent per annum, chiefly occasioned

---

* The Government year in all the Presidencies begins on 1 May; and, in commerce, the same date is adopted by individuals [*many houses at Calcutta, whereas the Bombay commercial year begins on 1 August.*]. In 1813–14, the Company altered it from 1 June, which had been the date of commencement previously to that time.

† I have supposed the whole export of opium 5,000 chests, a small deduction should therefore be made from these 3,700 for the consumption of the Moluccas.

Bengal exports brought over		lakhs 677·0
‡ China, with freight and charges, including insurance		155·0
	Carried forward	lakhs 832·0

by an advance in the quantity, or in the price, of opium. To the second and three subsequent years' export I have added a supply of cotton, of double the amount of the first of the five.

It remains for me to notice the inconsiderable but rising trade of New South Wales, whence a small import is derived, rather exceeding ½ lakh. The actual demand of this colony upon Bengal comes to about 3 lakhs* in sugar, rum, rice, Bengal piece-goods, a small assortment of spices, and sundries, capable of extension at the rate of full 10 per cent per annum. *[This trade has been much checked by the imposition of very high (perhaps prohibitory) duties on imported spirits by the local Government of New South Wales, a measure unknown to the author at the time.]* The preceding estimates, reduced into tables,† give the following general results.

		1822–23	1823–24	1824–25	1825–26	1826–27	*Average*
Imports	lakhs	288·6	301·3	314·3	328·2	343·2	314·7
Exports		835·6	908·9	911·3	906·2	916·1	895·6
Total trade in merchandise		1124·2	1210·2	1225·6	1234·4	1259·3	1210·3
Surplus export		547	607·6	597	578	572·9	580·9
Bills on Bengal treasury, Company's surplus remittance, private do., including Bombay and Madras		323	323	323	323	323	323
Balance to be received in bullion		224	284·6	274	255	249·9	257·9

It may possibly excite surprise that, while I have assumed a progressive increase of value on the import side amounting to nearly 55 lakhs, or 18½ per cent on a comparison of the last year of the series with the first, I should have taken the export at a fluctuating value, scarcely exhibiting any average increase whatever; and this, notwithstanding that, since the passing of the acts for extending the freedom of the trade, the latter have already advanced above a crore, i.e. about twice as much as the imports of the same period. I have already explained my

Bengal exports brought over	lakhs 832·0
* New South Wales, with charges, say	3·6
Total of export invoices	lakhs 835·6

† *Vide* Appendix G, H.

motives for calculating upon a constant decline in the price of indigo, which single article in my estimates causes a diminution of 57 lakhs between 1823–24 and 1826–27. Besides, it cannot be expected that the ratio of general advance during the period above-mentioned, stimulated as it then was both by the peace and by the energy of private enterprise, then for the first time awakened after a long night of exclusion and restriction, should be maintained for the five years in question, in a trade already pushed, as it should seem, beyond the bounds of prudent speculation. This consideration would make the advance allowed upon the imports appear too rapid, judging merely from past experience, were it not evident that the late increase in quantity has really been larger than the difference in value; British piece-goods being now imported at half, and actually selling at one-third, of the price they bore in 1814; and every other article from Europe, with scarcely a single exception, being reduced full 40 per cent in cost, and 50 per cent in saleable value. So that, making all due allowance for the country trade, if, in the eight years we have been examining, the total imports of merchandise advanced from 160 lakhs to 220 lakhs in *value*, i.e. in the ratio of $37\frac{1}{2}$ per cent, they have probably increased in *quantity* above 80 per cent; i.e. in the ratio of 290 to 160, which is above 11 per cent per annum. Whereas, the progression assumed for the next five years is little more than $4\frac{1}{2}$ per cent in value; and probably will not exceed 5 per cent, or half the former ratio, in quantity; as the cost of imported commodities is susceptible of very little further diminution.

It will moreover be observed that, while I have exactly balanced the Madras trade in conformity with the previous average of eight years, I have supposed a net annual transfer of capital from Bombay to Bengal of 7 lakhs, which is 21 lakhs short of the former average. The latter circumstance is explained by reference to the decreasing amount of bills drawn in that Presidency on the Bengal government, owing to the gradual diminution of the deficit in its revenue; by the consequent expectation of increasing difficulty in effecting remittances to Bengal, that may suffice to balance the growing demand for them as a channel of circuitous remittance to Europe; and by the consideration that hitherto the chief motive for transferring capital thence to Calcutta has probably been its investment in the Indian loans, which, until the last effected in 1819, had for some time occurred in almost annual succession. I have supposed that 23 lakhs may flow in from the Madras and Bombay Presidencies jointly, by inland operations; whereof nearly 20 lakhs may come from the former: and we have thus an annual influx of 30 lakhs, jointly from both;* which is probably not more than half the amount transferred during those years in which new loans were negotiated.

It may also be noticed that I have assumed 100 lakhs for the Company's surplus remittance: i.e. 20 lakhs in the shape of export to China, and 80 lakhs in their home investment: while I have allowed an equal sum for the external drafts upon the Bengal treasury.† Deducting from the latter item about 25 lakhs for disbursements not connected with commerce, we have thus a public contribution of 175 lakhs instead of about a million and a half sterling, the average annual demand of the home treasury: which amount is moreover virtually reduced, by the surplus trade profits lately transferred in bullion from London to India. It must, however, be remembered that, by the option enjoyed by part of the fundholders to demand payment of the principal in England, a claim has arisen, perhaps to the extent of 2 crore; the whole of which it will probably be requisite to discharge at home within the period of my prospective calculations; and which, divided into equal portions, at the exchange of 2s. 6d., may require an additional remittance of 50 lakhs per ann.

During the term of five years in question, I have reckoned a bullion import of between 224 lakhs and 287 lakhs per ann.: i.e. from 126 lakhs to 226 lakhs‡ from the country trade, South America and Mexico; and the balance from the United States and Europe. If the profits on the China trade originating in

---

* Perhaps a further sum should be allowed, for the cost and freight of salt from Madras; which I think would be fully covered by 1 lakh, or 1½ lakhs at most.

† I take 60 lakhs more than the average hitherto, as the drafts from China; and add thereto the lakh I annually deduct under the head of Bombay. The Company's increasing China trade can well employ the sum allowed.

‡ *Vide* Appendix H.

Calcutta compensate the risk and delays, we may look for an additional 10 lakhs or 15 lakhs per ann. from that quarter: and, in like manner, all bullion returns to Bengal from other parts are liable to an addition of interest and profit to the adventurer. But, though the annual amount of the bullion import should thus be swelled to an average of 300 lakhs, the contribution in specie from the United States and Europe would not be affected thereby; neither, on the other hand, would the latter be diminished or augmented by any fluctuation in the country trade, except in a very remote degree, which it is not necessary here to discuss, inasmuch as it can produce no immediate or sensible effect upon the exchange* with London.

By the assumed balances in the trade with Europe and the United States, we have to expect from them jointly a bullion import as follows:

Year		Rs
1822–23	lakhs	58·0
1823–24		76·3
1824–25		58·1
1825–26		34·3
1826–27		24·0
Total for years,		5)250·7(say, 50 lakh per ann.

which of course will be sent from those countries, whence it can be effected with the most advantage. But there is an essential difference between Great Britain and the rest; for, while all other markets appear to require a larger value in Asiatic produce than that of their own commodities available for exchange, Britain has a claim upon India greatly exceeding the difference; she, therefore, can have no motive to increase her claim by a remittance of bullion, unless to balance her commercial dealings with other nations; with whom we know that at present her

---

* I should expect however a very beneficial influence from the adoption of Mr Tucker's plan: *viz.* that the Company should grant bills on Canton in exchange for the bullion annually carried out by the Americans; and direct their super-cargoes to draw upon Calcutta to meet the London bills. Much bullion-freight and charges would thus be saved, both between America and China, and between the latter and Bengal, to the extent of more than half a crore, or perhaps even a crore of rupees, which is also the measure of the additional facility of remittance from Bengal to England, which this method would present. The distance almost precludes such an arrangement among private mercantile establishments, especially during the continuance of the present monopoly of the China trade.

dealings make her almost universally a creditor. On the contrary, her neighbours, in the order of their vicinity, will apply to her for bills, or letters of credit, upon Calcutta, to the extent of her surplus demand; because she has an evident interest in offering them such bills on cheaper terms, than those upon which they can remit bullion to India. If dollars sent from London to Calcutta yield an exchange of 2s. 3½d. per rupee,* as at present, France will call for such credits, on the principles of banking, when the Calcutta exchange shall be under 2s. 2¼d. or 2s. 2d.: the southern ports of Europe, when under 2s. 1¾d.;† and the United States of America, when under 2s. 1¾d.‡ Hence we may infer that, if in the first year, bullion to the extent of the joint balance of the United States, the Mediterranean and Spain be insufficient to cover the general balance of trade in favour of India, the difference being less than the balance against Portugal, the exchange upon London ought not to exceed 2s. 1¼d. The second year we have balanced with a trifling import of specie from France, which would raise the exchange to 2s. 2d. or 2s. 2¼d., unless Portugal remained still a debtor on account of the preceding year. The third, balanced in the same manner as the first, again reduces the rupee to 2s. 1¾d. And in the fourth and fifth, when even the United States might have recourse to such credits, it would probably average 2s. 1⅗d.

There are, however, many circumstances which tend to impress me with the expectation that the last is the highest rate of exchange we can look for during any part of the term. Commercial men are not always perfectly informed of passing events: nor, when possessed of complete information, do they avoid erroneous calculations. Foreign speculators have not always connexions in London: in their eagerness to secure funds for the purchases they contemplate, they may prefer, in some cases, a small sacrifice upon dollars, compared with the exchange, to the delay of procuring letters of credit, and the uncertainty of the due honour of the bills. A very small addition to the bullion import might shift the *onus* of covering the general trade

* *Vide* Appendix I, No. 1.
† *Vide* Appendix I, No. 2.
‡ *Vide* Appendix I, No. 3.

balance from one country to another; and perhaps an advantage of full ¼d. in the exchange must be allowed, as an inducement to prefer the circuitous, to the direct, mode of providing funds in the Bengal market. Besides, a custom prevails among the Calcutta agency houses, and likewise among their correspondents at home, to make a difference of 1d. to 1½d. in the rupee between the buying and selling exchange, which they probably deem a moderate and fair advantage. An American merchant who came provided with power to draw on Messrs Baring and Co., would probably not negotiate his bill under 2s. 1½d., although agents' and Company's bills were selling at 2s. 0½d. Aware of this circumstance, he imports bullion, so long as it costs him no dearer than his draft: and the same conduct being generally pursued, it seems probable that the exchange will never be above 2s. 1d. for government or agents' bills, so long as the claims of Britain for remittance shall exceed the surplus export to that country.

But it is possible that I have overrated her consumption of Asiatic products, and undervalued her power of disposing of her own in return. I may still more probably have assumed too small a sum for the remittable fund of Europeans in Bengal, which moreover is constantly increasing. Again, a larger amount than hitherto may be sent from the other Presidencies for similar investment. All or any of these circumstances would tend to depress the exchange. Nor can I overlook the prosperous state of the Indian revenue, which now yields a surplus of nearly a crore of rupees, say a million sterling, after paying all home and local charges whatever. No doubt, the surplus revenue will not for many years discharge the debt; but, since half its amount would afford a large and progressively increasing sinking fund, I cannot shut my eyes against the possibility that an arrangement may be proposed for the relief of our finances at home. *
The Act for renewing the Company's charter in 1793 provided for an annual payment of £500,000 to government, which in that year, and in that year only, was delivered into the ex-

---

* This anticipation has just been verified, by the parliamentary proposition for relieving Great Britain of £60,000 per annum heretofore chargeable for invalids, etc. etc. 4 Geo. IV. chap. . . .

chequer: and it has at one period been the favourite design of ministers, that India should be brought to aid the general finances of the empire.*

For these various reasons, I think it would be imprudent for an importer of merchandise from England to calculate upon an exchange higher than that of a return in bullion; i.e. 1s. 11d. to 1s. 11½d. per rupee.† Although there is some prospect of an average rate of 2s. to 2s. 1d. for a year or two longer,‡ I fully expect it will not maintain even this small advance, when, by the decline in price, the total value of indigo, as a return, shall have fallen 30 or 40 lakhs.

I am aware that some persons have considered the depression of the exchange as the mere transient effect of the oscillation of commerce. The immense import of bullion consequent upon the peace and the opening of the trade, and the knowledge that, during a whole century, specie was always deemed an essential part of the Company's outward investments, both to India and China,§ leave a natural impression that bullion must continue to be imported, and largely imported, from Europe, whose

* 'What I have stated will, I trust, relieve the Committee from all apprehensions on the subject of India. They will recollect the gloomy predictions that prevailed during the war, in respect to our possessions in that quarter becoming a charge upon the mother country; and they will also call to mind the repeated declarations of a noble friend of mine (Lord Melville), that the empire would lean on India, before India would require support from the empire.' Extract from a speech in the House of Commons, which introduced the Indian Budget of 1802. *Vide* Lord Lauderdale's 'Enquiry into the practical Merits of the System for the Government of India'. *Vide* also the stipulations of the last Act for Renewal of the Charter respecting surplus profits. 58 Geo. III. c. 155. [James Maitland (Lord Lauderdale), *An Inquiry into the Practical merits of the system for the Government of India under the superintendence of the Board of Control* (Edinburgh, 1809). – *Editor*]

† *Vide* Appendix I, No. 1.

‡ Not if the funds for discharging the untransferred portion of the Indian debt be wholly remitted within the five years embraced by my estimates.

§ Amount of silver bullion shipped between 1788 and 1807 from London:

		By the Company	By individuals
To India	oz.	20,802,910	11,831,089
To China		22,374,330	3,390,910
Or per annum India		1,094,890	622,689
China		1,230,228	178,469

besides a trifling amount in gold. The particulars here given were communicated to me at the India House.

consumption of Indian commodities is certainly capable of much further extension. We have, however, the example of a similar revolution in the China trade; which, according to a very exact statement lately received from Canton, has, in the last year, 1821–22, been fully balanced by an import of only 47,000 dollars, and an export of 45,400 dollars, as far as the Company and British subjects were concerned. But, admitting the probability of a very extended demand for the produce of Bengal in Europe, the exchange could not for any long time be raised above 2s. 4d., because dollars may be brought out and profitably exchanged for bills at 2s. 3½d. per rupee,* since the restoration of a metallic currency in England.

There is, however, another important alteration in the state of the question, caused by the emancipation of the Hispano-American colonies, and more especially of Mexico. I calculate that the returns thence to speculators in Calcutta will be received in bullion, so long as the exchange on London is but little below 2s. 1d.† Were the amount of this new connexion in trade very considerable, the opportunity of remitting through Mexico at more than 2s. per rupee would deserve attention, and certainly keep the exchange above that rate: but the more important consideration will be her capability of covering the whole balance of trade, by furnishing bullion at an exchange not exceeding 2s. 2⅔d. per rupee.‡ Upon her power of producing the precious metals it is unnecessary to expatiate. The annual coinage in silver and gold had reached twenty-eight million dollars at the royal mint of Mexico, previously to the political convulsions of 1810; and the total product of the mines, including fraudulent extraction, could not then be short of thirty millions. In 1812, the regular coinage was only four and a half millions: in 1819, however, it amounted to twelve millions, to which at least two millions more must be added for provincial coinage and for contraband: but the mines have again, since 1817, been steadily advancing in their product, and will very rapidly improve under a system of commercial freedom and political

---

* *Vide* Appendix I, No. 1.
† *Vide* Appendix I, No. 4.
‡ *Vide* Appendix I, No. 5.

independence, if the local taxes on the precious metals be reduced. The principal part of the external trade of Mexico, as of almost every other state, for some time to come, must be with Great Britain, whose metals and manufactures she chiefly requires; and the British exporter would gladly re-sell his dollars upon the spot, for bills of equal value on London. Firms engaged in the Indian trade have already contemplated the possibility of circuitous bullion-remittances to Asia, through the ports of Valparaiso, Lima, Acapulco, and Vera Cruz: and, should the Calcutta exchange be above 2s. 2⅔d.,* they would not forego the preferable opportunity that Mexico will offer, for the more expensive process of shipment of [*shipping*] dollars from England to Asia.

At the other Presidencies, it may happen that the exchange on London shall not exactly correspond with that of Calcutta, after allowing for the actual difference of their respective currencies only. According as the balance may lean on the side of demand for remittance, or demand for returns, in their respective relations with Bengal, we must add to that difference, or substract therefrom, the expenses of a transfer of bullion. On this principle it is, that the Bombay exchange upon Calcutta has, within the last twelve months, oscillated between 104½ and 111 rupees of Bombay for 100 sicca rupees – the reputed par being 108:† and the Bombay exchange on London had *fallen* to 1s. 10d. per rupee, some months before that of Calcutta was quoted below 2s. 1d.; whereas lately it has still continued to average 1s. 11d., while no merchant in Calcutta would draw at above 2s. A similar oscillation has occurred at Madras, where, the par being about 109 arcot for 100 sicca rupees,† the exchange on London has, during the last twelve months, been quoted at 1s. 9d. and 1s. 10d.; while at Calcutta it has vibrated from 1s. 11d. to 2s. 2d. I have already noticed the probability that the amount of

---

* *Vide* Appendix I, No. 5.

† I should have stated the par of Bombay and Madras at about 106 and 107, respectively, comparing the intrinsic value of the several currencies: but 2 per cent is added for the mint charge of recoining, in as much as the coin of the other presidencies can only be regarded as mere bullion in Bengal. Were the balance of trade reversed, the same percentage must be deducted for similar reasons; which would lower the par in each case to 104 and 105 respectively.

Company's bills drawn at those Presidencies upon Bengal will continue to decline. This resource failing, at the same time that the increasing demands of their European commerce will make them lean more and more upon the resources of Bengal for returns, it would follow that their rates of exchange with Calcutta should gradually attain a higher average, until they reach the constant rate of a bullion remittance. It will then be practicable to send home returns in bullion to Europe, from Bombay and Madras, although the Calcutta Exchange were at the same time maintained at 2s., or perhaps even at 2s. 1d. The case, indeed, has recently occurred in both those Presidencies, in private, as well as to the Company's, remittances.

In the foregoing calculations, I have presumed that all the Company's commercial operations will be guided by the same principles which govern those of individuals. This has not always happened: with the best opportunities of information, they sometimes suffer by the restrictions they impose upon themselves, especially by the rule not to admit private bills of exchange in any of their commercial transactions. Hence, when a sudden necessity arises to transfer funds from one treasury to another, the remittance is uniformly made in bullion,* whatever may happen to be the exchange on private bills; and hence we see them sometimes exporting specie, when individuals have ceased to find an advantage in so doing. Had the Company made use of private bills, in lieu of shipping bullion from

---

* In 1821–22, there were imported into Calcutta, on the Company's account, Rs.73,44,024 in bullion, according to the Custom-house valuations; and exported to London on the same account, Rs.110,00,000. The former was made up of the following items:

Rs.35,23,257	from	Canton
16,37,841		Bombay
11,80,305		Bencoolen
1,58,138		Singapore
4,76,408		Penang
3,655		Madras
29,420		Isle of France
2,80,000		Persian Gulph
55,000		Bussorah
Rs.73,44,024		

The amount of the drafts on the Bengal treasury, in the same year, from Bombay, China, and the settlements in the Archipelago, was very considerable.

Madras and Bombay, a few months back, they might have obtained them to a considerable amount in Calcutta, at 2s. 1d., and thus have prevented in a great measure the fluctuation which has occurred of 2d. per rupee; and they would have avoided the necessity of drawing from Bombay upon Bengal, at the disadvantageous exchange of 104½. It is very possible that the public funds could not have been remitted home to more advantage in produce: for, when they do not buy at a monopoly price the Company labour under great disadvantage from the very magnitude of their purchases; a disadvantage they experienced to the extent of about 10 per cent in their investment of indigo for last season. But it is strange they should forego the resource of private exchange operations, contrary to the practice of all European governments, and of every other trading company that we know of.

My prospective estimates are also founded upon the expectation of the continuance of the present fiscal systems of Great Britain and of other nations. Were the maxims of exclusive colonial policy universally abandoned; were all protecting duties, as they are termed, and partial prohibitions, sacrificed to the general rule of interest, which counsels to resort for the supply to that quarter, whence it can most cheaply be obtained, the products of India would gain an extension of consumption, to a degree that I will not attempt to calculate. By judicious regulations, the enterprise of individuals might be directed to the multiplication of the items of Indian production. The important articles of coffee, cocoa and cochineal might be made to enrich the commerce of the Ganges, and afford a return investment understated at a crore of rupees. Then, indeed, the Indian tribute to Great Britain would be paid at a more favourable exchange than we dare now anticipate. The policy of promoting such new products, so far as it can be effected by the legislature, requires no comment: the increase of the most valuable part of our mercantile navy; the increased rapidity of private accumulation, coupled with an advance in the interest of money;* the

---

* The more varied and extended employments of capital must have this effect or the analogous one, of preventing or retarding a fall, which progressive accumulation has a direct tendency to create.

augmented value of those savings for the purpose of home-remittance – these natural results of a system, which would extend the limits of demand for the products of British manufacture, and benefit the population of Hindustan, by clothing them at a less real cost in human labour, are well worth the attention of the merchant, the statesman, and the philanthropist.

In conclusion, I will offer a few suggestions upon the mode of drawing up the Calcutta trade reports. In their present form, the mass of information which they undoubtedly contain is less likely to serve any useful purpose, than to mislead by a cursory perusal. While the various branches of trade are classed in almost every possible way, the number of packages of imported woollens and silk and cotton piece-goods is omitted, together with some other quantities and articles capable of specification; such as the number of pieces of printed-calicoes, muslins, maddapolams, long-cloths, linen-shirting, white and coloured handkerchiefs, broad-cloth, purpets, kerseymeres, blankets, etc. etc. The want of these particulars renders it impossible to compare with any accuracy the consumption of British manufactures in India at different periods. But the chief defect is in the system of valuation, often varying, and never uniform or proximately correct: hence, the real amount of the commerce, in each department, as well as in the mass, can only be obtained by a minute and tedious investigation, like that I have above attempted; which, from the intricacy of the subject, is liable to many errors, and may disappoint the most patient inquiry.

Were all goods rated *ad valorem*, the Custom-house statements would require no other corrections than the allowance for estimated charges, and for the natural tendency to declare under the true value. A more accurate and more easy method of obtaining the desired information would be to keep a register of the total amount of every *invoice*, both inwards and outwards. Those of the import are now always required to be produced; and the same rule might be extended to the latter; which, if they could not conveniently be presented at the time of the ship's final dispatch, might, at all events, be afterwards exhibited, as they are always prepared in duplicate. This simple regulation would have the further advantage of not interfering with the method of levying the duties. Import invoices, made out in other currencies, should be converted into sicca rupees, at the exchange of the day, when practicable, or at the mint values of the respective coins; and the latter method should be adopted universally with regard to bullion. In the case of Portugal and Brazil, where a depreciated coin or paper form part of the circulating medium, their rates of exchange with England might serve as a guide: and, when the information should be wanting, the market-prices of the commodities.

It would also be desirable to publish an annual abstract of the commerce of Bombay, Madras and China, in three separate tables; and of any other considerable places of Asiatic trade, whence the requisite materials could be obtained. The additional labour thus incurred might be amply compensated by omitting the ships' names, and the particulars of each cargo, in the several statements; whereby two-thirds of the writing, and three-quarters of the paper, would be saved to the public departments.

The price-current is extremely defective, and in some articles incorrect. Why are indigo and piece-goods, and every other article of Bengal manufacture, omitted, while the prices of broadcloths and purpets are minutely given for every colour? Those who prepare the printed 'Exchange Price-Current' might furnish an annual one still more comprehensive.

I would further suggest that a commercial report, in a concise form, be annually printed.* This is done at a port less celebrated for enlightened society; I allude to Vera Cruz; and that on a plan very superior to any of our methods, each article being classed alphabetically, and estimated at its average market-price throughout the year. Without publication, the report affords scarcely a local advantage: it is merely a record to satisfy curiosity, not a means of reference for the public at large, nor a channel for the diffusion of important information.†

Calcutta, October, 1822

---

* This could certainly be prepared within two or three months after the conclusion of the year. The present voluminous details, with the remarks upon them, are scarcely completed within nine or ten months.

† The reports in their present form are sent home in triplicate, and may there perhaps be printed for parliamentary inspection. But I imagine that in practice they

Postscript[*]

Although the preceding remarks are expressly applicable to the trade of Bengal, it may be expected by commercial men that a memoir upon Indian commerce should not be altogether destitute of information respecting that of the inferior Presidencies. In Madras and Bombay, as well as in Calcutta, trade reports are annually prepared, of which besides the copies sent home to the Court, a copy is remitted to the office of the Territorial Secretary at Calcutta. To the latter I had free access: indeed, a series of Madras reports for eight years, 1813–14 to 1820–21, and of Bombay reports for the last four years of that period, were, during three months, in my possession; but they were so very voluminous, that my short residence in Bengal, and my other and regular occupations there, gave me little opportunity of examining them.

While the report upon the Bengal trade, confined as it is to the single port of Calcutta, is contained in a single folio volume, the Madras report occupies annually no less than six, besides a general statement with explanations, in consequence of the various places of commerce on both the Coromandel and Malabar coasts, comprehended within the limits of that Presidency. The Company's investments are nowhere noticed in the tables, which refer only to the private trade: there also appeared some confusion in the classification of the subordinate ports, prior to 1815–16, which I have consequently omitted. With these deficiencies, I have subjoined a summary of the external commerce of Madras,[†] during the years 1813–14 to 1820–21, according to the official valuations. The export of native piece-goods thence for three years, from 1818–19 to 1820–21 inclusive are added in detail.

---

rarely meet the public eye: for Mr Tucker appears to be unacquainted with the nature of the trade since his departure from Bengal, or he would hardly have put such questions as the following: 'Have they the large stock of specie which we possessed in 1810?' *Vide* p. 28 of his pamphlet, referred to *supra*.

[*] This P.S. and the statements in Appendix, from K inclusive, arrived only when the printing of the foregoing had been completed. Perhaps they may be found useful by the commercial and manufacturing classes.

[†] Appendix K.

The Bombay reports are put forth annually in one very thick folio, which, in 1819–20, contained forty-nine tables of external and sixty-five of internal trade, being three times as many as those of Calcutta. A separate report is made concerning the transactions with Great Britain, in which alone the Company's dealings are noticed. In the Appendix will be found also an abstract general statement of imports at Bombay and its subordinate ports, and of exports, from 1817–18 to 1821–22 inclusive.* To these are added statements of the private trade of Bombay with the United Kingdom between 1805–6 and 1821–22.† There is likewise subjoined a particular of the Company's transactions with the same [Presidency] from 1816–17 inclusive.‡ At foot of the last table I have introduced a summary of the whole trade with Great Britain, according to the official valuations, and I have added various corrections, partly taken from the price-current contained in the report books, which make a total difference of 45 lakhs in the balance of trade, excluding the year 1821–22, in which the corrections make a difference of 43 lakhs on the other side. Finally, I have added tables showing the tonnage and number of ships engaged in the commerce of Bengal and of Bombay respectively: the former from 1813–14 to 1820–21, the latter from 1817–18 to 1821–22, both inclusive.

The system of valuations at Madras I am unacquainted with. That of the Bombay Custom-house is fully as defective as at Calcutta. The consignees' affidavit is taken without exhibition of invoices; and, whereas in Bengal the pound sterling is converted into sicca rupees at the exchange of 2s., the Bombay rupee, nearly 7 per cent less in value, is assumed as equal to 2s. 6d.; so that an invoice from London, consisting of £100 in goods, besides £10 in charges thereon, is passed for 800 rupees; although, at the actual exchange of 1s. 10d., nothing short of Rs.1,200 net, besides interest, will cover the shipper. The French franc is considered as one-third of a rupee. The dollar, Spanish or American, is rated at Rs.216 per 100. The Portuguese reckon their import invoices at $17\frac{1}{4}$ to $17\frac{1}{2}$ rupees per

* Appendix L, *a* & *b*.   † Appendix L, *a*. 4 & *b*. 4.
‡ Appendix L, *c*.

99

meia dobra, which is about one rupee below the corresponding assay value of the currencies. The rupee of Madras is assumed as equal to that of Bombay; while the sicca rupee is converted into the latter at the current exchange. [*In fact the Rupee is usually taken as such without regard to its denomination and relative value.*] It follows, that import valuations are greatly underestimated with respect to the United Kingdom. But with regard to the trade of other countries, the deficiency is in some cases more than compensated by the regulation which subjects the cargoes of foreign vessels to valuation at an advance of 60 per cent upon prime cost; goods from the Coromandel coast, to an addition of 15 per cent; from China, to 20 per cent (at Calcutta, 30 per cent is added); from Malabar, without the province, to 10 per cent; from Goa, on the produce of Europe, to 60 per cent; from the Persian and Arabian Gulphs, on the like, to a similar advance, other articles to one of 15 per cent only; from Batavia, to 25 per cent; and from the Cape of Good Hope, to 30 per cent. Goods re-exported are valued as at the time of their introduction; and there are no fixed rates of valuation, except that of 120 rupees per candy of cotton.* [*And Rs.115 p. Candy of Pepper.*]

I have stated elsewhere that the value of the Bombay rupee in the exchange with Bengal may annually decline, until it shall reach the rate of a bullion remittance to Calcutta. The motives for this opinion are no-wise shaken by the recent negotiation of Bombay government bills upon the Bengal treasury at 100 Bombay rupees for 100 siccas at a time, when the merchants at Bombay were borrowing at high premiums, to make up their opium payments.† By a different financial arrangement, the sacrifice might have been avoided. The treasury of that Presidency is now amply provided and overflowing, although half the bills advertised were withdrawn; and we may not again have to remark an exchange fluctuating between 100 and 109 within eleven months, through the operations of the Local govern-

---

* Cotton of the first quality was, in 1820–21, sold as high as Rs.280 per candy of 7 cwt. Its present price is Rs.140 while the quality usually sent to China may be bought at Rs.115 to 120 per candy.

† In the beginning of Nov. 1822.

ment. It is now 105 to 105½, scarcely lower than before the transactions alluded to.

By the averages of a recent opium sale at Calcutta,* the price of that drug appears to have already fallen from Rs.4,500 very nearly to the rate which I have assumed for the next five years,† including the one now in progress. It is necessary to observe that the total quantity exported from Bengal will be much increased, by the late determination of the Governor-General in Council to sell and deliver at Calcutta one-half of the opium annually purchased in Malwa, instead of confining it to the port of Bombay, as hitherto since the establishment of the monopoly [*in 1820–21*]. The general trade of India with other countries will not be affected thereby: and, if the amount of bills drawn at Bombay upon the Bengal treasury be proportionally augmented, there will arise a demand exactly balancing the difference; because the aggregate amount of private drafts (by agents for Calcutta speculators and others) will be lessened in the same proportion [*The inference here seems to be that if a larger portion of the Malwa opium were sold by the Company in Bombay the excess would be bought entirely on Calcutta account which is neither a necessary nor very probable consequence, altho' it may be expected that part would be so purchased. But if the returns for such excess be made thro' Bombay or in Company's bills upon that Presidency the effect would be the same. This again is scarcely probable to the full extent, unless it be admitted that the import trade from China to Bombay both in merchandise and bullion is incapable of augmentation. The supracargoes' drafts have been a great resource during the current season (1823–24) in the early part of which they were made payable in Bombay to the extent of 37 lakhs including those which appeared at the close of 1822–23. They are still remitted to Bombay although now drawn extensively upon Calcutta – Bombay, 10 February 1824*].

During the present year, it would seem probable that the amount of public bills should be affected by the large bullion

* 1,900 chests sold 31 Dec. 1822;

Patna, at Rs.3,283 per chest;
Benares, Rs.3,257½ per ditto.

whereof ¾ were bought on speculation, and ¼ only for immediate shipment.

† Rs.3,000 per chest.

remittance,* said to be coming from Bengal in the Hon. Company's ship Ernaad. Drafts, however, from Canton, to nearly an equal amount, have already appeared against the treasury of Bombay, which, if occasioned by the destruction of the Company's property in the late fire at Canton, may not reduce the drafts of the supercargoes upon Bengal below the sum assigned in my estimates: on the contrary, the demands of the treasury at Canton may produce an extraordinary pressure upon the home treasury, and upon those of the other Presidencies, independently of the unusual resource above-mentioned.

I will conclude these observations by stating that the official value of British piece-goods imported from England at Bombay in 1821–22, though larger than any former year, was only about three-sevenths of the whole importation of piece-goods, without including what arrives from the subordinate ports of the Presidency:† the remainder chiefly provided from the Malabar Coast, Bengal and China. The proportion is, however, augmented to three-fifths, by estimating the British imports at the current exchange, and adding the invoice charges to the amount; and it is satisfactory to find that, with a similar correction, the British proportion is likely to exceed two-thirds of the whole (with the above exception) during the official year 1822–23. It is believed that the same class of imports has increased in an equal degree at Calcutta during the same period.

Bombay, 15 Feb. 1823

---

* About 15 [20] lakhs.
† About 12 lakhs.

Appendix A *General view of the external commerce of Bengal, according to the trade of 1800–21.*

	Imports				Exports				Bills on the Bengal treasury	Corrected Grand total	Balance of trade
Year	Merchandise	Company's bullion from London	Total bullion	Total	Merchandise	Bullion	Total	Grand total			
1813–14	1,58,21,599	—	57,55,366	2,15,76,965	4,64,08,319	42,750	4,64,51,069	6,80,28,034	1,77,39,272	8,57,67,306	− 71,34,832
1814–15	1,56,42,935	—	1,11,84,285	2,68,27,220	4,73,44,878	1,54,625	4,74,99,503	7,43,26,723	1,77,58,253	9,20,84,976	− 29,14,030
1815–16	1,64,48,657	—	1,94,49,746	3,58,98,403	5,63,95,085	15,750	5,64,16,835	9,23,15,238	1,33,42,861	10,56,58,099	− 71,75,571
1816–17	2,06,25,289	76,99,554	4,13,35,318	6,19,60,607	6,11,84,351	1,69,000	6,13,53,351	12,33,13,958	72,00,632	13,05,14,590	+ 78,07,888
1817–18	2,96,71,230	9,51,130	3,31,71,670	6,28,42,900	6,51,00,658	3,17,250	6,54,17,908	12,82,60,808	78,32,504	13,60,93,312	+ 52,57,496
1818–19	2,97,37,436	19,76,657	4,94,91,605	7,92,29,041	5,83,23,194	2,88,538	5,86,11,732	13,78,40,773	43,66,241	14,22,07,014	+ 2,49,83,550
1819–20	1,75,21,977	91,47,961	4,10,84,670	5,86,06,647	5,43,31,305	66,47,505	6,09,78,810	11,95,85,457	62,11,297	12,57,96,754	+ 38,39,134
1820–21	2,24,45,163	15,25,404	2,40,71,335	4,65,16,498	5,68,03,248	12,29,363	5,80,32,611	10,45,49,109	70,45,933	11,15,95,042	− 44,70,180
Total	16,79,14,286	2,13,00,706	22,55,43,995	39,34,58,281	44,58,91,038	88,64,781	45,47,55,819	84,82,20,100	8,14,96,993	92,97,17,093	+ 2,01,93,455
Average per ann.	2,09,89,286	26,62,588	2,81,92,999	4,91,82,285	5,57,36,380	11,08,097	5,68,44,477	10,60,27,512	1,01,87,125	11,62,14,636	+ 25,24,181

REMARKS

1. In the last column, excess of imports is expressed by + ; and that of exports by − .

2. The third and three last columns do not form part of the report statement, whence the rest are extracted.

3. The Company's bullion imports from London are supposed to consist of surplus profits on their trade, remitted to India for appropriation pursuant to Act of Parliament: except that of 1816–17, which was a balance of account received from the British government.

4. There is a deficiency in the amount of merchandise imported, by comparison with other statements in the trade reports distinguishing the Company's and private trade, to the extent of Rs.2,24,602 per annum, or Rs.17,96,816 in the aggregate: which difference is probably owing to omissions in the summing up, or to a different method of estimating the Company's imports for the first five years; these were not included in the Report statements of those years, but were taken into account when the statement was prepared, which has served as a basis for the above table.

Appendix B, No. 1   *Average annual amount of merchandise imported into Calcutta, from 1813-14 to 1820-21.*

Country	Mode of Custom-house valuation	Amount of ditto	Net amount corrected	Invoice amount obtained by adding 20 per cent
Great Britain	Rupee valued at 2s. instead of real exchange	1,08,65,633	84,82,810	1,01,79,372
France	10 Rs. valued at 24s. in lieu of 25 francs	2,07,721	2,01,412	2,41,694
Holland	Assumed at ditto, or a like ratio	23,160	22,234	26,681
Denmark	Ditto ditto ditto	46,781	44,910	53,892
Gibraltar and Malta	Invoices in dollars at 225 in lieu of 206¼ per cent	1,02,246	93,763	1,12,516
Cadiz	Do.	31,463	28,853	34,624
United States	Do.	3,91,890	3,59,378	4,31,254
Spanish America	Do.	3,24,288	2,97,384	3,56,861
Manilla	Do.	1,93,480	1,77,428	2,12,913
China (30 per cent added to cost)	Do.	28,12,351	19,83,869	23,80,643
Java	Do.	5,65,849	5,18,904	6,22,685
Coast of Sumatra	Do. or a similar rate	2,67,981	2,45,748	2,94,941
Penang and eastward	Do.	6,63,668	6,08,608	7,30,330
Ambroyna	Do.	17,864	16,382	19,658
Arabian and Persian Gulphs	Do.	9,92,861	9,10,490	10,92,588
Mozambique	Do.	52,104	47,781	57,337
Cape of Good Hope	Do.	9,240	8,473	10,168
Mauritius	Do.	5,13,328	4,70,741	5,64,889
Maldive Islands	Do.	1,37,047	1,25,677	1,50,812
Pegue	Do.	3,29,537	3,02,190	3,62,628
Ceylon	Do.	79,502	72,906	87,487
New South Wales	Do.	31,583	29,074	34,889
Lisbon	Do. in Reis*	2,71,503	2,48,978	2,98,774
Brazil	Do.	1,22,196	1,12,058	1,34,470
Coast of Malabar	Invoices in Bombay Rs. at 103½† instead of 108 per cent	9,05,133	8,84,177	10,61,022
Coast of Coromandel	Ditto in pagodas, at Rs.3¾ instead of 3·6¼ each, with an augmentation of 15 per cent on coast goods	8,06,275	say 6,50,000	7,80,000
Partial omission of the Company's imports in the tables of the first 5 years, Rs.21,26,033	Supposed an excess in the valuation and exchanges sufficient to cover invoice charges	2,65,754	2,50,000	2,65,754
Deficit (probably on the same account) owing to inconsistencies in the various trade reports	Do. do.	2,24,602	2,00,000	2,24,602
Total		Sa. Rs.2,12,55,040	1,73,94,228	2,08,23,464

Remarks

There being no printed Tarif, and the Custom-house valuations being governed by a written set of rules, liable to alteration, the corrections above applied are no doubt in some instances erroneous, as they have been assumed upon verbal information; but it is conceived the amount of such error cannot be very considerable. It must further be observed, that inaccuracies to a small extent may have arisen in calculating the mean annual importations of each country from the tables.
 * At Rs.2 14 as. per Mil-rea, worth 54 to 56d. † At the rate of Sa. Rs.94 13 as. 3 per cent per 100 Bombay rupees, which nearly corresponds with the above, and is the mint par.

George Alexander Prinsep

Appendix B, No. 2   *Total amount of merchandise imported into ditto from the United Kingdom.*

Year	Reported amount	Current exchange		Overcharge		Net amount corrected	Invoice amount obtained by adding 20 per cent
		s.	d.				
1813–14	85,89,121	2	7	22½	per cent	66,56,569	79,87,883
1814–15	77,03,798	2	8¼	25½	do.	57,39,330	68,87,196
1815–16	86,67,213	2	8½	26	do.	64,13,738	76,96,485
1816–17	94,96,650	2	7	22½	do.	73,59,903	88,31,884
1817–18	1,52,87,596	2	7½	24	do.	1,16,18,573	1,39,42,288
1818–19	1,72,26,316	2	7½	24	do.	1,30,92,000	1,57,10,400
1819–20	86,33,573	2	6	20	do.	69,06,859	82,88,231
1820–21	1,13,20,797	2	3	11	do.	1,00,75,509	1,20,90,611
Total	8,69,25,064	—		—		6,78,62,481	8,14,34,978
Mean	1,08,65,633	2	6¾	22 per cent		84,82,810	1,01,79,372

REMARKS

Possibly the Company may not load their invoices with charges so high as 20 per cent; but this rate is nevertheless probably within the real amount they incur.

By this table there appears an excess in the valuation averaging 6½ per cent; but hereafter they will fall short of the investments, while the exchange is under 2s. 5d.

Appendix C, No. 1 *Statement of the Custom-house, and corrected, valuations of the principal exports of Bengal.*

Year	Indigo				Piece-goods				Cotton			
	Reported amount	Custom-ho. valuation, per fac. md.	Estimated annual mean price	Corrected net amount	Reported amount	Custom-ho. valuation per piece	Supposed under estimate	Corrected net amount	Reported amount	Custom-ho. valuation per md. of 96 sicca wt.	Estimated annual mean price	Corrected net amount
						Rs. A.				Rs. A.		
1813–14	97,79,194	100	160	1,56,46,710	52,86,362	2 11	10%	58,14,998	39,92,036	13 3	13 6	40,01,706
1814–15	72,49,337	—	180	1,30,48,807	84,95,599	2 15	—	98,45,159	45,60,663	12 3¼	13 10	50,83,951
1815–16	1,28,91,953	—	150	1,93,37,930	1,31,56,587	2 12	—	1,44,72,246	38,21,475	11 11	13 4	34,26,893
1816–17	88,74,885	—	135	1,19,81,094	1,65,99,943	2 13	—	1,82,59,987	76,89,368	11 9	15 0	88,14,477
1817–18	80,31,855	—	130	1,04,41,411	1,32,94,725	3 1	—	1,45,58,198	1,10,13,074	11 0	18 0	1,80,36,616
1818–19	69,66,405	—	140	97,52,967	1,15,24,356	3 2	—	1,26,76,782	89,76,861	10 14	19 0	1,60,17,421
1819–20	99,49,895	—	125	1,24,37,369	1,16,66,071	3 2	8%	1,26,15,557	28,33,773	11 8	20 0	47,48,700
1820–21	75,92,919	—	150	1,13,89,378	1,08,40,652	3 5	—	1,17,07,904	44,40,881	16 0	20 0	55,66,380
Total	7,13,36,443	—	—	10,40,35,666	9,08,04,295	—	—	9,94,50,781	4,73,28,131	—	—	6,65,96,144
Mean	89,17,055	100	146	1,30,04,459	1,13,50,537	3 0	9¼%	1,24,31,348	59,16,016	12 4	16 8½	83,24,518

106

	Silk				Sugar			
Year	Reported amount	Custom ho. valuation per bazar seer	Estimated annual mean price	Corrected net amount	Reported amount	Custom ho. valuation per bazar md.	Estimated annual mean price	Corrected net amount
1813–14	17,17,126	6 5	10 0	70,68,401	12,17,108	7 12	8 8	16,08,202
1814–15	Cy. 43,48,201 / 33,12,709	11 7 / 6 2	11 7 p.f.s. / 9 2	79,74,256	Cy. 2,73,715 / 21,14,698	5 10 / 7 0	p.f.m. / 7 8	22,63,384
1815–16	Cy. 28,38,667 / 28,88,057	10 5 / 6 6	10 5 / 9 0	60,92,198	Cy. — / 23,23,927	— / 8 0	— / 9 8	—
1816–17	Cy. 20,22,891 / 77,72,525	10 0 / 5 8	10 0 / 9 8	53,18,552	Cy. 1,33,209 / 94,19,411	7 3¼ / 8 0	7 3¼ / 10 0	29,01,344
1817–18	Cy. 22,55,787 / 19,57,262	11 4 / 6 4	11 4 / 10 0	79,38,459	Cy. 15,309 / 38,81,397	7 11 / 8 8	7 11 / 10 8	43,01,746
1818–19	Cy. 47,98,597 / 18,53,975	11 15 / 5 12	11 15 / 10 12	71,76,677	Cy. 2,42,835 / 41,38,364	8 2¼ / 8 5	8 2¼ / 9 0	50,31,906
1819–20	Cy. 37,22,302 / 77,07,243	12 11 / 10 12	12 11 / 13 4	94,10,743	Cy. 2,42,699 / 44,83,897	7 9 / 8 0	7 9 / 10 0	51,21,996
1820–21	82,50,879	12 10	13 10	88,99,079	34,34,176	8 0	9 8	59,21,448 / 40,84,982
Total	5,54,41,251			5,98,78,365	2,59,24,738			3,12,35,158
Mean	69,30,156	7 8 / 11 4½	10 5 / 11 4⅓	74,84,796	32,40,592	7 14 / 7 4	9 3 / 7 4	39,04,395

REMARKS

The Company's sugar and silk are separately stated at their respective real cost, per *factory maund* and per *factory seer*: no addition therefore is made to the valuations; but in the two last years their trade is comprehended in the general mass. The Company, during the above period, exported no indigo. No specification has been obtained of their cotton and piece-goods. Piece-goods, both silk and cotton, are valued at the *aurung* prices, which it is believed are full 10 per cent too low, compared with those of Calcutta. The Company's charges being, however, presumed to be less, and their interest being included only in the tables of the two last years of the series, I have in them assumed a lower rate. The mean under-estimate of saltpetre appears to be about Rs.50,000 per annum.

Appendix C, No. 2 Statement, shewing the estimated invoice-value of merchandise exported from Calcutta.

Year	Valuation as per trade reports	Correction from above table	Inland duties (less drawbacks) supposed a charge upon foreigners	Export duties, deducting drawbacks upon re-exports	Cost of merchandise with duties	Estimated Calcutta invoice charges	Total	Remarks
1813–14	4,64,08,319	75,26,275	87,506	Deduct 4,344	5,40,17,756	11 per cent	5,99,59,709	Insurs. at war prems.
1814–15	4,73,44,878	91,43,893	1,41,229	Add 50,289	5,66,80,289	10 do.	6,23,48,318	Do. great pt. of this yr.
1815–16	5,63,95,085	98,92,712	218	do. 1,98,348	6,64,86,363	9½ do.	7,28,02,561	Commt. of Amer. trade ins. elsewhere
1816–17	6,11,84,351	80,48,578	—*	do. 4,27,301	6,96,60,230	9 do.	7,59,29,651	Do. French and Dutch do.
1817–18	6,51,00,658	1,26,46,845	—	do. 3,16,591	7,80,64,094	8½ do.	8,44,99,541	Trade of foreigners much increased
1818–19	5,83,23,194	1,33,20,881	—	do. 4,96,503	7,21,40,578	8 do.	7,79,11,824	Ditto.
1819–20	5,43,31,305	84,95,938	2,60,419	do. 3,44,617	6,34,36,279	7½ do.	6,81,94,000	Freights and prems. very low.
1820–21	5,68,03,248	70,88,166	2,37,376	do. 3,59,052	6,44,87,842	7 do.	6,90,01,991	Ditto.
Total	44,58,91,038	7,61,63,288	—	28,88,357	52,49,73,431	—	57,06,47,595	
Mean	5,57,36,380	95,20,411†	Say 2,00,000	2,72,545	6,56,21,679	8¼ per cent	7,13,30,949	

108

* In 1816 to 1819, the drawbacks are stated to have exceeded the amount of duties, no doubt because the former were returned always at Calcutta.

† The mean correction taken from the averages of the preceding table would be Rs.95,45,160; but so small a difference scarcely merits attention. Were a due proportion of the freight on the country trade and homeward-bound ships owned in Calcutta added to the total of Rs.7,13,35,949, and allowance also made for above half a crore of exports, not including opium, which though not enumerated, are supposed to have been likewise undervalued, it is probable the whole average export of merchandise would be found to exceed 750 lakhs during the above period. Grain alone is under-estimated to the extent of 8 or 10 lakhs at least, probably of 12 or 15; being valued at 1 rupee per maund, instead of 1¼ or 1⅓; besides 15 per cent charges, not inclusive of freight

Appendix D *Statement of the Bullion trade at the port of Calcutta.*

Year	Imports		Exports		Results	
	Reported amount	Value at Rs.203 per 100 drs.	Reported amount	Value at Rs.212 per 100 drs.	Total	Balance of trade
1813–14	57,55,356	51,92,610	42,750	40,280	52,32,890	51,52,330
1814–15	1,11,84,285	1,00,90,710	1,54,625	1,45,691	1,02,36,401	99,45,019
1815–16	1,94,49,746	1,31,03,549	15,750	14,840	1,31,18,389	1,30,88,709
1816–17	4,13,35,318	3,72,93,687	1,69,000	1,59,182	3,74,52,869	3,71,34,505
1817–18	3,31,71,670	2,99,28,084	3,17,250	2,98,920	3,02,27,004	2,96,29,164
1818–19	4,94,91,605	4,46,52,426	2,88,538	2,71,867	4,49,24,293	4,43,80,559
1819–20	4,10,84,670	3,70,67,502	66,47,505	61,45,249	4,32,12,751	3,09,22,253*
1820–21	2,40,71,335	2,17,17,693	12,29,363	11,58,333	2,28,76,026	2,05,59,360
Total	22,55,43,995	19,90,46,261	88,64,781	82,34,362	20,72,80,623	19,08,02,869
Mean	2,81,92,999	2,48,80,783	11,08,097	10,29,295	2,59,10,078	2,38,50,359

GENERAL REMARKS

1. The Custom-house valuation of the Spanish and American dollar is always 225 rupees per 100, both on import and export.

2. If the Bullion imported by the Company from London (*vide* Appendix A) be deducted, as being a remittance of profits, etc. for specific appropriation, and therefore not concerned in the balance of trade, the real value of the bullion imports will be reduced to about 224 lakhs, and the balance to about 213½ or 214 lakhs per annum, during the eight years comprehended in the above term.

* Rs. 65,00,000 of this year's declared exports being on the company's account I have valued the whole at Rs 208 par 100 dollars.

109

Appendix E   *Estimate of the external commerce of Calcutta, from 1813 to 1821.*

		Imports		
Year	Merchandise	Bullion	Bills on the Bengal treasury	Total
1813–14	1,65,14,272	51,92,610	1,77,39,272	3,94,46,154
1814–15	1,53,27,675	1,00,90,710	1,77,58,253	4,31,76,638
1815–16	1,59,56,685	1,31,03,549	1,33,42,861	4,24,03,095
1816–17	2,03,83,031	3,72,93,687	72,00,632	6,48,77,350
1817–18	2,89,02,288	2,99,28,084	78,32,504	6,66,62,876
1818–19	2,85,28,484	4,46,52,426	43,66,241	7,75,47,151
1819–20	1,73,94,719	3,70,67,502	62,11,297	6,06,73,518
1820–21	2,34,87,924	2,17,17,693	70,45,933	5,22,51,550
Total	16,64,95,078	19,90,46,261	8,14,96,993	44,70,38,332
Mean	2,08,11,885	2,48,80,782	1,01,87,125	5,58,79,792

REMARKS

1. The last column will be understood by reference to Appendix A, note 3, and Appendix D, note 2.

2. The figures of the first column were obtained, by adding to the annual imports from Great Brita

But Appendix B, which gave this ratio, having subsequently undergone correction, the proper multiplier seer

3. On comparing the balances resulting in this and Appendix A, there appears a difference Company's surplus profits, etc. remitted in bullion from London.

	Exports			Results	
				Excess of	Balance exclusive of the Company's
Merchandise	Bullion	Total	Grand total	exports	surplus profits, etc.
5,99,59,709	40,280	5,99,99,989	9,94,46,143	2,05,53,835	2,05,53,835
6,23,48,318	1,45,691	6,24,94,009	10,56,70,647	1,93,17,371	1,93,17,371
7,28,02,561	14,840	7,28,17,401	11,52,20,496	3,04,14,306	3,04,14,306
7,59,29,651	1,59,182	7,60,88,833	14,09,66,183	1,12,11,483	1,81,58,192
8,46,99,541	2,98,920	8,49,98,461	15,16,61,337	1,83,35,583	1,91,93,718
7,79,11,824	2,71,867	7,81,83,691	15,57,30,842	6,36,540	24,19,924
6,81,94,000	61,45,249	7,43,39,249	13,50,12,767	1,36,65,731	2,19,19,225
6,90,01,991	11,58,333	7,01,60,324	12,24,11,874	1,79,08,774	1,92,85,027
57,08,47,595	82,34,362	57,90,81,957	1,02,61,20,289	13,20,43,625	15,12,61,598
7,13,55,949	10,29,295	7,23,85,245	12,82,65,037	1,65,05,453	1,89,07,700

Appendix B) the annual reported amount of the residue, augmenting the latter in the ratio of $\frac{108,29,158}{105,69,817}$.

be $\frac{106,44,059}{103,89,407}$. Hence a small difference in the mean result.

s.1,90,30,385 in the annual average: which difference is augmented to Rs.2,14,32,632 by the exclusion of the

Appendix F *Estimate of the trade in merchandise of Bengal with Great Britain for the ensuing five years.* (Invoice value expressed in lakhs and decimals.)

		Imports				
Description of goods	Annual increase	1822–23	1823–24	1824–25	1825–26	1826–27
Cotton piece-goods	7 per cent	1. 40·0	1. 42·2	1. 45·8	1. 49·0	1. 52·4
Woollens	5 do.	25·0	26·2	27·6	28·9	30·4
Spelter	10 do.	8·0	8·8	9·7	10·6	11·7
Iron, steel, and nails	5 do.	6·0	6·3	6·6	6·9	7·3
Copper, pig, sheathing, etc.	5 do.	24·0	25·2	26·5	27·8	29·2
Lead	5 do.	3·0	3·2	3·3	3·5	3·6
Hardware, guns, etc.	5 do.	4·3	4·5	4·7	5·0	5·2
Earthenware	5 do.	2·0	2·1	2·2	2·3	2·4
Glassware of all sorts	5 do.	8·0	8·4	8·8	9·3	9·7
Clocks and watches	5 do.	0·7	0·7	0·8	0·8	0·9
Cordage and other naval stores, paints, lin-seed oil, tinware	4 do.	4·0	4·2	4·3	4·5	4·7
Oilman's stores, books, sadlery, hosiery, spruce, stationery, and other shop supplies for Europeans	3 do.	16·0	16·5	17·0	17·6	18·1
Malt liquor	3 do.	3·0	3·1	3·2	3·3	3·4
Wine, brandy, and liquors	at	10·0	10·0	10·0	10·0	10·0
Sundries, including new articles	10 per cent	4·0	4·0	4·8	5·3	5·9
Total	5·3 per cent	1. 1,58·0	1. 1,65·4	1. 1,75·3	1. 1,84·8	1. 1,94·9

REMARKS

As it is considered that some further economy may yet be obtained by the more general use of power-looms in the cotton manufactories, the competition of our fabrics with those of India is thought to be still capable of extension.

The annual augmentation on spelter is assumed at a high rate, because it will probably by degrees altogether supersede the imports of tutenague; the latter, however, may perhaps come from the Continent direct.

Description of goods	Annual increase	Quantity the first year	1822–23	1823–24	1824–25	1825–26	1826–27
Indigo	at	70,000 mds.	l. 151·2	{ 75,000 mds. l. 141·7 }	{ 75,000 mds. l. 121·5 }	{ 70,000 mds. l. 100·8 }	{ 70,000 mds. l. 94·5 }
Raw silk	5 per cent	15,000	78·0	81·9	86·0	90·5	94·0
Sugar	10 do.	3,000	24·0	26·4	29·0	31·9	35·1
Cotton	10 do.	100,000	—	15·0	16·5	18·2	20·0
Saltpetre	at	250,000	12·5	12·5	12·5	12·5	12·5
Silk piece-goods	at	150,000 prs.	10·5	10·5	10·5	10·5	10·5
Cotton ditto	{ decreasing 5 per cent	200,000	7·0	6·6	6·3	6·0	5·7
Lack dye	at }	10,000 mds.	3·0	3·0	3·0	3·0	3·0
Shell, stick, and seed-lack	at	10,000	2·0	2·0	2·0	2·0	2·0
Sundries, including new articles	10 per cent	—	11·0	12·1	13·3	14·6	16·1
Spices and other asiatic re-exports	at	—	12·0	12·0	12·0	12·0	12·0
Net cost			l. 311·2	l. 323·7	l. 312·6	l. 310·8	l. 306·2
Charges computed at 6 per cent			18·7	19·4	18·7	18·2	18·5
Total			l. 329·9	l. 343·1	l. 331·3	l. 320·0	l. 324·7

113

REMARKS

		1822–23	1823–24	1824–25	1825–26	1826–27
Per Maund	Rs.	240	210	180	160	150
Prices above allowed		216	189	162	144	135

Silk is valued above at 13 Rs. per factory seer
Sugar 6 per bazar maund
Cotton 15 do. do.
Saltpetre 5 do. do.
Cotton piece-goods 3¼ per piece, or Rs.70 per corge
Silk 7 do.

As most of the inferior indigo is shipped for England, the above valuations are 10 per cent lower than those assumed as the general average, viz.

Appendix G *Estimate of external commerce of Calcutta for the ensuing five years, exclusive of bullion.*

Imports, classed by the countries

Names		1822–23	1823–24	1824–25	1825–26	1826–27
France		4·0	4·2	4·4	4·6	4·9
Baltic ports		1·0	1·0	1·1	1·2	1·2
Portugal		1·0	1·0	1·0	1·0	1·0
Spain		—	1·0	1·3	1·6	2·0
Mediterranean		4·0	4·8	5·8	6·9	8·3
United States	Total lakhs	10·0	12·0	13·6	15·3	17·4
		2·0	2·1	2·2	2·3	2·4
Great Britain	Do. lakhs	12·0	14·1	15·8	17·6	19·8
		1,58·0	1,66·4	1,75·3	1,84·9	1,94·9
	Do. lakhs	1,70·0	1,80·5	1,91·0	2,02·5	2,14·7
Brazil		0·4	0·4	1·0	0·4	0·4
Mexico and South America		10·0	10·5	11·0	11·5	12·0
Cape of Good Hope		1·0	1·0	1·0	1·0	1·0
Mauritius		8·0	8·0	8·0	8·0	8·0
Arabian and Persian Gulphs		15·0	16·5	18·2	20·0	22·0
Maldive Islands		1·0	1·0	1·0	1·0	1·0
Ceylon		1·0	1·0	1·0	1·0	1·0
Coast of Malabar		11·0	11·0	11·0	11·0	11·0
Coast of Coromandel		8·0	8·0	8·0	8·0	8·0
Coast of Sumatra		2·6	2·6	2·6	2·6	2·6
Java		5·0	5·0	5·0	5·0	5·0
Pegue		2·0	2·0	2·0	2·0	2·0
Penang and eastward		10·0	10·1	10·2	10·3	10·4
Manilla		1·0	1·1	1·2	1·3	1·5
China		42·0	42·0	42·0	42·0	42·0
New South Wales		0·6	0·6	0·6	0·6	0·6
Grand total	lakhs	2,88·6	3,01·3	3,14·3	3,28·2	3,43·2

REMARK

Merchandise	Quantity the 1st year	Price	1822–23	1823–24	1824–25	1825–26	1826–27
Opium	5,000 chsts.	Rs.3,000	1,50·0	1,57·5	1,65·4	1,73·6	1,82·3
Indigo*	100,000 mds.	See note.* Rs. As.	2,40·0	2,52·0	2,34·0	2,08·0	1,95·0
Silk†	17,000 do.	12·11 per seer	86·3	91·0	96·0	1,01·0	1,06·0
Piece-goods, cotton	2,600,000 ps.	34·0 per pce.	84·5	81·0	78·0	75·0	72·0
Ditto silk	45,000 do.	7·0 do.	31·5	31·0	30·5	30·0	29·5
Sugar	6,000 mds.	8·0 per md.	48·0	52·8	58·1	63·9	70·3
Cotton‡	480,000 do.	14·0 do.	20·0	60·0	62·0	64·0	66·0
Saltpetre	380,000 do.	5·0 do.	19·0	19·5	20·0	20·5	21·0
Grain	1,400,000 do.	1·0 do.	14·0	14·5	15·0	15·5	16·0
Lack dye	13,000 do.	35·0 do.	4·2	4·4	4·6	4·8	5·0
Seed, stick, and shell lack	17,000 do.	—	3·0	3·1	3·2	3·3	3·4
Ginger	60,000 do.	5·0 do.	3·0	3·0	3·1	3·3	3·5
Gunnies	3,000,000 ps.	8·0 per 100	2·4	2·6	2·8	3·0	3·2
Sundries, including new articles	—	—	25·0	27·5	30·0	32·5	35·0
Asiatic and other merchandise re-exported	—	lakhs	7,30·9	7,99·9	8,02·7	7,98·4	8,08·2
			44·0	43·0	42·0	41·0	40·0
Total, prime cost	—	lakhs	7,74·9	8,42·9	8,44·7	8,39·4	8,48·2
Duties computed at	—		6·0	6·5	7·0	7·5	8·0
		lakhs	7,80·9	8,49·4	8,51·7	8,46·9	8,56·2
Commissions, and other charges at Calcutta, computed at	—	7 per cent	54·7	59·5	59·6	59·3	59·9
Total amount of invoices	—	lakhs	8,35·6	9,08·9	9,11·3	9,06·2	9,16·1
Deduct amount of imports as *supra*	—	—	2,88·6	3,01·3	3,14·3	3,28·2	3,43·2
Balance of exports	—	lakhs	5,47·0	6,07·6	5,97·0	5,78·0	5,72·9

115

* Indigo is estimated as follows		1822–23	1823–24	1824–25	1825–26	1826–27
	maunds	100,000	120,000	130,000	130,000	130,000
Price per maund	rupees	240	210	180	160	150

† Silk: only the low qualities are exported to Bombay and Madras; 15,000 maunds to England, at 13 rupees, and 2,000 elsewhere, at 10½; average 12·11 per seer.
‡ Cotton: the present year's export is assumed at 150,000 maunds to China, the next at 300,000 to China and 130,000 elsewhere.

Appendix H   *Estimate of the export to each country, balance of trade, and bullion-import of Bengal for five years.*

	1822–23				1823–24			
	Amount of exports	Excess of exports	Bills on Bengal govt.	Returns in bullion	Amount of exports	Excess of exports	Bills on Bengal govt.	Returns in bullion
China lakhs	1.55·0	1.13·0	60·0	33·0	1.84·0	1.42·0	61·0	61·0
Java	35·0	30·0	—	30·0	36·9	31·9	—	31·9
Penang and eastward	26·0	16·0	} 5·0 {	11·0	27·3	17·2	} 5·0 {	12·0
Coast of Sumatra	6·6	4·0		4·0	6·6	4·0		4·0
Manilla	4·5	3·5	—	3·5	4·8	3·7	—	3·7
Persian and Arabian Gulphs	60·0	45·0	—	45·0	65·0	48·5	—	48·5
Coast of Malabar	37·0	26·0	30·0	3·0	37·0	26·0	29·0	4·0
Coast of Coromandel	12·0	4·0	1·0	3·0	12·0	4·0	1·0	3·0
Ceylon	2·4	1·4	1·0	—	2·4	1·4	1·0	—
New South Wales	3·6	3·0	—	0·5	4·0	3·4	—	0·5
Mauritius	11·0	3·0	3·0	—	11·1	3·1	3·0	0·1
Cape of Good Hope	5·0	4·0	—	2·0	5·2	4·2	—	2·2
Maldive Islands	1·0	—	—	—	1·0	—	—	—
Mexico, Chili, Peru, and Buenos Ayres	35·0	25·0	—	25·0	42·0	31·5	—	31·5
Brazil	6·4	6·0	—	6·0	6·1	5·7	—	5·7
Pegue	1·2	*	—	—	1·2	*	—	—
Total Country Trade lakhs	4.01·7	2.83·9	1.00·0	1.66·0	4.46·6	3.26·6	1.00·0	2.08·3
United States	38·0	36·0	—	36·0	46·0	43·9	—	43·9
Mediterranean	10·0	6·0	—	6·0	12·0	7·2	—	7·2
Spain	1·0	1·0	—	1·0	2·0	1·0	—	1·0
Portugal	22·0	21·0	—	15·0	22·0	21·0	—	21·0
France	28·0	24·0	—	—	32·0	27·8	—	3·2
Baltic ports	5·0	4·0	—	—	5·2	4·2	—	—
Great Britain	3.29·9	1.71·9	—	—	3.43·1	1.76·7	—	—
Bills on the Bengal treasury (third column)	—	—	1.00·0	—	—	—	—	1.00·0
Company's surplus investment, including 20 lakhs to China	—	—	—	1.00·0	—	—	—	1.00·0
Remittable capital of individuals	—	—	—	1.00·0	—	—	—	1.00·0
Ditto Bombay and Madras. Ditto, received through inland bills on Furruckabad. Benares, and other treasuries	—	—	—	23·0	—	—	—	23·0
Total export lakhs	8.35·6	5.47·8	—	—	9.08·9	6.08·4	—	—
* Deduct surplus import from Pegue	—	8	—	—	—	8	—	—
Amount corresponding to surplus exports	—	5.47·0	—	5.47·0	—	6.07·6	—	6.07·6

1. The Bombay surplus remitted to Bengal, of 7 lakhs, is for commercial investment in produce. Besides commercial and capital remittances to Europe.

2. The small Ceylon balance may be covered by government colonial drafts; that of New South Wales in It appears above, that the first year is balanced by bullion from Portugal; the second by ditto from France; establish the exchange on London at 2s. 1¼d. at 2s. 2d. for drafts on foreign account, and (allowing the usual

	1824–25				1825–26				1826–27		
Amount of exports	Excess of exports	Bills on Bengal govt.	Returns in bullion	Amount of exports	Excess of exports	Bills on Bengal govt.	Returns in bullion	Amount of exports	Excess of exports	Bills on Bengal govt.	Returns in bullion
1.92·0	1.50·0	62·0	68·0	2.01·0	1.59·0	63·0	76·0	2.10·0	1.68·0	64·0	84·0
38·4	33·4	—	33·4	39·0	34·0	—	34·0	39·0	34·0	—	34·0
28·7	18·5	⎱ 5·0	⎧ 13·0	30·2	19·9	⎱ 5·0	⎧ 14·9	31·7	21·3	⎱ 5·0	⎧ 16·3
6·6	4·0	⎰	⎩ 4·0	6·6	4·0	⎰	⎩ 4·0	6·6	4·0	⎰	⎩ 4·0
5·1	3·9	—	3·9	5·4	4·1	—	4·1	5·7	4·2	—	4·2
60·0	41·8	—	41·8	55·0	35·0	—	35·0	50·0	28·0	—	28·0
37·0	26·0	28·0	5·0	37·0	26·0	27·0	6·0	37·0	26·0	26·0	7·0
12·0	4·0	1·0	3·0	12·0	4·0	1·0	3·0	12·0	4·0	1·0	3·0
2·4	1·4	1·0	—	2·4	1·4	1·0	—	2·4	1·4	1·0	—
4·4	3·8	—	0·5	4·8	4·2	—	0·5	5·2	4·6	—	0·5
11·2	3·2	3·0	0·2	11·3	3·3	3·0	0·3	11·4	3·4	3·0	0·4
5·5	4·5	—	2·5	5·7	4·7	—	2·7	6·0	5·0	—	3·0
1·0	—	—	—	1·0	—	—	—	1·0	—	—	—
46·2	35·2	—	35·2	46·5	35·0	—	35·0	48·5	36·5	—	36·5
5·8	5·4	—	5·4	5·6	5·2	—	5·2	5·4	5·0	—	5·0
1·2	*	—	—	1·2	*	—	—	1·2	*	—	—
4.57·5	3.35·1	1.00·0	2.15·9	4.64·7	3.39·8	1.00·0	2.20·7	4.45·1	3.45·4	1.00·0	2.25·9
46·0	43·8	—	43·8	46·0	43·7	—	34·3	46·0	43·6	—	24·0
14·0	8·2	—	8·2	14·5	7·6	—	—	14·3	6·0	—	—
3·0	1·7	—	1·7	4·0	2·4	—	—	5·0	3·0	—	—
22·0	21·0	—	4·4	22·0	21·0	—	—	20·0	19·0	—	—
32·0	27·6	—	—	30·0	25·4	—	—	28·0	23·1	—	—
5·5	4·4	—	—	5·0	3·8	—	—	5·0	3·8	—	—
3.31·3	1.56·0	—	—	3.20·0	1.55·1	—	—	3.24·7	1.29·8	—	—
—	—	—	1.00·0	—	—	—	1.00·0	—	—	—	1.00·0
—	—	—	1.00·0	—	—	—	1.00·0	—	—	—	1.00·0
—	—	—	1.00·0	—	—	—	1.00·0	—	—	—	1.00·0
—	—	—	23·0	—	—	—	23·0	—	—	—	23·0
9.11·3	5.97·8	—	—	9.06·2	5.98·8	—	—	9.16·1	5.73·7	—	—
—	8	—	—	—	8	—	—	—	8	—	—
—	5.97·0	—	5.97·0	—	5.98·0	—	5.78·0	—	5.72·9	—	5.72·9

REMARKS

which, 23 lakhs are supposed to arrive through the inland treasuries from Bombay and Madras jointly, for

the same way; and that of the Cape partly so, and partly by the drafts of Bengal invalids on Calcutta.
the third by ditto again from Portugal; and the fourth and fifth by ditto from the United States: which would
difference), 2s. at 2s. ¼d. for agents' and Company's bills.

Appendix I *Estimate of the Calcutta exchange by the balance of trade.*

No. 1. LONDON

(a) Invoice of dollars shipped at London *for Calcutta.*

Account of sale *at Calcutta.*

	£	s.	d.
100 dollars, bought at 4s. 9½d. per oz. or 4s. 2d. each	20	16	8
Brokerage, ⅛ per cent on purchase	0	0	6
Shipping charges, etc. say	0	0	6
Insurance premium, two gs. per cent on 23 lakhs	0	9	0
Policy Duty, ¼ per cent	0	1	2
Freight, 1 per cent on £20. 16s. 8d.	0	4	2
	£21	12	8
Interest at 5 per cent for 18 mos., from date of purchase to term of bill drawn at Calcutta in lieu thereof, at 6 mos.' sight, for purchase of produce, 7½ per cent	1	12	6
Total invoice cost	£23	5	2

	Rs.	Rs.
100 dollars at 205½* Rs. per cent		205·8
Commission ½ per cent	1.0.5 ⎫	
Ditto of account 1 per cent balanced by the saving of 1 per cent on drafts	— ⎬ 1·4	
Landing and petty expences	0.3.7 ⎭	
Net proceeds		Rs.204.4
		or
		2s. 3¼d. per R.

(b) Ditto, dollars shipped for London *from Calcutta.*

100 dollars bought at 206¼   Sale in London.

		Rs.	s.	d.
Rs. per cent* cost	Rs.206	5	4
Commission, ½ per cent	1	0	6
Shipping, etc. say	0	3	3
Insurance and commission, 3 per cent	6	2	11
Invoice cost	Rs. 213	12	0

Sale in London.	£	s.	d.
at 4s. 2d.	£20	16	8
½ per cent 2s. 0d. ⎫			
Brokerage ⅛ per cent 0 6 ⎬	0	6	8
Freight 1 per cent 4 2 ⎭			
Proceeds	£20	10	0
4 mos.' interest gained, at 5 per cent per ann.	0	6	10

Rs.213 12—at Exchange 1s. 11⅞d., equal to   £20 16 10

---

* The buying and selling prices are made to differ a little, less perhaps than the real difference occasioned by a demand for sale or purchase.

George Alexander Prinsep

Appendix I – *cont.*

No. 2. South of Europe

100 dollars shipped for London produce	£20	10	0
Saving in the insurance prm. compared with a bullion shipment for India 1½ per cent	0	6	2
Interest gained by lodging the money to be drawn upon from Calcutta, say 15 mos., at 5 per cent on £21	1	6	3
Total proceeds	£22	2	5

Deduct difference between 1 per cent commission at Calcutta on demanding bills, and ½ per cent on sale of drs., viz. ½ per cent on £22 2s. 5d.; also ½ per cent commission to the London acceptor

	0	4	5
	£21	18	0

£21 18s. at exchange 2s. 1¾d. equal to Rs.204·4 – the proceeds of 100 drs., if sent to Calcutta, as per No. 1.

No. 3. United States

100 dollars shipped for London produce	£20	10	0
Saving, as above (No. 2), at 1½ per cent	0	6	2
Interest gained, say 14 mos.	1	4	6
Total proceeds	£22	0	8
Deduct extra commissions in London and Calcutta, as per No. 2, 1 per cent	0	4	5
	£21	16	3

£21. 16s. 3d. at exchange 2s. 1⅗d. equal to Rs.204·4 – the proceeds of 100 drs., if sent to Calcutta, as per No. 1.

No. 4. Mexico – Calcutta Trade

(a) 100 dollars shipped at Vera Cruz on Calcutta account, and sold in London at 4s. 2d.   £20 16 8

Deduct agency at Vera Cruz, not incurred at Acapulco,

1 per cent	4s.	2d.			
Freight by ships of war, 2 per cent	8	4			
Insurance in London and policy, 2 per cent	8	4	1	6	1
Commission and brokerage on sale and expences, and 1¼ per cent on accepting drafts	5	3			

	£19	10	7
Add – gain of interest (*vide* No. 2) for 13 mos.	1	1	2
Proceeds	£20	11	9

(b) 100 dollars shipped at Acapulco for Calcutta as returns, are sold for   Rs.205.8

Deduct insurance at Calcutta, say 4 per cent Rs.8 3 6
Freight, say 2 per cent   4 1 9   12.8
Landing and petty charges, say   0 2 9

£20. 11s. 9d. equal to   Rs. 193·0 at 2s. 1d. per R.

Economic Development of India

Appendix I – *cont.*

No. 5. Mexico – British circuitous trade

100 dollars sold in London at 4s. 2d.			£20	16	8
Deduct freight and ins. from Vera Cruz, 4 per cent	16s. 8d.		0	17	8
Brokerage on sale and small charges, ¼ per cent	1 0				
			£19	19	0
Adding gain of interest (*vide* No. 2) 15 mos.			1	5	0
		Proceeds	£21	4	0

100 dollars shipped at Vera Cruz or Acapulco for
Calcutta are sold for   Rs.205.8
Deduct freight to Calcutta per ships of   Rs.5 2 2 ⎫
    war, 2½ per cent   ⎬
Ins. in England and policy 2½ per cent   5 2 2 ⎬ 14.9
Commission of sale, accounts, and ⎬
    drafts, 2 per cent   4 1 9 ⎬
Landing and petty charges, say   0 2 11 ⎭
          £21. 4s. equal to   Rs.190·15 at 2s. 2⅔d. per R.

Remarks on Appendix I

From the above statements it appears:

1. That, when the exchange on London is at 2s. 3¼d. and upwards, bullion will flow in commerce from Great Britain; and when at or under 1s. 11¾d. remittances may be made in bullion to Great Britain: and not otherwise in either case.

2. That bullion should cease to flow into Calcutta – from the south of Europe, when the exchange falls below 2s. 1¼d.; from the United States, when below 2s. 1⅗d.; and from Mexico, when below 2s. 1d. Want of foreign connexions will nevertheless sometimes induce small traders to ship bullion at some apparent disadvantage, in a moment of eager speculation: and allowance must also be made for want of information and error of judgment.

3. That, should the intercourse with Mexico continue free, bullion may be supplied thence to India, as a circuitous return for British manufactures, which will doubtless find a very extensive consumption in that country, whenever the exchange shall appear permanently to average above 2s. 2⅔d., perhaps even when at 2s. 2d., or 2s. 2¼d., per *sicca rupee*.

Appendix K General statement of external trade of the presidency of Madras, exclusive of the Company's investments.

Ports	1813–14	1814–15	1815–16	1816–17	1817–18	1818–19	1819–20	1820–21	1821–22
				Imports					
Fort St George	Rs. 65,50,999	54,56,855	58,45,142	47,95,526	71,68,480	55,46,883	43,52,878	45,63,899	66,89,565
Malabar and Canara	—	—	11,13,580	12,34,975	9,88,380	12,68,663	12,13,693	12,56,689	15,34,919
Subordinate ports	—	—	17,12,057	11,42,454	12,05,285	12,23,115	11,79,956	8,57,807	10,44,713
Total of merchandise	—	—	86,70,779	71,72,955	93,62,145	80,38,661	67,46,527	66,78,395	92,69,197
Fort St George	5,35,605	5,60,713	3,18,927	11,83,134	10,83,095	19,37,427	13,00,235	19,33,850	19,70,052
Malabar and Canara	—	—	12,01,427	14,68,947	15,49,946	16,62,387	23,12,571	19,87,493	14,90,690
Subordinate ports	—	—	6,64,417	4,06,106	4,49,194	2,97,829	4,11,459	4,48,300	5,44,989
Total treasure	—	—	21,84,771	30,58,187	30,50,235	38,97,643	40,24,265	43,69,643	40,05,731
Grand total imports	—	—	1,08,55,550	1,02,31,142	1,24,12,380	1,19,36,304	1,07,71,092	1,10,48,038	1,32,74,928
				Exports					
Fort St George	24,73,913	38,39,231	40,76,387	34,82,332	38,90,230	41,30,346	30,90,661	30,95,198	52,49,423
Malabar and Canara	—	—	47,22,962	45,90,002	46,56,710	48,85,656	55,47,363	57,53,232	55,49,233
Subordinate ports	—	—	29,95,977	32,91,418	31,11,156	29,44,745	20,03,752	28,20,259	59,12,710
Total merchandise	—	—	1,17,95,326	1,13,63,752	1,10,58,096	1,19,60,747	1,16,41,776	1,16,68,689	1,07,11,366
Fort St George	5,00,057	3,39,604	7,92,379	6,17,684	3,32,681	2,74,166	4,55,551	63,643	2,58,010
Malabar and Canara	—	—	63,563	73,830	1,64,368	98,674	71,109	87,843	19,118
Subordinate ports	—	—	3,480	—	1,616	10,230	3,267	—	—
Total treasure	—	—	8,59,422	6,91,514	4,98,660	3,83,070	5,29,927	1,51,486	2,77,128
Grand total of exports	—	—	1,26,54,748	1,20,55,266	1,21,56,756	1,23,43,817	1,21,71,703	1,18,20,175	1,69,88,494
Aggregate of import and export	—	—	2,35,10,298	2,22,86,408	2,38,14,852	2,42,80,121	2,29,42,795	2,28,68,213	3,02,63,422

Amount of native piece-goods exported from the Presidency of Madras.

	1818–19	1819–20	1820–21	1821–22
From Vizagapatam	2,78,041	1,98,537	75,621	2,67,248
Ingeram	5,71,764	5,23,972	6,46,879	8,45,695
Masulipatam	7,445	42,178	40,340	20,16,873
Madras	22,02,152	16,25,872	18,01,574	39,49,648
Cuddalore	3,37,567	4,90,405	5,20,944	8,98,425
Nagpore	3,53,919	4,88,035	3,59,650	5,39,139
Ramnad	86,228	92,866	62,493	66,133
Tinnevelly	1,88,891	1,90,644	1,61,783	3,79,627
Malabar	4,96,237	8,43,739	7,40,622	6,84,015
Canara	33,536	52,779	55,202	49,849
Total	45,54,780	45,49,027	44,65,108	92,96,653

NOTE – March 1824. The list of piece-goods exported in 1821–22 was sent me from Calcutta with the figures in the order I have placed them and without the names of places. I can only infer that probably they are rightly sorted. Why the third item is so extraordinarily increased compared with former years I cannot explain, nor whether the Company's investment not included in the list of 1821–22 and excluded in those which preceded. An extended demand for piece-goods in British colonies may have had some influence to increase the export.

Appendix L a. 1   *Abstract statement of imports of the Presidency of Bombay, exclusive of the Company's investments.*

1817–18

Places	Total	United Kingdom	Lisbon	France	Madeira	Cape of Good Hope	Brazil	Mauritius	China	Manilla	Penang and Eastern Islands
Bombay, including bullion	3,16,72,521	48,95,198	10,13,850	3,25,621	1,31,774	200	6,76,215	1,96,171	49,00,490	4,67,612	6,95,412
do. horses	1,01,04,969	4,55,225	6,19,253	1,81,343	—	—	5,77,600	1,04,646	12,17,674	30,641	4,360
Surat including external bullion	6,74,640	640	—	—	—	—	—	—	—	—	—
do. internal do.	24,38,843	—	—	—	—	—	3,31,495	—	—	—	—
	19,86,254	570	—	—	—	—	—	—	—	—	—
Broach	3,78,889	—	—	—	—	—	—	—	—	—	—
Bhownagur	1,87,849	—	—	—	—	—	—	—	—	—	—
Grand total, 1817–18	3,46,78,102	48,95,198	10,13,850	3,25,621	1,31,774	200	10,07,719	1,96,171	49,00,490	4,67,612	6,95,412

Places	Bengal	Coromandel Coast	Ceylon	Malabar and Canara	Goa and the Concan	Bassein and sundry ports	Cutch and Scind	Persian Gulph	Arabian Gulph	Coast of Africa	America
Bombay, including bullion	25,25,401	53,031	63,013	31,91,714	24,48,414	3,99,333	13,86,522	36,99,059	25,43,655	3,02,186	17,57,650
do. horses	225	—	—	23,513	2,92,351	76,572	—	25,95,630	21,16,259	2,43,800	15,45,877
Surat including external bullion	—	—	—	—	500	—	2,69,200	4,04,200	100	—	—
do. internal do.	—	—	—	3,851	—	2,54,059	3,555	27,753	16,57,895	1,60,235	—
Broach	—	—	—	—	—	2,79,365	—	—	—	—	—
Bhownagur	—	—	—	47,663	6,765	16,484	55,745	28,966	—	28,513	—
Grand total, 1817–18	25,25,401	53,031	63,013	32,43,228	24,55,179	9,49,241	14,45,822	37,55,778	42,01,550	4,90,934	17,57,650

Places	Total	United Kingdom	Lisbon	France	Madeira	Cape of Good Hope	Brazil	Mauritius	China	Manilla	Penang and Eastern Islands
Bombay	3,56,73,227	70,90,236	2,30,543	7,99,170	94,032	650	9,30,074	3,62,337	79,03,133	6,15,630	5,61,615
including bullion	1,57,02,511	33,68,536	2,30,543	6,06,567	—	—	9,04,977	1,19,279	33,71,691	1,03,028	31,370
do. horses	7,87,000	1,600	—	—	—	—	—	—	—	100	1,600
Surat	30,54,458	—	—	—	—	—	6,23,600	—	—	—	—
including external bullion	26,69,699	—	—	—	—	—	—	—	—	—	—
do. internal do.	11,400	—	—	—	—	—	—	—	—	—	—
Broach	3,03,463	—	—	—	—	—	—	—	—	—	—
Dollerah	2,57,434	—	—	—	—	—	—	—	—	—	—
Jamboosier, etc.	2,95,483	—	—	—	—	—	—	—	—	—	—
Grand total, 1818-19	3,95,84,065	70,90,236	2,30,543	7,99,170	94,032	650	15,53,674	3,62,337	79,03,133	6,15,630	5,61,615

Places	Bengal	Coromandel Coast	Ceylon	Malabar and Canara	Goa and the Concan	Bassein and sundry Ports	Cutch and Scind	Persian Gulph	Arabian Gulph	Coast of Africa	America
Bombay	26,48,167	1,58,454	46,534	35,01,414	2,77,033	—	13,29,099	52,12,544	16,94,753	1,49,181	20,68,628
including bullion	—	—	—	10,190	47,930	—	—	35,97,314	12,97,681	27,125	19,86,080
do. horses	—	—	—	—	—	—	99,500	6,82,400	1,800	—	—
Surat	—	—	—	2,036	43,453	—	—	22,560	19,98,542	—	—
including external bullion	—	—	—	—	—	—	—	—	—	1,67,764	—
do. internal do.	—	—	—	—	—	—	—	—	—	—	—
Broach	—	—	—	—	98,991	—	—	—	—	—	—
Dollerah	—	—	—	—	32,344	—	—	—	—	—	—
Jamboosier, etc.	—	—	—	—	2,44,234	—	—	—	—	—	—
Grand total, 1818-19	26,48,167	1,58,454	46,534	35,03,450	6,96,055	—	13,29,099	52,35,104	36,93,295	3,16,945	20,68,628

Appendix L *a.* 1 – (*cont.*)

1819–20

Places	Total	United Kingdom	Lisbon	France	Madeira	Cape of Good Hope	Brazil	Mauritius	China	Manilla	Penang and Eastern Islands
Bombay,	2,87,27,277	56,02,508	1,53,315	1,42,928	55,149	56,464	74,684	5,92,939	67,47,692	—	6,12,525
including bullion	56,21,409	6,05,768	82,720	87,700	—	—	72,000	1,38,769	14,83,716	—	1,40,226
do. horses	10,04,290	6,040	—	—	—	—	—	—	—	—	—
Surat,	17,57,559	—	—	—	—	—	97,582	—	—	—	—
including external bullion	14,68,768	—	—	—	—	—	—	—	—	—	—
do. internal	5,565	—	—	—	—	—	—	—	—	—	—
Broach	1,36,389	—	—	—	—	—	—	—	—	—	—
Dollerah	1,17,974	—	—	—	—	—	—	—	—	—	—
Jamboosier, etc.	2,70,809	—	—	—	—	—	—	—	—	—	—
Bhownagur	1,01,229	—	—	—	—	—	—	—	—	—	—
Grand total, 1819–20	3,11,11,237	56,02,508	1,53,315	1,42,928	55,149	58,464	1,72,266	5,92,939	67,47,692	—	6,12,525

Places	Bengal	Coromandel Coast	Ceylon	Malabar and Canara	Goa and Concan	Bassein and sundry ports	Cutch and Scind	Persian Gulph	Arabian Gulph	Coast of Africa	America
Bombay,	44,76,173	1,07,441	60,155	38,28,266	2,16,424	—	10,74,582	29,80,639	17,06,560	2,04,220	32,609
including bullion	160	—	—	12,586	14,200	—	—	16,77,334	12,41,328	64,902	—
do. horses	—	—	—	—	—	—	3,36,200	6,60,050	2,000	—	—
Surat,	—	—	—	11,848	74,284	—	1,550	13,169	13,18,056	2,41,070	—
including external bullion	—	—	—	—	—	—	—	—	—	—	—
do. internal	—	—	—	—	—	—	—	—	—	—	—
Broach	—	—	—	—	3,296	—	—	—	—	—	—
Dollerah	—	—	—	—	17,600	—	—	—	—	—	—
Jamboosier, etc.	—	—	—	—	2,20,105	—	—	—	—	—	—
Bhownagur	—	—	—	27,719	15,651	—	—	16,373	22,674	4,693	—
Grand total, 1819–20	44,76,173	1,07,441	60,155	38,67,833	5,47,360	—	10,76,132	30,10,181	30,47,290	4,47,983	32,609

Places	Total	United Kingdom	Lisbon	France	Madeira	Cape of Good Hope	Brazil	Mauritius	China	Manilla	Penang and Eastern Islands
Bombay including bullion	2,37,57,567	36,16,292	37,292	68,415	82,094	270	1,57,307	2,70,758	47,01,890	2,35,954	7,15,467
do. horses	49,24,312	80,173	19,800	25,464			86,800	5,194	6,37,075	3,973	1,34,260
Surat including external bullion	4,66,517										637
do. internal do.	20,84,087						2,18,125		330		85,985
Broach	4,300										
Dollerah	2,37,333										
Jamboosier, etc.	34,187										
Bhownagur	1,86,919										
	1,68,005										
Grand total, 1820-21	2,64,68,098	36,16,219	37,292	68,415	82,094	270	3,75,432	2,70,758	47,01,890	2,35,954	8,01,452

Places	Bengal	Coromandel Coast	Ceylon	Malabar and Canara	Goa and the Concan	Bassein and sundry ports	Cutch and Scind	Persian Gulph	Arabian Gulph	Coast of Africa	America
Bombay including bullion	30,47,206	94,434	46,640	39,18,656	2,28,296		6,42,519	34,87,754	18,63,817	5,42,579	
do. horses	5,500			6,875	35,440		8,500	22,08,661	15,54,910	2,11,687	
Surat including external bullion				29,130	51,082		1,31,600	3,33,950	15,46,194	1,25,325	
do. internal do.							2,688	25,558			
Broach					31,894						
Dollerah				1,397	17,030						
Jamboosier, etc.					1,84,729			63,279	66,620		
Bhownagur				9,536	20,670						
Grand total, 1820-21	30,47,206	94,434	46,640	39,58,719	5,33,701	—	6,45,207	35,76,591	84,76,631	6,67,904	—

125

Appendix L. a. 1 – (*cont.*)   *A statement of exports [imports] of the Presidency of Bombay, exclusive of the Company's investment.*

1821-22

Places	Total	United Kingdom	Lisbon	France	Madeira	Cape of Good Hope	Brazil	Mauritius	China	Manilla	Penang and Eastern Islands
Bombay including bullion	2,59,09,715	43,94,208	—	—	84,173	2,980	—	3,53,087	74,01,170	3,30,650	7,42,857
do. horses	39,59,173	86,420	—	—	—	—	—	66,000	2,16,128	—	65,951
Surat including external bullion	3,10,330	6,680	—	—	—	—	—	—	—	—	3,050
do. internal do.	14,91,663	—	—	—	—	—	—	—	—	—	10,880
	12,67,693	—	—	—	—	—	—	—	—	—	—
Broach	3,155	—	—	—	—	—	—	—	—	—	—
Dhollerah	1,56,043	—	—	—	—	—	—	—	—	—	—
Jamboosier	28,338	—	—	—	—	—	—	—	—	—	—
Bhownagur	2,20,246	—	—	—	—	—	—	—	—	—	—
	1,68,667	—	—	—	—	—	—	—	—	—	—
Grand total, 1821-22	2,79,74,672	43,94,208	—	—	84,173	2,980	—	3,53,087	74,01,160	3,30,650	7,53,737

Places	Bengal	Coromandel Coast	Ceylon	Malabar and Canara	Goa and Concan	Bassein and sundry Ports	Cutch and Scind	Persian Gulph	Arabian Gulph	Coast of Africa	America
Bombay including bullion	20,03,718	92,923	46,161	46,81,869	1,83,543	—	5,39,865	33,85,197	14,33,313	2,43,011	—
do. horses	—	—	—	7,955	11,046	—	5,100	22,65,954	11,58,312	76,307	—
Surat including external bullion	—	—	—	15,300	48,027	—	8,200	2,91,400	1,000	—	—
do. internal do.	—	—	—	—	—	—	4,387	13,256	12,06,304	1,93,500	—
Broach	—	—	—	—	29,439	—	—	—	—	—	—
Dhollerah	—	—	—	—	12,515	—	—	—	—	—	—
Jamboosier, etc.	—	—	—	—	1,82,613	—	—	—	—	—	—
Bhownagur	—	—	—	13,438	18,502	—	—	—	1,26,237	—	—
Grand total, 1821-22	20,03,718	92,923	46,161	47,10,607	4,74,639	—	5,44,252	33,98,462	37,65,854	4,27,511	—

1822–23

Places	Total	United Kingdom	Lisbon	France	Madeira	Cape of Good Hope	Brazil	Mauritius	China	Manilla	Penang and Eastern Islands
Bombay including bullion	2,67,16,000	56,24,719		1,09,938	1,80,855	24,948		3,46,890	70,44,708		6,31,651
do. horses	46,82,212	33,504		3,240				150	10,21,229		1,900
Surat including external bullion	4,71,370										
do. internal do.	11,38,843										
Broach	10,31,460										
Dhollerah	2,16,625										
Jamboosier, etc.	1,61,142										
Bhownagur	89,918										
Grand total, 1822–23	2,83,37,634	56,24,719		1,09,938	1,80,855	24,948		3,46,896	70,44,708		6,31,651

Places	Bengal	Coromandel Coast	Ceylon	Malabar and Canara	Goa and Damaon	Bassein	Cutch and Scind	Persian Gulph	Arabian Gulph	Coast of Africa	Guzerat ports subject to Mahrattas[1]
Bombay including bullion	20,77,725	88,341	23,202	41,78,665	2,60,596		5,57,024	36,70,169	16,14,645	2,72,918	
do. horses	45,800	6,480	3,900	42,588	940		11,221	24,42,314	9,51,403	44,734	
Surat including internal bullion					1,000	Included under Goa, etc. after the year 1817–18	83,100	3,92,200			
do. external do.				10,220	38,121		490	6,599	10,75,247	8,199	
Broach					18,963						
Dhollerah					14,223						1,97,662
Jamboosier, etc.				11,674	1,03,581						
Bhownagur					7,201			60,887			57,561
Goga					884						10,156
Grand total, 1822–23	20,77,725	88,341	23,202	42,00,565	4,43,569		5,57,514	36,85,728	27,50,779	2,81,117	2,65,379

1 [Added by Prinsep in 1824. – Editor.]

Appendix L a. 1 – (cont.) Abstract statement of exports from the Presidency of Bombay, exclusive of the Company's investments.

1822–23

Places	Total	United Kingdom	Lisbon	France	Madeira	Cape of Good Hope	Brazil	Mauritius	China	Manilla	Penang and Eastern Islands	Bengal	Coromandel Coast	Ceylon	Malabar and Canara	Goa and Concan	Cutch and Scind	Persian Gulph	Arabian Gulph	Coast of Africa	America	Guzerat ports subject to Mahrattas
Bombay including bullion	2,18,06,072	52,45,502	—	36,057	—	11,264	—	2,01,557	69,33,815	—	7,90,939	7,44,067	99,284	42,097	13,23,844	3,50,722	14,07,335	30,91,782	12,59,814	2,56,993	—	—
do. horses	6,47,773	60,414	—	22,800	—	—	—	26,004	20,500	—	39,970	22,675	—	—	1,48,697	83,753	3,500	—	2,12,000	7,560	—	—
Surat including external bullion	2,75,750	—	—	—	—	—	—	—	1,000	—	—	45,530	27,200	—	1,99,350	200	3,700	—	8,50,682	44,999	—	—
do. internal do.	9,60,990	—	—	—	—	—	—	—	—	—	—	—	—	—	3,770	57,269	3,197	2,073	—	—	—	—
Broach	26,810	—	—	—	—	—	—	—	—	—	—	—	—	—	—	3,525	—	—	—	—	—	—
Dhollerah	7,52,326	—	—	—	—	—	—	—	—	—	—	—	—	—	—	962	—	—	—	—	—	90,250
Jamboosien, etc.	93,775	—	—	—	—	—	—	—	—	—	—	—	—	—	—	79,807	—	—	—	—	—	—
Bhownagur	82,287	—	—	—	—	—	—	—	—	—	—	—	—	—	—	1,902	—	—	96,652	—	—	3,480
Goga	98,505	—	—	—	—	—	—	—	—	—	—	—	—	—	—	454	—	—	—	—	—	—
Grand total, 1822–23	2,30,44,105	52,46,502	—	36,057	—	11,264	—	2,01,557	69,33,815	—	7,90,939	7,44,067	99,284	42,097	13,27,614	5,04,641	14,10,532	30,93,855	22,07,159	3,01,992	—	92,730

George Alexander Prinsep

Appendix L *a*. 2   *Imports at Bombay from places within the Presidency.*

	Panwell and the Concan		Guzerat	Surat
1817–18	Bombay Rs.	26,17,321	70,55,494	20,53,480
1818–19		23,60,363	72,76,187	21,37,803
1819–20		35,54,232	39,82,597	29,83,440
1820–21		46,21,806	33,10,266	19,65,164
[1821–22		44,97,109	84,77,664	22,79,691]
[1822–23		46,41,928	60,15,491	24,94,195]

Appendix L *a*. 3   *Description of bullion imported at Bombay and Surat.*

	Value in Gold		Silver	Copper
1817–18	Bombay Rs.	5,61,338	1,15,35,160	425
1818–19		14,21,219	1,69,60,391	2,000
1819–20		4,95,079	66,00,664	—
1820–21		9,42,788	58,43,937	—
[1821–22		5,25,108	13,99,229	650]
[1822–23		4,02,036	10,24,873	—]

Appendix L *a.* 4   *Imports of Bombay from the United Kingdom exclusive of the Company's investments.*

Goods	1805–6	1806–7	1807–8	1808–9	1809–10	1810–11	1811–12	1812–13
Eatables	92,435	1,10,905	1,23,346	93,955	93,710	1,18,803	84,234	86,121
Glass ware	49,325	96,254	79,782	75,275	81,934	2,26,103	1,90,117	69,305
Metals	2,58,813	4,29,299	1,97,980	2,08,051	2,36,739	3,09,059	1,79,402	44,816
Piece-goods	—	—	—	2,51,762	72,576	1,22,297	1,54,534	29,705
Wear. Appar.	1,17,618	2,19,839	2,34,883	2,28,913	1,48,077	2,32,410	2,05,349	1,05,003
Wine	1,37,754	2,61,991	2,05,171	75,092	74,395	1,01,557	1,11,612	90,214
Woollens	362	6,513	—	—	—	—	7,790	—
Total of above By.r.	6,56,307	11,24,801	8,41,162	9,33,048	7,07,431	11,10,229	9,33,038	4,25,164
Bullion and goods not included above	12,82,919	16,13,641	13,27,528	10,43,879	8,53,237	12,87,070	11,25,904	6,45,237
Total By. Rs.	19,39,226	27,38,442	21,68,690	19,76,927	15,60,668	23,97,299	20,58,942	10,70,401

By a private Statement received from London, it appears that the official value of British cotton piece-goods exported to Bombay in all 1821 was as follows:

75,000 pieces of prints		£122,500
White goods, muslins, etc.		107,500
	Total	£230,000

Appendix L *a.* 5   *Statement of cotton imports at Bombay during ten years.*

	By individuals	
Year	Candies	Value in By. Rs.
1809	31,190	35,72,970
1810	32,235	37,71,945
1811	26,117	7,56,715
1812	15,040	17,39,220
1813	12,089	14,20,980
1814	14,211	16,30,785
1815	18,103	21,50,595
1816	29,032	34,02,150
1817	43,403	50,16,885
1818	74,333	86,10,525
Total	2,95,753	3,20,72,770
Average	29,575	32,07,277

1813–14	1814–15	1815–16	1816–17	1817–18	1818–19	1819–20	1820–21	1821–22
81,394	84,571	1,31,422	1,14,976	1,14,995	72,406	96,348	71,065	1,33,072
47,234	68,926	46,487	83,024	2,25,223	1,23,779	1,31,681	1,30,084	1,76,097
61,136	1,92,711	3,74,264	8,04,173	11,29,324	7,22,921	14,15,455	2,52,063	2,29,321
38,626	1,67,854	4,28,512	1,98,755	9,44,177	10,44,360	13,42,952	16,35,750	18,33,921
84,880	1,09,978	1,16,694	1,23,907	2,25,224	2,11,976	1,59,643	1,40,458	1,98,523
1,45,155	1,70,901	1,22,807	79,220	73,582	94,396	1,04,150	1,36,833	1,65,758
1,024	15,998	68,045	5,732	57,071	1,60,963	4,09,890	1,65,364	2,38,804
4,59,449	8,10,939	12,88,231	14,09,787	27,67,596	24,30,801	36,60,119	25,31,617	29,75,496
4,67,531	5,87,714	10,15,064	15,74,799	21,27,602	46,59,435	19,42,389	10,84,602	14,18,712
9,26,980	13,98,653	23,03,295	29,84,586	48,95,198	70,90,236	56,02,508	36,16,219	43,94,208

which corresponds almost exactly at the Custom-house exchange of 2s. 6d. with the imports of Bombay for 1821–22, *viz.* Rs.18,33,921, or £2,29,240. By a similar statement for 1822 there appears a surprising increase, the amount being nearly double, *viz.*—

1,22,000 pieces of prints	£182,000
Muslins, white goods, etc.	233,000
Total	£415,000

By the Company		Total	
Candies	Value in By. Rs.	Candies	Value in By. Rs.
11,229	13,47,480	42,419	49,20,450
4,578	5,49,360	36,813	43,21,305
9,306	11,16,720	35,423	18,73,435
7,077	8,49,240	22,117	25,88,460
14,858	17,82,960	26,947	32,03,940
8,450	10,14,000	22,661	26,44,785
15,584	18,70,080	33,687	40,20,675
14,835	17,80,200	43,867	51,82,350
13,343	16,01,160	56,746	66,18,045
17,619	21,14,280	91,952	1,07,24,805
1,16,879	1,40,25,480	4,12,632	4,60,98,250
11,688	14,02,548	41,263	46,09,825

1817–18

Places	Total	United Kingdom	Lisbon	France	Madeira	Cape of Good Hope	Brazil	Mauritius	China	Manilla	Penang, and Eastern Islands
Bombay including bullion	2,36,63,019	47,60,004	2,30,628	3,14,385	—	—	463	3,19,828	55,36,472	—	2,65,125
do. horses	15,50,084	3,000	—	—	—	—	—	5,232	46,240	—	21,900
Surat including external bullion	1,52,375	—	—	—	—	—	16,11,797	—	—	—	—
do. internal do.	31,58,488	—	—	—	—	—	—	—	—	—	—
Broach	29,750	—	—	—	—	—	—	—	—	—	—
Bhownagur	30,05,054	—	—	—	—	—	—	—	—	—	—
	78,219	—	—	—	—	—	—	—	—	—	—
	67,719	—	—	—	—	—	—	—	—	—	—
Grand total, 1817–18	2,69,67,445	47,60,004	2,30,628	3,14,385	—	—	16,12,260	3,19,828	55,36,472	—	2,65,125

Places	Bengal	Coromandel Coast	Ceylon	Malabar and Canara	Goa and the Concan	Bassein and sundry Ports	Cutch and Scind	Persian Gulph	Arabian Gulph	Coast of Africa	America
Bombay including bullion	7,50,906	2,12,291	1,99,857	9,49,613	41,23,301	3,94,231	16,79,550	19,24,928	12,79,580	40,870	6,80,987
do. horses	17,175	21,975	1,16,600	1,46,181	9,57,553	76,688	72,940	2,500	71,700	—	—
Surat including external bullion	44,200	10,500	—	73,525	20,100	1,050	2,746	7,052	13,08,923	96,293	—
do. internal do.	—	—	—	30,732	—	1,00,945	—	—	—	—	—
Broach	—	—	—	—	—	38,446	20,470	240	—	10,080	—
Bhownagur	—	—	—	30,488	—	6,091	—	—	—	—	—
Grand total, 1817–18	7,50,906	2,12,291	1,99,857	10,19,833	41,23,301	5,39,713	17,02,766	19,32,220	25,88,503	1,47,243	6,80,987

Places	Total	United Kingdom	Lisbon	France	Madeira	Cape of Good Hope	Brazil	Mauritius	China	Manilla	Penang and Eastern Islands
Bombay	2,18,76,389	77,36,115	—	3,22,251	—	—	2,00,208	5,46,649	45,38,002	—	2,73,279
including bullion	6,80,267			6,630					28,600		8,105
do. horses	1,76,500								1,000		
Surat	30,58,718						16,01,168				
including external bullion	28,300										
do. internal do.	25,83,620										
Broach	1,07,287										
Dollerah	75,862										
Jamboosier, etc.	1,49,138										
Grand total, 1818-19	2,52,67,394	77,36,115	—	3,22,251	—	—	18,01,376	5,46,649	45,38,002	—	2,73,279

Places	Bengal	Coromandel Coast	Ceylon	Malabar and Canara	Goa and the Concan	Bassein and sundry ports	Cutch and Scind	Persian Gulph	Arabian Gulph	Coast of Africa	America
Bombay	4,67,648	77,121	30,029	11,41,952	4,67,982	—	10,94,206	23,18,072	9,98,025	11,091	16,53,719
including bullion	31,000	55,000		2,32,242	1,87,832		1,30,858				
do. horses	35,500		2,000	1,38,000				18,287			
Surat				12,450	43,597				12,96,354	86,430	
including external bullion											
do. internal do.							432				
Broach					44,324						
Dollerah					3,604						
Jamboosier					1,29,871						
Grand total, 1818-19	4,67,648	77,121	39,029	11,54,402	6,89,378	—	10,94,638	23,36,379	22,94,379	97,521	16,53,719

Appendix L. b. 1 – (cont.)

1819-20

Places	Total	United Kingdom	Lisbon	France	Madeira	Cape of Good Hope	Brazil	Mauritius	China	Manilla	Penang and Eastern Islands
Bombay including bullion	1,75,81,113	56,80,608	31,615	2,73,963	—	49,012	90,290	89,442	30,55,259	—	4,23,594
do. horses	10,13,696	2,500	—	—	—	—	—	1,700	4,42,776	—	1,06,700
Surat including external bullion	15,07,987	—	—	—	—	—	1,11,956	—	—	—	66,403
do. internal do.	85,713	—	—	—	—	—	—	—	—	—	—
Broach	14,26,979	—	—	—	—	—	—	—	—	—	—
Dollerah	1,25,917	—	—	—	—	—	—	—	—	—	—
Jamboosier, etc.	18,488	—	—	—	—	—	—	—	—	—	—
Bhownagur	1,94,948	—	—	—	—	—	—	—	—	—	—
	59,347	—	—	—	—	—	—	—	—	—	—
Grand total, 1819-20	1,94,800	56,80,608	31,615	2,73,963	—	49,012	2,02,246	89,442	30,55,259	—	4,89,997

Places	Bengal	Coromandel Coast	Ceylon	Malabar and Canara	Goa and the Concan	Bassein and sundry Ports	Cutch and Scind	Persian Gulph	Arabian Gulph	Coast of Africa	America
Bombay including bullion	11,06,337	59,210	62,232	10,23,748	3,11,245	—	16,90,031	20,32,064	10,73,089	1,03,329	4,25,945
do. horses	2,09,599	34,700	—	1,83,330	8,997	—	40,000	19,800	—	—	—
Surat including external bullion	—	—	2,200	1,11,600	47,629	—	3,926	5,533	11,30,142	1,19,933	—
do. internal do.	44,700	—	—	22,465	—	—	—	—	—	—	—
Broach	—	—	—	—	1,174	—	—	—	—	—	—
Dollerah	—	—	—	—	2,922	—	—	—	—	—	—
Jamboosier, etc.	—	—	—	—	1,73,624	—	—	25,168	5,320	6,690	—
Bhownagur	—	—	—	—	10,998	—	—	—	—	—	—
Grand total, 1819-20	11,06,337	59,210	62,232	10,46,213	5,47,592	—	16,94,057	20,62,765	22,08,551	2,29,952	4,25,945

1820–21

Table 1

Places	Total	United Kingdom	Lisbon	France	Madeira	Cape of Good Hope	Brazil	Mauritius	China	Manilla	Penang and Eastern Islands
Bombay	2,18,29,054	14,89,728	—	88,754	—	2,100	—	74,576	96,57,461	—	6,52,596
including bullion	14,70,404	—	—	—	—	—	—	—	1,47,725	—	1,56,362
do. horses	1,85,350	—	—	77,700	—	—	—	—	—	—	5,000
Surat	12,36,395	—	—	—	—	—	—	—	—	—	—
including external bullion	53,932	—	—	—	—	—	2,26,056	—	—	—	—
do. internal do.	5,07,958	—	—	—	—	—	—	—	—	—	—
Broach	1,25,757	—	—	—	—	—	—	—	—	—	—
Dollerah	4,548	—	—	—	—	—	—	—	—	—	—
Jamboosier, etc.	2,11,015	—	—	—	—	—	—	—	—	—	—
Bhownagur	1,01,785	—	—	—	—	—	—	—	—	—	—
Grand total, 1820–21	2,35,02,554	14,89,728	—	88,754	—	2,100	2,26,056	74,576	96,57,461	—	6,52,596

Table 2

Places	Bengal	Coromandel Coast	Ceylon	Malabar and Canara	Goa and the Concan	Bassein and sundry ports	Cutch and Scind	Persian Gulph	Arabian Gulph	Coast of Africa	America
Bombay	17,43,676	2,63,304	94,943	12,97,620	3,72,396	—	22,09,192	28,39,193	8,66,840	1,76,675	—
including bullion	5,49,407	1,55,020	—	2,72,795	27,600	—	48,670	17,900	17,225	—	—
do. horses	83,050	5,700	26,000	64,700	900	—	—	—	—	—	—
Surat	—	—	—	—	—	—	—	—	—	—	—
including external bullion	—	—	—	6,631	66,272	—	2,529	3,901	7,43,304	1,81,702	—
do. internal do.	—	—	—	—	—	—	—	—	—	—	—
Broach	—	—	—	—	7,803	—	—	—	—	—	—
Dollerah	—	—	—	—	1,554	—	—	—	—	—	—
Jamboosier	—	—	—	—	1,97,843	—	—	57,118	27,917	—	—
Bhownagur	—	—	—	—	2,245	—	—	—	—	—	—
Grand total, 1820–21	17,43,676	2,63,304	94,943	13,04,251	6,48,113	—	22,11,721	29,00,212	16,38,061	3,58,377	—

Appendix L *b.* 1 – *(cont.)*

1821–22

Places	Total	United Kingdom	Lisbon	France	Madeira	Cape of Good Hope	Brazil	Mauritius	China	Manilla	Penang and Eastern Islands
Bombay including bullion	2,09,58,097	25,38,395	—	—	—	15,918	—	3,16,958	69,15,803	—	8,14,591
	14,20,726	2,57,874	—	—	—	—	—	29,000	—	—	1,63,400
do. horses	2,55,400	1,500	—	—	—	—	—	1,800	—	—	10,500
Surat	10,16,630	—	—	—	—	—	—	—	—	—	19,010
including external bullion	29,576	—	—	—	—	—	—	—	—	—	—
do. internal do.	4,74,685	—	—	—	—	—	—	—	—	—	—
Broach	1,07,885	—	—	—	—	—	—	—	—	—	—
Dhollerah	2,103	—	—	—	—	—	—	—	—	—	—
Jamboosier, etc.	1,72,326	—	—	—	—	—	—	—	—	—	—
Bhownagur	1,22,934	—	—	—	—	—	—	—	—	—	—
Grand total, 1821–22	2,23,79,975	25,38,395	—	—	—	15,918	—	3,16,958	69,16,803	—	8,33,601

Places	Bengal	Coromandel Coast	Ceylon	Malabar and Canara	Goa and the Concan	Bassein and sundry ports	Cutch and Scind	Persian Gulph	Arabian Gulph	Coast of Africa	America
Bombay including bullion	15,76,044	1,39,051	29,042	14,60,866	4,27,069	—	19,44,142	33,59,384	12,03,820	2,17,014	—
	5,94,654	37,400	—	2,03,445	1,18,230	—	2,500	4,500	13,250	—	—
do. horses	1,20,100	49,200	—	69,200	500	—	—	—	—	—	—
Surat	—	—	—	2,377	72,364	—	6,984	21,089	7,88,347	1,96,459	—
including external bullion	—	—	—	—	—	—	—	—	—	—	—
do. internal do.	—	—	—	—	—	—	—	—	—	—	—
Broach	—	—	—	—	4,172	—	—	—	—	—	—
Dhollerah	—	—	—	—	1,610	—	—	—	—	—	—
Jamboosier, etc.	—	—	—	—	1,54,611	—	—	—	—	—	—
Bhownagur	—	—	—	—	13,847	—	—	—	—	—	—
Grand total, 1821–22	15,76,044	1,39,051	29,042	14,63,243	6,73,673	—	19,51,126	33,80,473	20,94,613	3,23,473	—

George Alexander Prinsep

Appendix L *b*. 2   *Exports from Bombay to places within the Presidency.*

		Panwell and the Concan	Guzerat	Surat
1817–18	Bombay Rs.	40,75,873	53,23,285	42,33,043
1818–19		64,47,220	69,04,849	46,12,410
1819–20		45,95,288	58,48,484	32,21,921
1820–21		48,85,857	85,47,603	25,92,758

Appendix L *b*. 3   *Description of bullion exported from Bombay to Surat.*

		Value in Gold	Silver	Copper
1817–18	Bombay Rs.	1,87,035	43,97,378	475
1818–19		2,47,808	30,42,254	2,135
1819–20		2,07,385	23,19,003	—
1820–21		2,22,318	18,69,676	300

Appendix L *b.* 4 *Exports from Bombay to the United Kingdom, exclusive of the Company's investments.*

Goods	1805–6	1806–7	1807–8	1808–9	1809–10	1810–11	1811–12	1812–13
Camphor	26,750	1,18,777	7,410	17,422	94,274	22,292	28,700	—
Coffee	16,074	1,075	—	57,490	42,022	8,017	3,77,086	1,96,740
Cotton	5,88,725	2,89,665	7,82,835	6,93,182	12,10,844	10,55,935	39,900	—
Nankeens	—	—	—	—	—	—	—	—
Pepper	—	—	—	4,300	1,09,152	—	46,827	1,675
Raw silk	—	—	—	75,800	1,22,175	10,480	57,303	—
Sugar	2,860	—	—	—	—	—	—	—
Total of above By. R.	6,32,409	4,09,517	7,90,245	8,48,194	15,78,467	10,96,724	5,49,816	1,98,415
Bullion and sundries	1,53,659	2,81,697	2,66,529	3,56,848	8,15,167	2,58,131	9,87,984	5,75,208
Total By. Rs.	7,86,068	6,91,214	10,56,774	12,05,042	23,93,634	13,54,855	15,37,800	7,73,623

Appendix L *b.* 5 *Statement of cotton exports from Bombay in all 1818.*

To China, (about)	Bales	82,500
Great Britain		76,400
America,		23,000
France,		10,000
Lisbon,		11,000
Isle of France,		5,500
Penang		500
Total	Bales	2,08,900

George Alexander Prinsep

1813–14	1814–15	1815–16	1816–17	1817–18	1818–19	1819–20	1820–21	1821–22
16,479	17,224	59,800	11,400	26,974	12,152	31,268	—	—
3,59,024	5,99,775	1,48,423	11,460	1,46,938	1,80,451	40,718	19,014	82,082
18,347	96,205	1,90,617	11,36,395	37,04,234	65,86,197	28,00,470	3,33,588	8,40,586
38,596	17,671	23,244	—	390	48,300	2,27,502	67,963	33,760
4,58,675	11,88,009	7,72,736	4,01,573	2,40,234	2,87,221	2,75 802	5,746	1,85,311
1,71,829	1,32,480	3,11,150	72,622	1,60,062	26,171	4,09,823	2,32,500	2,92,716
—	2,33,301	2,42,653	97,400	69,999	82,468	8,81,533	1,32,055	17,301
10,62,950	22,84,665	17,48,623	17,30,850	44,48,831	72,22,960	46,67,116	7,90,866	14,51,756
19,88,593	4,91,226	8,46,052	2,87,613	3,11,173	5,13,195	9,13,492	6,98,862	10,86,639
30,51,543	27,75,891	25,94,675	20,18,463	47,60,004	77,36,155	55,80,608	14,89,728	25,38,395

Appendix L *c.* *Particular statement of the Company's, and summary of the whole, trade between Bombay and the United*

			Imports				
Goods	1816–17	1817–18	1818–19	1819–20	1820–21	1821–22	1822–23
Anchor and grapnels	2,298	—	—	—	—	—	—
Blocks	1,475	—	—	—	—	—	—
Buntine	1,343	—	—	—	—	—	—
Canvas	13,455	—	—	—	—	—	—
Cochineal	2,82,477	1,25,923	—	—	—	—	—
Colors and utensils	6,863	—	—	—	—	—	—
Copper, British, finc	3,08,740	1,99,434	2,49,927	—	—	5,06,709	2,16,468
do. Japan	—	41,192	—	—	—	—	—
do. plates	88,147	2,77,168	1,84,188	—	—	9,64,143	2,91,141
do. shot	—	15,979	—	—	—	—	—
do. foreign	—	—	—	—	62,020	42,115	38,760
Cordage	42,187	—	—	—	—	—	—
Figure heads	515	—	—	—	—	—	—
Glass ware	9,616	—	—	—	—	—	—
Iron, British	—	52,539	—	—	50,547	1,30,368	8,037
do. Swedish	70,810	56,208	49,342	83,595	1,14,338	70,133	—
do. kentledge	3,692	—	—	—	—	—	—
do. mongery	8,512	—	—	—	—	—	—
Lead	29,611	60,282	85,965	—	—	43,312	—
do. red and white	1,045	22,491	—	—	—	—	—
Piece-goods	—	—	—	—	—	4,071	19,794
Nails	645	—	—	—	—	—	—
Pitch and tar	2,280	—	—	—	—	—	—
Steel, British	25,775	—	—	—	—	—	—
do. Swedish	29,787	12,150	—	—	—	15,340	15,417
Screws	1,320	—	—	—	—	—	—
Tin	—	18,166	—	—	—	—	—
Wines and spirits	56,680	—	—	—	—	—	—
Woollens	3,70,655	2,10,534	1,85,232	65,890	1,41,863	13,32,398	4,79,122
Sundry marine stores	10,872	—	—	—	—	—	—
Horses	1,500	—	—	—	—	—	—
Treasure	—	—	—	—	—	—	—
Total of Comp's. imports	13,70,300	10,92,066	7,54,654	1,49,485	3,68,768	31,08,589	11,18,425
Do. of the commanders and officers of the company's ships	5,87,987	6,61,294	8,28,010	8,03,864	6,30,358	10,75,795	5,57,396
Do. by private-traders	23,96,599	42,33,904	62,61,236	47,98,644	29,85,861	33,18,413	50,67,323
Grand total, By. Rs.	43,54,886	59,87,264	78,43,900	57,51,993	39,84,987	75,02,797	67,43,145
	s. d.	s. d.	s. d.	s. d.	s. d.	s. d.	s. d.
Exchanges of	2 5	2 4	2 2	2 4	2 1	1 10	1 10
merchandise at the amounts to	—	59,27,185	51.65,024	55,13,812	46,85,777	1,01,13,241	91,49,570
Packages and charges omitted, say 20s. per cent	—	11,85,437	10,33,005	11,02,762	9,37,155	20,22,648	18,29,902
Bullion at 216 Rs. net per 100 dollars	—	4,37,016	32,33,795	5,81,537	77,966	82,963	32,164
Corrected total By. Rs.	about 53,00,000	75,49,638	94,31,824	71,98,111	57,00,898	1,12,18,852	1,00,11,576

			Exports				
Goods	1816–17	1817–18	1818–19	1819–20	1820–21	1821–22	1822–23
Almonds	—	—	—	—	4,758	—	—
Bovpoor (canvas)	—	—	129	—	—	—	—
Coffee	1,10,587	29,904	—	69,273	—	—	—
Cotton	26,026	—	28,923	6,30,841	2,50,216	9,946	—
Piece-goods	2,19,762	1,60,729	3,52,499	1,40,802	3,46,548	—	—
Rice	—	—	—	—	25,636	—	—
Saltpetre	1,01,085	1,05,573	62,077	1,53,550	2,81,185	35,621	—
Horses	—	—	—	—	—	—	—
Treasure	—	—	—	—	—	—	30,34,660

Total of Comp's. exports	4,57,460	2,96,206	4,43,578	9,94,566	9,08,343	45,567	30,34,660
Do. of the commanders and officers of the Company's ships	22,798	4,340	4,347	600	12,015	—	—
Do. by private-traders	19,95,665	47,55,664	77,31,808	56,80,008	14,77,713	25,38,395	52,46,502[1]
Grand total By. Rs.	24,75,923	50,56,210	81,79,733	66,75,174	23,98,071	25,83,962	81,81,162
Add for under-value of cotton, being the difference between 120 Rs. and the prices stated	Rs.160 3,87,474	Rs.175 16,97,777	Rs.180 33,07,560	Rs.225 30,02,397	Rs.200 3,89,203	Rs.150 2,12,633	Rs.140 4,01,702
Charges on the whole say	10 per ct. 2,86,340	9½ per ct. 6,07,860	9 per ct. 10,33,856	8½ per ct. 8,06,464	8 per ct. 2,22,982	8 per ct. 2,03,100	8 per ct. on private trade 4,19,720
Corrected total *at least* Rs.	31,49,737	73,61,847	1,25,21,149	1,04,84,035	30,10,256	29,99,695	91,02,584

A large export of bullion by the Company occurred immediately after the close of 1821–22, which has been noticed in the body of the 'Remarks'. No bullion was exported by individuals to Great Britain, during the first five years of the series; but in 1821–22 their bullion remittances amounted to Rs.2,57,847, chiefly gold.

[1] [Including Rs.24,10,219 in cotton and Rs.60,414 in bullion].

Appendix M *a.*   *1. Statement of ships and tonnage arrived at Calcutta during the following years.*

Flag	1813–14 Ships	Tonnage	1814–15 Ships	Tons	1815–16 Ships	Tons	1816–17 Ships	Tons
British	246	94,234	180	68,732	221	76,979	298	1,17,648
Danish	—	—	—	—	1	300	1	300
Portuguese	13	3,747	18	7,040	20	7,621	23	8,234
Spanish	2	724	1	196	1	604	1	293
Russian	—	—	—	—	2	829	—	—
French	—	—	—	—	—	—	3	1,843
Dutch	—	—	—	—	—	—	2	860
American	1	75	—	—	25	8,228	41	14,759
Arab and Dhony	343	56,280	244	40,475	218	36,850	154	26,715
Total	605	1,55,060	443	1,16,443	488	1,31,411	523	1,70,657

2. Ditto sailed from Calcutta during the same period.

	Ships	Tonnage	Ships	Tons	Ships	Tons	Ships	Tons
British	237	96,534	215	80,573	234	83,775	276	1,05,348
Danish	—	—	—	—	1	300	—	—
Portuguese	15	4,277	18	6,380	18	7,400	24	2,989
Spanish	2	781	2	321	1	604	3	1,523
Russian	—	—	—	—	2	829	—	—
French	—	—	—	—	—	—	4	2,518
Dutch	—	—	—	—	—	—	2	860
American	—	—	—	—	20	6,491	35	12,809
Arab and Dhony	345	57,600	245	40,575	213	35,150	153	26,878
Total	599	1,59,132	480	1,27,849	489	1,34,549	497	1,58,925

3. Statement of private tonnage shipped to Great Britain during the same period.

	Ships	Tonnage	Ships	Tons	Ships	Tons	Ships	Tons
By regular Indiamen	12	1,185	9	1,044	8	640	7	620
Europe extra ships	17	4,374	6	254	8	277	7	271
Bengal extra and licensed	19	8,594	30	17,704	34	18,670	58	27,344
Total	48	14,153	45	19,002	50	19,587	,72	28,236

George Alexander Prinsep

	1817–18		1818–19		1819–20		1820–21		1821–22		1822–23
Ships	Tons	Ships	Tons	Ships	Tons	Ships	Tons	Ships	Tons	Ships	Tons
340	1,33,923	290	1,22,234	239	97,705	209	89,265	214	93,205	213	97,803
3	1,240	6	2,946	2	836	2	562	1	353	1	468
17	5,904	16	6,728	12	5,900	13	7,207	12	4,783	15	5,940
2	530	3	2,203	1	396	1	610	—	—	1	270
—		—		—		—		—		—	
15	6,452	24	10,146	13	4,754	13	5,352	18	6,866	25	8,593
1	85	4	1,107	4	651	1	205	1	—	5	1439
40	14,233	54	16,498	24	6,977	13	4,320	19	5,508	15	4,605
165	29,188	166	29,104	187	32,845	69	15,946	189	28,258	146	21,900[1]
583	1,91,555	563	1,90,966	482	1,50,064	321	1,23,467	454	1,45,633	432	1,45,818

316	1,25,514	314	1,30,110	159	1,04,030	240	1,01,750	200	97,400	219	98,185
5	2,026	4	1,393	7	2,960	1	400	1	353	1	468
16	5,770	15	6,518	12	5,290	16	8,799	10	3,363	17	7,420
—	—	2	1,333	—	—	—	—	1	610	2	542
—	—	—	—	—	—	—	—	19	6,973	12	4,812
14	6,421	23	9,740	13	4,636	11	4,361	2	473	24	8,367
1	190	3	962	5	846	1	683	19	5,694	5	800
38	13,538	53	16,129	36	10,937	1	3,695	192	34,504	15	4,510
162	28,778	166	30,426	186	32,745	67	15,958	1	350	146	21,900
552	1,82,237	580	1,96,611	418	1,61,444	347	1,35,646	465	1,49,782	441	1,47,004

9	376	8	339	6	338	—	—
2	1	3	47	1	2	—	—
114	55,928	104	48,728	74	34,335	53	26,734
125	56,305	115	49,114	82	34,675	53	26,734

1 [Evidently under a wrong class].

Economic Development of India

| | 1817–18 | | | | 1818–19 | | | |
| | Total | | From Great Britain | | Total | | From Great Britain | |
	Ships	Tons	Ships	Tons	Ships	Tons	Ships	Tons
English	113	52,226	39	23,508	138	60,619	36	21,428
Portuguese	11	5,030	—	—	9	3,661	—	—
French	6	2,611	—	—	6	2,903	—	—
American	11	4,554	—	—	20	7,011	—	—
Turkish	1	300	—	—	—	—	—	—
Arab	2	864	—	—	9	1,141	—	—
Dutch	—	—	—	—	—	—	—	—
Total	144	65,585	39	23,508	176	75,335	36	21,428

2. *Ditto, sailed from Bombay*

| | Total | | From Great Britain | | Total | | From Great Britain | |
	Ships	Tons	Ships	Tons	Ships	Tons	Ships	Tons
English	115	50,812	28	12,151	133	61,186	41	19,126
Portuguese	3	900	—	—	6	2,900	—	—
French	5	2,282	—	—	6	2,401	—	—
American	9	3,152	—	—	21	7,538	—	—
Turkish	—	—	—	—	—	—	—	—
Arab	3	1,364	—	—	2	1,611	—	—
Dutch	—	—	—	—	—	—	—	—
Total	135	58,510	28	12,151	168	75,636	41	19,126

George Alexander Prinsep

| | 1819–20 | | | | 1820–21 | | | | 1821–22 | | |
| Total | | From Great Britain | | Total | | From Great Britain | | Total | | From Great Britain | |
Ships	Tons	Ships	Tons	Ships	Tons	Ships	Tons	Ships	Tons	Ships	Tons
145	66,280	41	26,975	120	58,792	23	16,155	118	56,643	21	17,404
6	2,516	—	—	8	2,870	—	—	4	1,090	—	—
5	1,676	—	—	1	162	—	—	1	341	—	—
1	464	—	—	—	—	—	—	—	—	—	—
—	—	—	—	—	—	—	—	2	862	—	—
5	1,795	—	—	4	1,720	—	—	5	1,927	—	—
—	—	—	—	1	300	—	—	—	—	—	—
162	72,731	41	26,975	134	63,644	23	16,155	130	60,863	21	17,404

during the same period.

| | 1819–20 | | | | 1820–21 | | | | 1821–22 | | |
| Total | | From Great Britain | | Total | | From Great Britain | | Total | | From Great Britain | |
Ships	Tons	Ships	Tons	Ships	Tons	Ships	Tons	Ships	Tons	Ships	Tons
145	65,159	31	14,187	111	52,121	17	7,595	129	62,268	16	7,939
6	2,574	—	—	7	2,266	—	—	4	1,658	—	—
5	1,997	—	—	2	434	—	—	—	—	—	—
4	1,704	—	—	—	—	—	—	—	—	—	—
—	—	—	—	—	—	—	—	2	862	—	—
5	1,917	—	—	5	2,080	—	—	6	2,857	—	—
—	—	—	—	1	300	—	—	—	—	—	—
165	73,351	31	14,187	126	57,201	17	7,595	141	67,645	16	7,939

1822–23

| | Arrivals | | | | Departures | | | |
	Ships	Tons	Ships	Tons	Ships	Tons	Ships	Tons
English	110	48,187	22	15,800	114	52,219	26	13,743
Portuguese	8	2,121	—	—	7	1,631	—	—
French	5	1,230	—	—	5	1,349	—	—
American	1	321	—	—	1	321	—	—
Turkish	—	—	—	—	—	—	—	—
Arab	11	3,757	—	—	9	3,687	—	—
Dutch	—	—	—	—	—	—	—	—
Total	135	55,616	22	15,800	136	59,207	26	13,743

Second Postscript[1]

I am now enabled to add to the series of past years the commercial tables of 1821–22* and 1822–23† extracted from the Custom-house reports with corrections as before, and to offer a comparison of the actual with the estimated trade of the latter year, the first of my anticipated series. No very near approximation could be expected, first because the operations of trade between distant countries are never balanced within the year. Goods are frequently many months on hand, or are sold on credit; there might be large sums unremitted or over-remitted on speculation at the beginning or close of the year or both – a source of error dissipated in proportion to the length of time embraced. And secondly, because the report tables of 1821–22 were not under my inspection when my estimates for the subsequent period were prepared. ‡

That chasm in my information was peculiarly unfortunate. Important changes had already occurred, the knowledge of which must have influenced my opinions respecting futurity. The imports of merchandise from China had fallen off considerably, partly owing to the establishment of a more direct intercourse with Europe through Singapore, while those of Great Britain, chiefly under the head of cotton piece-goods, were increased 59 lakhs compared with the year preceding, being even 23 lakhs more than any very liberal estimate for 1822–23. In exports there had been a great falling off under the head of sugar, particularly to Great Britain, while I was calculating upon an advance in this and other less important items which had also begun to decline. Hence I set out with an import estimate for 1822–23 something short of the total imports of 1821–22 and very much below them under the separate head of Great Britain. My export estimate however, although founded

* Those of Bombay have already been given.
† Except Madras.
‡ The Calcutta exchange price-current contains a monthly and of some articles a weekly list of exports and imports. None of them were in my possession.

[1] [Goldsmiths' Library of Economic Literature, Senate House, University of London, MSS 694. The handwritten postscript is now bound with the printed copy of the *External Commerce of Bengal. Editor*]

on erroneous data in the particular above noticed and containing by inadvertence a very incorrect valuation for grain does by a remarkable coincidence agree to a lakh* with the actual total amount and very nearly with the amount of exports under the head of Great Britain.†

Such a concurrence is not likely to happen again. Some articles, for instance spelter, may be closer to the estimate. In that commodity indeed it is exceeded during the current year,‡ although so large a deficiency appears in the last, and already shipments of cotton have recommenced as I ventured to predict. In grain a very considerable excess will occur in 1823–24 in consequence of the large export to meet the scarcity at Madras. But the item of indigo, which in quantity by 8,000 maunds and in value by 20 to 30 lakhs has exceeded the estimate for last year, will probably be deficient 40,000 maunds and in value 40 to 50 lakhs this season. That item may have been overvalued on the whole; it is at least doubtful to judge from the actual state of the home market, although something be allowed for panic, whether an average crop of 120 to 130,000 maunds would bear the average prices I have assumed.

The chief difference however will be in opium. I took the whole exports of that drug in 1822–23 at 5,000 chests *viz*.:

Patna and Benares	3,000
Malwa	1,500
	5,000

Assuming an average valuation of 3,000 rupees per chest with an augmentation (in quantity on price) of 5 per cent per annum. Supposing as I did that 1,500 chests of Malwa opium be also sold in Bombay and 1,200 or 1,300 shipped at Demaon, the total supply would be about 8,000 chests including 200 or 300

---

* Aggregate amount of exported merchandise lakhs 834·9 *vide* Appendix O.
Estimated amount of exported merchandise lakhs 835·6 *vide* Appendix H and P.
† Actual amount exported to Great Britain lakhs 342 *vide* Appendix H and N.
Estimated amount exported to Great Britain *lakhs* 329·9 *vide* Appendix H and N.
 N.B. estimate for 1823–24 lakhs 343·1 *vide* Appendix H and N.
‡ The quantity already amounts to about 71,000 maunds according to the statements in the price current, calculated up to 24 March.

147

from Turkey. Rather more of the last has been brought to Asia in consequence of the high prices of 1822, but that source of supply is likely to be nearly abandoned since the hope of profit has vanished. Of the quantity exported from Bengal my estimate assigned to

China	3,700 chests
To Penang and Java, etc. 1,300 of which a portion might be re-shipped for the same destination say	300
Shipments from Bombay and Demaon 2,750	
Deduct portion of the same probably consumed in the Islands 500	2,250
Turkey opium	250
	6,500

Now the consumption of China appears to be almost stationary, extending to about 6,000 chests; so that, had the company limited their sales thereto, the assumed average price of 3,000 rupees in Bengal might probably have been supported. Their additional 1,500 chests have had the effect of raining the market and destroy at least four-fifths of their opium revenue. The mischief has been augmented by the vain attempts of the speculators of 1822 to keep up the prices in China by holding back, and the consequent influx into that market of more than the excess in the total supply, the imports of last season being stated at 9,000 chests to meet a consumption of 6,000. If the Company devise means hereafter to reduce the total quantity of Malwa opium from about 5,300 to about 3,000 chests, prices may again come round, although there must still for some time be a dead stock of former years unsold.

The amount of bills on the Bengal treasury corresponds in the total very closely with the estimate of 100 lakhs, although differently distributed. Yet that estimate was formed with the knowledge of a much smaller amount having been drawn in 1821–22.* Those of the supracargoes in China may perhaps in the present year exceed the assumed amount of 60 lakhs. The exigencies of the Canton treasury in consequence of the fire induced them to negotiate upon Bombay alone in 1822–23

* Rs.73,44,025. *Vide* Appendix P.

no less than 37 lakhs; but their drafts are now drawn exclusively upon Bengal.

The most considerable discordances will be found where we should expect to find them in comparing the various trade balances with the ingress and egress of bullion. * To effect this it was necessary to separate the bullion operations of the Company whose declared exports under that head (Rs.113,16,410 in 1821–22 to Great Britain and the Mauritius and Rs.50,94,620 in 1822–23 to Madras and Bombay) are considered as mere financial remittances.† Their entire commercial balance is also excluded from the column of calculable returns,‡ and added to the amount of their surplus remittances. From the same, column deductions are likewise made as in the estimate under the heads of Ceylon, New South Wales and the Cape, in consideration of the government and private bills§ likely to have formed part of their returns to Bengal. With these corrections the country trade promised returns in bullion to the amount

	in 1821–22	and	1822–23
of	lakhs 125·0	and	154·3
and gave only	97·4	and	76·7
shewing a deficiency of	27·6	and	77·6
in their bullion imports respectively.			

The former is less than $8\frac{1}{2}$ per cent upon the total amount of exports to the countries comprehended in this class. It includes, moreover, some private trade remittances from Bengal to England thro' China, Singapore, Java, etc. besides the whole value of the investment of the officers of the Company's China ships. The latter is $21\frac{1}{2}$ per cent upon the similar exports of its corresponding year, but scarcely exceeds half the value of the opium export, one-third of which is supposed to have been lost altogether by the speculation, while returns for the remainder are known to have been unusually delayed.

The commerce of Europe and the United States, exclusive of

* *Vide* ditto.
† The bills from Sumatra properly belong to the surplus remittance account: so indeed do all those from China. In fact the whole item of bills may be resolved into 'surplus remittance'.
‡ *Vide* Appendix P, fourth column of each year.
§ For pay and salaries of invalids of the Bengal establishment.

bullion and the Company's transactions exhibits a balance of exports to the extent of*

	in 1821–22	and	1822–23
	lakhs 140·6	and	241·8
Our estimate gave for private remittable capital	123		123
And the Company's actual surplus remittance in merchandise appear to have been	102	and	125·5
Deficit of exports	lakhs 86·5	and	6·7

Comparing the actual exports with the remittance demand which amounts respectively must be diminished by the value of the surplus private exports to China, etc. for remittance to Europe, being thus rendered about 70 lakhs in the former year while the latter becomes changed into an excess of 5 or 10 lakhs, we might perhaps in both years allow a considerable difference between the actual net proceeds and the gross amount invoices, which, especially in the case of shop articles and British piece-goods, have usually been attended with loss during that period. A deduction of 15 per cent from the whole (a pretty large abatement) would still leave a balance of full 40 lakhs short in 1821–22, but by a similar computation there would appear a surplus about equal thereto in the following year. Taking them together, with every allowance, we find that the course of trade did not require an import of bullion at Calcutta from any part of Europe or the United States. A considerable supply did however arrive from both, attributable certainly to ignorance and miscalculation and amounts less bullion exported in 1821–22 to 94·8 lakhs† and 1822–23 to 48·3. No wonder that in the former year the exchange on London so rapidly declined with a surprise remittance demand exceeding 130 lakhs, while the total resource from the negotiation of Company's interest bills, then for the last time granted at the option of stockholders, did not in all India exceed 120 lakhs.‡ The financial arrangements of 1822 which cancelled that option did not throw into the market any large amount of bills for principal paid off, almost all the resident

---

* *Vide* Appendix P.
† *Vide* Appendix P, last column of each year.
‡ *Vide* p. 23.

holders of Company's paper having accepted the option of transfer into the new loan. These bills certainly contributed with a speculative demand for indigo of which a good deal was shipped on Calcutta account, to create a temporary rise in the exchange from 1s. 11d. to 2s. 2d. between February and June 1822; but the rise was soon afterwards counteracted by bullion imports from America and at the close of the year 1822–23 the exchange returned to the rate of a bullion remittance as from the above calculations we should expect it to have done.

The merchant then began to look about for that description of bullion which offered the most favourable exchange as a remittance, gold mohurs promised nearly 2s. per rupee: always a small portion of the circulation, the coin bore a high premium. Spanish dollars were next in request. They also have advanced from 205½ to 210½ and 211 rupees per 100 and if the Europe imports continue on their present scale, will permanently maintain their relative intrinsic value of 210¼ rupees* or even a little more, being preferred at par to the rupee of the country.

In Bombay the expedient of remitting rupees has already been resorted to by the principal agency houses on several occasions within the last six months, it being impossible to collect preferable descriptions of bullion at short notice in sufficient quantity. The total imports of that Presidency (and of Madras in 1821–22) show a considerable augmentation, although the Company sent out to the former only one-third of the value of their investment of the previous year. The increase in the Bombay private trade imports from Great Britain is very large, nearly 50 per cent; so that, although the exports of the same class have been doubled, both in the article of cotton and in the aggregate, they are overvalued by the former deducting therefrom the investments of the Company's officers the proceeds of which they carry on to China, even though we augment the Bombay export with a proportion of the pepper and other produce shipped for England at the Malabar port under the Madras government. But in 1821–22 and 1822–23 it is known

---

* The sicca rupee contains 175·9 grains of pure silver and the dollar according to Kelly 370·9. The mint charge at Calcutta is 2 per cent on silver and the mint value of the Spanish dollar is thence computed at 206¼ rupees per 100.

that several lakhs were remitted home through Calcutta and in the former year something may have been sent also through China. Then also the Company's bills afforded a resource.* All these allowances however seem insufficient to make up the deficit in the amount of merchandise shipped for Great Britain adding to that deficit the Bombay portion of private remittable capital.†

I have not attempted and I shall not now undertake to submit the trade of Bombay in its several branches to the same scrupulous examination adopted with that of Bengal, nor have I the means of subjecting that of Madras to a similar analysis. Both seem to keep pace with Bengal in the period and degrees of their expansion and contraction. Some financial operations however deserve notice as they have materially affected the exchange between one Presidency and another.

It is elsewhere stated that in the course of 1823 bills appeared from Canton drawn upon the Bombay treasury to the extent of 27 lakhs. To meet them, two remittances in cash of 20 lakhs each were sent round from Calcutta in the Company's cruisers *Ernaad* and *Investigator*, leaving a surplus of 3 lakhs for general purposes. In the interval between them, namely in July and August, tenders were accepted for bills on Bengal to the extent of about 20 lakhs, negotiated at 104, 105 and 106 Bombay rupees for 100 siccas, but mostly at 103: so that the total aid received from Bengal appears to have been about 60 lakhs and only 23 lakhs exclusive of the amount absorbed by the China bills. A further sum has been obtained from the Malabar treasuries by transfer of the Madras government. But in the same period the Company have sent home $9\frac{3}{10}$ lakhs in gold coin from Bombay and have forwarded to China, besides their usual investment, a large consignment of their woollens imported in 1821–22. It appears therefore that with the resource of the annual opium sale the Bombay government does not in ordinary cases require more than half the aid from Bengal assigned to it in any estimate. The price of opium is now so much fallen that the

---

* In 1820–21 Rs.8,67,082, *vide* note to p. 24. The amount must have been greater the following year of which the particulars are wanting.

† Estimated at 42 lakhs for Madras and Bombay jointly, *vide* note to p. 17.

produce of the sale just concluded is above 8 lakhs short of the last and some recent naval equipments may in a slight degree further augment the deficit of 1823–24.*

Notwithstanding the comparatively small amount of government drafts negotiated upon Calcutta, the Bombay exchange with that Presidency during the year in question has at no time been higher than 106½. The rise which occurred in September was soon afterwards checked by an influx of China bills drawn upon Bengal and remitted as returns to Bombay, or to Calcutta on Bombay accounts, which cause contributed with the approach of the opium sale gradually to pull down the exchanges very nearly to par,† whence it has again started upwards. On the whole there appears to be much less demand for bill remittances to Bengal than in former years,‡ whether owing to the opportunity of investing capital in the Company's loans no longer existing, or to what other cause, it is not my present purpose to examine.

In the Bengal trade reports there is an item of Rs.31,18,617 exported in bullion to the Coromandel coast in 1822–23 on government account, intended probably to make up the deficit in that treasury occasioned by the 40 lakhs withdrawn for remittance to England per H.M.S. *Glasgow*. The very large importation of grain at that Presidency has lately much affected its exchanges with Bengal and Bombay: the former was for a short time at par previously thereto; the latter has been depressed thereby from 102 to 96 Bombay for 100 Madras rupees in the Bombay bazar. The exchange with England has throughout the year ranged lower at Madras than at the other Presidencies.¶

* The Bombay deficit is partly of a commercial nature and so far depends upon the relative amounts of the Company's imports from Great Britain and exports to China. Both vary considerably.

† Towards the end of March some bills were negotiated at par in the bazar.

‡ In 1814–15 the Bombay public drafts on Bengal amounted to sr. Rs.64,28,843 and in 8 years prior to 1820–21 they averaged 38½ lakhs, *vide* Bengal trade reports. In 1819–20 they amounted to Rs.37,82,520 while the exchange with Calcutta ranged between 108 and 113.

¶ Calcutta in 1822–23 2s. 2d.–1s. 11¼d.   in 1823–24 1s. 11d.–1s. 10d.
   Bombay   do.   1s. 11d.–1s. 9½d.   do.   1s. 10d.–1s. 8d.
   Madras   do.   1s. 10d.–1s. 9d.   do.   1s. 8d.

The Bombay and Madras rupees are nearly of equal value, it is in contemplation

Remarkable fluctuations were observed in the prices and supply of Europe goods in all the Indian markets almost simultaneously; but those of Calcutta exhibit the greatest extremes. The year 1818–19 is that in which the largest sacrifices were made. Its imports with those of 1817–18 far exceeded the demand in every article not excepting cotton goods considering their relative cost at the time. The disappointment of speculators produced the usual consequence, a partial abandonment of the Indian trade for a year or two and in some commodities a supply to the extent of only one-third or one-fifth and even one-tenth of the value of the largest importation. The accumulated stocks were gradually expended and prices again rose, or a great reduction took place in the original cost, especially of cotton and woollen fabrics. One or both causes revived the languid spirit of adventure. Again the markets are overloaded and again the merchant is compelled to choose between sacrificing his consignments at a miserable discount and suffering them to rot in his warehouse, while a falling exchange threatens every day to augment the loss on his returns. It seems therefore impossible to hope that the average amount of Europe imports for the last two years will be maintained. On the contrary there is reason to fear that in this particular my estimate will prove little if at all undervalued during the remaining years of the series they embrace.

Bombay, 31 *March* 1824

to make them pass current indifferently under the former Presidency. Their contents in pure silver are as follows:

Bombay 164·63 ⎱
Madras 165 ⎰ *vide* Bombay Calendar.

The Furrackabad rupee containing 160 grains of pure silver is now declared so current by Proclamation dated 9 April 1824.

George Alexander Prinsep

Appendix N *Bengal trade with Great Britain.*

IMPORTS

Description of merchandise	Estimates for 1822–23	Actual amounts corrected with 20% for charges	
		1821–22	1822–23
	Lks.		
Piece-goods, silk and cotton	40·0	56,18,244	78,92,835
Woollens	25·0	30,13,794	24,18,506
Spelter	8·0	2,12,665	4,92,470
Iron, steel and nails	6·0	5,55,755	5,30,669
Copper, pig sheathing, nails, etc.	24·0	29,57,351	22,84,279
Lead	3·0	29,753	4,68,063
Hardware, guns and ironmongery in general	4·3	4,81,553	6,61,745
Earthenware	2·0	57,830	86,724
Glassware of all sorts	8·0	5,58,359	5,34,267
Clocks and watches	0·7	48,587	83,552
Cordage, paints and other naval stores and tinware	4·0	4,01,548	4,02,224
Oilmans stores, books, stationery, sadlery, spinning hosiery and other shop articles for Europeans, medicines, carriages, jewellery and plated ware	16·0	22,54,040	33,42,584
Malt liquor	3·0	4,32,912	7,05,575
Wine, brandy and other spirits and liqueurs	10·0	10,57,711	14,52,236
Sundries, including new articles	4·0	5,16,488	3,56,603
Total sicca rupees	158·0	1,81,96,591	2,17,18,333

Economic Development of India

REMARKS

1. The items of oilman's stores, etc. and beer were certainly undervalued with reference to their average importation.

2. Some idea may be formed from the table shown opposite of the fluctuations that have occurred in several articles and the difficulty of estimating their annual consumption. The Custom-house values are given. They include the Company imports in the last four years only.

3. The total imports of Madeira wine in 1820–21 are stated at Rs.5,04,004. That year above 3 lakhs and in 1814–15 about 4 lakhs were imported otherwise than under the head of Great Britain which usually absorbs nearly the whole quantity. The average re-exports for 8 years to 1820–21 inclusive were Rs.3,70,984 being in 1819–20 Rs.10,36,705 including Rs.9,75,522 to Great Britain.

4. The fashion of drinking sherry commenced only two or three years back.

Year mentioned below		1816–17	1817–18	1818–19	1819–20	1820–21	1821–22	1822–23
Piece-goods	—	3,13,102	11,20,902	26,55,192	15,85,890	25,55,908	46,81,870	65,77,279
Cutlery	—	59,749	1,66,198	2,56,747	48,548	46,931	58,925	1,46,440
Earthenware	—	1,60,906	4,62,300	5,08,984	50,519	31,613	48,192	72,270
Glassware	—	4,95,990	11,21,205	10,29,612	2,27,909	4,03,981	4,64,071	4,40,731
Sadlery	—	1,35,995	1,82,056	2,11,315	1,33,865	99,647	1,06,230	1,77,078
Confectionery	—	46,847	91,615	1,21,249	37,324	40,008	62,538	91,651
Hosiery 1815–16	48,389	1,40,784	2,40,947	3,11,894	55,262	51,548	83,782	1,74,306
Hats 1814–15	23,133	1,24,348	2,17,321	2,69,241	57,717	26,054	58,283	1,86,548
Medicines do.	26,328	72,788	1,01,538	1,16,825	16,713	40,655	70,676	1,34,093
Oilman's stores		2,11,679	2,95,014	3,39,911	1,13,990	1,05,056	2,59,963	3,19,963
Perfumery 1815–16	27,687	62,720	1,35,269	1,31,566	21,420	25,022	42,250	1,14,296
Stationery 1814–15	68,049	1,92,634	3,08,986	2,77,510	47,938	78,023	1,48,752	3,30,340
Beer do.	1,72,481	4,87,907	4,63,783	3,83,639	1,45,255	1,95,855	3,60,760	5,87,980
Port wine 1813–14	2,59,959	1,09,496	1,58,573	2,16,338	91,810	74,839	1,15,579	1,58,962
Madeira do.	9,49,125	4,08,575	5,27,730	2,51,600	1,69,369	2,90,119	1,29,496	3,18,448
Perry and sherry 1814–15	9,687	22,172	42,212	20,685	18,945	16,392	75,576	1,61,725
Rum 1815–16	8,862	8,078	7,139	3,769	3,208	2,386	3,796	44,057
Brandy do.	47,090	68,077	85,321	1,54,796	1,42,914	1,69,204	1,01,220	78,032

Description of merchandise		Estimates for 1822–23		Actual exports in 1821–22			Actual exports in 1822–23		
		Quantity	Value	Quantity	Deduced value	Corrected value	Quantity	Deduced value	Corrected value
			Lks.			Lks.			Lks.
Indigo	Fy. Mds.	70,000	1,51·2	51,177	54,20,123	92·1	79,992	1,00,26,300	1,72·8
Raw silk	B. Mds.	15,000	78·0	13,954	73,10,129	75·1	15,786	77,03,799	86·6
Sugar		3,00,000	24·0	1,97,570	15,52,365	15·8	1,73,118	14,05,646	13·8
Cotton		—	—	18,953	3,54,962	3·5	22,904	2,88,486	3·7
Saltpetre		2,50,000	12·5	1,87,210	11,16,682	9·4	2,17,004	13,76,812	9·2
Piece-goods, silk	pieces	1,50,000	10·5	77,617	8,05,032	8·7	1,01,967	8,94,121	9·7
Ditto cotton		2,00,000	7·0	1,85,648	6,46,690	7·0	1,46,909	4,52,627	4·9
Lack dye	B. Mds.	10,000	3·0 ⎫						
Shell lack, etc.		10,000	2·0 ⎬	—	5,32,423	5·5	—	3,08,905	3·2
Sundries including new articles		—	11·0	—	4,77,136	5·0	—	8,45,754	8·8
Spices and other Asiatic re-exports		—	12·0	—	7,53,211	8·1	—	9,27,071	10·0
Net cost		—	3,11·2	—	1,89,68,752	2,30·2	—	2,42,29,515	3,22·7
Charges at 6 per cent		—	18·7	—	—	13·8	—	—	19·3
Total	lakhs	—	3,29·9	—	—	2,44·0	—	—	3,42·0

Remarks

1. The Bengal report tables give the aggregate value of exported merchandise under denominations of quantity different from those of the tables which specify the quantities exported to the several countries. In the above, the average contents of packages are taken as follows:

		1821/22	valuation	1822/23	valuation
Indigo	Chests	12,635 @ 4½ Mds. ea.	180	19,571 @ 4½ Mds. ea.	216
Raw Silk	Bales	6,972 @ 2 ,, ,,	13½ – 11½	7,893 @ 2 ,, ,,	14 – 12½
Sugar	Bags	79,228 @ 2½ ,, ,,	8½	69,247 @ 2½ ,, ,,	8
Cotton	,,	5,415 @ 3½ ,, ,,	18	5,544 @ 3½ ,, ,,	16
Saltpetre	,,	93,605 @ 2 ,, ,,	5	108,502 @ 2 ,, ,,	4.12 as
Piece-goods, Silk,	Boxes	704 @ 110½ pieces	add 8% to declared value	950 @ 107⅓ pieces	add 8% to declared value
,, ,, Cotton,	Bales	1,668 @ 111¾ ,,		1,354 @ 108½ ,,	

2. Assuming the bales of silk to average 2 maunds, those shipped for other places will average in 1821–22 nearly 3 maunds and in 1822–23 rather less than 1 maund, which cannot be in either case. At my valuation of 13 rupees per seer in the estimates the supposed number of maunds would give Rs.72,56,080 and Rs.82,08,720 respectively. But the mean prices are quoted 13·4 and 14·12. So that in 1821–22 unless the usual size of the bales was reduced which is contrary to the above inference, there cannot have been much exported to Great Britain on private account which also I know to be correct, since the Custom-house valuation except on the Company's [raw silk] is only 6 and 7 rupees per seer. Perhaps 1,000 maunds in the former and 4,000 in the latter year might be the extent of the private trade and I have accordingly added for correction 5 and 6 rupees per seer respectively upon those quantities.

3. My estimate for cotton piece-goods agrees almost exactly in the valuation per piece with that of the Custom-house. In silk piece-goods it is much too low if the total number of pieces divided by that of the boxes give the true average contents of packages exported to Great Britain. This does not however seem probable from the similarity in amount and diversity in the number of pieces so obtained. Dividing the aggregate value by the latter we have Rs.5·11 and Rs.5·7 per piece and 143,000 and 168,000 pieces respectively for Great Britain.

4. The Company exported in 1821–22 3553 maunds and 1822–23 8,284 maunds of indigo, an article which for many years had not formed part of their Bengal investment.

Appendix O   *General commerce of Bengal exclusive of bullion.*

IMPORTS

		1821–22		1822–23	
Names of countries	Estimate for 1822–23	Declared value	Corrected value	Declared value	Corrected value
	Lks.		Lks.		Lks.
France	4·0	7,42,561	8·5	7,20,248	8·3
Baltic ports	1·0	7,636	0·1	22,945	0·3
Portugal	1·0	63,455	0·7	2,56,941	2·8
Spain	—	—	—	—	—
Mediterranean	4·0				
sicca rupees	10·0	8,13,652	9·3	10,00,134	11·4
United States	2·0	2,90,477	3·2	2,43,013	2·7
Sa. Rs.	12·0	11,04,129	12·5	12,43,147	14·1
Great Britain	1,58·0	1,51,63,826	1,82·0	1,80,98,011	2,17·2
Sa. Rs.	1,70·0	1,62,67,955	1,94·5	1,93,41,758	2,31·3
Brazil	0·4	72,842	0·8	50,197	0·5
Mexico and Spanish South America	10·0	9,37,448	10·7	8,57,977	9·8
Cape of Good Hope	1·0	34,066	0·4	80,014	0·9
Mauritius	8·0	6,47,448	7·2	6,93,572	7·7
Arabian and Persian Gulphs	15·0	11,62,152	10·8	16,48,853	18·3
Maldive Islands	1·0	1,83,475	2·0	1,49,043	1·6
Mozambique	—	19,923	0·2	10,320	0·1
Ceylon	1·0	48,485	0·5	1,14,856	1·3
Coast of Malabar	11·0	15,51,205	18·1	4,76,835	5·5
Coast of Coromandel	8·0	8,87,221	9·5	7,14,170	7·7
Coast of Sumatra	2·6	1,23,872	1·4	2,05,387	2·3
Java	5·0	6,46,292	7·2	5,55,691	6·2
Pegue	2·0	4,54,403	5·1	3,58,624	4·0
Penang and Eastward	10·0	4,88,776	5·4	6,46,334	7·2
Manilla	1·0	82,460	0·9	44,185	0·5
China	42·0	22,88,959	19·5	12,30,310	10·5
New South Wales	0·6	6,617	0·1	38,113	0·4
Grand Total Sa. Rs.	2,88·6	2,59,03,399	2,94·3	2,72,16,239	3,15·8
Supposed true Totals of 1822–23				Sa. Rs. 2,68,66,538	3,11·8

George Alexander Prinsep

REMARKS

1. The excess in my estimates of sugar, lack, ginger and gums is attributable in great measure to the want of the report for 1821–22 and all information relative thereto when they were prepared. I was thus ignorant of the rapid decline which had already occurred in the exported quantities of those articles.

2. My valuation of 1 rupee per maund in grain was an oversight. In a note to Appendix C No. 2 it is stated that grain had been undervalued at 1 rupee to the extent of 4 to 8 annas and I knew that the prices were generally advancing from year to year.

3. No addition is made to the valuation of re-exports because they include a large proportion of British goods reshipped for a market, being unsaleable in Bengal except at a loss. British goods indeed have rarely been sold otherwise within the last two years, although for the most part at a nominal advance upon invoice calculated at 2s. 8d. per rupee.

Description of merchandise		Estimate for 1822–23		Actual trade of 1821–22			Actual trade of 1822–23		
		Quantity	Value	Quantity	Declared value	Corrected value	Quantity	Declared value	Corrected value
			Lks.			Lks.			
Opium	chests	5,000	1,50·0	2,590	91,19,220	91·2	4,42¼	1,42,08,153	1,42·1
Indigo	Fy. Mds.	1,00,000	2,40·0	81,857	87,57,907	1,47·3	1,09,198	1,31,21,699	2,62·1
Raw silk	B. Mds.	17,000	86·3	16,030	81,70,638	89·7	16,461	81,64,933	94·6
Silk piece-goods	pieces	4,50,000	31·5	5,95,229	33,28,218	35·7	5,61,419	30,67,277	33·7
Cotton ditto	Mds.	26,00,000	84·5	25,26,846	77,01,319	82·1	28,09,780	79,99,521	84·3
Sugar		6,00,000	48·0	3,95,407	32,16,316	31·6	2,90,145	22,57,228	21·8
Cotton		1,40,000	20·0	2,39,131	34,24,311	37·1	95,244	12,44,980	13·8
Saltpetre		3,80,000	19·0	2,88,578	16,25,435	14·4	3,42,861	20,24,726	16·3
Grain		14,00,000	14·0	14,95,141	15,57,579	24·3	15,05,294	15,15,373	22·5
Lack dye		13,000	4·2 }						
Seed, stick and shell lack		17,000	3·0 }	20,325	6,33,168	6·5	10,988	3,21,923	3·3
Ginger		60,000	3·0		41,155	0·4		34,708	0·4
Gummies		3,00,000	2·4		1,25,699	1·3		1,24,974	1·3
Sundries including new articles			25·0		19,42,538	20·0		21,55,203	22·0
Total prime cost	Sicca rupees		7,30·9		4,96,37,503	5,79·6		5,62,40,698	7,18·2
Asiatic and other re-exports			44·0		39,15,620	39·2		56,10,780	56·13
Total amount of invoices	Sa. Rs.		7,74·9		5,36,53,123	6,18·8		6,18,51,480	7,74·3
Duties computed at			6·0						—
Commission and other charges at Calcutta	Sicca rupees		7,80·9			6,24·8			7,80·3
			54·7			43·7			54·6
Total amount of invoices	Sa. Rs.		8,35·6			6,68·5			8,34·9
Deduct Amount of imports			2,88·6			2,94·3			3,11·8
Balance of exports	lakhs		5,47·0			3,74·2			5,23·1

George Alexander Prinsep

REMARKS

1. The imports from France show an extraordinary advance compared with former years, having never before exceeded Rs.5,27,182 which is the reported amount for 1818–19. In 1819–20 the declared amount was Rs.3,34,245 and in 1820–21 only Rs.2,32,183.

2. Spain was estimated to recommence her imports into Bengal in 1823–24. The late events in that country render it probable that her name will continue blank on the list for some time longer.

3. From the Mediterranean returns ought soon to arrive for the large exports of both years if not transferred to the account of Great Britain.

4. My data for 1822–23 were obtained before the Bengal report for that year was completed and are found to be not free from error. In our table the aggregate imports of merchandise are stated at Rs.2,68,66,538 which is also the sum of the values of the articles. But deducting the amount of bullion Rs.1,69,39,678 according to the particulars given from the stated amount of aggregate imports from the several countries we have Rs.2,72,16,239 being a difference of Rs.3,49,704. In another table the items of Spanish America and Manilla being stated at Rs.10,82,548 and Rs.44,187 respectively instead of Rs.8,57,977 and Rs.44,185 augment the total amount of merchandise to Rs.2,74,40,814. I have taken the first Rs.2,68,66,535 as the true aggregate of merchandise and Rs.1,72,89,382 as that of bullion imported in 1822–23.

5. The following are the valuations assumed for the principal articles.

Appendix P *Bengal exports to the several countries, balance of trades and bullion imports.*

Names of countries		Estimates for 1822–23			Actual trade	
	Amount of exports	Excess of exports	Bills on Bengal	Return in bullion	Corrected amt. of exports	Excess of exports
China lakhs	1,55·0	1,13·0	60·0	33·0	1,15·0	95·5
Java	35·0	30·0	—	30·0	23·0	15·8
Penang and Eastward	26·0	16·0	⎱ 5·0 ⎰	11·0	30·0	24·6
Coast of Sumatra	6·0	4·0		4·0	5·8	4·4
Manilla	4·5	3·5	—	3·5	9·9	9·0
Persian and Arabian Gulphs	60·0	45·0	—	45·0	40·0	29·2
Coast of Malabar	37·0	26·0	30·0	3·0	28·5	10·4
Coast of Coromandel	12·0	4·0	1·0	3·0	20·0	10·5
Ceylon	2·4	1·4	1·0	—	1·3	0·8
New South Wales	3·4	3·0	—	0·5	3·1	3·0
Mauritius	11·0	4·0	3·0	—	21·0	13·8
Cape of Good Hope	5·0	4·0	—	2·0	5·0	4·6
Mozambique	—	—	—	—	—	−0·2
Maldive Islands	1·0	—	—	—	1·0	−1·0
Mexico, Peru, Chile and Buenos Ayres	35·0	25·0	—	25·0	20·0	9·3
Brazil	6·4	6·0	—	6·0	1·7	0·9
Pegue	1·2	−0·8	—	—	4·0	−1·1
Total Country Trade lakhs	4,01·7	2,83·1	1,00·0	1,66·0	3,29·3	2,29·5
United States of America	38·0	36·0	—	36·0	56·0	32·8
Mediterranean	10·0	6·0	—	6·0	8·9	8·9
Spain	1·0	1·0	—	1·0	—	—
Portugal	22·0	21·0	—	15·0	5·0	4·2
France	28·0	24·0	—	—	22·0	13·5
Baltic Ports	5·0	4·0	—	—	—	−0·5
Great Britain	3,29·9	1,71·9	—	—	2,44·0	62·0
Bills on the Bengal Treasury	—	—	—	1,00·0	—	—
Company's surplus Investment	—	—	—	1,00·0	—	—
Remittable Capital of individuals	—	—	—	1,00·0	—	—
Ditto of Bombay and Madras through inland Bills	—	—	—	23·0	—	—
Totals lakhs	8,35·6	5,47·0	—	5,47·0	6,65·2	3,70·1
Add differences explained in the notes	—	—	—	—	3·3	4·1
Amounts corresponding with the surplus exports				lakhs	6,68·5	3,74·2

	of 1821–22				Actual trade of 1822–23		
Bills on Bengal	Returns calculated in bullion	Corrected actual ditto	Corrected amt. of exports	Excess of exports	Bills on Bengal	Returns calculated in bullion	Corrected actual ditto
35,23,257	41·0	33·2	1,47·0	1,35·5	45,16,959	79·0	24·0
—	15·8	7·3	29·5	23·3	—	23·3	12·1
4,76,408	} 9·8	{ 6·2	32·5	25·3	6,44,422	} 2·8	{ 6·6
13,38,443		{ −1·5	4·9	2·6	18,31,204		{ 1·3
—	9·0	1·4	3·0	2·5	—	2·5	3·4
3,35,000	25·9	22·6	43·0	24·7	5,54,000	19·2	20·3
16,37,841	−2·0	6·4	49·0	43·5	29,22,817	19·8	1·6
3,656	10·5	—	11·5	3·8	5,303	3·8	0·4
—	—	—	1·6	0·3	—	—	—
—	0·5	—	3·5	3·1	—	0·5	0·9
29·421	6·0	0·9	17·0	9·3	—	3·0	0·7
—	0·6	0·1	10·0	9·1	—	7·1	—
—	−0·2	—	—	−0·1	—	−0·1	—
—	−1·0	—	0·7	−0·9	—	−0·9	—
—	9·3	17·0	3·3	−6·5	—	−6·5	2·1
—	0·9	3·8	2·2	1·6	—	1·6	3·3
—	−1·1	—	3·2	−0·8	—	−0·8	—
73,44,026	1,25·0	97·4	3,61·9	2,77·3	1,04,74,705	1,54·3	76·7
—	—	45·8	44·0	41·3	—	11·6	45·8
—	—	—	8·0	8·0	—	—	—
—	—	—	—	—	—	—	—
—	—	12·3	28·0	25·2	—	—	19·7
—	—	21·5	50·0	41·7	—	—	11·2
—	—	—	1·0	0·8	—	—	0·2
—	—	15·0	3,42·0	1,24·8	—	—	1·4
—	73·4	73·4	—	—	—	1,04·7	1,04·7
1,02·0	1,02·0	1,02·0	—	—	1,25·5	1,25·5	1,25·5
1,00·0	1,00·0	1,00·0	—	—	1,00·0	1,00·0	1,00·0
23·0	23·0	23·0	—	—	23·0	23·0	23·0
2,98·4	4,23·4	4,90·4	8,34·9	5,19·1	3,53·2	5,19·1	5,08·2
75·8	−49·2	−1,16·2	—	4·0	1,69·9	4·0	14·9
3,74·2	3,74·2	3,74·2	—	5,23·1	5,23·1	5,23·1	5,23·1

Economic Development of India

REMARKS

1. The sign minus (—) implies deduction. Thus in column 2 there is supposed an export deficiency of 0·8 lakhs under the head of Pegue and in column 5 of 1821–22 there appears an import of bullion from Sumatra exceeding the export by 1·5.

2. The amount of bills drawn from the Coast of Sumatra includes Rs.1,58,138 in 1821–22 and Rs.3,59,470 in 1822–23 from Singapore.

3. All imports and exports by the Company are excluded in computing the returns due, but included in the accounts of imports and exports.

4. The Company's surplus investment or the excess of their Bengal exports beyond their imports is composed as follows, exclusive of bullion.

5. Under the heads of Ceylon, New South Wales and the Cape of Good Hope allowance is made as in the estimate for British government and private bills (of Bengal invalids) computed to form an important part of the returns from those places to Bengal.

6. Under that of Mauritius there was in 1821–22 a bullion import of Rs.103,900 according to the Custom-house valuations and a bullion export of Rs.3,25,410 including Rs.3,16,410 by the Company. The net corrected value of the surplus private importation was therefore about Rs.86,000. To the aggregate exports of merchandise to the Mauritius 2 Lakhs are added for short valuation of grain and 4 for charges including freight. Of these 6 lakhs, 4 belong to the trade of the Company who supplied the grain in question or which is the same thing paid for the quantity landed at a contract price.

7. The exports to France include 2,443 chests of indigo in 1821–22 valued at 200 rupees per maund and 4,563 in 1822–23 valued at Rs.240. Both valuations are probably too low. By increasing the first to about 213 rupees per maund the difference in the sum of the exports (3·3 lakhs) would be made to disappear. *Vide* Appendix O.*

8. In summing up the column of 'Excess of exports' for 1821–22 there is a further deficit of 0·8 compared with the preceding table. In the same column for 1822–23 appears a deficit of 4 lakhs, the exact amount of the difference between the total corrected imports resulting from the sum of the commodities and the aggregate imports from the several countries according to the particulars sent me from Calcutta. *Vide* Appendix O.

9. By the third, fourth and fifth columns of actual trade of both years it will be perceived that the bullion imports and trade balances differ very considerably from each other. The several additions at the bottom of the column shew

  (1) that the trade would have been balanced with a bullion importation of Rs.75·8 lakhs in 1821–22 and Rs.169·9 lakhs in 1822–23;

  (2) that exclusive of the country trade, with a bullion export of Rs.49·2 lakhs in 1821–22 and import of 15·6 lakhs in 1822–23;

  (3) that the aggregate bullion imports differ from the trade balance on the amount of returns calculable in bullion, by an excess of Rs.1,16·2 lakhs in 1821–22 and a deficit of Rs.14·9 lakhs in 1822–23, supposing the errors noticed above (notes 8 and 9) to affect only the items of commerce with Europe and the United States.

10. The estimated amounts of Bombay and Madras transfers of capital for remittance through Calcutta are preserved in the tables of actual trade; but they are believed to be overrated with reference to 1822–23 and the future years of the series, since the cotton of Bombay may for a time supply Europe returns for Bengal

* The prices of the time seem to warrant the increase, as only indigo of good quality is sent to that market.

equivalent to the Bombay orders for indigo, sugar, saltpetre, etc. During 1823, however, merchant bills on London have been negotiated to a considerable amount in Bombay on Calcutta account.

11. Under the head of Mexico, Chile, etc. there appears a bullion import of lakhs 19·1 taking both years together, while the balance of trade required only 2·8 lakhs. The excess of 16·3 lakhs may perhaps be accounted for partly by the unremitted returns oᵀ former years, but has doubtless been owing principally to circuitous remittances from Spanish America through Bengal to Europe and the United States which remittances were very profitable while the Indian exchanges continued high.

2

Thomas Tooke, A History of Prices, and of the State of the Circulation during the Nine Years 1848–56, Volume VI (1857)

Appendix XXIII

Shipments of silver to India and China during the six years 1851–56; special circumstances affecting the eastern trade during those years; influx of gold and silver into India during the eight years 1841–54; and silver coinage of India during the twenty years 1836–45.

I

Among the most remarkable commercial phenomena of the last five or six years has been the large and increasing annual shipments of the precious metals, but chiefly silver, from Europe to India and China.

The continuance of these shipments for so long a period, and to so large an extent, has naturally excited much attention, and has led to discussions, the result of which cannot be said to have been so far very satisfactory.

The problem, in truth, does not admit of any clear solution, except by means of an extensive and careful collation of facts scattered over a somewhat wide surface.

In the series of Tables A to O attached to this Appendix I have endeavoured to deal with the subject in this mode; and I have sought to render the evidence as complete as possible, because it is quite manifest, that upon a satisfactory explanation of the causes of the drain of silver to the east since 1850 will depend, in a great measure, the answer to be given to several of the most important questions arising out of the effect, up to the present time (close of 1856), of the gold discoveries.

I will state, first, the general nature of the tables appended.

The first, Table A, and the subsidiary statements, B and C, set forth, on the data carefully compiled by Mr Low, the shipments of gold and silver from Europe to the several ports of India and China, during each year 1853–56, and in totals, during each year 1851–56. Considering the special nature of the mode of transit (by the large steamers) for these shipments, it is probable that the figures in Tables A, B and C set forth with reasonable accuracy the whole of the bullion exports.

In the three Tables D, E and F will be found the leading facts connected with the import and export trade of China during the six years 1850–55, as regards the trade with the United Kingdom. The figures are official; and I believe that the statements given as regards the trade with India and the United States are substantially near the truth.

The three Tables G, H and I exhibit very fully the import and export trade of the whole of British India; in the first place, in Tables G and H, from the records of the India Custom houses; and in the second place, in Table I, from the records of our Board of Trade.

The five Tables K, L, M, N, and O relate to the imports and exports of gold and silver into and from the whole of India; and to the extent of the silver coinage of India during the whole or portions of the period 1834–55. These tables have been derived from the data contained in the valuable paper by Colonel Sykes on the External Commerce of India, inserted in the Statistical Journal for 1856, and from data with which I have been furnished by Colonel Sykes' direction as chairman of the East India Company; and I am glad to have this opportunity of expressing my obligations to Colonel Sykes, and to the official persons at the India House, for the readiness with which they have met my inquiries.

II

It will facilitate the explanations to be given, to introduce, in the first instance, the following general summary of the facts contained in the tables.

India and China Trade, 1850–55   *Approximate statement of the imports and exports as they affect the United Kingdom; being a general summary of the details contained in the annexed Tables A to O.*

Description	1855	1854	1853	1852	1851	1850	Totals
1	2	3	4	5	6	7	8
	Mlns.	Mlns.	Mlns.	Mlns.	Mlns.	Mlns.	Mlns.
	£	£	£	£	£	£	£
(1)							
Exports from China:							
to United Kingdom	8·6	9·2	6·7	6·2	6·2	5·0	41·9
to India	1·5	1·5	1·5	1·5	1·5	1·5	9·0
to United States	2·6	2·1	1·9	2·6	2·2	2·0	13·4
	12·7	12·8	10·1	10·3	9·9	8·5	64·3
Exports from India:							
to United Kingdom	12·7	10·7	9·0	8·0	8·5	8·0	56·9
Total	25·4	23·5	19·1	18·3	18·4	16·5	121·3
(2)							
Imports into China:							
from United Kingdom	1·3	1·0	1·7	2·5	2·1	1·6	10·2
from India	3·6	3·7	3·6	4·2	4·2	4·2	22·5
from United States	0·3	0·3	0·3	0·3	0·3	0·3	1·8
	5·2	5·0	5·6	7·0	6·6	6·1	34·5
Imports into India:							
from United Kingdom	10·3	9·6	7·7	6·9	7·4	7·0	48·9
Drafts by E. I. Co.	3·7	3·8	3·3	2·8	3·2	2·9	19·7
	19·2	18·4	16·6	16·7	17·2	16·0	103·1
Ascertained shipments of gold and silver from Europe	9·0	5·7	6·5	3·6	1·8	0·5	27·1
Totals	28·2	24·1	23·1	20·3	19·0	16·5	130·2

In 1856, the shipments of gold and silver amounted to 14½ millions sterling.

It is quite clear on the face of these figures that the derangement of the eastern trade since 1851 has arisen almost wholly from the increased consumption in this country and the United States of the productions (chiefly tea and silk) of China; and from the decreased consumption in China of the manufactured goods (chiefly cotton manufactures) sent from England.

The trade with China is what is technically called a triangular trade; that is to say, that while America buys largely of China (almost wholly tea), America sells but little direct to China. America settles its annual debt to China by additions to the exports of American goods to England. In other words, England becomes the channel through which the trade between China and America is adjusted.

Further, while India sells more merchandise (chiefly opium and cotton) to China, than China sells to India, the balance due from China to India is made to a considerable extent available for adjusting the balance due from England to China.

That balance is very large; and since 1851 has become larger every year.

England has consumed the tea and silk of China to the amount, in 1855, of 8½ million sterling; while the consumption of English goods in China has been little more than 1 million.

It would be very difficult, if not impossible, to untwine the separate threads which are involved in this intricate commerce; nor would such an effort answer any useful purpose.

The whole of the eastern trade must be considered in one mass; and probably the arrangement exhibited in the summary just given is as convenient a form as can be adopted.

It is important to introduce (as is done) the amount of the annual drafts on India sold in London by the East India Company. I have explained, in Appendix xxi, the circumstances under which those drafts arise, and why they are to be included among the exports to India.

Including the amount of those drafts, it appears – contrary to what is the general supposition – that, for the six years 1850–55, the balance between India and England has been in favour of England; and that but for the excess of imports into England and America, from China, the current of the precious metals would have been from India to England, as the result of the ordinary trade in merchandise and India House drafts between the two countries.

But, besides this ordinary trade, there has been, since 1852, the effect, year by year, of the investments of English capital in Indian railways.

I have no accurate means of ascertaining the amount of funds lodged with the East India Company in London during the last four or five years – say during the years 1852–56 – as payments of capital by English and European shareholders, in pursuance of shares held in Indian railways. The amount, however, must have been considerable.

There have been two principal railway companies established as relates to India, and three or four minor companies.

The original company, and the largest, is the 'East India Railway Company', incorporated by act of parliament in 1849, for the construction of a great trunk line from Calcutta towards Agra and Delhi, and the north-west frontier. The amount of capital, authorized (by various modifications) to be raised by this company, is about 10 millions sterling; upon nearly the whole of which the East India Company guarantee rates of interest of 5 and 4½ per cent per annum. About 40 miles of the line at the Calcutta end were opened in September 1854; and a further portion of 120 miles to the Ranegunge collieries was opened in February 1855. The works are vigorously in hand over all or most of the sections towards Delhi; and, as far as I can judge, the payments of capital in England, 1851–56, have been about 5 or 6 millions sterling. Of these payments a large portion has been expended in England for iron rails, locomotives and machinery; and that portion would not affect the Indian exchanges. But by far the larger portions of the payments, it is to be presumed, have been remitted to India to provide for the immense disbursements there, for wages, salaries, materials and charges.

The second company is the 'Great Indian Peninsular', also incorporated in 1849 for the construction of a great trunk line from Bombay to various parts of the west coast, and the interior. The East India Company guarantee interest at 5 and 4½ per cent per annum, on amounts of capital equal to 3 or 4 millions; and the payments on account of capital in England in 1851–56 would seem to have been about 3 millions sterling. A length of 37 miles of the line was opened from Bombay in 1854.

There are other companies for constructing railways in Madras, Central India, Sind, the Punjab, and other regions; some of them under guarantees of interest, and others as merely private enterprises.

It seems to be probable, therefore, and is, I believe, the fact, that during the five years 1851–56, the capital paid in London for Indian railways has been not much less than 10 or 11 millions sterling; that the remittances to India, in pursuance of these payments, must have been at least 5 or 6 millions; and that of this sum of 5 or 6 millions there has been remitted in the two years 1855 and 1856, probably $1\frac{1}{2}$ millions a year – that is to say, that the payments in 1855–56 have been far heavier than in 1851–54.

It is highly probable that these remittances of $1\frac{1}{2}$ millions per annum may have been accomplished by direct shipments of silver to some extent, bearing in mind the natural desire of the East India Company to obtain the best possible rate for the bills sold by them in London.

Under any circumstances, it is perfectly plain that the railway remittances of 1851–54, and still more of 1855–56, have materially affected the position of the eastern trade; and it is abundantly obvious, that to whatever extent these railway remittances have proceeded, they have *pro tanto* turned the stream of silver in favour of India.

We see, indeed, from Table I that the increase in the real value of the England exports to India has been nearly or quite as rapid as the increase in the imports from India. The exports were 7 millions in 1851, and $10\frac{1}{3}$ millions in 1855.

The imports from India were $12\frac{1}{2}$ millions sterling in 1855; but in that year they were largely increased by the augmented importation from India of cotton, wood, rice and seeds, in consequence of special disturbances of the price of those articles in this country.

But not only has the transit of silver to the east been occasioned by an adverse mercantile balance against England, but it has been occasioned by the peculiar position of the exchange markets. In the first place, the East India Company, in London, have been enabled, by the railway funds, to keep up a selling rate so high, that it has been profitable to remit silver. In the second place, the state of the exchanges in China has offered great inducements to exchange operations by means of bullion.

I arrive, then, at these conclusions, *viz.*:

173

(1) That down to the close of 1850, the eastern trade – that is to say, the trade between China, India, the United States and England – adjusted itself, year by year, very closely by means of the India House drafts.

(2) That, during the five years 1851–55, the trade between England and India, including the India House drafts, has exhibited a balance rather in favour of England than of India.

(3) That, during those five years, the exports of merchandise from England to India have increased as rapidly as the imports into England from India.

(4) That this ordinary trade has been interfered with by the arrangements for transferring to India the investments of English capital in Indian railways.

(5) That the great cause of disturbance in the balance of the eastern trade since 1850, has been the very large and rapid increase in the consumption, in England and America, of the tea and silk of China.

(6) That this disturbance has been materially increased by the impediments occasioned by the civil war in China to the consumption of European goods.

(7) That it has been further increased by the confused and barbarous systems of currency prevalent at the leading ports in China.

(8) That it has been yet further increased by the inducements held out by the fluctuations of the rate of exchange in India and China to exchange operations by means of silver remittances.

(9) That as the general result of the whole of these circumstances, we may correctly describe the efflux of silver to the east during the six years 1851–56, as occasioned fundamentally by the increased demand for the tea and silk of China excited in England and the United States, principally in consequence of the enlarged employment and expenditure in those countries arising out of the gold discoveries.

Part of the gold of California and Australia has been employed in the purchase of larger quantities of those necessaries (tea) and luxuries (silk) of which China afforded the readiest supply; and England, occupying the chief position in the eastern trade – performing the functions of an intermediate country, through which nearly all the rest of the world obtain their supplies of Asiatic commodities, and adjust the balances due from them for these supplies – has been, of necessity, the country most largely concerned in the bullion operations of the last six years. On the one side, England has received from China and India the products for which there has been an active European and American demand; and, on the other side, England has collected and forwarded to the East the amounts of gold and silver required to adjust the general account of each year.

It is needful to remember, however, that until the year 1856, the remittances of gold and silver to the east were comparatively not of any excessive amount.

For the five years 1851–55, the average annual remittances were:

	£
Gold	500,000
Silver	4,500,000
	5,000,000

and towards this annual remittance there were the increasing supplies of silver from Mexico and South America.

In the year 1856, the remittances have been,

	£
Gold	500,000
Silver	14,100,000
	14,600,000

and this 14½ millions is, beyond doubt, a drain of the most remarkable character; and very amply accounts for the rise in the price of silver in London; for the drain of silver from France; and for the absorption, at once, of all arrivals of silver by the American packets.

Of the 14 millions of silver shipped in 1856, very nearly 5 millions was sent to Bombay; and only 3½ millions to Calcutta. It must be recollected, that the mere circumstance of the silver being sent in the first instance to India does not justify the absolute inference, that therefore the remittance is intended to remain in India. The probability is that a very considerable proportion of the silver remittances of the last four or five years have merely touched at Indian ports on their way to China. The combinations rendered necessary by the varying rates of exchange, when two or more places are concerned, are so intricate that it is almost impossible to infer the real destination of specie from the first point of debarkation.

The remittances of the whole of the six years 1851–56 amount to:

	£
Gold	5,000,000
Silver	36,500,000
	41,500,000

The circumstances which will determine the future magnitude of the annual drain of silver to the east are:

(1) The continuance of the present consumption of tea and silk in England and the United States; that consumption depending in some intimate degree upon the abundance of the supplies brought forward in China. The consumption of China silk, at least in 1857, will be very large, in consequence of the failure of the silk crop in Italy. The abundance of employment in England and America is likely to maintain a large consumption of tea at moderate prices; but any important rise in the price of tea, whether occasioned by failing supplies, or the cost of the silver remittances required to be paid for it, would, as in the article of sugar in 1855, produce an immediate effect on the consumption.

(2) The continuance of the remittances to India of English capital for investment in railways – the effect of these remittances being to maintain the selling rate in London of the drafts of the East India Company at a point favourable to the remittance of silver.

(3) The extension of the exports of British and foreign merchandise to India and China, but especially to India; and every extension of railways in India will powerfully assist the diffusion of European merchandise.

(4) The establishment of an effective system of currency in China; the revision of the present treaties with China; and the termination of the civil war which has ranged for ten or twelve years in the central provinces of the Chinese empire. All these

are results, the attainment of which will probably be promoted by the collision between the British and Chinese authorities at Canton, commenced in October 1856.

So long, however, as the present drain of silver to the east continues, it must be ascribed to its true cause, namely, a redistribution of silver between the west and the east, arising wholly out of the large and sudden demand in the west for Asiatic commodities.

III

The four Tables K, L, M and N exhibit very fully the bullion trade of the whole of India for the eight years (ended 30 April) 1846–47 to 1853–54.

The general result was as follows during those eight years – and they may be considered as an ordinary period under present circumstances; *viz.*

India, 1846–47 to 1853–54. Average annual –

	£
Imports of gold	1,170,000
Exports of gold	46,000
Net imports	1,124,000
Imports of silver	2,960,000
Exports of silver	1,070,000
Net imports	1,890,000
Net balance of imports of gold and silver into India	3,014,000

It appears from the summary in Table L of the more extensive details contained in Tables M and N, that of the £1,170,000 imports of gold about one half comes from China, and the other half from Ceylon, Singapore, and latterly from Australia.

Of the small amount of £46,000 exports of gold, one half seems to be sent to England, and the other half to a variety of small places.

Of the large sum of £2,960,000 imports of silver, nearly 50 per cent is also obtained from China; 25 per cent only (or say ¾ of a million sterling) was obtained in the eight years from

England; and the remaining 50 per cent was chiefly obtained from Ceylon.

The export of £1,070,000 of silver is similarly accounted for.

It is clear, therefore, that the net import of silver and gold may be stated to have been, down to 1853–54, not more than the comparatively moderate amount of 3 millions sterling; and that, in general terms, 2 millions are derived from China in payment for opium.

It is necessary, therefore, to receive with great caution the statements which are frequently made of the large annual absorption of silver in India, as the balance due to India upon its external trade not only with China but with Europe.

In Table O, there is a statement of the coinage of silver in the whole of India during each of the twenty years 1835–36 to 1854–55.

The average annual coinage is $3\frac{3}{4}$ millions sterling; and the annual amounts present no extreme variations.

The money of legal tender in India is the silver coin called the 'Company's rupee', introduced 1 September 1835, in supercession of the numerous varieties of rupees (Sicca, Surat, etc.) which were previously current. The Company's rupee contains 165·92 grains pure silver, and 15·08 grains alloy; and is worth, reckoning silver at 62d. per oz. 23d. sterling. It is popularly converted into sterling at the rate of 2s.

A gold coin was also introduced, 1 September 1835, called a 'mohur', equal to 15 rupees. The mohur contained 165·92 grains pure gold, and 15·08 grains alloy, and is worth £1 9s. 2d. sterling.

Previous to the measure of September 1835, gold, as well as silver, was a legal tender in India; but under the law of 1835, silver was adopted as the exclusive standard.

In 1841, however, the Indian governments found it expedient to authorize their collectors to receive gold mohurs whenever tendered. But in December 1852, a public notification was issued, that gold coins would be no longer received by the public officers. The effect of this notification, which is still in force, is again to render silver the single standard metal in India.

The origin of the change of December 1852 is said to have

been a somewhat sudden increase in the quantity of gold coin tendered by the public, and an apprehension, on the part of the government, that they might possibly be led into the predicament of having to accept all payments made to them in gold as the cheaper metal, and to make all payments to others in silver, the dearer metal, and the only form of legal tender.

The question is an intricate one; but it seems to be probable that the notification of December 1852 was somewhat hastily adopted.

The quantity of silver coin in use in India is quite enormous. The mass of silver coin held as the cash reserves of the several public treasuries, in various parts of India, frequently amounts to 12 or 15 millions sterling. The introduction of railways and telegraphs will materially economize these reserves.

But the principal form in which silver is absorbed in India is as personal ornaments – bracelets, brooches, hair-pins, etc.

There are no means of ascertaining, by any authentic data, the amount of silver in use in India as coin and ornaments; and any attempts at numerical statement are little better than mere conjectures.

It is, however, quite conceivable that the mass of silver may amount to 400 millions sterling; and considering the nature of the forms in which it is principally found, we can scarcely estimate the annual loss by wear and abrasion at less than 1 per cent, or say, 4 millions per annum.

Upon such a basis the net imports of 2 millions sterling per annum of silver would only half suffice to replace the annual loss on the existing stock.

And I am inclined to think that, for a very long period of time, the imports of silver into India have been barely adequate to maintain the level of the previous enormous quantity.

I have referred, in a former Appendix (App. ii), to the importance of the element of wear and tear in all questions relating to the precious metals; and India is, I believe, one of the most striking illustrations of the vast consequences involved in this consideration.

The total shipments to the several countries given in Table A will appear from the summary shown in Table B.

Table A   *Shipments of gold and silver to India and China from the United Kingdom and from ports in the Mediterranean, during each of the six years 1851–56, according to the returns compiled by Mr James Low, exchange broker, 5 Austin Friars.*

Shipped from England	1856 Gold	1856 Silver	1855 Gold	1855 Silver	1854 Gold	1854 Silver	1853 Gold	1853 Silver
1	2	3	4	5	6	7	8	9
	£	£	£	£	£	£	£	£
Per P. & O. C. steamers to –								
India:								
Bombay	8,	4,748,	1,	2,267,	—	202,	2,	1,574,
Madras	28,	213,	18,	177,	—	28,	22,	173,
Calcutta	1,	3,417,	—	2,300,	—	100,	—	814,
	37,	8,378,	19,	4,644,	—	330,	24,	2,561,
Straits:								
Penang	—	52,	—	23,	—	20,	—	48,
Singapore	30,	514,	27,	283,	90,	362,	9,	460,
	67,	8,944,	46,	4,950,	90,	712,	33,	3,079,
China:								
Hong Kong	130,	1,443,	214,	625,	227,	916,	93,	670,
Canton	—	520,	—	532,	2,	1,342,	18,	826,
Shanghai	—	1,203,	21,	200,	—	120,	—	6,
	197,	12,110,	281,	6,307,	329,	3,090,	144,	4,581,
Other places	208,	8,	667,	103,	812,	10,	516,	39,
	405,	12,118,	948,	6,410,	1,141,	3,100,	760,	4,620,
Per G. N. S. N. C. Steamers	—	—	—	—	33,	31,	134,	226,
Total from England	405,	12,118,	948,	6,410,	1,174,	3,131,	894,	4,846,
Total from Marseilles, Gibraltar, and Malta	74,	1,990,	243,	1,524,	48,	1,451,	92,	847,
	479,	14,108,	1,191,	7,934,	1,222,	4,582,	986,	5,693,

NOTE. The three figures at unit end are omitted: thus 8 represents £8,000.

And the general abstract, shown in Table C, compiled from the tables furnished by Mr Low, will show the total exports of gold and silver to the east, as far as ascertained during the six years 1851–56.

In addition to these tables, derived from the circular of Mr Low, I gladly avail myself of certain returns published in the *Daily News* of 24 January 1857, as compiled by the city

Table B *Summary of Table A as regards shipments from United Kingdom per P. and O. steamers, 1853–56.*

Places	1856 Gold	1856 Silver	1855 Gold	1855 Silver	1854 Gold	1854 Silver	1853 Gold	1853 Silver
1	2	3	4	5	6	7	8	9
	£	£	£	£	£	£	£	£
India	37,	8,378,	19,	4,644,	—	330,	24,	2,561,
Straits	30,	564,	27,	306,	90,	382,	9,	508,
China	130,	3,166,	225,	1,357,	230,	2,378,	111,	1,502,
Other Places	208,	8,	667,	103,	812,	10,	516,	39,
	405,	12,118,	948,	6,410,	1,141,	3,100,	760,	4,620,

editor of that paper, relative to the arrivals of gold and silver in the United Kingdom during each month of 1856. From these returns I have drawn out Table C*. The *Daily News* is honourably distinguished among the journals of the present time for the ability with which financial questions are discussed in its columns. I have not the good fortune to acquiesce in many of the doctrines put forward; but I fully appreciate the calmness, intelligence, and impartiality with which the investigation is pursued by the writers in this journal.

Table C *Gold and Silver. Total shipments to east, 1851–56.*

Years	Gold From Great Britain	Gold From Mediterranean ports	Gold Total	Silver From Great Britain	Silver From Mediterranean ports	Silver Total
1	2	3	4	5	6	7
	£	£	£	£	£	£
1851	102,	not given	102,	1,716,	not given	1,716,
1852	922,	,,	922,	2,630,	,,	2,630,
1853	880,	93,	973,	4,710,	848,	5,558,
1854	1,174,	48,	1,222,	3,132,	1,451,	4,583,
1855	948,	243,	1,191,	6,409,	1,524,	7,933,
1856	404,	74,	478,	12,118,	1,990,	14,108,
	4,431,	460,	4,888,	30,718,	5,813,	36,528,

Table C* *Gold and Silver, 1856. Imports into United Kingdom from Australia, United States, and from West Indies and Mexico, according to the data collected by the city editor of the* Daily News.

1856	Gold from		Silver from West Indies, Mexico, etc.	Total gold and silver
	Australia	United States		
1	2	3	4	5
	Mlns.	Mlns.	Mlns.	Mlns.
	£	£	£	£
Jan.	0·67	0·12	0·80	1·63
Feb.	0·32	0·07	0·72	1·15
Mch.	0·65	0·37	0·36	1·41
	1·64	0·56	1·88	4·18
Apl.	1·12	0·35	0·69	2·18
May	1·66	0·78	0·36	2·94
June	1·29	0·92	0·88	2·90
	4·07	2·05	1·93	8·02
July	0·71	1·18	0·63	2·76
Aug.	1·14	1·60	0·54	2·67
Sept.	0·67	0·69	0·75	2·17
	2·52	3·47	1·92	7·60
Oct.	0·37	0·80	0·35	1·58
Nov.	1·27	1·10	0·43	2·70
Dec.	0·36	0·60	0·38	1·54
	2·00	2·50	1·16	5·82
Total of 1856	10·25	8·60	6·82	25·63

NOTE. The four unit figures are omitted: thus, 0·67 represents £670,000.

The imports from China into India (including treasure) are stated to have been about 1½ millions, during each of the four years, leaving, therefore, a balance against China of about 2 millions sterling in favour of India.

The quantity of tea exported from China to the United States during the eight years 1849–56 is stated in Table E.

The imports into China from the United States are very limited in amount. The payments due to China from the United States are almost wholly provided for by means of the trade of the United States with England.

The total value of the imports into the United Kingdom

Table D *China (including Hong Kong), exports to and imports from, as regards the Unite d Kingdom, five year 1850–54.*

Cotton manufac-tures and yarn	Woollen manufac-tures	Metals	All other articles	Total exports	Years	Tea	Silk	Tea	Silk	Total imports

	Exports to China (declared value)					Imports from China				
						Quantities		Estimated value		
Cotton manufac-tures and yarn	Woollen manufac-tures	Metals	All other articles	Total exports	Years	Tea	Silk	Tea	Silk	Total imports
1	2	3	4	5	6	7	8	9	10	11
£	£	£	£			lb.	lb.	£	£	£
1,020,	404,	48,	102,	1,574,	1850	49,368,	1,770,	3,110,	1,332,	4,442,
1,596,	373,	75,	117,	2,161,	1851	69,487,	2,055,	4,200,	1,540,	5,740,
1,904,	433,	65,	101,	2,503,	1852	65,295,	2,418,	3,920,	1,810,	5,730,
1,406,	203,	40,	101,	1,750,	1853	68,640,	2,838,	4,080,	2,175,	6,255,
640,	156,	62,	142,	1,000,	1854	83,301,	4,576,	5,380,	3,320,	8,700,
882,	126,	126,	133,	1,277,	1855	81,560,	4,436,	5,118,	3,013,	8,131,

NOTE. The Declared or Real Value of the Exports of Opium and other merchandise from Bengal to China during the four years 1853–56, is estimated as follows:

Year ended 30 June	£
1852–3	3,830,000 real value.
'53–4	3,271,000 ,, ,,
'54–5	3,006,000 ,, ,,
'55–6	3,284,000 ,, ,,

And to these exports to China must be added the exports from Bombay and Madras.

from China has been about £500,000 beyond the amounts set forth in col. 11 of Table D.

The general result, therefore, of the China trade during the six years 1850–55, may be estimated as shown in Table F.

The abstract (Table H) will collect, in a concise form, the results of the preceding Table G for the several periods of years into which it is divided.

Table E *Tea exported from China to United States.*

Year ended 30 June	lb.	Estimated value £
1848–49	18,072,000	1,170,000
1849–50	21,757,000	1,430,000
1850–51	28,700,000	1,880,000
1851–52	34,334,000	2,221,000
1852–53	40,974,000	2,665,000
1853–54	27,867,000	1,820,000
1854–55	31,515,000	2,010,000
1855–56	40,246,000	2,600,000

Table F   *China Trade, 1850–55. Estimate of the amount in millions sterling of the total China trade during each of the six years.*

	1855	1854	1853	1852	1851	1850	Total
1	2	3	4	5	6	7	8
	Mlns.	Mlns.	Mlns.	Mlns.	Mlns.	Mlns.	Mlns.
	£	£	£	£	£	£	£
Exports from China to:							
United Kingdom	8·6	9·2	6·7	6·2	6·2	5·0	41·9
India	1·5	1·5	1·5	1·5	1·5	1·5	9·0
United States	2·6	2·1	1·9	2·6	2·2	2·0	13·4
	12·7	12·8	10·1	10·3	9·9	8·5	64·3
Imports from China from:							
United Kingdom	1·3	1·0	1·7	2·5	2·1	1·6	10·2
India	3·6	3·7	3·6	4·2	4·2	4·2	23·5
United States	0·3	0·3	0·3	0·3	0·3	0·3	1·8
	5·2	5·0	5·6	7·0	6·6	6·1	35·5
Balance in *favour* of China	7·5	7·8	4·5	3·3	3·3	2·4	28·8
	12·7	12·8	10·1	10·3	9·9	8·5	64·3

In connexion with Table G, made up from the returns of the Custom houses in India, we may usefully consider the statement of the trade with India, as made up by our own Board of Trade.

With the year 1854 the Board of Trade commenced a system which enabled them to ascertain the real value of the imports, as well as the exports, to India and other Countries. Prior to 1854, the quantities of the articles imported can only be given.

In the subsidiary Table I, I have given an abstract of the English returns for the five years 1851–56, enumerating the leading articles both of import and export.

The rapid expansion of the value of the exports to India, from 7 millions sterling in 1851 to 10 millions sterling in 1855, is a result which will arrest attention.

As regards the last five of these Tables K, L, M, N and O, I desire to draw the attention of the reader to the statements contained at pages *ante*, relative to the real nature of the bullion trade of India, and of the comparatively limited coinage of India.

Thomas Tooke

Table G *British India. Statement (in millions), according to the books of the East India Company, of the real value of the imports and exports of merchandise and treasure into and from the whole of India, during the years (ended 30 April) 1834–35 to 1854–55; omitting the mere port to port trade from one part of India to another.*

Years ended 30th April	Merchandise — United Kingdom Impts. from	United Kingdom Expts. to	Other countries Impts. from	Other countries Expts. to	Totals Impts. from	Totals Expts. to	Treasure (gold and silver) whole world Impts. from	Treasure Expts. to	East India Co.'s drafts — Bills sold in London by E. I. Co.	Bills bought under hypothecation in India
1	2	3	4	5	6	7	8	9	10	11
	Mlns. £	Mlns. £	Mlns. £	Mlns. £	Mlns. £	Mlns. £	Mlns. £	Mlns. £	Mlns. £	Mlns. £
1834–35	2·7	3·0	1·6	4·9	4·3	8·0	1·9	·2	·7	not given
1835–36	3·1	4·0	1·6	7·1	4·8	11·1	2·1	·1	2·0	—
1836–37	3·8	4·9	1·7	8·3	5·5	13·2	2·0	·2	2·0	—
1837–38	3·2	4·3	1·8	6·9	5·0	11·2	2·6	·3	1·7	1·6
1838–39	3·5	4·5	1·7	7·2	5·2	11·8	3·0	·3	2·3	0·8
1839–40	4·3	5·9	1·5	4·9	5·8	10·8	1·9	·5	1·4	1·0
							13·5	1·6	10·1	—
1840–41	6·0	7·0	2·4	6·4	8·4	13·4	1·8	·3	1·2	1·2
1841–42	5·4	7·1	2·3	6·7	7·8	13·8	1·8	·5	2·6	0·4
1842–43	5·3	5·8	2·2	7·7	7·6	13·5	3·4	·2	1·2	0·6
1843–44	6·3	7·7	2·5	9·5	8·8	17·2	4·8	·7	2·8	0·2
1844–45	7·9	7·2	2·8	9·3	10·7	16·6	3·7	1·1	2·5	0·6
							15·5	2·8	10·3	3·0
1845–46	6·5	6·6	2·6	10·3	9·1	17·0	2·5	·8	3·1	0.5
1846–47	6·4	6·5	2·5	8·8	8·9	15·3	2·9	·7	3·1	1·3
1847–48	5·8	5·7	2·8	7·6	8·6	13·3	2·0	1·4	1·5	not given
1848–49	5·5	6·2	2·8	9·9	8·3	16·1	4·2	2·5	1·9	,,
1849–50	7·6	7·0	2·7	10·3	10·3	17·3	3·4	1·0	2·9	,,
							15·0	6·4	12·5	—
1850–51	8·3	8·1	3·2	10·0	11·5	18·1	3·8	·5	3·2	not given
1851–52	9·2	7·1	3·0	12·7	12·2	19·9	5·0	·9	2·8	,,
1852–53	7·2	8·4	2·7	12·1	10·1	20·4	6·8	1·0	3·3	,,
1853–54	8·4	7·7	2·7	11·6	11·1	19·3	4·9	1·5	3·8	,,
1854–55	9·6	6·9	2·8	11·4	12·4	18·3	2·0	1·9	3·7	,,
							22·5	5·8	16·8	—

NOTE. The five unit figures are omitted: thus, 9·6 represents £9,600,000.

Table H *Summary of Table G, according to the annual averages of the periods of years 1834–35 to 1854–55.*

Groups of years ended 30 April	Merchandise — United Kingdom Imports from	United Kingdom Exports to	Other countries Imports from	Other countries Exports to	Totals Imports from	Totals Exports to	Treasure (gold and silver) whole world Imports from	Treasure Exports to	Bills sold in London by E. I. Co.	Bills bought under hypot. in India
1	2	3	4	5	6	7	8	9	10	11
	Mlns. £	Mlns. £	Mlns. £	Mlns. £	Mlns. £	Mlns. £	Mlns. £	Mlns. £	Mlns. £	Mlns. £
1835–40	3·4	4·4	1·7	6·5	5·1	11·0	2·3	0·4	1·7	1·0
1841–45	6·2	6·9	2·4	7·9	8·6	14·9	3·1	0·6	2·1	0·6
1846–50	6·3	6·3	2·7	9·4	9·4	15·8	3·0	1·3	2·5	1·0
1851–55	8·5	7·6	2·9	11·5	11·4	19·2	4·5	1·2	3·4	not given

NOTE. The cols. 10 and 11, which exhibit the amount of the drafts of the East India Company sold in London (col. 10), and the amount advanced in India by the East India Company on the hypothecation of goods (col. 11), have been already explained in Appendix XXI. The figures in col. 11 cannot be obtained for the whole period.

Table I *Whole of India (exclusive of Ceylon and Singapore). Statement of the real value of the imports from, and exports to, as regards the United Kingdom, according to the returns of the Board of Trade.*

(1) Imports from India, real values.

Articles	1855	1954	1953	1952	1851
1	2	3	4	5	6
	Mlns.	Mlns.			
	£	£			
Cotton, raw	2·24	1·64			
Hemp	0·57	0·67			
Hides	0·48	0·40			
Indigo	1·52	1·54			
Oils	0·34	0·21			
Saltpetre	0·26	0·60	Real value not given for		
Rice	1·56	0·87	1853, 1852, and 1851.		
Seeds	1·88	0·77			
Silk, raw	0·56	0·40			
Silk, manufactures	0·26	0·28			
Sugar	1·03	0·88			
Wool, sheep's	0·50	0·40			
All other articles	1·47	2·00			
Totals	12·67	10·67			

(2) Exports to India, real values.

	1855	1954	1953	1952	1851
Beer and Ale	0·44	0·30	0·26	0·17	0·15
Copper	0·36	0·16	0·18	0·20	0·30
Cotton manufactures	5·84	6·56	5·07	4·70	5·04
Iron	1·24	0·45	0·35	0·18	0·27
Machinery	0·40	0·10	0·09	0·04	0·03
Woollen mnfs.	0·27	0·36	0·27	0·21	0·27
All other articles	1·39	1·19	0·09	0·97	0·95
	9·95	9·12	7·32	6·48	7·02
Foreign and Colonial Produce	0·40	0·50	0·40	0·40	0·40
	10·35	9·62	7·72	6·88	7·42
India House Drafts	3·70	3·80	3·30	2·80	3·20
	14·05	13·42	11·02	9·68	10·62
Deduct apparent balance in favour of United Kingdom	1·38	2·85	—	—	—
	12·67	10·67			

Table K *Gold and silver. Imports and exports, by sea: whole of India (Bengal, Madras and Bombay), during the eight years (ended 30 April) 1846–47 to 1853–54.*

Total of gold and silver		Years ended 30 Apl.	Gold		Silver	
Imported	Exported		Imported	Exported	Imported	Exported
1	2	3	4	5	6	7
£	£		£	£	£	£
2,940,	714,	1846–47	852,	3,	2,088,	711,
1,972,	1,426,	1847–48	1,048,	10,	924,	1,416,
4,204,	2,539,	1848–49	1,402,	53,	2,802,	2,486,
3,396,	971,	1849–50	1,160,	65,	2,236,	906,
3,811,	541,	1850–51	1,155,	2,	2,656,	539,
5,052,	919,	1851–52	1,339,	71,	3,713,	848,
6,831,	1,055,	1852–53	1,335,	169,	5,496,	886,
4,848,	788,	1853–54	1,078,	4,	3,770,	784,
4,132,	1,119,	Average (8 years)	1,171,	47,	2,960,	1,072,
33,054,	8,953,	Total (8 years)	9,369,	377,	23,685,	8,576,
25,101,	—	Excess of Imports	8,992,	—	15,109,	—

Table L *Whole of India. Imports and exports of gold and silver. Summary, eight years, 1846–47 to 1853–54.*

(1) GOLD

IMPORTED into the whole of India		From or To	EXPORTED from whole of India	
Average	Total		Total	Average
£	£		£	£
40,000	324,000	United Kingdom	206,000	26,000
8,000	62,000	Foreign Europe	—	—
5,000	42,000	America	—	—
594,000	4,758,000	China	12,000	1,000
522,000	4,180,000	All other Places	156,000	19,000
1,169,000	9,366,000		374,000	46,000

(2) SILVER

Average	Total	From or To	Total	Average
665,000	5,325,000	United Kingdom	2,269,000	284,000
28,000	225,000	Foreign Europe	8,000	1,000
8,000	63,000	America	7,000	1,000
1,356,000	10,850,000	China	452,000	56,000
898,000	7,183,000	All other Places	5,832,000	729,000
2,955,000	23,646,000		8,568,000	1,071,000

Table M *Whole of India.* (1) Gold imported and exported (*by sea*) from and to the following countries, *viz.*

Years ended 30 April	United Kingdom		Foreign Europe		America		China		All other places		Totals	
	Imptd. from	Exptd. to	Imptd. from	Exptd. to	Imptd. from	Exptd. to	Imptd. from	Exptd. to	Imptd. from	Exptd. to	Imptd. from	Exptd. to
1	2	3	4	5	6	7	8	9	10	11	12	13
	£	£	£	£	£	£	£	£	£	£	£	£
1846–47	—	—	2,	—	16,	—	460,	—	347,	3,	851,	3,
1847–48	23,	3,	—	—	20,	—	516,	—	490,	6,	1,049,	9,
1848–49	15,	38,	—	—	6,	—	934,	—	445,	14,	1,401,	52,
1849–50	10,	36,	—	—	—	—	634,	—	515,	28,	1,159,	64,
1850–51	22,	—	—	—	—	—	695,	—	438,	2,	1,155,	2,
1851–52	72,	—	—	—	—	—	693,	—	573,	70,	1,338,	70,
1852–53	130,	129,	60,	—	—	—	568,	10,	576,	30,	1,334,	169,
1853–54	52,	—	—	—	5,	—	258,	2,	769,	3,	1,077,	5,
Ave.	40,	26,	8,	—	—	—	594,	1,	522,	19,	1,170,	46,
Total	324,	206,	62,	—	42,	—	4,758,	12,	4,180,	156,	9,364,	374,

(2) *Silver: whole of India.*

Years ended 30 April	United Kingdom		Foreign Europe		America		China		All other places		Totals	
	Imptd. from	Exptd. to	Imptd. from	Exptd. to	Imptd. from	Exptd. to	Imptd. from	Exptd. to	Imptd. from	Exptd. to	Imptd. from	Exptd. to
1846–47	1,	—	—	—	7,	—	1,450,	—	628,	709	2,086,	709,
1847–48	35,	704.	1,	—	21,	5,	520,	32,	346,	674,	923,	1,415,
1848–49	21,	1,460,	1,	—	12,	2,	2,174,	—	595,	1,023,	2,802,	2,485,
1849–50	16,	82,	18,	6,	6,	—	1,692,	60,	520,	757,	2,235,	905,
1850–51	480,	10,	58,	—	3,	—	1,150,	1,	1,003,	527,	2,654,	538,
1851–52	969,	6,	22,	—	13,	—	1,608,	3,	1,064,	838,	3,712,	847,
1852–53	2,210,	—	155,	2,	1,	—	1,862,	21,	1,400,	865,	5,495,	886,
1853–54	1,593,	7,	28,	1,	—	1,	394,	335,	1,627,	439,	3,769,	783,
Ave.	665,	284,	28,	—	8,	1,	1,356,	56,	898,	729,	2,959,	1,071,
Total	5,325,	2,269,	225,	8,	63,	7,	10,850,	452,	7,183,	5,832,	23,676,	8,568,

Thomas Tooke

Table N   *Whole of India year 1853–54. Detail of the total, representing the imports and exports in the column headed 'All other places', in the preceding Table M.*

Gold			Silver	
Imported	Exported	From or to	Imported	Exported
1	2	3	4	5
£	£	£	£	£
—	—	Malta	3,000	—
20,000	—	Suez	450,000	5,000
16,000	—	Aden	93,000	8,000
119,000	2,000	Ceylon	835,000	294,000
44,000	—	Penang	21,000	—
—	1,000	Malacca Straits	—	63,000
29,000	—	Arabian Gulph	45,000	4,000
134,000	—	Persian Gulph	113,000	7,000
2,000	—	Africa	14,000	4,000
3,000	—	Cape of Good Hope	—	—
70,000	—	Mauritius	21,000	54,000
2,000	—	Bourbon	31,000	—
350,000	—	New South Wales	1,000	—
769,000	3,000		1,627,000	439,000

Table O   *Silver coinage for the whole of India (that is, of the three mints of Calcutta, Madras and Bombay), distinguishing the bullion delivered by the public and the uncurrent coins cancelled by the treasuries, 1835–36 to 1854–55.*

Years ended 30 April	Silver received from public	Uncurrent coins from treasury	Silver coinage	Years ended 30 April	Silver received from public	Uncurrent coins from treasury	Silver coinage
1	2	3	4	1	2	3	4
	Mlns.	Mlns.	Mlns.		Mlns.	Mlns.	Mlns.
	£	£	£		£	£	£
1835–36	1·35	1·46	2·27	1845–46	2·26	1·43	3·84
1836–37	1·25	2·25	3·81	1846–47	1·78	1·41	2·92
1837–38	1·81	1·78	3·19	1847–48	0·62	0·88	1·78
1838–39	1·99	1·59	3·85	1848–49	0·94	0·65	2·58
1839–40	1·92	1·22	3·14	1849–50	1·93	0·57	2·41
Average	1·66	1·66	3·25	Average	1·50	0·99	2·71
1840–41	1·66	1·15	2·84	1850–51	2·27	0·99	2·61
1841–42	2·10	1·87	3·29	1851–52	3·73	0·96	4·24
1842–43	3·07	0·48	3·30	1852–53	5·45	0·49	5·51
1843–44	3·54	0·94	4·67	1853–54	3·28	0·80	5·25
1844–45	3·56	1·21	4·70	1854–55	0·42	0·61	1·36
Average	2·78	1·13	3·76	Average	3·03	0·77	3·79
Totals ten yrs.	22·25	13·95	35·06	Totals ten yrs.	22·68	8·79	32·50

3

John Horsley Palmer, Minutes of Evidence taken before the Select Committee on the Affairs of the East India Company

Veneris, 16° die Martii, 1832

THOMAS HYDE VILLIERS, ESQ., IN THE CHAIR

John Horsley Palmer, Esq., called in; and examined

1281. Mr Palmer, you are Governor of the Bank of England, and partner in the East India house of Palmers, Mackillop and Company? – Yes.

1282. Will you be so good as to state whether, in your opinion, it is necessary for the East India Company to carry on trade in order to make their financial remittances to this country? – I should think the financial remittances to this country might be made with perfect facility, without the necessary consequence of the Company carrying on trade to the extent to which I understand it to exist.

1283. Do you consider that there would be a facility of remittance from India or through China to the amount of three millions and a half sterling, and if so, will you have the goodness to state the mode in which you think that might be done? – I should think that three millions and a half sterling might be remitted without difficulty from China and India together; and the mode in which I would submit that should be done would be with reference to bullion and the general exports. The trade itself will furnish a value of three millions and a half sterling as at present existing; and provided bills of exchange secured upon that trade were tendered to the Company at the bullion price, I see no reason why those goods should not be deposited in the possession of the Company until the bills were paid. The invoice

190

value of the goods upon which I found that opinion are three millions and a half, or nearly so, from Bengal, and two millions from China.

1284. What, in your opinion, would be the average exchange at which such remittances could be effected in that matter? – I think they ought to be effected at the bullion price, which would be from 1s. 11½d. to 2s. per sicca rupee.

1285. Do you not also think it necessary to make allowance for the interest in the interval between the money being advanced in one country and the repayment being made in the order? – Distinctly not. All exchange operations in bills have reference to the actual produce of the remittance in bullion in the country to which those remittances are sent.

1286. Can you state any conclusions which you may have formed with respect to the value of the Sycee silver as compared with the sicca rupee, and of the rupee in sterling? – It so happens that we have very lately, within the last six weeks, received a remittance from Bengal in both those species of bullion, one was Sycee silver, and the other was the Bengal sicca rupee; and if the Committee will allow me, I will state precisely the out-turn of those two remittances. The Sycee silver is found to have, upon an average, about 12 grains of gold in a pound of silver, troy weight. The Sycee silver was sold in this market at 4s. 11d. seven-eighths per ounce British standard, including eight grains of gold.

1287. What do you mean by including eight grains of gold? – Because the buyers take no cognizance of any quantity not exceeding eight grains.

1288. Then no additional value is given to it unless it has more than eight grains? – No; all above eight grains is paid for in the additional value of the silver, and therefore the silver was virtually sold, containing the 12 grains, at 5s. 0½d. per ounce.

1289. It contained 12 grains? – Twelve grains.

1290. Now, can you state its fineness? – No, I cannot; I do not know whether the Sycee silver is better or worse.

1291. Do you say that it was sold for 5s. 0½d. per ounce? – Yes, per ounce standard; reduced to standard; that Sycee silver, containing 12 grains of gold per pound, sold at 5s. 0½d. per ounce standard silver, gave an exchange of 1s. 11d. five-eighths per sicca rupee, calculated against a bill at six months' sight.

1292. Will you explain those words, 'calculated against a bill at six months' sight'; was interest taken off the proceeds for the period of six months, at five per cent? – I think it was five per cent.

1293. So that that makes it equivalent to a bullion remittance? – Yes.

1294. Upon the general run of remittances from India, comparing bullion with bills, and supposing bills to come to you at six months' sight, what percentage should you think fair to charge for the average risk upon bad bills on a merchant? – I should prefer a bill at the same rate, and would give no premium for bullion. Every person who takes a bill of exchange believes it to be good; and if he does not believe it to be as good as bullion he will not take it. If I have the opportunity of taking a bill at the same rate of exchange which bullion would give, I would take the bill of exchange in preference to a remittance in bullion, from the security of the payment of the bill by the triplicate copies.

1295. Have not you the same security as to the certainty of specie remittances by the practice of either insuring in London, or of making insurances in Bengal payable in London? – You have, certainly; but still there is always a certain degree of risk in the recovery of a policy; independent of the security of the person who has to pay, there are always legal questions to which the holder of a policy is liable, which would induce me to give the preference to a bill.

1296. What should you consider to be the charge per sicca rupee for the expense in bringing the bullion from India to London? – There are various charges.

1297. Can you state the rate of insurance now? – I think two per cent, and the freight a half per cent.

1298. Then 1s. 11d. and five-eighths per rupee, you state to be the net return, after the expense of bringing the bullion to England has been deducted? – Yes.

192

1299. In that you have taken the weight of the Sycee silver, containing the same weight of fine silver as if it had been a sicca rupee? – It is always turned into British standard.

1300. That is, you mean, supposing a sicca rupee and not Sycee silver to have been sent from India, it would have realized to you 1s. 11d. and five-eighths? – Not a sicca rupee; I am speaking merely of Sycee silver.

1301. But then you ought to tell us, with a rupee how much silver you bought in India, otherwise it gives us no criterion? – The Sycee silver cost in Calcutta 96 sicca rupees per 100 sicca weight.

1302. Are you able also to state what is the degree of fineness of the Sycee silver? – The Sycee silver was about eight penny-weights better than English standard.

1303. Are you aware that Sycee varies as to its intrinsic fineness very much in China, and that some buy it in China of a much finer and a much coarser quality? – No; upon my inquiry of the bullion brokers in London, I could not find that to be the case.

1304. What was the date of this transaction? – I think it is about six weeks ago.

1305. You have stated the quantity of gold that was in this Sycee silver; can you state what is the general quantity of gold in the Mexican dollar? – I cannot, but I think not more than four grains.

1306. So that the quantity of gold in the Sycee silver is evidently greater than in the Spanish dollar? – Certainly.

1307. Therefore the Sycee silver in China cannot be the Spanish dollar melted down in that country and exported? – Certainly not.

1308. Should you conclude from that, that it must be the silver of the country itself, of the mines of Asia? – Yes.

1309. What is the smallest quantity of gold which you understand it is worth the refiner's while to extract from silver under the improved process with sulphuric acid? – I think it is five grains; I believe four grains pays the expense, and it may be worth the refiner's while to buy it and refine it for that quantity; but it would not be worth the while of other people to do it under six or seven grains. I have stated that the Sycee silver gave at the price stated 1s. 11d. and five-eighths per sicca rupee; the sicca rupee at the same time, sent as coin from Calcutta, was sold at the same price of 4s. 11d. and seven-eighths per ounce British standard, and gave an exchange equal to 1s. 11¼d. per sicca rupee.

1310. Was the rupee of full weight? – Fair average weight.

1311. Coined at the Company's mint? – Yes.

1312. Melted down when it was sold, and brought to the same standard, of course? – Yes.

1313. What quantity of gold was there in the sicca rupee do you suppose? – Nothing worth extracting; I think it was about four grains.

1314. Talking of the par of exchange of a sicca rupee, you are of course aware it must depend in London on the market price of silver? – Yes; that which was sold six weeks ago at 4s. 11d. and seven-eighths per ounce, would not now sell for more than somewhere about 4s. 11d. and one-eighth; but that is under the circumstance of an unusual high exchange with Paris.

1315. Which at present exists? – Yes.

1316. Then it has fallen within six weeks? – Yes, the market price of silver.

1317. Have you any reason to expect in future a larger import of silver bullion from India than heretofore? – I should say certainly, in the present state of the exchange in India, particularly in Calcutta.

1318. Are there any peculiar circumstances that are likely to lead to an extension of the import of bullion into this country from India, that have come to your knowledge? – No, otherwise than by the reference to manufactured goods sent out, which have been remitted within the last 10 or 12 months at from 1s. 10¼d. to a halfpenny per sicca rupee by bills at six months' sight, the consequence of which has been, that orders have been transmitted from England to remit rupees or other silver bullion from India to England, which it is proved will give 1s. 11¼d. per rupee, and upwards.

1319. Has there been any order sent also to China to the same effect, to your knowledge? – I believe that the remittance from

China will be so small for proceeds of manufactures sent from this country, that it will hardly attract notice.

1320. Are there any silver mines worked in the Indian peninsula? – Not that I am aware of; I do not know.

1321. You conclude, that the sicca rupee is coined of Spanish American silver? – I do not know; I cannot answer that question; that information must be derived from the Calcutta mint.

1322. If you employ a refiner to extract the gold on the account of the owner of the silver, what percentage does he charge for making the separation? – There is a great deal of discussion going forward upon the question at the present moment, and therefore I cannot answer the question correctly. I think the quantity used to be about five grains.

1323. But they deducted the value of five grains? – Upon reference, I find that the refiners took three-fifths of eight grains, and gave the proprietor of the silver two-fifths, and all above eight grains; that was the proportion; but there is, as I have already said, a negotiation now in progress which may alter that proportion.

1324. Do you know that there has been heretofore any prejudice existing in the trade against the remittance of bullion to this country? – Certainly on the part of the Indian merchants.

1325. Do you consider that is still the case? – Yes, I consider an attempt has been made by the Indian merchants to retain the bullion in India, which it is quite impossible for them to do.

1326. Under what idea do you consider they have been anxious so to retain it? – From the scarcity of money that would ensue from the exportation of the metal.

1327. Does not the same prejudice obtain in all parts of the world among merchants, that the exportation of bullion from the country, and more especially of the coin of the country, has an immediate tendency to diminish the quantity of money in the market, and thereby to affect the prices of commodities, and produce what is called commercial distress? – Certainly; the knowledge that that will be the result is beyond dispute. But the question in India has been of a different character; there has been (perhaps the word prejudice was not a proper word to use) an idea in the minds of the native merchants, that they could by their own act retain the bullion in the country, and regulate the remittance by arbitrarily fixing their own rate of exchange.

1328. Although you entertain no doubt that any effort unnaturally to retain the bullion would be ineffectual, you do not entertain a doubt that the exportation of the bullion, and more especially of the current coin, has the effect of producing an immediate scarcity of money? – Distinctly so.

1329. Do you conceive that if the gold coin of this country could be introduced generally in India, that that measure would have a tendency to facilitate the operations of trade in any way? – No; I do not see in what way commerce would be promoted by our coin; it is quite immaterial what the coin is when the fineness is once known.

1330. You are aware that there are various descriptions of currency in India? – Still they all have their respective values.

1331. Do you consider that answer equally applicable to the gold as to the silver? – I apprehend that gold neither does nor will circulate to any extent as current coin in India, where silver forms the actual currency, and is a legal tender.

1332. Might not the effect of introducing, if it were possible, a gold currency in India, have an effect to raise the market value of gold all over the world, by introducing a large and extensive new application of it? – It might have the effect; but I should be directly opposed to an opinion of the propriety of introducing gold into India as the current coin of the realm.

1333. Are you not of opinion that between two countries like England and India, having very extensive and intimate commercial intercourse, that as far as that intercourse is concerned, there would be an advantage in having the legal standard in the same metal? – Certainly; and I think it would be much more beneficial for the world at large, that the same metal should universally prevail as the legal tender.

1334. Should you apprehend that any material inconvenience would necessarily arise to the circulation and currency of this country, supposing it at any time to become necessary to effect any considerable operation here in Indian finance, such for example as the transfer of any portion of Indian debt to this country, or the raising of a loan for the service of India? – Not if it is done with due regard to the existing circumstances at the time. The expenditure of India in this country is stated to be about three millions a year; therefore so far as regards those three millions, there would be no difficulty in raising a loan to that extent, paying off the Indian debt to the same amount by the revenue of India. An arrangement of that kind would, I conceive, be the least objectionable mode of transferring any portion of Indian debt to this country.

1335. But such an operation would not at all affect the difficulty, if difficulty there be, in the means of India to remit the three millions, or whatever sum India may have to remit to Europe, excepting in as far as the interest of the debt, by being borrowed in England, may be at a lower rate than the debt in India? – Certainly; there is no other advantage.

1336. Besides the two methods that you have mentioned of making remittances from India to England, namely, those of sending bullion, or of making advances in India upon the security of cargoes shipped by private merchants; would there not be a third, namely, that of the India Company drawing bills in England upon its Indian treasuries, and disposing of those bills in England to merchants? – The answer to the question of the Company drawing bills on India, would depend a good deal upon the state of their own imports from India and China to this country; if they are not importers themselves of produce, then I apprehend that a certain portion, and perhaps a considerable portion, might be obtained by their own bills on the treasuries of India.

1337. Supposing the India Company to give up trading both with India and with China, would not such a mode of remittance afford great accommodation to the private merchant carrying on those trades? – To a certain extent, I think it would; especially so far as may relate to the European and foreign capital embarked in the Indian and China trade.

1338. Would it not interfere with the exports from this country? – No.

1339. If you take bills payable in India or China, will there be as much exported from this country as there would be without that? – I think so, upon this ground, that the export trade to India and China does not seem to admit of much increase so long as we are receiving from India and China the sum required for the territorial purposes, which is brought in trade; if the Company are not the traders, other persons will, for their own profit, bring that supply which the demand requires.

1340. But is it not your opinion that India would bear a much larger export from this country than now takes place, if returns could be found for that which is sent from this country? – I do not know what articles of export from this country India could take more than are now sent.

1341. Is at present any considerable portion of the exchange business between England and India carried on by drafts in London? – I believe not to any considerable extent.

1342. Is it not in the nature of a trade with a distant country for the exchange operations to originate in the distant country, and not in London? – To a considerable extent.

1343. And more especially when the operations are mostly for the account of that distant country? – Yes.

1344. Are you aware that, in nearly all our commercial transactions with distant countries, with India, with America, and even with Russia, the exchange operations almost wholly originate in those countries, and that bills are seldom drawn from England upon them? – I think that it must be known to those persons engaged largely in trade, that very extensive credits have been taken from London prior to the parties leaving Europe for distant markets, which answer nearly the same purpose as taking bills from England.

1345. Is not that mode rather the means of carrying on the other operations of drawing from the distant country itself? – The Company are supposed to abandon trade, and still to have a large fund to bring from India to England; now, the consequence of the measures originating in India, and the parties not taking any quantities of money or bills from hence, would be throwing an excessive amount of bills into the market of India, which might so raise the exchange as to force bullion from this market for the purpose of meeting those bills in the event of their not being readily taken out of the market for the Company's remittances to Europe.

1346. Do you not think that if the Company were to abandon their trade with India and China, and that they were to be constantly offering bills drawn on their Indian treasuries for sale in this country, that that would probably give rise to houses established for the very purpose of negotiating such bills, and negotiating such bills with a view to facilitate the mercantile transactions of other houses? – I can only reply by stating, that I still believe a considerable portion of bills could be negotiated in this country in that state of the trade which has been supposed.

1347. Supposing there be any alteration made by which the trade should be transferred from the hands of the Company to individuals, the amount of trade being the same, there must always be the same means of remittance into whosoever hands it may fall? – Certainly.

1348. Although the means of remittance might be the same, should you not apprehend, if the Company were entirely debarred from trading either to India or China, and were left to rely upon remittances by bills from India, or drafts from England on India, the effect of the narrowness of the Indian market and the few houses transacting the business, together with the power they would have from the smallness of their number of combination, and the knowledge of the extent of the wants of the Company, and in many instances of the precise period when those wants occur, would lay the Company too much at the mercy of the combination in their operations? – My original answer was not intended to be confined to the Indian trade, but it was given under the presumption that the Company be debarred from all trade. The imports from China as well as India, about five millions and a half sterling, furnishing the means for making the Company's remittances, I do not apprehend any effect from combination, presuming the Company will at all times order bullion to be transmitted, if bills are not procurable at the bullion rate.

1349. Do you not suppose that the number of houses, which are now few at Calcutta, would be considerably augmented if the Company were to cease to export from India? – I entertain considerable doubt whether any great increase would take place.

1350. How many houses are there in Calcutta whose bills the Company might be reasonably supposed to take? – I do not believe that the Company will take the bills of any one house in Calcutta without very good security being attached to it.

1351. Is it your opinion, as a merchant connected with India, that the Company could with safety, year after year, take so large a sum as they would require of the houses established in Calcutta without collateral security? – I think they ought not to do it.

1352. If in your opinion it would be necessary in many cases to take collateral security, would it not in fairness, and to prevent reflections upon individual credit, become necessary to make it a general rule that in all cases there should be security? – Certainly.

1353. Could you state how many respectable houses there are in Calcutta? – I cannot answer that question; there have been several respectable houses established since the renewal of the charter.

1354. Do you apprehend that there would be any difficulty in the Company taking security with the bills they might take from these houses? – I apprehend not.

1355. Now, if the advances made by the Company upon bills drawn upon England were secured upon the bills of lading of the cargoes, and the Company were allowed to charge the insurance upon the cargoes, and to insure, would it be necessary that the Company should be very nice in its selection of the houses to which it made advances? – I think it is necessary that all mercantile transactions should be with houses of credit.

1356. But would not the circumstance of the bills being secured by the bills of lading on the cargoes make it much less necessary for the Company to be extremely nice in its selection? – I still think it would be necessary that the Company should act with houses of credit, otherwise they would have imposed upon them the duty of examining more nicely than might be convenient the quality of the goods that were so shipped, and the correctness of the invoice cost.

1357. Supposing the Company not to advance to the full

amount of the value of the article shipped, but to the amount only of two-thirds, would not that lessen the necessity of any rigid examination of the nature of the cargo? – The best answer I can give is with reference to our own individual case as merchants advancing money upon goods shipped from this country: it is the credit of the party with whom we act which guides us in our proceedings, and obviates the necessity of that examination as to the quality and price that would attach to a house of an inferior kind.

1358. You have stated that bills from India are available for the purpose of the territorial remittances by means of a security given on bills of lading; do you conceive that bills from China may be made equally available by means of any similar provision? – Certainly.

1359. Have you considered at all how you could effect that security? – I believe the Company have adopted that system in a limited degree from India.

1360. Have you considered how the territorial government of India could avail itself of bills from China with equal security as upon the bills of lading from India? – That would depend a good deal on the nature of the Company's agency in China. If the Company abandon all connexion with China and have no servants in Canton, of course there could be no persons to transact their business; but if they retain any part of their agency in China, either for the purpose of remittances or other occasions, then those parties would have the same power of attending to the securities as they have in the different parts of India.

1361. Supposing the commercial character of the Company to cease, do you conceive that the territorial government of India could establish an efficient agency at Canton for the purpose of effecting the remittances through those bills? – I have not given that subject any consideration; but I apprehend there would be no difficulty in making such an arrangement; the extent of the funds realized in China from India produce being very considerable, and which are necessarily to be returned to the different presidencies of India.

1362. And the returns to India are now made to a considerable amount in bullion, are they not? – There is a considerable amount of bullion sent. I have only seen the last two or three years; but a considerable amount of bullion has been sent from China to Bengal and Bombay.

1363. Is not the balance of trade between India and China considerably in favour of India? – Certainly, so far as it is exhibited by the remittance of bullion.

1364. Would not the necessity you mentioned of the Company's attending to the quality of goods which they should take as security, particularly in China, make it necessary for them to look almost as carefully at those goods, and to have nearly the same establishment for the purpose as if they were making purchases on their own account? – I think not, provided the house with which they were dealing were equally respectable with those with whom they would have the power of acting in different parts of India.

1365. Is it in your opinion probable that houses would establish themselves in a place like Canton of sufficient respectability? – I think so.

1366. When these goods arrive in England, supposing them to arrive to the extent and value to make them efficient for the purpose of the Company's remittances, would it not oblige the Company to keep a large establishment of ware-houses of some description, and a large establishment for the transaction of business to receive those goods until the bills were either paid, or security for the payment given? – I should think not; I think the Company should retain possession of those goods in the bonded warehouses of London and the outports, and they should never part with them until the bills be paid: but they should afford to the proprietors in the intermediate time every reasonable facility for the sale of the property.

1367. Taking all the circumstances into consideration, is the Committee to understand that it is your opinion that no material difficulty would arise to the Company's getting home, without trading itself, the means of making their payments in Europe? – Distinctly so; I beg to say that that answer is simply as regards the remittances, it is no opinion as to the policy of the Company abandoning any part of their present China trade.

1368. Do you consider that the necessity of realizing in

England a large amount for the use of the territory has been a great impediment to the growth of a profitable export trade from this country to India? – I do not believe that it has had any such effect.

1369. When this country is required to make a large expenditure upon the Continent, a more than ordinary expenditure on the Continent, has that any tendency to increase the export trade of this country? – If we export a large amount of the precious metals from hence so as to affect materially the prices of this country, and reduce them below the prices of other countries, it is probable that an export of commodities will take place to bring back the precious metals that have been so exported.

1370. And from the cause that you have stated, is not the effect of making a large continental expenditure generally this; to occasion a large increase at the time of the export of commodities? – A large export of commodities may follow from the course I have mentioned, but I am not prepared to answer the question, and say, that such export has been profitable to this country; it may have been so, but I do not feel able to answer the question decidedly.

1371. But has not that reduction of prices of which you spoke, consequent upon a great foreign expenditure, been materially to increase the export to the Continent of our commodities? – I should imagine it may have increased the export of commodities, but it probably diminished the imports at the same time.

1372. If therefore there was occasion, in case of war in India, for a large extra expenditure, should you not apprehend, that from the very cause that you have stated as applicable to this country, it would lead to an eventual large increase of the export of commodities from India to this country? – Does the question mean that we are furnishing the pecuniary means from England of carrying on this large Indian expenditure. If I understand the question, it is this: whether, in the event of a large pecuniary supply being required from England for the purpose of carrying on a war in India, that would not force a large export of commodities from England.

1373. No, the reverse; whether it would not occasion a large export of commodities from India to England, placing England in the situation of the Continent and placing India in the situation of this country. The question is, in case of a war requiring a large advance to be made on account of the territory of India in this country, whether that would not occasion a large export of commodities from India to England? – I do not consider the immediate export of commodities from India to be a necessary consequence of the case supposed. If bullion were likely to afford a more favourable remittance than goods, in payment of the supplies required from England, then bullion would be sent. It is probable that the effect of such a transmission of bullion would subsequently increase the exports and diminish the imports of India, from the fall in general prices likely to ensue in that country, and thereby cause a return of bullion to the extent previously exported.

1374. Supposing it was desirable upon general principles, upon the renewal of the Company's charter, to put an end to the Company's trade both with India and China, might it not be useful to leave them the occasional power of making a remittance by goods, not for the purpose of traffic, but for the purpose of occasionally securing their independence in the markets from which they might have to make those remittances? – I see no objection to the power being left, but I imagine that the Company would never use it if they were debarred from trade generally.

1375. What effect has the exercise of that power often had on the price of the commodities in which they made their investment, as upon indigo? I think it has not been beneficial.

1376. Has it not had the effect of occasioning the most enormous fluctuations in prices of the commodity, when it was known that the Company were in the market? – I think it is always prejudicial in a great body like the Company acting occasionally upon the market in India, by orders transmitted from this country.

1377. Did this country during war find it necessary to make consignments of merchandise for the purpose of meeting its foreign expenditure? – No, I believe not. I certainly do not think it desirable that the Company should continue purchasers of indigo and other principal articles in India, upon the system which has hitherto been pursued, which has had the effect of raising prices considerably, and thus stimulating an extra production, which, from an unfavourable out-turn attendant upon the sales in this country, has been subsequently checked, the extra quantity so produced thereby occasioning a glut in the market of India, and consequently an undue depreciation.

1378. And if the general rule were, that they were to abstain from making investments of merchandise, would not the effect of their suddenly breaking through that rule have a much worse effect in occasioning a great fluctuation of price than if it was their constant practice to be making investments in any article such as indigo? – I am not prepared to say there may not be occasions when the Company might, beneficially to the public, become purchasers, though I think, generally speaking, that their purchases in India have not been of that character.

1379. Is a practice to be justified, if you show that in particular instances it might have been productive of benefit; is not the best mode of determining the policy of any practice, to look at the general result after a series of years? – I think it is.

1380. You have stated that the exports from India and China amount to five millions and a half? – I believe them to be about that amount.

1381. Do you remember what the exports from this country to India and China may be? – My information is taken from the year 1828–29; I think in the year 1828–29 they were near three millions sterling to India.

1382. And to China? – And including China, to about £3,700,000 or £3,800,000.

1383. And that leaves what? – That leaves about £2,000,000; but then you must keep in view that the private merchant acts extensively with the foreigner, and thereby he relieves himself by the foreign trade for that which he would give to the Company as a remittance.

1384. Then if your exports from England were to increase considerably beyond your exports from India to this country, it would throw a difficulty in the way of remittance, would it not? – Except in bullion.

1385. You say that you expect a large exportation of bullion from India to take place? – Yes.

1386. Has India any natural means, except by its trade, of gaining bullion? – No, not that I am aware of.

1387. Then suppose that there is a great demand for bullion upon India, either unexpectedly or quicker than it can supply the deficiency, what will be the effect on the people of India under those circumstances? – Considerable pecuniary distress.

1388. Would not that pecuniary distress at last amount to an impossibility of further remittance? – No; I believe that it would have the effect of lowering the prices of commodities in India; both those sent from England and those produced in India, until an influx of bullion restored the prices to their former level.

1389. Suppose that the people of India at this moment are taxed to the greatest extent they can bear, and that bullion is exported from India to a large extent, so that all commodities are lowered in price, and they are still obliged to pay in the original sum, will not that have a very severe effect upon the community in general? – It would have a corresponding effect to that which would be produced in this country under similar circumstances.

1390. Will not everything that facilitates the export of articles the produce of India to China or other countries, be the best mode of relieving them from the danger of such an emergency? – Certainly.

1391. Will not facilitating the export trade of opium to China, and in return for such opium the obtaining large returns of bullion, be one of the most effectual means of preventing India from suffering in the manner presumed by the former question? – China can afford no more to part with her bullion to any unreasonable extent than India; bullion is the regulator of every description of trade throughout the world, and it will regulate the Indian trade, though in the course of that regulation the parties carrying on the commerce of India may occasionally sustain considerable inconvenience.

1392. If bullion is demanded from India as a regular mode of making the remittances to this country, in what manner can

India obtain that bullion but by exchanging her produce for the precious metal? – I hold it to be quite impossible that any country ever did or ever can permanently export its bullion.

1393. Do you mean by that answer to deny that a country can permanently continue to export bullion, even in the cases where that country regularly exports either its produce or manufactures in order to purchase bullion? – I mean simply that it cannot continue to export more bullion than it receives.

1394. If China obtains a considerable quantity of bullion, either by means of its mines, or in return for the tea that it exports, and if India sends a large quantity of opium, for which it receives in return a large quantity of bullion from China, may not India continue to export to this country a large supply of bullion? – Certainly; because there is no excess or deficiency on either side.

1395. And will not, therefore, everything that gives facility to India for obtaining bullion in exchange for opium, or any other of its produce, tend to facilitate the territorial remittance which India has constantly to make to this country? – Everything that tends to facilitate and promote the trade of India must be beneficial to India, and enable that country more readily to meet all its engagements.

1396. Are you aware to what extent the trade in opium has been increased since the year 1826 between India and China? – I really have not attended for the last four or five years to the details of trade with India, but I believe that the trade in opium has been very considerably increased.

1397. Are there not some articles of consumption of which the quantity consumed may not always be dependent on the question of price? – Certainly.

1398. May not opium be an article of that description? – Probably it is; the importation into China being prohibited, it is smuggled into that country to a very great extent.

1399. Now spices are articles of that description, are they not: you do not suppose that persons would use spices in any proportion to the diminution that might take place in their value? – I think certain spices would increase very much in point of consumption by reduction of the prices; pepper is an article which would be likely to increase considerably in consumption.

1400. Now for instance, pepper being now at 3d. a pound, do you suppose if it were reduced from 3d. to 2d. it would materially increase the consumption? – It is 3d. without duty; it is the duty that prohibits the use of pepper. If it could be sold for home consumption at 3d. or 2d. a pound, I apprehend a large increased consumption would take place in this country.

1401. Are you aware that the Dutch Company formerly, upon that principle, used to burn their spices, from a conviction that an increase of quantity would produce them no benefit? – That was the notion, certainly.

1402. May not opium, from the nature of the article, and of the impediments put in the way of its sale by the Chinese government, be an article of which the consumption might not increase in proportion to the diminution of price? – The trade of Canton is so peculiar from the character of the government, that there is no article carried to that port which might not be materially impeded in point of consumption.

1403. Are you not aware that opium is an article which becomes so necessary for those who consume it, that when once they begin it they cannot leave it off? – I believe that to be the case.

1404. Without knowing the particular details of the opium trade, are you not aware that since 1826 there has been a very great increase in the consumption of opium, at the same time that the price has fallen? – I do not know that the price has fallen; I believe there has been a great increase in the export from India.

1405. In a country like India, where the people have fixed money payments to make, would not the distress arising from the constant export of bullion take place, before the remedy which you allude to might reinstate the equilibrium of the precious metals? – I think India would sustain a very considerable degree of inconvenience, from their supply being a distant one.

1406. That therefore, taking into consideration the general condition of India, any system which should constantly expose it to an exportation of bullion, must occasion considerable permanent distress in the country? – A constant exportation of bullion I believe cannot take place from any country; the moment the pressure is felt, that moment the commencement of the remedy arises.

1407. The question and answer presumes that there will be a distress arising from the constant exportation of bullion; in that answer, you mean that distress would arise if bullion were exported to such an extent as to diminish the quantity required for the currency of the country, but you do not apprehend that distress would arise if there were constant imports beyond the quantity required for the currency, and a constant export of that same excess? – No.

1408. But does not the distress consequent upon the diminution of the currency precede the remedy? – Certainly.

1409. And therefore must be felt before the remedy can come in play? – Clearly so.

1410. Are you aware when there has been a considerable exportation, that the price of bullion has risen in India when the demand has been considerable? – The demand I rather think has been temporary, and during that temporary demand the price has probably advanced. I am not prepared to speak to the present price without reference.

1411. Would not all difficulties thrown in the way of the export trade of opium, very materially tend to prevent the acquiring by India of any surplus quantity of bullion for the exportation? – If you destroy the export trade from India to the place from whence it receives its bullion, so far you injure the power of India to supply bullion to that part of the world where it is required.

1412. And to that extent you would inflict an injury upon the natives of India? – Certainly, always adverting to a surplus export of bullion.

1413. But does not an export of bullion consequent upon a political payment, differ very much in its effect upon a country from any export arising from a commercial payment, in as far as the commercial payment is apt to cease with the difficulty, but the political payment is one which must be made without reference to the means of the country making it? – I do not draw the distinction, because a payment made politically in bullion, has the same effect upon the currency of the country as if made commercially, and if continued will so contract the currency of that country as to affect the whole of its prices.

1414. But does not that suppose that that country has some production which other countries must take? – There is hardly a country in the world the productions of which will not find a market at a certain value. If a country is supposed to have no productions, then there is an end of the power of payment. Bullion can only be taken as the medium; the payment must be made by the industry of the country; and I can draw no distinction between the payment such as the Committee alludes to, namely, a political payment by India, or a payment for foreign war by England. If our expenditure on the continent of Europe be thirty millions or fifty millions in the year, it is quite impossible to furnish that in bullion, and therefore by the same reasoning, I maintain it is quite impossible for any other country to continue to furnish politically any payment of bullion that the produce of that country will not re-supply.

1415. Applying the case to a very poor country like Norway, and supposing Norway to have a political payment to make of two millions and a half, would any effort that those people could make, raise anything which the world would take in fulfilment of such a payment? – If Norway has nothing to offer in payment of those continued remittances, there is an end to the existence of Norway as a nation: if she has no productions, the money is tantamount to production as long as it exists; when that is gone, there is an end of her power to pay.

1416. Then would follow an absolute inability to make the payment? – Yes.

1417. Is there not therefore an end to the principle, that there must be the means of making any payment for which there is an obligation, but that it must depend at last upon the ability of the country to produce those means? – No country can pay without the means of paying.

1418. Your theory then is that it is not finite? – My opinion is more practical than theoretical; theoretically, the Committee are right in the mode in which they put the question; but practically speaking, I doubt whether every country which has the power or the credit to incur a debt such as the Committee allude to as being required to be paid, has not within itself the means of payment from its own industry.

1419. In what respect does the tribute which India pays differ from the remittances which Ireland has to make to the resident absentees in this country? – I do not imagine there is any material difference.

1420. And the greater the tribute any country has to pay, whether it be a political payment, or whether it be rents, the greater the necessity, is it not, for giving to that country every facility for disposing of its produce for the purpose of making good such payment? – Certainly.

1421. If this country were to prevent the export of the cattle or the butter to this country from Ireland, would there not be the greatest difficulty to the Irish of making good their payments? – I suppose so.

1422. Upon the same principle, everything that tends to prevent India from disposing of her opium, must tend to prevent her making good the political payment to this country? – Everything that tends to check the trade in the productions of India, is certainly prejudicial with reference to its engagements.

1423. The exports from India and China to England being five millions and a half, and the returns from England to India and China three and a half, it would appear that that leaves a surplus of two millions only for territorial remittance to England; but in considering the whole territorial power of remittance, must you not take into account the balance of the trade between Calcutta and Canton? – The power of remittance is intimately connected with the whole trade between foreign countries and India; the balance of the trade with China, so far furnishes the means of remittance in bullion. There are three millions and a half of exports from England to the different presidencies of India, and China; and the returns from thence to England are about five millions and a half, to which is to be added the balance of the foreign trade with India, as part of the means for furnishing the remittance which the Company require.

1424. But then beyond it, do you not conceive that the return in bullion from China to India would be available as a territorial remittance to England? – It facilitates the operation of the whole trade.

1425. And must you not take it into account in considering the balance of remittances? – It is taken into account. The trade between India and China is merely one of an internal character (if I may use the expression); the bullion brought back from China, if it be brought back to India, facilitates the remittance of bullion from Bengal to Europe or to England; that is merely part of the general trade of India.

1426. Supposing the private trader to be admitted to a participation with the Company in the China trade, are you aware of any peculiar disadvantages to which the private trader might remain subject, arising out of the system upon which the Company's trade is carried on? – If the question refers to any supposed inconvenience which the private trader would sustain in the port of Canton connected with the Company, I am not prepared to say he would sustain any inconvenience; but if I were to give an answer upon a more enlarged character, it would be that he is under great delusion as to the real advantage to be derived upon opening the trade with the port of Canton, particularly so far as regards the export trade from England in manufactures, and from other parts of Europe in articles of general produce for sale in Canton, for the purpose of purchasing the return cargo. I am disposed to think that he will not find that beneficial market which he contemplates for European articles; and as regards the article of tea constituting his return cargo, he will sustain this further inconvenience: the East India Company, under the regulations of the existing charter, are called upon to hold a very large stock (I believe a year's) in advance. Now, the consequence of that system will be, that after having sustained the natural effects of competition in the purchase at Canton (on advanced prime-cost), he will be met in this market by the Company's stock, which must necessarily be brought into the market for sale, when no longer required by law to retain it in the warehouses. Therefore, while the private trader is bringing by a competition an article of a high cost from China, he will be met in this market by a double quantity, and consequently a low price of sale.

1427. The difficulty you have mentioned would apply only to the first few years of the opening of the trade? – Only to the first two or three years.

1428. Would it not also apply to the importation from the continent of Europe when tea is at a remarkably low price, even under what it cost in China? – All the import, whether it be from the Continent or from China, or from the Company's warehouses, will meet in this country to the prejudice, while it lasts, of the private trader.

1429. What is your opinion with regard to the increased consumption in this country, supposing that the price of tea were to fall to a very great extent? – I believe you might increase the consumption to almost any extent.

1430. What is the reason that it is decreasing in America, where the price is very low? – Perhaps they like coffee better. I only refer to this country where the consumption is so universal among the lower orders, and I believe (though I speak subject to correction) that our importation is principally of the lower quality of tea. Seeing the manner in which the common people in this country consume tea, and the price they pay for it, there appears no reason to suppose that, if they could obtain double or treble the quantity at the same price, they would not take it.

1431. Now, suppose that some of the tea imported by individual merchants should prove to be of very inferior quality, so that the people of this country became disgusted with it, is it then your opinion that they would continue to drink tea, and that the consumption would increase? – I think that question would principally apply to the higher class of persons, and which relates, I believe, to the smallest part of the consumption.

1432. Are you aware that on the continent of Europe, for a considerable number of years past, the consumption of tea has been gradually decreasing, and that the whole imports of tea to the continent of Europe, by sea, does not exceed eight millions of pounds annually? – I am not aware of the actual quantity consumed on the continent of Europe. I have always understood the beverage of the continent of Europe has been principally coffee, and therefore they have taken tea more as a substitute for coffee than from any particular partiality to the commodity.

1433. You are not aware that the quantity of tea that has been consumed on the Continent has been decreasing rather than increasing? – No, I am not aware of that circumstance, but I can very easily understand it would be so from the extreme cheapness of coffee.

1434. Are you aware that the price of tea on the Continent is extremely cheap also? – Yes; but still coffee has fallen in that degree that it will enable all persons to double their consumption.

1435. Though in this country the coffee has also fallen to the same extent of cheapness, yet the tea has been, from some circumstances, continuing to increase in its demand? – Coffee has also increased in this country, but the consumption of both tea and coffee has, I imagine, been increased by the low prices at which they are afforded to be sold.

1436. Are you aware that by reducing the duty on coffee to one-fourth, the consumption of coffee has increased twenty fold? – I believe it has increased very largely.

1437. Do you believe any people in the world drink a worse article in the shape of tea than our poor people in most villages in England? – I believe it is very bad indeed.

1438. Supposing that the Company, by any arrangements it could make, were to transfer a portion of its territorial payments from England to India, the necessity of remittance from India to England would remain the same, but as the Company itself would have fewer remittances to make, would not the danger that has been apprehended by some of a combination amongst the merchants to enhance the rate of remittance, be much diminished by so diminishing the payments to be made in England? – I have always considered it to be a matter of surprise that the Company have not long since transferred part of these payments to India; I mean payments to officers on furlough, and retired civil and military servants, etc., which will amount to half a million, if not more.

1439. If there be any danger to be apprehended from a combination on account of the large payments to be made, would not that danger be diminished to the extent of the amount to be transferred? – Certainly.

1440. This would be another mode, then, in which the Company, if it gave over trade, might assist itself in making remittances from India to England, by diminishing the amount to be remitted by itself? – Certainly, it would not only diminish the amount to be remitted, but at the same time would tend to a better regulation of the exchange.

1441. Do you think it likely that a country like India shall be drained to the extent of two or three millions every year for the purpose of political payments to another country in Europe for which it receives no equivalent, without gradually and certainly impoverishing that country? – I think the power of production in India is so great, and the commodities themselves are so valuable, that there is never likely to be any difficulty in making the required payments through the commercial products of the country.

1442. Although that may afford the means of making the remittances, does not the necessity of one country making an habitual and perpetual political payment, for which it is to receive no equivalent, produce the impoverishment of that country? – Not if it is made in the articles of production of that country; I think it is evident that the money levied in the shape of tax upon the population of India, is re-exported in the productions of India for which a demand arises in Europe, and therefore, though the drain to a certain extent does exist, still it is so small as not materially to affect the prosperity of the country.

1443. Does it not amount to this, that it becomes a tribute in kind, and would not France, for instance, if a tribute were imposed upon France, payable in a given quantity of wine and oil every year, for which no equivalent was returned: would not that have the same tendency to the impoverishment of the country upon which that tribute was imposed, in the same manner as if it were paid in money? – Not to the same extent, because the actual expenditure in growing the wine and oil will remain in France.

1444. Supposing therefore the perpetual condition of the

relation between India and Europe to be that that country is to make a political annual tribute, does it not bring with it a condition of a perpetual injury to that country to the extent of making it almost impossible for it ultimately to bear it? – No, I think not; I think the pressure is on the individual tax payer; I think he is the person who is prejudiced and damnified by the sum he pays, but the agriculturist who produces the indigo or the silk, is paid for his labour and for the production of those articles, through which the payment of the tribute is made.

1445. But as between country and country he has to give the value for which he receives no compensation? – Therefore that part of the population which pays the tax suffers to the extent of their payment.

1446. In what respect does that differ from the remittances constantly made from the agricultural part of the country to the residents in great towns for the rents; does it not entirely depend upon the proportion? – Certainly.

1447. The proportion which such remittance bears to the value of the whole annual produce of the country? – I do not think it has any material effect on the real prosperity of a country.

4

John Crawfurd, A Sketch of the Commercial Resources and Monetary and Mercantile System of British India, with suggestions for their improvement, by means of Banking Establishments (1837)

Chapter I

Extent and population of India. Coast, harbours, and rivers. Statistical view of the British possessions. Climate and soil. Character and industry of the people.

The British territories in Hindostan have been computed to contain upwards of 480,000 square miles, and a population exceeding eighty millions. Besides this, we have territory beyond Hindostan exceeding 50,000 square miles, and containing 300,000 inhabitants: our Indian dominions are, therefore, about five times the extent of the two British Islands, and contain more than three times their population.

This is, however, not all: there is a tributary territory in Hindostan of above 580,000 square miles, with more than fifty-four million inhabitants; and this territory, from being intermixed with our own, and from the political ascendency we exercise over it, is hardly less British than that of which we directly administer the government. We have, of the same description, beyond Hindostan, above 50,000 square miles, with 400,000 inhabitants; so that, in all, the territory over which we virtually exercise dominion is ten times as great as the British Islands, and the population above five times as great.

With the independent states on our immediate frontier we have commercial treaties, and, of course, commercial relations.

Of this description, bordering on Hindostan, there is computed to be 137,000 square miles, with seven million inhabitants, and beyond Hindostan 180,000 square miles, with two-and-a-half millions. The reader may see the computed figures, at a glance, in the following table:

	Area	Population	Population per square mile
British territories in Hindostan*	432,483	80,636,371	186
Tributary do. do.	563,610	54,271,092	96
British territories beyond Hindostan	50,117	297,054	6
Tributary do. do. do.	50,000	408,000	8
Independent states, in or bordering on Hindostan	137,000	7,000,000	51
Independent states beyond Hindostan	180,000	2,500,000	14
Total	1,413,210	145,112,517	102*

With very small exceptions in favour of the people of Sinde, of the Portuguese, Danes, French, and Burmese, the whole of a coast, of not less than 4,800 miles in extent, from the mouth of the Indus to the eleventh degree of north latitude, and ninety-ninth of east longitude, is under our dominion. Maritime intercourse and external commerce, therefore, to the nations of the interior is almost wholly under our control. Indeed, from the eleventh degree of latitude down to the extreme point of Asia, touching on the equator, we exercise, commercially, through the possession of three naval and commanding positions, an influence almost as great as if we had the actual dominion of the whole of the intermediate coast.

In the vast coast now stated the number of good harbours is but small, not exceeding in all a dozen, of which the most important, or best, are Calcutta, Bombay, Sincapore, Penang, Malacca, Martaban, Tavoy, Mergui, Trincomalee, Galle, and Cochin. The great rivers of India, or of the neighbouring countries, are about ten in number, of which the most important, for

* Besides this there are upwards of 90,000 square miles of British territory, or a country larger than Great Britain and Ireland, of the population of which there is no estimate (Population Returns, in Appendix to the Report of the Select Committee of 1831, p. 762; Report by C. E. Trevelyan, Calcutta, 1834).

external and internal navigation, are the Ganges, the Indus, and the Irawadi.

The following sketch will give the reader some notion of such of the principal rivers of Hindostan as are fit for internal navigation, and which, by the facility they afford to internal communication, contribute, more or less, to promote the industry of the country. The largest have their source in the great chain of northern mountains, and the rest, with few exceptions, in the table land of central and southern India, which is supported by the two chains of mountains called the Ghauts. Few of them, it is to be observed, are navigable for considerable shipping, further than the influence of the oceanic tide; and, indeed, generally, not so far. Many of them, however, are suited for steam navigation to a large extent; and in three – the Ganges, the Berramputre, and the Irawadi – the experiment has been successfully made, in a length of 750 miles for the first, and of 500 for the last, Of the Indus, although the experiment has not been yet tried, quite enough is known to warrant us in believing that it is far better suited than any of these. Steam navigation upon this great river, is probably, practicable to the extent of at least 1,000 miles, which makes it, in this respect, more like the great navigable rivers of America than those of Asia. For three quarters of their course the Indian rivers are probably all of them suited to, what would be called in this country, canal navigation; and there are few of them that do not, either by their periodical floods, or by artificial irrigation, contribute to fertilize the lands they pass through. In this latter respect, the Ganges and the Caveri, watering, in their progress, lands which through their agency, are rendered not inferior in productiveness to Egypt, are the most distinguished.

The following are the chief rivers of Hindostan, and the countries which border upon it, with their computed length of course. In northern India we have the following – the Ganges 1,500 miles, the Berramputre 1,600, the Jumna 780, the Gunduck 450, the Cosi 300, the Gogra 300, the Goomtee 300, the Sone 300, the Betwah 300, and the Chumbul 500. In southern India there are the Taptee 460, the Nerbudda 700, the Mahe 380, the Sabrematta 200, the Godavri 850, the Krishna 700, and the

Caveri 700. In Pegu we have the Saluen above 900 miles. In the neighbouring countries we have the Indus and its largest tributary making, together, about 2,000 miles, and the Irawaddi about 700.

In a country like India, embracing twenty-seven degrees of latitude; containing extensive plateaux, elevated from two to three thousand feet above the level of the sea; some of the most extensive plains in the world, almost on a level with, or rising but a few hundred feet above the level of the ocean; the highest range of mountains in the world; tracts of bare rock; deserts of mere sand; and dense forests of primeval wood, it is almost unnecessary to insist that there is great diversity, both of soil and climate. Europe itself, from Gibraltar to the North Cape, is not more varied in soil and climate than this vast region. The most fertile tract of land in India is the valley of the Ganges, extending from the sea to the first range of the northern mountains, and bounded to the south by the Vindya chain, running from the twenty-fourth to the twenty-sixth degree of latitude. This contains an area of not less than 180,000 square miles, or near half as much more as the area of Great Britain and Ireland. The true value of British India consists in this great valley, watered throughout by the artery of the Ganges, and its numerous tributaries. Here lies the best part of the population of India, whether for number, civilization, or industry. Without possessing this portion, we could not have achieved the conquest of the rest; nor, supposing us to have achieved, could we have retained it, or found it worth retaining. The largest portion of British India is within the tropics, and, in climate and production, the whole has more or less of a tropical character. Beyond the twenty-seventh degree of latitude, however, there is an approach to the climate, and, consequently, to the products of Southern Europe. Within the tropics there are two seasons, a dry and a wet; and beyond them three, consisting of a sultry summer, a wet autumn, and a serene winter, cool everywhere, and, to the north, nearly equal to the coldness of the climate of Greece and Italy.

The inhabitants of India, although markedly distinguished from those of other parts of the world in physical and moral character, are scarcely less varied among themselves than their soil and climate. A native of Bengal is at least as different in language, manners and religion from a native of the Tamul country, as a Spaniard is from a Russian, or a Russian from a German. The most numerous of the Indian nations are those speaking the Hindi or Hindustani language; a dialect formed on the basis of an ancient Hindu tongue by superadding Persian, introduced by the Mahomedan conquerors, exactly as our own language has been formed by the addition to the Saxon of Norman-French. The process, it is remarkable, commenced about the very same period, and, probably, was completed in nearly the same length of time – that is, in about 250 years. This people occupy the whole of the upper valley of the Ganges, to the extent of 174,500 square miles, and their number has been estimated at about thirty-one millions, of whom about twenty-two millions are British subjects, the remainder being tributaries intermixed with them. The next most populous nation is that speaking the language of Bengal. This occupies the whole of the delta of the Ganges, or more strictly the whole tract of the inundation of that river, to the extent of 80,000 square miles; and its number has been computed at twenty-five millions. In southern India, the most numerous people are those speaking the Telinga language. Their numbers may amount to about eight millions, while they occupy at least 100,000 square miles. Occupying the extreme south of India and its neighbourhood, we have the Tamul nation, whose numbers are probably not less than five millions. To the north of the Telingas and to the south of the Bengalees, we have another nation, the Oorias, whose number cannot be less than four millions. We have two other great nations in the south whose numbers have not been computed – the Carnatas and the Mahrattas – but the majority of whom are now subjects of the British government. To these great indigenous nations are to be added many minor ones – a variety of wild and wandering races with a crowd of foreign settlers, or their descendants, or mixed descendants; as Arabs, Persians, Afghans, Turks of Zagatay, Armenians, Jews, Portuguese, English, and other northern nations of Europe.

The reader is not to imagine that the population which is now described is, or has been, stationary in numbers. The inhabitants of the lower portion of the delta of the Ganges under our dominion have enjoyed a peace of more than seventy years, and they have increased in numbers, as any other people, having room enough, would have done under the same circumstances. The only great checks to this increase have been the famine of 1771, and the pestilence of 1817. In 1765, their numbers were estimated at twenty millions; in 1790, at twenty-four millions; and in 1824, at above thirty-seven millions and a half. Thus, in the first period of twenty-five years, the increase had been 20 per cent, and in the second period of thirty-four years above 50 per cent. There is no doubt but that at present the population is at least forty millions; so that, in a period of little more than seventy years, it has doubled its numbers. A census made of the population of the Madras territory in 1823 shewed its amount to be, in round numbers, thirteen millions and a half; and a recent one raised it to fifteen millions; so that, in a period of about ten years, it had increased above 11 per cent, which is at about the same rate as the increase in the principality of Wales.

The distribution of the population is exceedingly unequal, varying with the fertility of the land, its other natural advantages, and the industry of the people. The country watered by the Ganges and its tributaries, subject to the British government, although embracing but 231,000 square miles, out of the 432,000 which constitute the British territories, contains near sixty millions, or three-quarters of the whole inhabitants. In the delta of the Ganges, in its widest extent, there is a population of 276 to the square mile; but, in particular districts, where the land is fertile and easily cultivated, and water abundant for navigation and irrigation, there is an extraordinary density of population. In the district of Hoogly, for example, there is a population of 549 to the square mile; in that which contains the city of Calcutta 562; and in Burdwan 594; which last exceeds the populousness of any province of China but one, Chekiang. As we proceed northward and westward, along the course of the Ganges, from the twenty-fifth degree of latitude, the language and character of the people, and the quality and productions of the soil change. Excluding a hilly district unconnected with the Gangetic plain, we have here a population of 236 to the square mile; which rate probably extends, with very little interruption, through the rest of the valley of the Ganges, up to the foot of the hills. The entire valley of the Ganges, taken together, contains about 260 inhabitants to the square mile; which is within eight of the vaunted population of the Chinese empire, estimated at the highest.

The countries of the south are far less populous. Those under the Madras government contain, on an average, but 105 to the square mile. Here also, there is a much greater inequality in the distribution of the population than in the Gangetic plain. In the rich province of Tanjore, so peculiarly favoured by perennial irrigation, there are 225 inhabitants to the square mile. In Malabar, a country with a considerable foreign commerce, and well irrigated, there are 146. In the countries situated in the great plain between the sea and the eastern ghauts, and which are well irrigated through means of artificial collections of water, there are about 103 inhabitants to the square mile. In the countries on the great table land, the population is but 78 to the square mile; and in the sandy provinces about the southern promontory but 74.

The territory under Bombay has the same rate of population as that under Madras, or 105 per square mile. Here also we have a great diversity in its distribution. In our territories in Gujerat there are about 180 inhabitants to the square mile; in those under the western ghauts but 90; and in the newly acquired provinces on the tableland, above them, but 86.

Notwithstanding, then, the vast apparent population of Hindostan, generally, and of the British possessions in particular, the country cannot be considered a populous one: on the contrary, it is even under peopled, if we consider only the vast extent of good land which it contains, and of which a great deal is still uncleared, and unreclaimed. Were the British dominions only as populous as France, they ought to contain ten million inhabitants more than they do. What is applicable to the British dominions is still more so to these, taken along with the Tributary States; for the truth is that in course of conquest we have, naturally enough, picked up the most fertile and populous portions of the land. The united dominions thus described ought, if as populous as France, to contain half as many more inhabitants as they do; while, in fact, they are much less populous than so poor a country as Switzerland; and do not in this respect surpass Portugal, a country far from remarkable for its fertility, or its industry.

Hindostan, it is needless to say, is much more an agricultural than a manufacturing country. It has been reckoned to contain twenty-six great towns, of which all belong to the British government except six, and these belong to Tributary States. The population of these twenty-six towns has been very roughly estimated at about four-and-a-quarter millions. If we reckon, however, every place as a town that contains 4,000 inhabitants and upwards, as would be done in Europe, this is greatly to underrate the towns of India. There is no doubt, however, but that the proportion of the town to the rural population is very small. If we should estimate the first for the British territories at five millions, it will form but one-sixteenth of the population – a vast disparity, if compared to the proportions in any European country. The rural population of India live invariably in villages, a practice still rendered but too necessary for the protection of life and property.

Physically viewed, the people of Hindostan may be considered as inferior in strength and stature to the European race. They have, generally speaking, neither the same strength, nor the same endurance of toil that Europeans possess; nor the same skill in economizing and applying their physical powers. A great deal of the inferiority, it should be added, ought to be charged to the inferiority of their civilization. Their minds are acute and subtle, rather than solid or practical. If, consequently, the comparison, either physical, intellectual, or moral, be made between them and some of the less civilized nations of Europe, as the Russians, the Greeks, and others, and it is unquestionably fairer to make the comparison with these than with the more advanced nations of Europe, the disparity will be found to be by no means so great; and, indeed, in many cases the parallel will be to their advantage. One peculiarity of a people in such a state of society as the Hindoos, and it more or less belongs to the nations who are permanently settled among them, is a patient although slow industry, and a degree of frugality which, in a great many cases, amounts to parsimony. Hence, the whole mercantile classes are distinguished by economy, shrewdness, expertness, and diligence; and the merchant, the banker, the accountant and retail dealer approach much nearer to the same parties in Europe than any other classes of the community. In the towns of Calcutta and Bombay, many of the native merchants have made themselves acquainted with the English language and literature, and speculate largely and boldly in foreign commercial adventure. The docility and submission of the whole race is great, and the indisputable proof of it is our conquest, and our ability to maintain that conquest, without much difficulty, by numbers which have never exceeded *a sixteen-hundredth* part of the conquered. Among the Indians themselves, there is, of course, a great diversity of character. The people of Bengal are the smallest and feeblest, and the most timid; but they are not the least ingenious, acute, or industrious. A great many of the military, and other higher classes of the Hindoos, beyond Bengal, possess high courage, and this character obtains both to the north and the south; but still, docility, incapacity of combining for their common defence, and a preference of peace and submission to a painful and persevering struggle for national independence, is the characteristic of the whole. Hence, during the long period of eight centuries, they have, considering their numbers, become an easy prey to mere handfuls of foreign invaders. There is, in fact, no numerous people in the world, the Chinese excepted, so easily overrun, subjugated, and retained in subjection, as the Hindoos; nor, it must be added, so rich a prize to the conqueror.

With the character which we have ascribed to the Hindoos, it would be mere extravagance to compare the amount of their productive industry with that of almost any European nation. The mere labour of a Hindoo is not to be compared to that of any European, and still less with that of any of the more civilized European nations. An Englishman hears that the ordinary pay of an Indian agricultural labourer is from 30s. to 40s. a year, without food, clothing, or habitation; and, without further examination, he at once jumps to the conclusion that the wages of labour are proportionably low in India, and that consequently the profits of stock must be in the same proportion, high. He never takes into account the imperfect tools which the Indian employs; the time he takes to perform his labour; the careless and slovenly manner in which he executes it; and the extraordinary superintendence necessary to protect his employer from the sloth, habitual carelessness, and chicanery of one who is so wretchedly rewarded. In a word, such an observer does not consider the amount of labour well executed, the only criterion of the real price of wages. In the most ordinary mechanical drudgery, such as that of a porter, it would be very difficult to estimate the labour of three Indians as equal to that of one Englishman. In our Indian shipping four Lascars, or Indian mariners, are reckoned to be equal to only one English seaman; and here it may be observed that no Indian has ever been found fit for employment as a steersman, a circumstance arising from a want of firmness and self-possession, not very easily accounted for. In all skilled labour, the disproportion between Indians and Europeans is, of course, still greater than in ordinary day labour. But the Indians are not excelled by Europeans alone, but by some other Asiatic people, and particularly by the Chinese, who are greatly their superiors in strength, ingenuity, diligence, and perseverance. The labour of one Chinese carpenter or cabinet maker in Calcutta is equal to that of from four to six natives of Bengal, and his wages are, of course, in proportion. While the Indian earns no more than from £3 12s. to £6 per annum, the Chinese will earn £48. The nature of the climate, and still more, the small number of European artisans, who are always employed as superintendents, and receiving in that capacity not less than £100 a year, does not admit of our drawing a fair comparison between the skilled labour of a native and of an Englishman. Perhaps, however, we shall not greatly err in estimating the labour of an European carpenter or cabinet maker as being half as valuable again as that of a Chinese, or £72; which is equal to that of fifteen Indians. Under this view of the state of society in India, we may safely consider that the attempt to introduce the complex manufactures of Europe into India, notwithstanding cheapness of raw material, and apparent low price of wages, may be looked upon as a signal commercial blunder. A cotton mill, for the spinning of water twist, was introduced into Bengal a few years ago. The machinery fell into the hands of its present owners at a very low cost, and, consequently, they are enabled now to work with native hands, and to produce, even with native cotton, a very tolerable yarn. Under ordinary circumstances, however, it is admitted that it must have been a ruinous speculation. The Russians have introduced into St Petersburgh and Moscow a very considerable number of cotton mills, with a policy, in so far as the nation is concerned, as questionable as their introduction into Bengal; but more prudently, in so far as the speculators are interested, since the manufacture is conducted under the protection of an enormous duty on foreign yarn. Even such a manufacture as that of a newspaper, which enjoys a sort of natural monopoly, is of very high cost in India. It has been established for near sixty years, and yet the cost of a newspaper, wholly untaxed, is at least four times as great as in the United States, and the article, in many respects, of an inferior quality. The Indian paper is unfit for printing, and that used by Europeans, both for printing and other purposes, is imported from China and England. In a country where the raw material is so abundant no paper manufactory has been attempted by Europeans; one only excepted by some English missionaries at a Danish settlement. The proportion for skilled labour, however, it is evident, will not hold with respect to rural labour, that of the great mass of the labour of India. Perhaps we may here take – after allowing for the superiority of the implements of European husbandry – the proportion of five natives to one Englishman. The Indian artisan hardly ever confines himself exclusively to his business. The weaver, the carpenter and the tailor are for the most part agriculturists; and the loom, the adze and the needle are constantly interchanging with the plough, and the harrow, and the hoe.

It should be observed that the quantity of labour performed, and the money wages of labour, are very far from being the same throughout India. We have hitherto been speaking of

Bengal; but many of the other people of India are of more robust frames, more laborious, and more persevering. They receive higher wages, but their condition is, notwithstanding, not superior, for they pay a higher price for the necessaries of life. When we speak of the wages of labour in India, it is of course with reference to the cost of the necessaries of life, which, in so far as corn is concerned, is probably not above one third part of what it is in England. 30s. and 40s. a year for rural labour, therefore, mean £4 10s. and £6, in so far as the interests of the labourer are concerned. Upon the whole, we may conclude that rural labour in India, of the most ordinary kind, is not above one third part of its cost in England; that when it takes the character of a manufacture, as in the instances of indigo, sugar, and silk, the disparity is not nearly so great; and that in skilled labour it is for the most part a great deal higher than in England. This is exactly such a result as we should expect.

This test, applied to our Indian population, will show its effectual productive amount. Let us suppose, for example, that of the artisans, mechanics, and cultivators of India, on an average four are equal to one Englishman, and then our great population of eighty millions virtually dwindles to twenty millions, or one fifth less than that of the population of the United Kingdom. Some facts may be adduced in corroboration of this view of the relative productiveness of Indian industry. The whole of the Indian land tax for eighty millions of people is, in round numbers, about twelve millions sterling. With some partial exceptions, this land tax is, in reality, the rent of the land, and in a great many cases it is a rack rent. The land rent of the United Kingdom, not including houses or mines (not always excluded in India), is believed at present to exceed forty millions: thus, then, the real rental of British India does not much exceed one fourth part that of a country which is little more than one fifth part of its extent.

Let us, however, apply another test to the comparative industry of Britain and India. The total gross amount of the taxes of India is about eighteen millions; and the people are taxed to the utmost they can pay; and certainly, at all events, they are taxed more highly, in proportion to their means, than the people of England. Their taxation per head is 4s. 6d. Now, our taxation, at present, amounts to about forty-five millions; and estimating our population as high as twenty-five millions, the taxation per head is 36s., or eight times as great as that of the Indians. Considered as an index of comparative wealth this test would reduce our Indian population from eighty to ten millions; but in this estimate much allowance ought certainly to be made for the great superiority of the English fiscal system; at once less oppressive and more productive than that of India.

Of the state of agriculture and arts amongst the Hindoos we shall now give a very brief sketch. The cultivation of India is very extensive, but very rude. Almost everything that is the produce of Indian rural labour is, when compared with that of people in a more civilized and favourable state of society, crude and unmarketable. The value of the Indian plough is about 2s.; of the implement called a harrow, about 1s.; and, of the pair of oxen employed to draw them, about 20s. The work performed by a plough and a yoke of oxen is valued at 3d. per day. The corn is everywhere trodden out by cattle, and not threshed. The great body of the cultivators or occupants of India, whether under the denomination of tenants or proprietors, are pretty much in the condition of the *Metayers* of southern Europe, paying to the landlord, and that landlord most generally the government, a share of the crop as rent, and that share amounting to a fifth, a third, or one half, according to the quality and condition of the land – often taken in kind, but, by the British government, usually converted into a money payment. Directly or indirectly, the cultivator must have advances from some party or another, or he cannot carry on his cultivation. This is done by the government,* by a middleman, by the proprietor, where there is a permanent settlement of the land-tax, and, more frequently than all, by a professional money-lender. What must the European agricultural reader think of a system of husbandry carried on by farmers, whose whole stock in trade may not exceed 60s. in value, who cannot move a step unless they receive an advance to buy seed-corn or cattle, and whose operations may

---

* Advances are as much discouraged as possible by the British government, but their amount is still not less than £200,000 a year, much of which, of course, is never recovered.

be arrested by the death of a bullock, or the loss of a wife, who has been performing the lighter part of the drudgery?

The success of the Indian husbandry, such as it is, is mainly attributable to the fertility of the land, the heat of the climate, and, above all, the command of water, which, when it is not supplied at once by the hand of nature, as is often the case, is applied by artificial means; not skilfully, indeed, but laboriously and extensively. Water alone multiplies the produce of the land, according to the nature of the soil and crop, and the facility of applying it, from two to ten-fold. Without this command of water India would have been a desert, and its inhabitants a few wandering tribes of savages. Of all the branches of the agricultural industry of India, we take this opportunity of observing that there is not one which is so capable of rewarding the application of skill and capital as irrigation. In rude embankments, and tanks upon a large scale, the experiment has been tried by the natives and succeeded; but hitherto, British industry has never been directed to this, in a warm climate, all-important department of industry. The art of irrigation in India is still in its infancy. In the lower provinces of Bengal, the British government, the great proprietor of the land, because it receives the principal part of the rent, lays out but £40,000 a year in the repair and maintenance of works of irrigation. In the Madras provinces, it expends in the same way about £80,000 a year; so that the total expenditure upon such works does not, for all British India, as far as it is given in the public returns, exceed £120,000 a year. In the western provinces of Bengal, with the exception of one old canal, recently re-opened with great advantage, there are no great works of irrigation. It is the same with the territory under Bombay. The truth is that the irrigation of India is for the most part carried on by miserable wells, from which the water is drawn by a single wretched bullock with a leathern bucket. There are particular works of irrigation in Italy and the south of France more valuable than those of all India put together. What a field is there not here, then, for the application of British skill and capital.

One advantage belongs to Hindostan, in common with every warm country which will readily occur to the intelligent reader; the capacity of the soil for cultivation nearly throughout the year, uninterrupted by any rigour of climate. Two crops, generally, of different products can always be raised within the year, when the soil is good, frequently from the same land.

What is applicable to agriculture is applicable to every branch of industry. Such is the general poverty of the people, that no industrious movement can be made without a previous advance of funds, lent in one form or another, at an exorbitant interest, to cover great risks and great profits. With European capital, and under the direction of European skill, a better system of rural industry is in course of introduction; directed, at present, to the articles of indigo and silk; and promising soon to be extended to the staples sugar, cotton, coffee, and even tea. In such undertakings higher wages, generally double the ordinary amount, are usually given, and, as invariably happens in such circumstances, more labour, better executed, is performed.

The state of the other useful arts in India is not more advanced, and scarcely, indeed, upon a level with agriculture. In four arts alone, the Indians early excelled other nations; the manufacture of cotton fabrics, shawls, cotton dying, and calico printing; to all which, they seem to have been invited either by the possession on the spot, or by an easy access to raw materials, which no other people at the time commanded. Where they have not possessed these natural advantages, the useful arts among them are in the rudest state. Their woollen cloths are execrable; their pottery, always unglazed, as bad as can be described, and every description of hardware as rude as can be imagined. Their attempts in glassware are wretched. An enumeration of the different arts, professions and occupations practised in an Indian town will give the reader by far the best notion of the actual state of the arts in India. A census of the town of Bareilly was carefully taken for the purpose of ascertaining this fact.[1] The town contains 66,000 inhabitants, is situated between the twenty-eighth and twenty-ninth degree of latitude, is the capital of a great and fertile province, constituting

[1] [The reference is to an article by Robert Thomas John Glyn, published in the *Transactions of the Royal Asiatic Society*, see Crawfurd's footnote at the end of p. 234. – *Editor*]

one of the most improved and productive portions of British India. The trades practised in it were found to be the following:

Goldsmiths
Braziers
Blacksmiths
Carpenters
Distillers
Curriers
Shoemakers
Saddlers
Washermen
Barbers
Stone cutters
Bricklayers
Potters
Cotton weavers
Silk weavers
Carpet weavers
Dyers
Basket makers
Cotton dressers
Painters
Cutlers
Tailors
Confectioners
Oil makers
Bankers
Manufacturers of leather bags and bottles
Bow and arrow makers
Palankeen bearers
Vendors of precious stones
Hoe and mattock diggers
Stone masons
Spirit dealers
Falconers
Javelin men
Turband makers
Farriers
Tobacco-pipe makers
Bakers
Gardeners
Embroiderers
Horse-cloth makers

Money changers and brokers
Rope makers
Silk and cotton mercers
Fire-work artificers
Colour makers
Leather dealers
Kite makers
Torch bearers
Sugar refiners
Grocers, perfumers, and druggists
Manufacturers of shel-lac ornaments
Grass sellers
Flour and meal-men
Ironmongers
Tobacconists
Fruiterers
Lacemen
Corn merchants
Bards
Scourers
Tinmen
Armourers
Brewers
Tent makers
Water carriers
Land measurers
Calico printers
Turners
Bamboo splitters
Wire drawers
Brush makers
Physicians
Goatskin dressers
Kid-butchers
Ox-butchers
Shawl menders
Refiners of dross of metals
Horse breakers
Whip makers

'On a view of the detailed classification above exhibited,' says the very judicious and experienced author of it, 'it cannot but immediately strike the observation, how very backward and imperfect is the subdivision of labour; and how very few are the trades and manufactures in this, the chief town of the very extensive and populous province of Rohilkund.' The same remark is, indeed, applicable to all the principal towns of Hindostan; the same indisputable signs of deficiency of capital and want of industry are found in all. Compare any town in the civilized parts of Europe containing a population of 66,000 inhabitants with Bareilly, and how many more varieties of trade and manufacture will be found in it than this statement shows! This is, no doubt, in some measure to be attributed to the nature of the climate, in which man has less occasion for quantity and variety of clothing, food and household furniture than in Europe. The Hindu religion, that so strictly inculcates the dread of pollution, both in food and in dress, does, also, materially contribute to diminish the number of trades in Indian towns:* still, although these circumstances do certainly tend to restrict the multiplication of handicrafts, the poverty of the people and their low advance in civilization must be admitted to be the principal cause. The very limited diffusion of wealth, and consequently the little demand for the conveniences and luxuries of life, limit the number of trades and manufactures to a very insignificant amount. The natives of Europe have very little idea of the actual condition of the inhabitants of Hindostan; they are more wretchedly poor than we have any notion of. Europeans have hitherto been too apt to draw their opinions of the wealth of Hindostan, from the gorgeous pomp and splendour of a few emperors, sultans, nabobs, and rajas; whereas a more intimate and accurate view of the real state of society would have shewn that these princes and nobles were engrossing all the wealth of the country, whilst the great body of the people were

---

* Actuated by this superstitious notion, the greater part of the Hindoos cook their own victuals, make and mend their own clothes, and wash their own linen; and even the higher classes chiefly employ their own private servants in those offices, instead of resorting to shops for the supply of their wants. Hence, butchers and bakers are wanting, and tailors and washermen not numerous, in the Hindu part of the community.'

earning but a bare subsistence, groaning under intolerable burthens, and hardly able to supply themselves with the necessaries of life, much less with its luxuries. The statement of monthly earnings given in this enumeration is rather over than underrated; but it may serve to convey some notion of the comparative poverty of the people. The average rate of earnings appears to be from 5s. to 8s. per month (valuing the rupee at the exchange of 2s.). What is the food of the higher classes in Hindostan? (by Hindostan, is meant the northern provinces of our Indian empire, between the Nerbudda and the Setlej): but though wheat is three times cheaper in Hindostan than in England, yet the earnings of both the middling and lower classes are too scanty to enable either class to live on such an article of luxury. The former mix with wheat, split pease, vetches, and other vegetable productions; the lower classes subsist upon barley, millets, maize, tares, vetches, etc. But this is luxury compared with the food of the lower classes in the villages; their earnings, rising only from 4s. to 6s. per mensem, forces a recourse to the vilest food. The more scrupulous castes are obliged to mix with the coarse grains above mentioned wild roots, herbs, and insects; while the outcasts, as the numerous race of Chumars, Kanjars, Dusads, etc., scruple not to eat vermin, dead fish, carrion, etc.'*

Other parts of the country, and other situations, are still more backward. In the richest portion of all India, the province of Burdwan in Bengal, not seventy miles from the British capital, on an inquiry into twenty-six great villages, or rather towns, containing 40,000 inhabitants, and, consequently, between 1,500 and 1,600 inhabitants for each, it was found that the division of employments, professions and trades amounted only to thirty-three; and this included, besides day labourers, such employments as officiating priests, religious mendicants, bards, astrologers, snake charmers, and outcasts.† Among these there was neither butcher, baker, tailor, shoemaker, or bricklayer. It

* Enumeration of the various classes of Population, and of Trades and Handicrafts, in the Town of Bareilly, in Rohilkhund (read 18 March, 1826; Transactions of the Royal Asiatic Society, vol. I).

† Asiatic Researches, vol. IX.

will be observed that a bookseller or a stationer are trades not to be found in either list, and still less a newsvender or a tavern keeper. In lieu of these, we have kite makers, falconers, astrologers, and snake charmers: such is the state of the arts in British India.

Chapter II

Inland trade. Roads and bridges. Cost of transporting goods. Corn and other grain. Cotton and cotton manufactures. Sugar. Salt.

The internal trade of India comprehends not only the commercial intercourse between one portion of the British dominions and another, and the trade of the latter with the tributary and independent states of Hindostan, but also the trade along a land frontier of at least 2,000 miles. Including Sinde, Cabul, Lahore, Nepaul, Boutan, and the Burmese dominions, we have here an area of at least one million and a half square miles, and a population of about a hundred and fifty-six millions. From the circumstances we have already described, there are very few foreign, or tropical productions, which the foreign nations included in this statement, the Burmese excepted, can receive, but through their commercial connexion with us.

With the exception of a few military roads constructed by the English, of small importance in a commercial point of view, there are no good carriage roads in any part of India. What are called high-roads in that country are, in truth, little better than broad and bad pathways. The number of bridges, in a country which, in many parts, is intersected by a prodigious number of rivers or streams, is small, and the few that exist are bad. 'At some distance from this', says the late Dr Francis Buchannan Hamilton,

I crossed the Capine, by a bridge which is here looked upon as a prodigy of grandeur: in Europe it would be considered as a disgrace to the architect of the meanest town: the arches are about five feet span, the piers are of nearly an equal thickness, and do not present an angle to the stream. The sides of the arches have scarcely any curvature, but are composed of two planes meeting at an acute angle. The parapet is rude, and the whole is composed of an irregular mixture of brick and stone. The pavement consists of rough and irregular flags, which form a very bad road. The bridge is, however, both long and wide, and is a great convenience for foot passengers, or merchants, conveying their goods on oxen.*

To ferry goods, cattle and passengers, one has sometimes the good fortune to meet a boat: at other times two canoes are lashed together and used as a ferry boat: ruder, and more unsafe, and more tedious contrivances are not less frequent. 'The *Caveri* here', says the last writer quoted,

is at present, a fine large and deep river, flowing with a gentle stream, about a quarter of mile in width. In the hot season it is fordable, but after heavy rains, it rises above its present level ten or twelve feet perpendicular and then its channel is completely filled. The only ferry boats on this large river, are what are called *Donies*, or baskets of a circular form, eight or ten feet in diameter, and covered with leather. They transport, with tolerable safety, men and goods, but cattle must swim, which is both a fatiguing and a dangerous enterprise.†

'It cannot be said', observes the governor general, in 1823, in a public minute,

that there is any want of occasion for government to extend its liberality, from their being no objects to which it could be directed with a prospect of extensive benefit. The simple fact of their being *no roads* in the lower provinces of Bengal, which open for a space of twenty miles together, a land carriage throughout the year, is a sufficient answer to any such objections.

Throughout the whole plain of the Ganges, from the hills to the sea, but chiefly in the middle and lower part of it, there is an extensive inland navigation; and on the rivers of the south there is a considerable one also, although much inferior in amount. Many of the minor streams, however, are rendered dangerous or impracticable by falls, shoals, and rapid currents; and much of the navigation, even of the larger rivers, is impracticable everywhere, except during the four months of the rainy season, owing to the evaporation produced by long continued droughts, and to the absorbing character of the soils through which they pass. The greater part, therefore, of the

---

* *Journey through Mysore, etc.*, II, 147.
† *Ibid.* II, 163.

inland trade of India must be carried on by land. Goods are conveyed, to a small extent, in carts, or rather, very rude cars, drawn by one or more pairs of oxen. According to the computation of Dr Buchannan Hamilton, a cart drawn by eight oxen in India will not convey a greater load than an English cart drawn by a single horse.* Much the greater proportion of goods, however, are carried by pack-bullocks. On the north-western frontier, camels and horses are employed; and in the mountains bordering Hindostan, to the north, small horses, and even goats, are employed. In all the mountainous and hilly districts, porters are still more in use in the conveyance of merchandise than any description of cattle. The charge for conveying goods by land carriage, in the plains, has been estimated, on an average, at about 56s. per ton per hundred miles; and by the navigation of the Ganges, at about 2s. per ton for the same distance; that is to say, about one twenty-eighth part of the amount of the charge of the land carriage. Thus, then, the cost of conveying merchandise for 100 miles by land, in India, is equal to more than half the charge of conveying the same merchandise by sea from Calcutta to London, a distance of about 12,000 miles; and the *rate* of freight on the Ganges, by native navigation, is three times as costly as its rate between London and Calcutta.

The source of the internal trade of India, it is almost superfluous to say, is like that of all other trade, the difference in the character of the productive industry of the different countries carrying it on. In the British dominions alone, there are from eighty to ninety districts generally following the old Mogul divisions. These may be more justly termed provinces, or even kingdoms, than districts; for few of them contain less than half a million inhabitants, while some contain one, two, three, and even four millions. The products of the greater number differ from each other; and hence there is, to a greater or smaller degree, an interchange of commodities between them. Then there is the usual intercourse between town and country; and the distribution of foreign commodities, imported by sea or land, together with the furnishing of the tropical products of

* *Ibid.* III, 321.

India, the products of Indian arts, and foreign merchandise to the countries to the east, west, and north of it, in exchange for their national commodities.

Corn, cotton, oil-giving plants and sugar are the most important of all the productions of India, in so far as the inland trade and inland consumption are concerned. Rice is the first object of husbandry in every country of India, south of the twenty-fifth degree of latitude, wherever there exists a sufficient supply of water, natural or artificial, for its culture. But the country which is most remarkable for its production, and in which the chief commerce in it is conducted, is the tract of the inundation of the Ganges. To the north of the twenty-fifth degree of latitude, it gradually gives way to wheat and barley. In some of the elevated and dry lands of south India, we have the place of these three grains occupied by the *Cynosurus* or *ragy*. The quantity of millet grown (for the poor are mostly fed upon it) is very great. Of this grain, ten species, at least, are cultivated: pulses also are an article of extensive growth and consumption; and of these there are more than a dozen commonly cultivated. If we estimate the daily consumption of our eighty million British subjects at three quarters of a pound a head of every kind of corn, millet, and pulse, we shall have an annual consumption of 48,900,000 quarters, to which, if for seed corn, we add about one-tenth part more, we shall make the total produce no more than fifty-four millions, which is probably not more than the present estimated produce and consumption of the United Kingdom with twenty-five million people. We shall, perhaps, not underrate the average value of all kinds of corn and pulse at 12s. per quarter; and, in this case, the annual value will not much exceed thirty-two millions sterling. In this estimate we have omitted the corn consumed by cattle, for this reason, that the vast majority of the cattle of India get no corn. We have also omitted the grain used in distillation, because it is still more inconsiderable. These sums indicate the defective husbandry of India, the poverty of the people, the small amount of their food, and the want of capital for every industrious undertaking.

In 1790, when the population of the lower provinces of the Gangetic plain amounted to twenty-four millions, Mr Colebrook estimated the value of the corn annually transported from considerable distances, and, therefore, excluding the supplies drawn by towns from their immediate neighbourhoods, at two millions sterling.[1] This rate would give, for all British India, at present, between six-and-a-half millions and seven millions sterling, and for our own territories and Tributary States united, about eleven-and-a-quarter millions; which, however, as an estimate of the annual value of the Indian corn-trade, under the limitations stated by Mr Colebrook, would probably be a great deal too high, as other parts of India have not the same amount of surplus produce as Bengal, nor the same facility of transporting it to distant places. Even supposing, however, that there were no exaggeration in this statement, the amount will appear exceedingly small, for so vast a population, inhabiting a country of which the physical and geographical characters, and consequently produce, are so widely different. In a single year there has been imported into Great Britain, struggling against its corn laws, grain to the value of twelve millions sterling and upwards. Such is the vast disproportion between a rich and a poor country; between one with an active and enterprising commerce, and one with a sluggish and torpid one; between one abounding in capital, and one that is but too obviously deficient in it.

The cotton plant, of a great many varieties, is grown from one extremity of the British possessions to another; from Ceylon, in the sixth degree of latitude, up to the Himalaya mountains in the thirty-second. There is perhaps no plant whatever, unless tobacco, of such universal production, within the limits which we have just developed. There are many parts, however, in which it is produced much more cheaply and of better quality than in others; and hence it forms a very large branch of the internal trade. The upper portion of the valley of the Ganges and the country lying south of it, as far as the twenty-first degree of latitude, are those which produce it in the greatest abundance: and from these countries a large trade is carried on in it, to the lower valley of the Ganges, to the banks of which river it is

[1] [Colebrook, *Remarks on the present state of the husbandry and commerce of Bengal* (Calcutta, 1795), p. 129. – *Editor*]

occasionally conducted by a land journey of from 400 to 500 miles. From this article a prodigious variety of fabrics are woven; varying in almost every district, from some that are coarser than anything that we know of in this country, up to the fine muslins of Dacca, which we cannot yet imitate. The last named fabric is prepared from a cotton wool grown in the neighbourhood, and of which the locality is very limited. Mr Colebrook, in 1790, estimated the annual value of the clothing of the people of Bengal at six millions sterling. As the rest of the people of India are fully as well, if not better clad, than the people of Bengal, it will be no exaggeration to state the whole value of what is manufactured by the British population at twenty millions; nor that by the whole population subject to our control, British and Tributary, at near forty-four millions. This, supposing exportation and importation to balance each other, would make the annual value of the dress of each individual but 5s.: but it must be recollected that the children, for the most part, up to six or seven years of age, go naked; and that a great number of the labouring classes have raiment enough only to cover their nakedness; the male sex a single clout and the female sex two. The inhabitants of the Three Kingdoms are supposed to consume, yearly, about twenty millions worth of cotton goods, so that, in proportion to numbers, they consume much more than three times the value of what is consumed by our Indian subjects, who have the raw material on the spot, who have been possessed of the manufacture for 3,000 or 4,000 years, and who have hardly any other clothing. This will not much surprise those who have seen, in England, more looms under a single roof than exist in a whole Indian province, and each power loom making as much cloth as a dozen Indian weavers.

If the value of the manufactured fabric of India be taken at thirty-four millions, which, by the way, is about the same as the computed value of the cotton manufactures of Great Britain, we shall have the means of estimating the value of the raw material produced, exclusive of what is exported. The value of the raw material in this country is supposed to be about one-fifth part of the fabric; but, in India, this would be far too small a proportion, as the great bulk of the manufactured article is of a far coarser texture, or contains more raw material than with us. Of the coarse cotton goods manufactured in the United States half of the value consists of the raw material. One-third perhaps will be a fair average for India, where the goods, although coarse are of a loose fabric. This will make the value of the raw material between eleven and twelve millions sterling.

It has been said that the importation of British cotton manufactures has destroyed the manufactures of India, and been injurious to its people. It is obvious to anyone who will take the pains to inquire, that there is no foundation for such an assertion. The following refutation of this popular prejudice will be sufficient. We furnish the Indians annually with cotton goods, which, on the spot, may be worth two millions sterling; that is to say, we furnish them to the extent of one-seventeenth part, or about 6 per cent of the whole of their own manufacture. To the Indian manufacturer the apparent damage done is to that amount, and no more: but, in truth, there can be no injury done at all to artizans who have been, heretofore, weavers and agriculturists, in reducing them, in a country where land is still abundant, to the necessity of devoting their time to one employment only, and that the one best suited for the country they live in. The real falling off, after all, in the export of cotton fabrics from India does not exceed three-quarters of a million sterling per annum. This, in so far as Europeans are consumers, could not be helped, for the high price and inferior quality of the Indian fabrics would forbid their consumption, unless a high bounty were paid upon their importation. Even here, however, the falling off is more apparent than real: it is the apparent value, and not the quantity, which has fallen off, while the decreased value is compensated to the consumer by an equivalent decrease in the price of every foreign commodity which he receives in return. As to the Indian people generally, they are clear gainers; or they would surely not take the British goods, unless they were either cheaper or better than their own. They obtain a market for their domestic produce to the amount of the two millions which they pay. At the same time we consume to the yearly value of a quarter of a million's worth of their cotton wool; and, in China, we find a market for them, for the same article, to the amount of a whole million.

Sugar is the next most important article of the inland trade. The sugar cane, in India, at least, has as wide a limit for its growth as either cotton, or tobacco; but, with very partial exceptions, its growth, for the manufacture of sugar, is confined to the great plain of the Ganges. Here it succeeds only in dry rich lands not subject to inundation: any land fit for the culture of wheat is fit for the successful culture of the cane; which is a plant of the same natural family. Its geographical limit, however, is perhaps wider than that of wheat; for it will thrive from the equator to the thirty-second degree of latitude; whereas wheat on the level of the sea will only succeed from the twenty-fifth to the fifty fifth at the utmost. All the high and dry lands of India, which have a soil of sufficient fertility, are, therefore, fit for the growth of the cane as an object of husbandry. Heretofore, it has succeeded best in the province of Benares, between the twenty-fifth and twenty-sixth degrees of latitude. But it is known that it will equally succeed, and does in reality succeed, up to the twenty-eighth degree; while many of the higher lands, even in the immediate neighbourhood of the tract of the inundation of the Ganges, are well suited for its growth. The art of granulating sugar appears to have been introduced from China, and the art of crystallizing it from the Arabs or Persians; facts which are distinctly pointed at by the foreign names of the two commodities. That which is mostly used by the natives themselves is a foul mass of sugar from which the molasses have not been separated; but a great deal of imperfectly granulated sugar is also prepared, and forms an article of the inland trade, as well as of the foreign trade, by land and sea. Sugar is also made in India, from several of the palms; and, on the whole, the consumption of this article, of one kind or other, is very considerable, chiefly in the form of sweetmeats. The price of sugar in India may be perhaps, about one-third part of what it is in this country, allowing for the inferior quality of most of what is used, or about 10s. per cwt. Let us suppose that, in this case, the whole of the people of India, British and Tributary consume but about one-third of what is consumed in England, or 8 lb. per head, and still the consumption will amount to above 480,000 tons, and its value will exceed £3,857,000. A committee of the principal civil officers of the Indian government, about thirty years ago, made the daily consumption of a family of eight persons, earning £48 a year, about 8 oz. of sugar, with 16 oz. of sweetmeats, which probably would make, in all, about 1 lb. a day; that is 2 oz. for each individual, or better than 45 lb. per head per annum. A man with an income of £48 a year, however, is a man of the middle class; and the great mass of society being very poor, such an amount for the whole population would be extravagant. The average consumption of salt, a highly taxed article, is known to be about one-quarter of what it is for a person with the income which we have above described. Taking the same proportion for sugar, which is not now a taxed article, and which, unlike salt, is for the most part produced on the spot, we shall have an average consumption of between 11 lb. and 12 lb. per head, which maybe considered a corroboration of the estimate already made, or, at least, a proof that that estimate is not an exaggerated one.

There are a great number of other articles, the produce of India, such as indigo, opium, silk, tobacco, saltpetre, salt, oils and oil skins, drugs, hides, lime, timber, etc. which are objects of the inland trade. Of one part of India, a few of the productions are peculiar to itself. This is the coast of Malabar, to which, with a few exceptions, as far as Hindostan is concerned, the production of teak, sandal-wood, black pepper, and cardamoms is confined. The most important of the articles now enumerated will be considered under the head of the export trade; and for the rest a particular description of them is not necessary in a sketch of this nature. The corn, cotton, sugar, and other articles of the inland trade are paid for in the productions of the coast, which are almost always those of the tropics; in the production of foreign tropical countries of Asia; and in the produce and manufactures of Europe and China.

Of the commodities above stated, the most important is salt. By far the greater part of this is produced on the coast of India, or imported landways from foreign countries. It is chiefly paid for everywhere in corn. Taking the consumption of salt, legal and contraband, at 15 lb. a head for the British and Tributary population, which is not too much for a people who have few other condiments, we shall have an annual consumption approaching to a million tons. Of this quantity, the wholesale price to the consumer, including tax, which is generally 300 per cent on the prime cost, cannot be estimated at less than £8 per ton, and, therefore, the whole extent of the trade will be about eight millions a year.

The tropical or foreign commodities, which pay for the Indian produce already enumerated, consist of the areca nut, spiceries, the metals, iron, zinc, tin, copper, and lead; woollens, and cottons. Such is a rapid view of the inland trade of India; and we regret that nothing more explicit and distinct can be given, for the subject is one of great difficulty and obscurity, for an obvious reason that, until within the last three years, Europeans were not only precluded from holding landed property, but even interdicted by law from engaging in some of the principal branches of the trade. 'The mercantile interests of the interior of the country in particular', says Mr Trevelyan, now one of the secretaries of government, in an able and luminous report,

are involved in great obscurity. The merchants of the upper provinces know nothing of the trade of the lower provinces. The merchants of the lower provinces know nothing of what is passing above Mirzapoor, and the maritime trade is a branch separate from both. The trade with England, which is in the hands of our countrymen, is an object of daily attention; but, as we have not had any concern with the internal commerce of the country for many years past, nobody has thought of making it his study.[1]

Until within the last year, the whole inland trade of British India was subject to transit duties, which the last-named writer describes as 'a monstrous system of universal excise, under the name of custom-duty, which subjects the industrious classes of the community to the most cruel penalties and restrictions, and the farmer carrying his goods to market, and the petty dealer collecting his investment and transporting it to the local mart, as equally exposed to its baneful influence'. These have been happily and wisely abolished within the provinces subject to Bengal; and, if they are not, ought to be abolished in the other parts of the British possessions, where their operation is well

---

[1] [C. E. Trevelyan, *Report upon the Inland Customs and Town Duties of the Bengal Presidency* (2nd ed., Calcutta, 1835), p. 174. – *Editor*]

known to have been still more oppressive and pernicious. There still remain for abolition the monopoly of the manufacture and sale of salt; and of the culture of the poppy, and the preparation and sale of opium, imports which yield two millions of yearly revenue, but a poor compensation to the state, for the injury which they inflict on the industry and comforts of the people; and the less defensible, since it is notorious that an equal amount could easily be raised from the same commodities by less objectionable methods.

Chapter III

External trade. Value of imports and exports. Value of imports and exports of foreign Asiatic ports. Remarks on articles of export, viz. indigo, silk, opium, saltpetre, sugar, corn. New articles of export.

The foreign commercial relations of India are with the following countries, which we give in the order of their relative importance: Great Britain, China, Persian and Arabian Gulfs, France, United States, East India Islands; other continental nations of Europe than France, Cape of Good Hope and Mauritius, Birman Dominions, Siam and Cochin China, South America, New Holland. There are no public documents in existence which give a comprehensive view of the whole amount of the import and export foreign trade of India. In 1828–29, the value of the export and import trade of the four principal ports of British India was stated, in official documents, as follows:

	Imports £	Exports £
Calcutta	5,062,506	5,644,771
Madras	381,255	445,226
Bombay	853,394	839,762
Sincapore	1,961,120	1,804,660
Total	£8,258,275	£8,734,419

This, however, it must be observed, is a mere Custom-house valuation; something like our own official value in fixedness, but differing from it, in the commodities being undervalued instead of overvalued; and this, indeed, to such an extent, that in some cases of staple articles, not one half the real value is given. It is also to be added, that the trade has considerably increased since the date of the statement.

We shall add to this inadequate view an account of the trade of those foreign ports of India which hold the chief commercial intercourse with the British possessions, namely, Canton, Java, and Manilla, and in which British merchants, or British mercantile agents, are settled. In 1832, the British and American trade with Canton was as follows:

Imports	£4,951,560
Exports	4,278,380

Of this amount, the import trade, from British India alone, amounted to about three-and-a-half millions sterling, which of course was paid for in goods, bullion, or bills to the same amount. In 1835, the first year of British free trade with China, the imports and exports, according to the official statements of the superintendents, were as follows:

Imports	£4,712,428
Exports	4,065,954

Thus, so far from the capital of the Company being missed in China, the British trade alone is, within £450,000, as great as the united private British, Company's, and American trade, was three years before.

The export and import trade of Java, in 1828, was as follows:

Imports	£1,498,007
Exports	1,458,278

The trade of Manilla, the capital of the Philippine Islands, in 1831, was as follows:

Imports	£304,120
Exports	271,587

With the three ports in question, then, Europeans had, at the periods alluded to, a trade, the imports of which approached to seven millions sterling, and which, now, in all likelihood, greatly exceed this amount. By far the larger portion of this trade is British, and is carried on by British merchants, and British shipping.

With this view of giving the reader some general notion of the commercial importance of the countries with which the above ports are connected, we give their computed populations:

The eighteen provinces of China	370,000,000
Java and its dependencies	7,000,000
Philippine islands and dependencies	2,500,000
Total	379,500,000

To complete the statement of imports and exports in the Indian trade, we give those of the United Kingdom, for 1832, which were as follows:

Imports	£6,337,098
Exports	3,750,280

This statement excludes China, but includes other portions of India eastward of the Cape of Good Hope, which are not British possessions – the trade with which, however, in comparison to that with our own possessions, is very inconsiderable. We have here, then, an aggregate, not of trade, indeed, for it is evident that the same branches are repeated, but of commercial transactions, and operations, to the amount of near forty millions sterling a year. The object of our statement, in fact, is to point out the extent and importance of a branch of commerce which may truly be said to be yet in its infancy; the freedom of no part of it dating farther back than twenty-two years, and that of the whole being only of three years standing.

The character of the import trade of India is so well known to the British merchant, that it would be superfluous to enter upon the subject in this sketch. In reference to it we shall simply observe that time and experience have now fully ascertained, that the much-apprehended prejudices and antipathies of the population of India had no real foundation in fact; that the Hindoos are very much like other people in their tastes and wants; that they consume, with few exceptions, the productions and manufactures of foreign countries to the extent of their means; and that the British merchant has not been found wanting, in enterprise and ingenuity, to supply their wants.

A few observations on such articles, the produce and manufacture of India, as are fitted for the consumption of foreign nations, and which have not been already considered, will, however, be of some value, as an illustration of the resources of India, and its capacity for foreign commerce. Most of the commodities in question have been rendered available to the consumption of civilized nations, solely through the agency of the capital and ingenuity of British subjects.

The most important of these commodities is indigo. The plant which produces the Indian indigo, or the *indigofera tinctoria*, grows luxuriantly from the equator to the thirtieth degree of latitude; and, wherever the soil is fertile enough, and the climate warm enough, will yield, although with much caprice as to soil, season and moment of manufacture, a good and abundant dyeing material. From the earliest period of our intercourse with India, it would appear that we exported indigo from that country; but the drug being of native, and therefore of unskilful manufacture, it was, in due time, expelled from the markets of Europe, by the competition of the more skilfully prepared drug of America and the West Indies. Soon after the peace of 1783, the West India process of manufacture was introduced into Bengal; and, nearly from that time, and, until the last five or six years, when the exported opium has surpassed it in value, indigo has constituted the principal article of the exports of India. Shortly afterwards it was introduced into the north-western provinces of the Gangetic plain; and, in later periods, into some of the Madras provinces – into Java, and into the Philippine islands; all of which now produce indigo for the European, American, and even Persian and Arabian markets, to the very general exclusion of the indigo of tropical America, which, as already stated, had once superseded it. The quantity produced everywhere else is very secondary, both in quantity and quality, to that which is raised in Behar and Bengal; the rich soil and warm climate of which seem to be peculiarly congenial to the plant. The territory most favourable to the production of indigo lies between the twenty-third and the twenty-seventh degrees of north latitude and between the eighty-fourth and ninetieth of east longitude. Whether from inferior skill or unsuitableness of soil and climate, or both of these, what is now produced to the northward and westward of the limits thus described is of a very inferior quality. The annual produce of all the Bengal provinces has been estimated at about nine million pounds weight, produced on about a million and a quarter acres of cultivated land; the planters, on an average, farming about 2,500 acres each. The prime cost of the article, to the planters, has been estimated, by themselves, at £1,680,000; yielding a gross profit, including risk and charges, to the port of exportation, of above 40 per cent, and thus making the export value about £2,400,000.* This is surely striking and conclusive evidence of the resources of India, when elicited by the application of European skill and capital.

The next most important article of the export produce of India is raw-silk, at least for European consumption. The production of silk in India is confined to Bengal, and even here to a very limited space – a few spots here and there, on the banks of the Ganges, raised for the purpose of cultivation, above the inundation of the river, and lying between the twenty-third and twenty-fifth degrees of north latitude. The species of silk worm, and the species of mulberry it feeds upon, are both peculiar to Bengal; and this is, probably, at least one cause why the raising of silk has not been more extended, and why the Indian silk is inferior, as it confessedly is, to that of China, Italy, and France – all equally produced from the *Bombyx mori*, feeding on the white mulberry.

The Italian mode of winding silk, and the machinery necessary for it, were introduced into Bengal by the East India Company about sixty-five years ago, and from this time dates the exportation of silk from Bengal. The trade from that time has been, for the most part, in their hands; few natives and a still smaller number of Europeans venturing to enter into competition with them – another substantial ground for the inferiority

---

* Letters from British Settlers in the Interior of India; London, 1831. [The reference is to Letter xxvi, 6 November 1829, p. 93. – *Editor*]

of Indian silk in quantity and in quality. In the year 1828–29, the quantity of raw silk exported from Calcutta was 1,597,440 lb.; and its value £956,117. Of this amount, the silk of the Company constituted nearly four-fifths of the whole. Besides this, about £200,000 worth of manufactured silk goods were exported; so that the whole value of silk is not equal to one half that of the indigo.

The silk manufacture of this kingdom has been in a state of prosperity since the freedom secured to it, in 1825; and its annual value, at present, is estimated at seven millions sterling. Our manufacturers justly express their dissatisfaction at the small amount, and inferior quality, of the supply of the raw material, which they receive from the British possessions in India. In truth, the progress of the manufacture has depended, chiefly, upon the raw silk brought from China, a country which, as long as silk was an article of the East India Company's exclusive investment, hardly contributed any quantity worth naming to our supply.

As soon as the East India Company have disposed of all their silk filatures, which is at present in progress, the produce, and trade of raw silk, will necessarily fall into private hands; and there is fair ground to hope for an extension of both. Silk, and even the best silk, is produced in China, as far north as the thirty-second degree of latitude, in a more elevated, and, there-fore, in a much colder country than India. In Europe, the culture of the mulberry for feeding worms, extends to the forty-seventh degree; and it would seem, indeed, to succeed best between the forty-second and forty-third degrees, judging by the produce of Italy. There can, therefore, we should presume, be no reason whatever, for not expecting that the culture of silk might be extended from its present narrow limits, to the most northerly portions of our dominions, and wherever the soil is rich enough for the growth of the mulberry.

Opium is an article calculated to become of vast importance to the agriculture and commerce of India. The growth of the poppy is, at present, confined to a few districts of the lower provinces of Bengal, pretty much in the same way as the growth of tobacco is confined to a few districts of France, for the purposes of the government monopoly in that country. In the great province of Malwa, however, in the centre of India, it is now freely cultivated, paying an export duty; and to this we, in fact, owe the vast increase which has taken place in the trade in it, within the last twenty years. In India there is a considerable local consumption of this article, especially in some of the north-western provinces; but the great marts for its consumption are the Malayan islands, the countries lying between India and China, and above all, China itself. We believe we shall not over-rate the whole export produce of opium from India, at 24,000 chests a year; nor the export value of every chest, at £120 sterling; making a total value of £2,880,000. The wholesale price of the article to the consumers will certainly amount to a sum of not less than three-and-a-half millions sterling. This is probably a larger sum than is paid by foreign nations for all the wines exported from France, Spain, and Italy. In Indian agriculture, the poppy may be said to take the place of the vine and olive, in southern Europe. It is ascertained by experience, that it may be grown in any good dry soil, in India, from the thirtieth degree of latitude, to the twenty-fourth; and, indeed, in high lands to a much lower latitude. The freedom of its growth, therefore, would be of vast advantage, both to the agricultural and commercial industry of India, and one which ought not to be sacrificed, even were there a necessity for the sacrifice, for an annual revenue of £700,000 or £800,000, which is the utmost amount of it. The present consumers either cannot, on account of soil or climate, or are not permitted by municipal laws, to cultivate the poppy. Among these customers, who extend from the seventh degree of south to the fortieth degree of north latitude, and from the ninety-fifth to the one hundred and twentieth of east longitude, and whose numbers cannot well be estimated at fewer than 400 million people, opium has been more or less an article of consumption ever since we knew them. During the last fifty years it has been constantly on the increase – in the first thirty, slowly; but in the last twenty so rapidly, that the quantity has multiplied at the least fourfold. It would be absurd, then, we repeat, to suppose that a liberal government should, by the exercise of a petty monopoly, producing but a few hundred thousand pounds of revenue, sacrifice a great national advantage, the amount of which might be realized by an export duty of some 30 per cent, levied on strangers directly, without detriment to its own subjects. For the last thirty years the opium revenue derived from the monopoly has been stationary, or rather, indeed, declining – a monstrous state of things, when it is considered that within the same period, the quantity of the article exported has multiplied tenfold, and the value at least fivefold; but such is the sure result of all monopolies.

Saltpetre is an article of the foreign trade of which Bengal had a natural monopoly, until the recent discovery of cubic nitre, or nitrate of soda, in South America, interfered in a small degree with it. Wherever the severity of the hot winds prevail, from the eastern limit of Behar, in about the eighty-eighth degree of longitude, to the western limits of India; and from the twenty-fifth degree of latitude, nearly up to the northern mountains, this commodity is produced, abundantly, in dry and sterile soils, unfit for cultivation. In 1828–29, the quantity exported from Calcutta was about 14,000 tons, valued at about £160,000. About forty years ago, the exportation amounted to little more than half this amount; so that, in fact, the trade in this commodity has been doubled in that period. Forty years ago, the quantity used in England, on an average of years of peace and war, was short of 1,900 tons; it is now, after twenty-three years of peace, between 7,000 and 8,000, or four times as great. The difference is easily accounted for by the increase of arts and population among us, and by the difference in price between the produce of a free commerce, and a close monopoly.

We shall now sum up the amounts and values of the staple articles of foreign export; and, from these, the reader will be enabled to form a more competent idea of the resources of India for foreign trade, than from the perusal of the meagre statements of the Custom-house.

Upon some of these articles, already described under the head of the inland trade, a few remarks will not be out of place, viewed as articles of foreign consumption. The Americans export about 350,000,000 lb. of cotton, worth about £7,000,000;

Opium, 24,000 chests, of about 140 lb. weight each	£2,880,000
Indigo, 10,000,000 lb.	2,500,000
Cotton wool, 100,000,000 lb.	1,500,000
Cotton manufactures	250,000
Raw silk, 1,600,000 lb	950,000
Silk manufactures	200,000
Corn and grain, 468,750 qrs.	375,000
Sugar, 16,000 tons	256,000
Saltpetre, 14,000 tons	160,000
Total	£9,071,000

so that a branch of American industry, of little more than forty years standing, exceeds the corresponding branch from all British India, in the proportion, as to quantity, of $3\frac{1}{2}$ to 1; and as to value in that of 7 to $1\frac{1}{2}$. Indian cotton, generally, is the lowest in quality of all the kinds known in the markets of Europe; being, in comparison to all others, dirty, and coarse and short in the staple. Generally speaking, it is not above half the average value of the cottons of other countries. Considerable improvement has been made of late years in the marketable value of Indian cotton; but there is still wide room for improvement. India has similar soils, climates, and physical localities to those countries which produce the best cotton: it produces itself, in some localities, very fine cotton, and it must be clear, therefore, that its present inferiority can have no other source than a slovenly and barbarous cultivation and preparation; for which, the obvious remedy is abundant capital, skilfully directed.

The quantity of sugar exported from all British India is less than one-third part of what is exported from the little island of Mauritius; and the average quality of what is exported is much inferior to that of almost any other exporting country. As in the case with cotton, the careless culture and manufacture of small and poverty striken cultivators and manufacturers, are the chief causes of this inferiority. In this article, as well as in cotton, there has been a considerable improvement of late years; and the best qualities of East Indian sugars in the English market (a very small proportion, however, of the whole) are now scarcely inferior to the best qualities of West Indian. Until last year they paid one-third more duty than the latter; that is, a cwt. of East India sugar, worth 32s., paid a duty of the same amount, or cent per cent upon the value; while a cwt. of West Indian sugar, of the same price, paid but 24s., or 75 per cent. In short, there was a bounty of 25 per cent in favour of the one, and against the other; and this is, indeed, a very favourable view of the fiscal arrangement, which, for more than twenty years, operated against the consumption of the produce of India. The sugars are now put upon an equality, in so far as concerns the exports of Bengal, being the produce of the British possessions; but still, excluding from the advantage, the export of every other part of British India, an unjust, absurd, and mischievous distinction, which ought immediately to be abandoned. Under the old system, out of a yearly consumption in this kingdom of 180,000 tons, the whole consumption of Indian sugar was less than 4,000 tons – one forty-fifth part of the whole quantity! With the high cost of producing West Indian and colonial sugars, there is no doubt but the quantity of Indian sugar consumed in England will be very greatly increased under the new arrangement of duties. Indeed, it may be observed that if we take into consideration all the circumstances of abundance of land, fertility of soil, and cheapness of labour, there is no country in the world so well suited to the growth of the sugar cane, as a very large proportion of our Indian territory. The distance of the voyage will go for little or nothing, since, unlike the tropical countries of the western world producing sugar, India has a large body of consumers of British produce and manufactures; from which it necessarily follows, that a great share of the home freight is paid for by the profits of the outward investment.

The corn of India, both rice and wheat, is inferior to that of other countries, for the very same reason that Indian cotton and sugar are inferior, viz. that they are the produce of a rude husbandry, and rude preparation. Rice is scalded instead of being kiln-dried; and wheat is subjected to no process of drying at all, except what it receives from desiccation in the sun. The rice, in husking, instead of being carefully separated from the husks, is broken and damaged by using the rudest instruments in the process. Although, therefore, the finest sorts be nearly equal in quality to Carolina, in the market of England, the great bulk of what is imported is scarcely of one half the value. It is needless to add, then, that there is a wide field here for more capital, and its concomitant, skill. The value of all descriptions of corn and grain, under whatever name or denomination, exported from the United States of America, is, on an average of years, about two-and-a-half millions sterling, which approaches to about seven times the amount of all that is exported from British India. India, however, has, without doubt, the capacity of becoming a large corn exporting country, with proper improvements in its agricultural industry. We have pointed to the means of effecting such improvements; the chief of which, we may repeat, is a skilful and extended system of irrigation.

Were the corn laws abolished in this country, it is not improbable, but that even Indian wheat might be imported into England. The export price at Calcutta – for this grain is brought by an easy voyage down the Ganges, near the banks of which lie some of the best wheat countries – does not exceed 12s. per quarter, or, allowing for its inferiority to European wheat, 16s. At the ordinary prices which have prevailed of late years, 16s. more would pay freight to England, and allowing 8s. for charges and profits, it might, consequently, be produced in the English market at 34s. per quarter, or, allowing for inferiority, at 40s. In fact, between 5,000 and 6,000 quarters of Indian wheat were imported in 1831, a year in which the average prices in this country exceeded 66s. a quarter. We may take this opportunity of observing, that the productiveness of the Gangetic provinces – an advantage which by no means belongs to many other parts of the British possessions – is subject, comparatively, to very little fluctuation from year to year. The soil and the seasons are congenial to husbandry; there is no year in which Bengal does not export corn; there have been few scarcities in any part of the country; and no actual famine for near seventy years.

It must be evident enough that improvement in the old and tried articles of the production of India must be of far more consequence to the agricultural and commercial industry of the country, than the introduction of new ones, although we would by no means be thought to deprecate enterprise in the latter. Besides silk and indigo, which are virtually new commodities, introduced through European skill and capital, the following articles have been actually introduced, or are in the course of introduction – dye and shel-lac, largely used in the arts in England; linseed, very largely imported into England, within the last three years; safflower; castor oil; sal-ammoniac; coal, so indispensable to the success of steam navigation in India, and of which the already ascertained fields are very extensive, and conveniently situated; hides, of which, last year, there were imported to the number of 377,488, which is little short of half the importations from South America, the old staple of our supply; coffee, introduced into Malabar, Mysore, Ceylon, and Bengal, and of which, last year, there were already imported into England 5,783,880 lb. weight; and tea, of which plants have been recently introduced into Bengal, in some of the countries, on the north-east frontier of which, the native plant has been discovered, and where, therefore, the soil and climate bearing a considerable resemblance to the tea countries of China, it is not unlikely to succeed. From other parts of the British dominions, tin, an article, in a great measure, new to the consumers of Europe; and of which, last year, no less than 783 tons were imported, and of which, indeed, generally there is imported, one-quarter of the quantity produced by the Cornish mines; antimony, first discovered about twelve years ago, and of which last year, 1,500 tons were imported, and 825 used at home; catechu, or terra japonica, recently imported and now largely used in calico printing, and of which last year, the quantity imported was about 1,500 tons, and that taken for consumption upwards of 500 tons; with pearl sago. These are all articles which have been discovered, or brought forward, for the foreign trade, by the enterprise of Europeans. This rapid sketch will give the reader a general notion of the capacity of India for foreign commerce; and prove, we trust, to his satisfaction, that the field for a judicious application of capital is vast, and, in a practical sense, inexhaustible.

Chapter IV

Monetary system of India consists of silver two-shilling pieces, or rupees. Indian banking and bills of exchange. Usual rates of interest charged by Indian bankers. Hoarding and buying of treasure. Expense of counting, examining, and transporting of treasure. Expense of coinage. Estimate of the advantages of a paper circulation for India.

The standard currency of continental India consists of silver in coins, generally of the value of about 2s.; on which are invariably impressed, in Persian characters, and in the Persian language, the name of the reigning Mogul, the year of his reign in which they are struck, and name of the place where they are coined. This is the well known rupee – a word of Hindoo origin, meaning silver. There are copper coins (counters, of course), representing one sixty-fourth part of the rupee, or the quarter of the sixteen parts into which the rupee of account is divided. In native transactions the smallest change is represented by shells, called cowries, of which eighty go to the smallest copper coin, and, consequently, no less than 5,120 to the rupee. The use of so minute a denomination of money is an index of the poverty of the people, and of the low price of wages, and necessaries of life among them. In this country, a farthing, equal in value to more than fifty cowries, is hardly of any use as money. The shells thus used are species of Cyprea, imported in cargoes, as an article of trade from the Maldive and Laccadive islands, and are the same as are used in some parts of Africa for the same purpose.

Silver coins, and most probably silver money, were first introduced by the Mahomedan conquerors. Gold, as far as they had coins at all, was the money of the Hindoos; and, in the southern parts of India, rude coins of this metal, from the value of 6d. up to 7s., known to Europeans by the name of pagodas and gold fanams, are still in circulation.

Since the fall of the Mogul empire, and very probably also before it, every petty prince coined his own money, and fixed his own standard. Dr Kelly has given a list of above eighty different kinds of rupee, varying in the quantity of pure silver they contain, and varying also in sterling value, from 1s. 2d. up to 2s. 2d.; but, on an average, their worth is somewhat under 2s.[1] Until last year the British government had no less than five mints – three in Bengal, and one in each of the other presidencies at each of which rupees of different values were coined – to perplex their subjects and puzzle themselves. The whole of the rupees, new value, coined in the British territory, are reduced to one nearly 2s. each – a very great improvement.

Paper money, whether in bills or notes, forms a very small proportion of the Indian circulation. Bills of exchange have been known to the Hindoos from very remote periods. They are known to Europeans under the name of Hoondee, a corruption of the Indian word Hindwi, or Hindoo; a word which is Persian, and, therefore, evidently given to them by the Mahomedan conquerors. In every large town of India are to be found native bankers, or shroffs, who deal in bills of exchange, and who have correspondents, not only in all the great towns of Hindostan itself, whether British, tributary, or independent, but even in Cashmere, and some parts of Persia. The Hoondee, or bill, it may be observed, is drawn out in a written character, peculiar to the class of bankers, and illegible to anyone else. Very generally the Indian bankers distrust the conveyance by the European letter post, and have *estaffettes*, or special couriers, of their own.

The business of banking among the Indians is chiefly confined to the issuing and discounting of bills of exchange, money lending, and money changing, or the exchanging of one description of coins for another. The receiving of deposits can hardly be said to be part of their business; and the issuing of notes, payable to bearer, or paper-money, has always been unknown to the Indians; and, as will be presently seen, these two forms of banking exist, even under our government, but to a very limited extent, hardly affecting the general conclusion that the whole money of India is in silver coin; and that, with a

---

[1] [Partick Kelly, *Oriental Metrology, comprising the monies, weights, and measures of the East Indies and other trading places in Asia reduced to the English standard by verified operations* (London, 1832). – *Editor*]

single exception, that of the Treasury of the British government, there is no place of absolute safe deposit for money. India, in fact, may be said to be exactly in the same state that Great Britain would be in, if the whole circulation of the latter were in half-crown pieces, and that there were no place of deposit for money but the public stocks, and the coffers of individual merchants and speculators, exercising, on their own responsibility, in this respect, the functions of bankers.

The profits of the *shroffs*, or Indian bankers, are very large; and they constitute, now, and have always constituted, by far the wealthiest class of the Indian people. The richest are to be found in the towns of Calcutta, Benares, and Bombay; but many wealthy persons, of the same class, are to be found, also, in the cities of Delhi, Agra, Lucknow, Patna, Surat, Dacca, Mirzapore, and others. The number of this class, of every sort, is indeed very great, for they are not only found in every town, but also in every considerable village. In Calcutta there are five or six, said to be worth a million sterling each, although this is perhaps an exaggeration; and, at Benares, they are still more wealthy.

Among the Mahomedans, as is well known, all interest is deemed to be usury, and therefore illegal – a law, however, which, if not more honoured by them in the breach than the observance, is more frequently broken than observed. With the Hindoos, on the contrary, the profit on money lent, or interest, is not only legal, but the amount which can be exacted, may, in general terms, be described as unlimited. British subjects alone are limited by law to an interest of 12 per cent. The rate of interest in India, between native and native, is variable, but always enormous; a great part of the amount, however, consisting, not in the profit of the capital lent, but in the risk of lending to a needy borrower, in a country where the administration of justice always has been, and still is, very imperfect.

Of the class of small bankers, the best account we have seen is that in *Hamilton's Hindostan*, and which we believe is taken from the manuscript statistical account of Bengal, by the late Dr Francis Buchannan Hamilton. 'Potdars, or money changers', says Mr Hamilton, are a very numerous class, but many of them having no shop, sit in the open market, with heaps of cowries placed before them. In the more rural quarters, the money changer goes to market with a bag of cowries on his head; or, if a rich man, with a loaded ox, which, if strong, may carry to the value of an hundred and fifty rupees. All the early part of the market, he sells cowries for silver, to the people who wish to purchase goods, and in the evening the various hucksters bring back their cowries, and change them for silver. In the morning the money changer usually gives 5,760 cowries for a rupee, and in the evening he gives a rupee for 5,920 cowries, which is a profit of one thirty-sixth part on every good mint rupee, besides a fluctuating batta, or exchange on all others. It is also customary with the money changers to advance cowries to all servants who have monthly wages; and at the end of the month, when the wages become due, they return the loan in silver; for all this class, if trusted, anticipate their income. To these improvident persons the money changer gives only seventy puns of cowries for his rupee, so that he realises four seventy-fourths per month, for the use of the money; but occasionally loses his principal. *

The discount charged may here be taken at about 3 per cent on each operation: if the market be held, therefore, once a week, this gross profit on the capital is repeated fifty-two times every year; and if it be a twice a week market, as is more probable, 104 times. What Sir James Stewart said of government payments, in his time, it appears, therefore, is still applicable to the ordinary disbursements of the great bulk of the people. 'The money paid by the labourers of the ground', observes he, 'is, at present interrupted, in its course, at every change of hands, until, by the repeated *shroffage* (discount), it comes at last reduced, as I may say, to a shadow, into the company's treasure.'†

We shall give examples from different parts of India of the rates of interest usual exacted by the Indian money lenders, the great mass of the borrowers being, of course, the occupants of the soil, because they constitute the great majority of the people. The late Sir Thomas Munro, who had better opportunities of judging, and a mind and acquirements better fitting him to judge of such matters, than perhaps any other European sojourner in India, gives the following official description of

* *Ibid.* I, 40.
† Page 72 [Sir James Stewart, *Principles of Money as applied to the present state of the coin of Bengal* (London, 1772). – *Editor*]

transactions of this nature, in a country subject to his own authority, more extensive than the kingdom of Scotland, and containing two million people. 'Almost every ryot', says he, has an account with a bazar-man (money-lender) and a balance against him. This account often runs through two or three generations, and is rarely paid off entirely. It usually originates in a small advance by the bazar-man, who probably gives seventy or eighty rupees, and takes a bond for an hundred with interest, at two and a half per centum monthly. The ryot, in return, makes payment in grain, cotton, or other articles, which are usually valued against him, and he receives, occasionally, from a bazar-man, small sums for the discharge of his *kists* (instalments of tax). After going on in this way, for a number of years, the ryot finds, that though he is continually paying, he is only getting deeper into debt.*

The medium interest here exacted is not 30 but 40 per cent; while the banker, in receiving payment of it, turns merchant, and, in that character, exacts a further interest. Both the borrower and the state are plundered, by this most miserable system.

If we go to Bengal, the richest and best known part of India we shall find the state of things to be exactly the same. Our evidence here shall be taken from the work of the late Mr Alexander Fraser Tytler, whose information was deemed, by the historian of British India, to be superior in value to any which had ever been laid before the British public; and whose early death he deplored, as not only a loss to his country, but to human kind. 'The great mass', says Mr Tytler,

of the people of Bengal, the peasants and tradesmen (who are also cultivators of the land, and whose gains can only increase with the wealth of the peasantry) are unable to purchase European articles of commerce. They live from day to day, and nine-tenths of them are forced to borrow their daily food, and corn to sow their lands, from the mahajuns (banker merchants). On the grain supplied for their family consumption, the mahajuns charge the peasant fifty per cent, on that furnished for seed a hundred per cent. Besides this, by false accounts, and by taking an inhuman advantage of the situation of the ryots, they often keep them in balance.†

* Report of Sir Thomas Munro; 1807. Selection of papers from records of the India House; vol. ɪ, p. 237.

† Considerations on the Present Political State of India: London, 1815. The vituperation of the Indian bankers by Mr Tytler, and others, is not justifiable. The Indian bankers are just what the nature of their position makes them, and, neither better nor worse, than what any other class of men would be, under similar circumstances. The celebrated political economist, Sir James Stewart, in the Project

So far for the provinces under the governments of Madras and Bengal. We have equally good testimony for those under that of Bombay. Colonel Sykes,[1] who for years conducted a minute and extensive survey of the Deccan, containing between three and four million people, gave, fresh from that survey, the following evidence before a Committee of the House of Commons:

What is the rate of interest paid by the cultivator for the advances of capital, and what persons are in the habit of making those advances? About two per cent a month, but it is sometimes much higher; and, in borrowing seed-grain, it is frequently an hundred, to a hundred and fifty per cent. The lenders are Brahmins, and that class of shopkeepers called *warees*, who correspond to grocers and grain dealers in Europe. Are the ryots in such a situation as to make it necessary for them frequently to borrow at this most extravagant rate of interest? I am afraid they are, as there is a great deal of improvidence in the ryot. *

For all India, we have the testimony of the late Mr Mill, an historian, a philosopher, and a practical statesman, after twelve years acquaintance with the official details of Indian finance, and at least thirty years acquaintance with India, generally.

Are the zemindars in the habit of raising money by loan, in the way of mortgage? They raise money by way of loan: to what degree it can be considered mortgage, I do not feel myself competent to speak. Do they raise it upon mortgage bearing interest, and so that the creditor can come in, and take possession by means of foreclosure? Mortgage, I imagine, among the zemindars is, by no means, a common thing. The interest of money is exceedingly high to the zemindars: at this time, when money is borrowed by government at four per cent, it is reported that twenty-four

of an Indian Bank, which he published sixty-five years ago, gives a juster verdict. ' In this view ', says he, ' the Bank will be a check upon every one who may have it in his power to oppress the labourer, or the manufacturer; because the profits of the bank will depend much upon the credit of the inhabitants, and upon the preservation of their property. . . . What a new phenomenon in Bengal, a Shroff director of a bank, from a blood-sucker is become the protector of the labouring man! Interest does all. He sucks the blood because it is his interest so to do: he gives his protection from the same motive. By directing the interest of individuals to a proper object, good government is established.' The Principles of Money, applied to the present state of the Coin of Bengal, etc. etc. 1772, page 81.

* Minutes of Evidence before the Select Committee on the affairs of the East India Company, in 1832.

[1] [William Henry Sykes (1790–1872), served in the Indian army, and was appointed official statistical reporter to the Government of Bombay in 1824. He became Chairman of the East India Company in 1855. See *D.N.B. – Editor*]

per cent and even thirty per cent, is a common rate paid by the zemindars in Bengal. Upon what security does the zemindar raise money? Upon his personal security and his property, which is sold for debts to his private creditors, as well as to government. A zemindary will be sold in the execution of a decree, as well as for arrears to government.*

In a country with so rude and clumsy a monetary system as we have described, and where there was a great deal, and there still is, much anarchy, the hoarding and burying of treasure are, of course, very frequent. There is hoarding both by private individuals and by governments, and burying by the former. These modes of misapplying capital are, in fact, inevitable in such a state of society, and have prevailed in every age and every country similarly circumstanced, as well as in India. It would be in vain to attempt any estimate of the amount of the precious metals wasted in this manner; but evidence of the existence of both practices is easily adduced. In the ten years ending with 1823–24, the net importation of bullion – that is, the importations, deducting the exportations – amounted to the enormous sum of 233,773,231 rupees, for Calcutta alone, exclusive of what was imported into Madras, Bombay, and other ports. This, at the sterling value of the rupee, will give an average annual importation little short of two-and-a-half millions sterling. 'Such parts of this – and', says the home government, 'they must be very considerable – as do not remain in circulation can only be accounted for by supposing they are retained in the *hoards* of individuals, or disposed of by the abundant use of bullion ornaments, in which the natives of India indulge.'† The imports of bullion into Bombay, in excess of the exports, seem to amount yearly to about a million sterling; so that, allowing the imports and exports, at all other ports, and on the frontier, to balance each other, we shall have a clear sum of three millions and a half sterling as the annual consumption of the precious metals in India.

A frequent practice with all classes in India, and especially with the lower classes, is to melt down gold and silver coins into

* Minutes of Evidence before a Select Committee of the House of Commons, 1831.

† Letter from the Court of Directors to the Governor-General, 24 September 1828.

ornaments, for themselves, wives, and children, but especially for the latter; and hence, the origin in India of a crime unknown in Europe – the murder of children for the gold and silver ornaments they wear. When an Indian peasant, or artizan, happens, by good fortune, to save a few rupees, having no means of safe custody, and still less the means of investing the money to advantage, he melts the coin down to make ornaments for his wife and children; and hence the rude and massy armlets, bracelets, anklets, collars, and nose ornaments, which are so frequent. Of the hoards of private individuals, of course, we can know nothing; but of those of government we have a considerable mass of evidence. It appears, from an official statement, that, in the ten years ending with 1826–27, and taking the first day of May as an example, there existed, in the provincial treasuries of fifty-four collectorates of Bengal and Madras, a sum in hard silver money of £1,702,195, which is declared by the home authorities, in so far as Madras is concerned, to have been constantly half a million more than the exigencies of the public service required. From 1821 to 1824, the balance in the Indian treasuries, throughout, almost every rupee of it in silver or gold coin, amounted to ten millions sterling. The balance of the precious metals lying in the British treasuries is, indeed, never short of seven millions sterling, as may be seen by the following official statement of the cash balance, on 30 April in each year:

1832	7,453,360
1833	7,232,515
1834	7,377,766
1835	7,916,031
1836 estimate	8,999,641 *

The greatest hoarder of treasure in India is the king of Oude better known as the nabob of Lucknow. His principality contains an area of about 24,000 square miles, and a population of about seven millions. This prince was supposed, some years ago, to hoard annually about half a million sterling, which he was enabled to do by maintaining hardly any military establishment:

* East India Annual Revenue Accounts, 1836.

paying very little to his civil officers, whose chief employment was the collection of his revenue; and exacting everything he could from his subjects. In 1814–15, out of this hoard, he lent the British government two millions sterling; and, in 1827, he gave them another million, for which he received, in return, some barren and unhealthy lands, under the Himalaya mountains.

The capture, by the British, of the strongholds of the natives has often afforded evidence of the extent to which these princes carried the practice of hoarding; although, in almost every case, much of the hoards was expended in the hostilities which led to the captures. In 1781, there was found in the strongholds of the chief of Benares, a mere zemindar, or collector of the land revenue, a sum little short of a quarter of a million sterling. In 1799, there was found, in Seringapatam, near a million sterling, in the precious metals, after three expensive wars with the English, and after the loss of a great extent of territory. In one of the many strongholds of the Mahratta chief Scindia, there was found, in 1803, £330,000 in hard specie; and, in 1826, in Bhurtpore, the capital of a small Hindoo principality, about £900,000. Throughout all Asia, indeed, the practice of hoarding is general. The king of Ava, the sovereign of a very poor people, was supposed, before his war with us, to have accumulated a treasure, in gold and silver ingots, amounting to above a million and a quarter sterling. In the stronghold of one petty prince of Java, the British found a treasure, in specie, of £200,000.

From these samples, the reader will be enabled to judge of the extent to which hoarding is carried on by the Indian governments.* On the subject of burying treasure, Mr Tytler, whom

---

* The amount of the royal treasure, carried away by Nadir Shah from Delhi, in 1739, is alleged to be greatly exaggerated; but we really see no ground for this conclusion. The event took place within thirty years of the death of Aurungzebe, and while the empire was still tolerably entire. The mark of the royal treasury was the first, in the period of two centuries, and yet the whole amount taken was but three and-a-half millions in specie, and a million and a half in plate; making a total of five millions, or but five times as much as was captured in the capital of the petty prince of Mysore, in 1790. As to the value of a million, set on the peacock throne, fifteen millions on jewels, and eleven millions on other property, they are obviously arbitrary, and even fanciful, and ought not to be taken into the computation.

we have already quoted, states, with respect to the country-people in Bengal, 'Any improvement in their circumstances marks them out as victims for the dacoits (gang-robbers). They, therefore, bury their gains, till they have become considerable, and then spend them in the manner above described – in expensive religious ceremonies and shows, and in feeding the Brahmins.' The evidence of Mr Sinclair, a civil officer of the Indian government, whose official duties were exercised in Tanjore, the richest province of the Madras presidency, is to the same effect. He thus expressed himself, before a committee of the House of Commons, in 1831.

Are any of the meerassydars men of prudent, saving habits? In general, they are not; the great meerassydors are like great landlords, elsewhere, they are very often encumbered with debt; and on the occasion of a marriage, or other great ceremony, they do not limit their expenses by any regard to the future. In the event of their accumulating any capital, what means have they of disposing of it? I believe they generally bury it. There is no means of their employing it to any extent, and there is no place where they would feel disposed to deposit it. Would they be disposed, if the government gave them facilities, to deposit it in the coffers of the government? No; and it would be exceedingly troublesome to have such a complicated account. Would it not be attended with great advantage to that province, if banks were established? I think a bank might be of use. *

In every country, indeed, where property is insecure, and the monetary system imperfect, the burying of the precious metals is sure to take place. Throughout Europe, as everyone knows, it prevailed to so great an extent, for at least twelve centuries, so that treasure trove was considered a regular branch of the royal revenue; and yet the anarchy, in its darkest ages, is not to be compared to that of the East, at all times. The observation especially refers to India, which, in every period of European connexion with it, has been deemed the peculiar tomb of the precious metals; because the singular frugality of the natives induced them to hoard that which the badness of the government did not enable them to keep for beneficial purposes. Even among so poor a people as the Burmese, our military officers, serving

* The practice, now followed, of prefixing the name of a member to the question he puts in Committee, was not in use when this evidence was taken, or we should have had the pleasure of recording the name of the representative who put the last very sensible and judicious question.

in the war with them, had ocular demonstration of the extent to which the burying of treasure was carried. The inhabitants of Rangoon had but a few hours' warning of the approach of the English expedition; yet, in these few, they contrived to bury considerable quantities of ingots of silver; which the proprietors, afterwards, exhumed with the sanction, and in the presence, of the British authorities, immediately before the restoration of the place, and after the conclusion of peace. Most of the parties, making application, recovered what they had buried; but, in several instances, the spot where it had been deposited could not be identified, and the money was, of course, lost, to be recovered, perhaps, as treasure-trove, by some future generation.

The counting, and the transport, of treasure, in a country where there is little assistance from paper-money, and but an inconsiderable accommodation from bills of exchange, must, of necessity, be a source of great public inconvenience, and great public loss. The difficulty of counting is aggravated, in India, by the whole currency, or nearly so, being in silver – even in small pieces of that metal. Even supposing the whole of such pieces to be of the same standard value and denomination, every piece ought to be counted and examined, although in great payments this becomes impracticable, and recourse must be had to weighing, which, of course, excludes examination.

A few years ago, the British government issued an order that no rupees should be received into the public treasury that had lost any part of their weight, as all metallic money must, sooner or later do, by friction, unless on payment of the ascertained difference, in the shape of a discount. This was a glorious opportunity for the native servants of the public treasuries – for the money-changers and for the money-lenders. Every piece had to be examined and weighed, and a discount charged on each (for few were allowed to be of the full weight) at the rate of from $\frac{3}{4}$ to 2 per cent. The treasury establishments of money-counters and examiners had to be increased, while the money-lenders advanced light money to the tax-payers, and exacted payment in money of the full weight; so that the ignorant contributors to the taxes had to pay a new impost, under very vexatious circumstances.

It has been stated, as the result of an experiment, that it would take an inexperienced person, at the rate of eight hours a day, for every working-day, a whole year to count a million of sovereigns, to say nothing of weighing and examining them. It would, of course, take ten times as long to count the same value in rupees. Although a practised money-counter will do the same thing, with infinitely more expedition, this fact is quite sufficient to demonstrate the prodigious inconvenience of such a currency as that of India. Of the inconvenience resulting from this state of things, let the transactions of the British government be taken as an example. The gross revenue, in round numbers, is, with trifling exceptions, paid and disbursed in silver pieces, of 2s. value, of which the number is 180 millions. The number of treasuries is, at least, 140; and, in some cases, the coins are paid, over and over again, between one treasury and another. The 180 million pieces are first counted by the tax contributor, and then by the collector. But these treasuries also disburse, and the whole disbursements nearly balance the whole receipts. The treasurer, in disbursing, counts once more, and the party receiving counts also. Thus, the operation of counting is performed four times over; so that, to say nothing of the intermediate countings between one treasury and another, the virtual number of pieces counted will amount to four times the amount of the revenue, or 720 millions. At every one of the 140 treasuries, there is a distinct establishment for the express purpose; and at all the principal treasuries very numerous and expensive ones. The three head treasuries of India – although those of Calcutta and Madras receive considerable assistance from the use of paper-money, and although they be mere offices of receipt and disbursement – consist of about 200 persons, and cost about £25,000 a year.

Then comes the charge of transporting money over an area of near a million square miles, on bad roads, and through countries sometimes so dangerous that a strong military escort is often necessary; even with the assistance of which, examples have occurred of the treasure being plundered. In Bengal, the expense on this account is diminished by payments made by European merchants at Calcutta, for drafts on the provincial collectors, on account of advances for cotton, indigo, and other produce. At Madras, where there is little trade, the expenses appear to be very heavy; for we find, in the public accounts, the single item of extra pay to the European officers in charge of treasure escorts, amounting yearly to upwards of £10,000. Independent of the actual outlay in these cases, there must be taken into account the disorganization which such detachments produce in the military force, and the known injury and inconvenience which their march occasions to the inhabitants.*

Besides the treasure transported by land, a great deal has also to be conveyed, by long sea voyages, to London, and occasionally to seven separate settlements to the eastward; and to Madras and Bombay, the revenue of every one of which is short of their expenditure; making an aggregate annual deficit of two millions and a half which Bengal has, one way or another, to supply. It is true that this is done, generally, by granting bills on the Bengal treasury, to merchants and others having payments to make in Bengal; but, (in the case of London especially) the coin is not unfrequently transported: and on military expeditions it is always so.

The inconvenience arising out of a metallic currency constitutes of course, a most material item in the charge of collecting the public revenue; and that that charge itself is enormous, and demands reduction in every shape in which it can be effected, will be made apparent to the reader, by the following brief statement drawn from the latest official documents upon the subject.

Indian revenue and charges of collection for 1833–34.

Territory	Gross revenue £	Charge of collection £	Net revenue £	Per centum On gross revenue	On net revenue
Bengal	11,366,028	1,996,745	9,369,283	17½	21¼
Madras	4,641,491	561,203	4,080,288	12	13¾
Bombay	2,441,707	294,300	2,147,406	12½	13¾
Total	18,449,226	2,852,248	15,596,977	15½	18¼

* Of 356 removals which took place in 1829 (in Bengal), 39 were, or might have been, made by water. Treasure is always accompanied by a military escort, and that employed on the 39 removals above mentioned amounted to 90,000 men,

This however exhibits, neither the correct revenue, nor the charge: there are annuities in the shape of allowances and assignments, paid out of the gross revenue as above given. These are, properly speaking, the price paid by the present possessors of India for the fee simple of the territory; and they amounted, in the year already given, to the following sums, for the three governments of India.

Bengal	£525,042
Madras	634,764
Bombay	442,670
Total	£1,602,476

Thus, the real net revenue of India is actually short of fourteen millions; and the charge upon this, above 28 per cent.

Coining is another heavy drawback upon a country like India, with a silver currency, and little or no paper money. In the public accounts, the annual loss sustained on this account, after deducting a revenue derived from a charge on refining, and a seignorage of 2 per cent, is about £30,000 per annum. But in this is not included the rent of expensive buildings, and the interest, wear and tear of very expensive machinery, imported from England. If we are rightly informed, the buildings and machinery have not cost less than a million sterling. In a country such as India, where the real interest of money is high, rent, interest, and wear and tear of machinery cannot be estimated at less than 20 per cent; which, therefore, together with the sum already named, would make the actual loss on coining not less than £230,000 per annum. The assay and coining of money are, in fact, nice and difficult operations, of the nature of manufacture, and can neither be done well, nor cheaply in such a country as India, and we have not the least doubt but that the currency of India would be much more cheaply and far better coined in England.

with their officers, for one day. These troops, besides the wear and tear to which they are exposed, and the expense of their conveyance, are allowed extra batta during the whole period of their employment on this service. In steam vessels, such an escort would not be required. (Precis of Reports on the Navigation of the Rivers of India, by Lt. J. H. Johnstone, R.N.) [See Minutes of Evidence before the Select Committee of the House of Commons, Parliamentary Papers, 1831–32, vol. 10 (ii), Part 1, p. 139. – *Editor*]

From the facts now stated, the reader will see the extent of the inconvenience which is sustained from the present metallic currency, the absence of an adequate supply of good paper money, and the want of a competent amount of banking establishments. Although it be impossible to form any correct estimate of the real loss sustained by the present system, we may, at least, suppose a case which will illustrate it. It has been stated,* and the statement is supposed to be rather under than over-rated, that if there existed no paper money in England, it would require 200 millions worth of gold and silver to perform, without performing half so well, the functions which are now performed with fifty or sixty millions of the precious metals, and bank notes. From 120 to 130 millions of capital are thus disengaged, or in other words, a machine worth fifty or sixty millions sterling performs the whole work of a machine costing 200 millions, and with infinitely more convenience and dispatch. If we estimate the charge of interest, wear and tear, and coining, on the medium sum saved, or 125 millions sterling, at 5 per cent per annum, the yearly saving will amount to six-and-a-quarter millions sterling.

It would be absurd to suppose that in a poor country like India, the services to be performed by money would be, in proportion to population, what they are in a rich country like England. Let us suppose, however, that with our eighty million Indian subjects, the precious metals required in circulation would be in the proportion of one-eighth part what is required in England, which is in the proportion of the respective taxation of the two countries. In this case the active circulation of India would amount to about eighty millions, which perhaps is not overrating it, when we see a sum approaching to one-quarter of it paid annually into the British treasury. To this amount, however, ought to be added the sum which is withdrawn by hoarding and burying, and the use of which is lost to the public. Let us take this at the moderate amount of twenty millions, public and private, and we have already seen that the

* M'Cullocks Commercial Dictionary, p. 65. [J. R. McCulloch, *A Dictionary, practical, theoretical, historical, of commerce and commercial navigation* (London, 1832). *Editor*]

sum in the British treasury alone amounts to above seven millions of this amount. This will make a round sum of 100 millions, which will hardly be deemed an extravagant estimate of the circulation of a country, which has every year a net importation of three-and-a-half millions of gold and silver, to make up for wear and tear of coin, hoarding, and burying. If the same banking system were introduced into India, as exists in England, twenty-five or thirty millions sterling would perform the same functions which are now performed by 100 millions; and from seventy to seventy-five millions would be disengaged, which, reckoning interest, wear and tear and coinage at 12 per cent, would produce a yearly saving, on the average, of the two sums stated, equal to £8,700,000.

To introduce the refined and extensive system of English banking to such an extent in India, would, however, be wholly impracticable, until the country be better ordered, and confidence better established; and, therefore, we must suppose the displacing of the precious metals, and the substitution of a paper money to a much smaller extent. Let it, then, merely for the sake of illustration, be supposed practicable only to one half of the extent which we have supposed, and still the annual saving will, in a pecuniary point of view, be £4,350,000, to say nothing of the advantages of dispatch and facility, in almost every mercantile transaction.

The real difficulty of introducing a good paper currency among such a people as the Indians will, we are quite certain, not be very great. A paper currency, although not a sound one, is of very general use in Russia, where it forms the ordinary money, not only in the most civilized parts of the Empire, but even among the rudest of its tribes; parties, not only ignorant of the Russian language, but even of the arts of reading and writing. For the last thirty years it has been extensively used in Java, among seven million people, not one man out of a hundred of whom understands the writing, or the language in which the notes are printed. But the experience of India itself, as far as it has gone, is to the same effect. Among the natives of the towns of Calcutta and Madras, paper money is even preferred to metallic, and in so far as the first of these places is concerned, the notes issued in it have a circulation which extends to Benares, 560 miles above Calcutta. In fact, they are more or less known among a population of some forty million people.

Chapter V

Manner in which European mercantile transactions were conducted previously to the extinction of the Company's monopoly. Population of European emporia. Mercantile and exclusive character of the government, before the cessation of the monopoly. Description of the great European mercantile firms, which sprang up under the monopoly, and fell with it.

We have next to consider a very important branch of the subject, the manner in which the mercantile transactions of Europeans are conducted. These are, of course, carried on at the great ports of the foreign commerce, where the main body of European merchants resides, while the comparatively small number of Europeans in the provinces are, for the most part, but agents and correspondents of the mercantile firms of those places. With an exception for the law of inheritance, which is native for natives, the laws here in force are the common and statute laws of England, administered by English professional judges appointed by the crown. The places alluded to, and their computed populations, are as follows:

City of Calcutta	265,000
Town of Madras	160,000
Town and Island of Bombay	162,570
Town and Island of Sincapore	25,000
Town and Island of Panang	57,400
Town and territory of Malacca	33,800
Total	703,770

The following is the number of mercantile British firms at the several ports of British India: Calcutta, before the failure in 1830, fifty; at present sixty-two: Bombay, seventeen: Sincapore, fifteen: Madras, ten: Penang, two. To these, perhaps, we ought to add Canton, where a large body of English merchants are settled, amenable, to a certain extent, to English laws. We have here no less than eleven English firms, some of them very wealthy; besides six American houses of great respectability; and a considerable body of Persee merchants, who are British subjects.

In describing the mode of carrying on business, we shall chiefly confine ourselves to the principal port, Calcutta. The reader will recollect that, previously to the year 1814, the East India company enjoyed, by law, a monopoly of the trade of every place, from the east coast of Africa to the west coast of America inclusive. In so far as regarded the trade between the East Indies and Europe, there was very little relaxation in this monopoly for a period exceeding 200 years. But in the local trade of India, British, foreign and native, the East India company had not, for a great number of years, interfered; and although they meddled in the trade of staple articles, the produce of India, they did not exclude the competition of Europeans in them, except in so far as the latter were precluded from engaging in the inland corn, salt, and tobacco trades. It will be recollected, at the same time, that the restrictions on the residence of Europeans in India were severe and oppressive, that Europeans were liable to expulsion for any offence given to the government, and indeed, to expulsion, without any offence at all, and on bare suspicion. It was the settled policy of the government to make the number of European residents as small as possible; and, consequently, their number, up to the period in question, was very inconsiderable. Such a system was sufficient to paralyse all industry; and when we now look back to it, we are rather disposed to wonder more that the commerce of India was so considerable, than that it was so small. It was under this state of things that the great mercantile firms of Calcutta, as they were called, sprung up. Although now extinct, it will be impossible to understand the present mercantile position of India without some account of them. The relaxation which took place in the monopoly, and in the restraints upon European settlements, by the Act of 1813, brought upon the old established firms a host of active competitors, carrying on business on different principles; and the absolute cessation of the monopoly in 1833 completed the revolution which commenced in 1814; so that the trade of India is, at the present moment, upon a totally different footing to what it had ever been before. It became, in fact, free for the first time, after a lapse of 230 years.

The great houses of Calcutta, the failure of which, for vast sums, is so well known to the public, had, for the most part, been established about fifty years, before their fall in 1830, and the three subsequent years. They were six in number, and their partners, generally from three to four, consisted, in many instances, of civil, military, and medical officers of the East India Company; who, tempted by the large fortunes which had been realized in them, had quitted the public service, and entered them. Although generally men of talent and acuteness, and, indeed, selected on this account, they were, for the most part, destitute of mercantile training or experience. It should be observed that the partners retiring with fortunes to Europe had set up mercantile establishments in London; so that each of the six Calcutta firms had a corresponding firm in England – not, indeed, in partnership, but intimately connected with them in business.

As long as the East India Company's monopoly existed, the great mercantile houses were placed under circumstances which, naturally, secured to them a kind of sub-monopoly. Nearly the whole European and American business fell into their hands. They were agents for the whole civil and military service: they were agents for the planters and merchants settled in the provinces. They were bankers receiving deposits; and bankers making advances for the produce of the interior; and frequently bankers issuing paper money. They made large advances on ships, shipments, and indigo factories; and as general merchants, they not only acted as the agents of others, but speculated largely to every quarter of the world, on their own account. By foreclosing mortgages, on the ruin of speculators, to whom they had made advances, on ships, houses, and factories, they became, eventually, and to a very great extent, ship-owners, house-owners, farmers, and manufacturers.

On the original establishment of the great houses, the partners were, of course, without capital of their own; and, indeed, the deposits from the savings of the civil and military servants may be said to have contributed throughout, the principal fund with which their business was conducted. An intimate and friendly intercourse and connexion had always subsisted between the great firms and the Company's civil and military servants, who, before 1814, constituted nearly the whole European community. To these officers they were always kind, useful, and obliging, and frequently essentially serviceable. Commanding their respect and friendship, with strong claims on the gratitude of many, and possessing the unbounded confidence of all, it is little to be wondered at, that the great annual savings of the servants of the government were poured in upon them – more especially after the great reduction which took place in the interest on investments in the public funds, and which, in seventeen years' time, had fallen from 10 to 5 per cent. The established firms possessed, no less, the confidence of the great monied natives of Calcutta, as well as of many of the provincial towns; and, it must not be forgotten, that among the partners of those firms there existed many individuals whose honour, probity and generosity were well entitled to all esteem and confidence.

At the period in question, the savings of the public officers of the government, instead of being invested in the public securities, or remitted to Europe, as at present, came, to a large extent, into the hands of the Calcutta firms, continued in the country, and were invested in mercantile speculations. What the amount of these must have been may be judged of, when it is explained that the salaries of the European civil officers of Bengal considerably exceed a million sterling a year, and those of the military European officers, certainly to no smaller a sum. Induced by the higher rate of interest paid in Calcutta, and the greater supposed security of investment there, the civil and military officers of Madras and Bombay also invested their funds, to a considerable extent, in the Calcutta houses; and as the salaries and pays of these two presidencies united do not fall much short of those of Bengal, we may safely estimate the whole fund, from which deposits were drawn, at little less than four millions sterling per annum. Successful European shopkeepers, tradesmen, planters, ship-owners and ship-masters deposited their savings in the great houses also, which, moreover, drew largely from native sources, for the confidence reposed in them by all parties was unlimited.

With the large funds thus received by the great houses, in their capacity of bankers, they made advances to speculators for indigo, cotton, silk, opium, etc. to the annual amount, it has been computed, of full five millions sterling. The interest which they allowed on deposits was, generally, not less than 10 per cent; and that charged on advances 12 per cent, besides a commission on the advance. As long as the houses were secure from competition, they made great profits under this system, which enabled the partners to retire to Europe, from time to time, with fortunes of £100,000, or £150,000 each – sometimes, indeed, of a quarter of a million, or even half a million. In short, as every one who knows the mercantile history of India for the last thirty years must remember, to get admission into one of these houses as a partner was considered as the making of a man's fortune, and a large one too.

After the cessation of the Company's close monopoly, and when the great houses were subjected to the competition of more active and economical traders, the same system would no longer work. Improvident advances were now made to prodigal public officers of the government, and to needy and ignorant private adventurers, who, having themselves nothing to lose, recklessly entered into any sort of speculation on which advances could be obtained from the Calcutta firms. They even obtained additional advances, in order to extricate them from the difficulties in which their rash speculations had involved them: this went on from year to year. The balances against the speculators, increased by heavy interest and charges, were yearly brought to the new books of the establishment, as if they were real assets, until death either reduced the amount, by recovery of the sum insured on the life of the party, or cancelled the debt, when no insurance was effected.

The competition of the more prudent and cautious commercial traders of Europe, which followed the change of 1814, enabled the latter to engross a considerable share of the export trade, heretofore nearly monopolized by the six principal firms.

It was then that, deprived, to a considerable extent, of the ordinary mode of employing the large amount of deposits, which still continued to flow in upon them, they felt themselves obliged to resort to other and more precarious means. Tempted by temporary high house rents in Calcutta, they invested largely in houses: they also invested largely in indigo works, coal mines, ships and ship-building, breweries, tanneries, distilleries, spice and coffee plantations, clearing desert islands as proprietors, and even in cotton mills, rice mills, flour mills, and saw mills. The value of these descriptions of property rose in proportion to the influx of capital. In this manner was locked up a great share of their funds; which, when the moment of pressure upon them arrived, could not be realized, except at most ruinous sacrifices. Such funds were, consequently, wholly unavailable to meet their obligations. To these imprudent speculations is to be ascribed the immense amount of nominal balances which appeared on the books at the credit of the partners of the concerns, at the time of their failure.

Although the competition they now had to sustain in the export trade involved them in loss for a series of years, yet, such was the unlimited confidence still reposed in them by the Indian community, that they continued to receive deposits as usual; nor did even the failure of Palmer and Co., in 1830, affect the remaining houses so immediately as was at first apprehended owing to the assets of that house, which it had been long the habit in India to regard as insolvent, turning out nearly equal to one half its liabilities.

Nevertheless, public confidence had become unsettled, and while deposits were rapidly decreasing, the depositors, whose balances had accumulated, began gradually to retire them. Remittance to Europe was usually the alleged excuse for withdrawing, and as drawing on England was the most convenient mode of meeting such demands, bills were freely granted, until checked by remonstrances from correspondents in England.

Such remonstrances were occasioned by the rapid increase of the amounts of the debts of the Indian houses, in consequence of the drafts given by them in favour of Indian constituents. These were far beyond the permanent advances which, it appears, the

London houses were usually in the habit of making to the Calcutta houses, and which ranged from £100,000 to £400,000 each. The object of such advances was to enable the latter to continue those extensive consignments to England, from which, besides receiving 5 per cent interest on the advance, 2½ per cent commission on the sale of the consignments, and 1 per cent on accepting bills, and making payments on credits, the English corresponding firms derived other very considerable advantages.

The utter inability of the Calcutta houses to liquidate the heavy balances against them in England compelled them, in compliance with the understood conditions of the advance, to continue their shipments to Europe, in the face of certain loss, and long after they would otherwise have abandoned them, while the increasing demands of their banking constituents forced them to draw against each consignment to its full invoice amount, which being more than, at the time, the goods frequently realized in England, contributed to augment their home debt, and gave rise, not only to fresh remonstrances, but to the appointment of special agents authorized to demand security for the debt, and the conclusion of arrangements which should insure a gradual liquidation of the whole.

In several instances the demand for security was complied with; and mortgages were granted, by which an undue preference was given to a few creditors, at a time when, it is alleged, that even the most sanguine members of the Indian firms ought to have been satisfied – from the notorious inability of their debtors to pay them, from the sacrifices they had been already obliged to submit to, and from the admitted depreciation which had taken place in the value of their remaining property – that their assets never could realize the amount of their liabilities.

Had the Indian houses stopped payment, while their property was yet unencumbered by mortgages, and before unavailing sacrifices to support their credit had still farther dissipated their assets, instead of the miserable pittance which, in a period of nearly four years, has been doled out in the shape of dividends, a considerable amount would have, at once, been received by each creditor, and much misery and distress averted.

When all confidence in the old firms was, evidently, at an end

– when they no longer continued to receive deposits, and when their banking constituents were becoming every day more and more clamorous for payment, with an infatuation, not unusual in such cases – they still went on borrowing funds at heavy sacrifices, by pledging every description of property within their power. With the funds thus raised, besides satisfying the most pressing demands, they still continued making extensive shipments to Europe, on the faith of which many of their most clamorous creditors took bills on England in satisfaction of their demands. In this manner they continued to struggle on, until the suspicion of their more distant constituents, in the interior of India, being fully roused by the frequent excuses and pretexts with which their repeated orders for payments and remittances were evaded, these also proceeded to take prompt steps for their own security, and appointed special agents to enforce immediate payment of their claims. Many were fortunate enough to succeed; for some of the houses went on raising money at most ruinous sacrifices, until, there being no more property to pledge, and no money left to pay with, they were, at length, compelled to stop.

The folly and substantial injustice of the course pursued, throughout their struggles, by the great firms, are, if possible, aggravated by the reflection that those parties who were restrained by delicacy, personal regard for the individuals, or confidence in their judgment, from pressing them in their difficulties became the principal victims. The next greatest sufferers were those who, on the faith of the shipments to England, had taken bills. In ignorance of the customary mode of transacting business, the goods were not hypothecated to them, but received by, and carried to the credit of the shippers, while the bills, duly protested, returned to India with additional charges, as claims against the now lapsed houses. By the time those bills reached Calcutta, with protests for non-payment, the whole of the estates were in the Insolvent Court, and official assignees appointed, by whom the fixed property has since been in part realized; but in consequence of the poverty and distress occasioned by the failures, and the immense amount of property thrown at once into the market, at a reduction on the actual cost, which, were there no records to prove the fact, would seem incredible. Consequently, after discharging the mortgages and sums for which the property had been pledged, but little remained for the general creditors. In short, these great houses, which had been the principal channel of conducting the export and import trade of India for half a century, fell, one after another, in the course of three short years, and, in the aggregate, for the enormous sum of twenty millions sterling; of which 5s. in the pound will certainly never be recovered; so that we may safely conclude that there has been an actual sacrifice of the capital by which the Indian commerce had previously been conducted, to the amount of fifteen millions sterling.

Chapter VI

Present mode of transacting European mercantile business in India. Cessation of the Company's trade. Amount of remittance of public revenue, for tribute and other purposes. Manner in which the capital of the old firms, and of the Company, has been supplied by their successors. Mode in which business is conducted by the latter. Manner in which the public revenue is remitted to England. Remittance of private fortunes. Manner of remitting funds to the interior of India. European banking establishments, and paper money. Comparison of these, with those of England and America. Estimate of the rates of interest in India. Want of secure investments for deposits.

Besides the loss of funds for carrying on the Indian trade which followed the failure of the great houses, another event, not indeed to be deplored, soon followed, the total cessation of the East India Company's commerce. The capital which the Company used to estimate that it had engaged in the commerce of India and China amounted to between twenty-two and twenty-three millions sterling (£22,636,585*). Such extravagant and factitious estimates are obviously of no value whatever. Had such a capital, along with the fifteen millions lost through the

---

* Papers relating to the East India Company's Charter, 1833, page 38; printed by order of the General Court, for the information of the Proprietors.

fall of the great houses in India, been withdrawn at once from the Indian trade, we can hardly suppose that trade not to have suffered heavily from the loss, making every allowance for the rapidity with which the redundant capital of England may have flowed in to occupy the channel. The trade of the East India Company was, in reality, carried on with the Indian revenue; the Company, in a word, traded with the public taxes of India, while it paid its dividends, and the interest of its home bond debt, by a clumsy tax levied upon the people of England, on the article of tea. This was, in a word, the substance and character of what was miscalled the Company's trade. The total value of all the imports of the Company into England at their English valuation, was, in 1832, but £1,107,787; and the total value of their exports from China, in the same year, amounted to within a fraction of two millions sterling (£1,960,799). Making due allowance for the English valuation of the Indian exports, we shall perhaps not underrate the extent of the gap which the withdrawal of the East India Company had produced, and which was to be filled up by private capital, at the amount of two-and-a-half millions sterling.

The reader is of course aware that the territorial revenue of India has to contribute largely to expenses incurred in England; some of these of a permanent and some of a fluctuating nature. For the year 1835, the permanent charges were as follows:

Dividends of proprietors of East India stock, chargeable upon the revenues of India, Act 3 and 4, Will. iv. cap. 85.	636,826
Interest on the home bond debt, ditto	92,858
Invoice value of stores consigned to India	234,341
Transport of troops and stores, deducting freight charged in invoice	40,944
Furlough and retired pay to military and marine officers, including off-reckonings	521,316
Payments on account of King's troops serving in India	120,000
Retiring pay to King's troops	60,000
Charges general, deducting charges of establishments put upon outward invoices	404,890
Absentee allowances to civil servants of the Indian establishments	38,633
Miscellaneous	5,133
Total	£2,154,941 *

* East India Annual Revenue Accounts; printed 24 June 1836.

We have, here, a sum exceeding two millions sterling; but it is believed that, including the fluctuating charges, a sum of at least three millions must be annually remitted to England. The whole of this has been called a tribute, but improperly. The civil and military charges evidently are not so, except in so far as they may be extravagant, and there is not the least doubt that they are so, considering the poverty of the country to which they relate. Neither are the charges of the home government, under the same limitation, to be called tribute; although, here, from the inevitable nature of our connexion, both pecuniary loss and injury cannot but accrue to a country, the principal branch of whose government is paid at 12,000 miles distance from the governed. There are, however, obviously, portions of the Indian remittance that are nothing but a tribute; as the dividends paid to the proprietors of India stock; the interest of the commercial bond debt; and such part of the charges of establishment as consist of pensions paid to commercial officers. It is very remarkable that the aggregate of these items approaches to *double* the amount which the East India Company became bound to pay the nation, by act of parliament in 1793, as a compensation for the enjoyment of the territorial revenue, which they never paid but once; and from making payment of the balance, on a declaration of total incapacity, they were exonerated in 1813 to the amount of nine millions and a half sterling. It seems, then, from what we have above stated, that it is not only fair and just, but even very profitable for governments to abjure trade.

The existence of the tribute to which we have referred is distinctly indicated in the vast difference between the real value, in England, of the exports to, and imports from, India. In a free commerce, between any two countries, and when there is nothing but commerce concerned, the exports and imports ought to balance each other, as no country can be expected to get from another, what it does not receive an equivalent for. This is so far from being the case in the trade between England and India that, in every year, the imports exceed the exports: thus, in 1832, the exports amounted only to £3,750,286, while the imports were £6,337,098: the excess of above two-and-a-half millions obviously consists of tribute, or at least funds remitted for political purposes, or the remittance of the private fortunes of public officers, for which India receives no equivalent, or at all events none in the shape of mercantile equivalent.

The manner in which the capital of the great houses which failed, and the withdrawal of the capital of the East India Company, has been supplied by their successors, must now be described. On the fall of the first of the great houses, which preceded that of the others by about three years time, a promising field for the formation of new establishments, in Calcutta, seemed to present itself, and several were almost immediately formed, composed of parties, highly respectable in point of character and talent, and, in some instances, well connected in this country, but not known, or ever reputed, to possess property or capital of their own. The subsequent failures gave rise to the formation of farther establishments of the same description. Besides this, capitalists in England, some anxious to preserve, and others to establish, a commercial connexion with India, took immediate measures to form establishments in India, in direct connexion with, and dependent on themselves.

Besides the permanent advances of English capital, on which these several Indian establishments are founded, there is also a very large amount of funds constantly passing through their hands, for the purpose of being worked for the advantage of both establishments, and the usual course of operations is as follows.

The establishments in this country, having dependent establishments in India, send agents, or, as they are usually called, *drummers*, to the manufacturing districts, to beat up for consignments to India. As an inducement to speculation, advances are frequently made upon such consignments, by bills, at six and twelve months, to the extent of from two-thirds to three-quarters of their value. The consignee is always liable for whatever amount the consignment may realize, short of the advance, but he is sometimes guaranteed against failure in India. The charge for sale, guarantee and remittance is from 7 to 10 per cent, of which the home establishment receives two-fifths or one-half, as may have been agreed upon, and, in return, allows the Indian establishment a like proportion of the commissions on all consignments from India.

The consigner's instructions are, generally, to realize and remit in good bills, while the consignee, having authority from his friends to value on them, for the amount realized from such consignments, whenever funds are required for other operations, and the exchange is favourable, usually remits the net proceeds in such bills accordingly, and the amount passes to the credit of the house at home, in an account kept under the head of 'A. B. & Co., *their* account'. This account is also credited with the proceeds of bonds of the Company's 4 and 5 per cent loans, which are occasionally obtainable in this country, at 1d. to $\frac{1}{2}$d. in the exchange, under the Company's bills, although the one carries interest from the day of purchase, while the other is only payable at sixty days sight. The balance of this account is further augmented by bills, drawn by individuals in this country on their relations or agents in India for money received by them, either under credits from the houses in India, or on the faith of accounts current, exhibiting balances in their favour, or company's securities lodged in their name. In all such cases the exchange generally ranges from 1d. to 3d. per rupee, under the Company's rate, besides the usual commissions.

Through the above, and other sources which it would be tedious to enumerate in detail, a large amount of funds is constantly accumulating in India, belonging to the home establishments, on which they receive Indian interest, the Indian establishment having the advantage of employing it, *but at their own risk*, in making the necessary advances on produce, etc.

Being placed in circumstances to make such advances is of great consequence to both establishments, but particularly to the Indian; for, besides charging $2\frac{1}{2}$ per cent on the advance, $2\frac{1}{2}$ per cent on the sale or shipment of the produce, and 12 per cent interest, they, as one of the conditions under which the necessary advance is usually made, secure to themselves the uncontrolled management of the produce, the bona fide proprietor – unless in tolerably independent circumstances, which is rarely the case – having no voice in the matter.

The Indian establishments thus become the principal holders

of produce, and are thereby enabled to establish a virtual monopoly, which, by a mutual understanding amongst the body,
gives them an uncontrolled power of regulating the rates of
exchange, as well as the prices of produce, a state of things
which, however beneficial to the parties, is most prejudicial to
the general interests of the country.

When the shipping season arrives, the produce is either sold,
or taken over by the agent, at the market price of the day, or it is
shipped on account and risk of the proprietors. If shipped to
Europe, the agents advance and charges are repaid by bills
drawn against it, in favour of the London establishments – to
whom it is, of course, consigned – but at an exchange of from
2d. to 3d. per rupee, that is, from 10 to 12 per cent more than
their own bills transmitted to the manufacturers in return for
consignments from England. But if the produce be taken over by
the Indian establishment, and shipped on their *own account*, as is
not unfrequently done, the funds of the home establishment are
remitted to them back in bills against the shipment, at the same
exchange as the bills in favour of the manufacturers. This not
unfrequently gives rise to warm altercations, which, however, it
being the interest of neither party to expose to the public by an
appeal to law, the affair is usually compromised by mutual con-
cession.

A considerable amount of produce is purchased by the occasional speculators from Europe and America, whose principal
reliance for the means of purchasing is on their negotiations,
either under credits with which they have been provided, or
under security of two-thirds of the cargo. The principal part of
the credits is usually granted by establishments at home, on the
strength of funds in the hands of their friends in India. But
whether they are or not, there being no other extensive holders
of produce than the merchants on the spot, and even if there
were, there being no other establishments possessed of the
means of cashing such bills to any extent, however undoubted the
authority under which they are drawn, the speculators or traders
in question find themselves under the necessity of referring the
purchase of cargo, as well as the negotiation of bills, to one or
other of the establishments. The exchange, in such cases, is

usually fixed by a sort of circular note addressed to a few of the houses, at from 1½d. to 3d. per rupee above the Company's rate, and above the rate of their own bills in favour of manufacturers, and other constituents in this country, besides being subject to a charge of 1 per cent for negotiating. There are supplemental charges of from 7 up to 13 per cent.

If the cargo is hypothecated as security for the bills, it is, of course, consigned to the corresponding establishment at home, in whose favour the bills are drawn.

Unless when accounts from Europe, or an unusual influx of speculators from abroad, raises the price of produce and the rate of exchange beyond the ordinary limits, the establishments in India are, themselves, the principal shippers on their own account, not so much for the sake of the profits they anticipate, as to accomplish the ends for which they were established, and on which the existence of many of them is entirely dependent, viz. that of *making business* for their friends at home. It is well known, indeed, that the annual amount of funds supplied from this country, and on which the principal business of the Indian establishments is dependent, is regulated by the yearly amount of consignments from India, which, whatever may be the result of the speculators, is always profitable to the home establishment, and gives them, moreover, the power, whenever circumstances may render it expedient, or necessary, for their own security, of receiving and realizing such shipments to the credit of the parties in liquidation of the balance due to themselves, leaving the holders of the bills drawn on the faith of the shipments, but having no lien on them, to their recourse on India.

In the above remarks we have not included those establishments which confine their operations to the internal commerce of India, or those principally engaged in what is commonly called the *country trade*, that is, the international Asiatic trade, with a portion of the coasting trade. Of the first of these concerns patronized and employed by some of the principal manufacturers of this country, as agents for the sale of their goods, perhaps it is enough to observe that as long as they have confined themselves exclusively to the legitimate objects for which they professed to be established, that of simple agents, the promptness and regularity with which they have effected a remittance of their sales, as early as realized, as well as the rate of exchange of such bills as they have been at times able to procure in the market, have been most favourably contrasted with the occasional tardiness in remitting, and, generally, unfavourable rates of exchange of those establishments which remit their own bills on their correspondents in England.

The remittance of the territorial revenue by the Company constitutes an important element in the present mode of conducting the India trade. There are two modes of effecting this remittance, viz. by drawing bills in England on India, and by making advances of cash in India, for bills on England, the cargoes of the drawers being hypothecated to the government as security. In 1835–36, the bills drawn in England on the Indian treasuries were as follows:

Bengal	£1,655,650	17	6
Madras	223,385	5	1
Bombay	166,217	12	1
Total	£2,045,253	14	8

The remittances from India by merchants bills, were, in the same year, as follows:

Bengal	£1,090,378	12	4
Madras	11,750	6	8
Bombay	31,099	9	4
Total	£1,133,228	8	4

But besides these modes, Indian revenue is also remitted to England through the China trade. The Company, for this purpose, maintains a very expensive establishment of agents at Canton, costing, we believe, not less than £20,000 a year, which draws bills on the Indian treasuries for money received of merchants on the spot; which money is again advanced for private bills, on England, the cargoes being hypothecated to the Company as security, in the same way as is done in India. The amount of such bills, in 1835–36, was £1,338,028 10s. 4d. *

In this manner, it will appear that, in the year in question, a sum exceeding four-and-a-half millions sterling (£4,516,510

* East India Revenues and Remittances; ordered by the House of Commons to be printed, 28 July 1836.

13s. 4d.) of the revenue of India was remitted to England. This affords a curious and striking refutation of the East India Company's arguments in favour of continuing their trade, and their oft repeated assertion that it would be impossible to remit revenue, to any considerable amount, through means of merchants' bills. It would appear that they not only remit to any extent they please, but on far more favourable terms than when they were merchants themselves. According to their own showing, on the average of the three years ending with 1829–30, it appears that the exchange realized on indigo and raw silk, the two staple articles in which they dealt in India, was something short of 1s. 8d. for the sicca rupee.* In 1835–36, the rate of exchange which the government received in India for its rupee was 2s. 1d., and 2s. 2d. giving an average of 5d. on each rupee, beyond what was realized by their commercial transactions. To say nothing of the advantages of prompt payment and no risk, the clear gain of the Company by the loss of their trade is about 25 per cent. By being precluded from dabbling in the trade, in 1835–36, the Company, in fact, improved their resources by a sum little short of £1,125,000.

The following are the conditions on which advances are usually made to merchants in India, by the government, for bills. On handing over to the Treasury bills of lading, and other shipping documents duly executed, making the shipment deliverable to the holders in London, the parties receive two-thirds of the value of such shipment for their bills on their correspondents in London. The Court of Directors, in whose favour the bills are drawn, on receiving payment, whether under discount, or at maturity, hand over all the documents along with the bills to the parties paying them.

The obvious effects of this system are to exclude all parties shipping to other ports than London from participating in the accommodation thus afforded; and to exclude from its advantages all parties who principally rely on the negotiation of their bills for the means of effecting their purchases.

It must, therefore, be evident that if establishments existed in India, possessing extensive capital and resources, from which

---

* Report and Appendix of the Select Committee of 1831, pp. 655 and 656.

parties, requiring remittances, could at once obtain bills on England, even temporary deposits would not be risked, except with such establishments or with parties who confined their business exclusively to agency. The salutary separation of agency from mercantile and other speculative operations, which would be effected by such means, would assuredly give a stability and security to every description of business hitherto unknown in India.

The agent who scrupulously abstained from all manner of speculation on his own account would soon acquire the unlimited confidence of a numerous constituency, while the merchant and speculator would have every facility in obtaining, on moderate terms, capital to carry on his speculations to the full extent which the means at his disposal rendered safe and prudent. No longer in a situation to obtain the means of speculating, except through the usual recourse to the money market, their transactions would be more generally known, and as the moneylenders and their brokers would be more cautious in coming under advances to those who had no adequate security to offer, their operations would, necessarily, be limited to the extent of their credit and resources, a result which could not fail to have a wholesome effect upon all legitimate mercantile transactions.

Independent of the remittances effected through the Company, it is believed that a sum ranging from one to two millions is annually remitted on account of private parties, principally civil and military officers of the government. A great part of this sum, as already observed, used formerly to continue in India, on account of the high interest which the old houses were accustomed to give for it; and the great confidence reposed in them. The same confidence is, unquestionably, not reposed in their successors, while the low rate of interest given in the Company's securities, scarcely higher than in England, presents no temptation to leave the funds in India. The interest given by the present houses of agency, in Calcutta, is 8 per cent. It is an acknowledged fact that few or no deposits are made with them, even with this temptation; or, if made at all, only for the purpose of being immediately remitted to Europe.

The accommodation which the English merchant at present

possesses in receiving from or remitting money to the interior; and that which he receives from the use of paper money, may here be described. If money has to be remitted from one part of India to another, there are, except by sending bullion, but two modes of effecting it – either by Government bills, or by Hoondees. If a merchant of Calcutta, for example, has to remit funds to his correspondent in the interior, for the purpose of purchasing produce, which, as we have already seen, is done annually, to the amount of several millions sterling he offers his money to the Treasury, for an order upon a collector of the land-tax or customs, perhaps 100 miles off, and he receives accommodation, or otherwise, according to the circumstances of the different treasuries. This is just as if purchases of corn, cottons and woollens, on behalf of the merchants of London, were to be carried on by making the Treasury in Downing Street, giving orders upon the collectors of customs, excise, assessed taxes and land-tax, the banking agents of the parties. But it may so happen, and it very often does, that even when the government is disposed to give the accommodation, the residence of the European correspondent may not be within many miles of a collector's treasury. In such a case, the party must send a native accountant to count and examine the treasure, piece by piece, and in a great number of cases – in almost every case, indeed – he must send an armed escort to convey it safely to his own place.

When the European merchant can obtain no accommodation from the government Treasury, he goes to an Indian banker for a Hoondee, or native bill of exchange. The nature of these Hoondees is best described by examples. A Hoondee, drawn at Bombay, is usually payable at Calcutta at fifty-one days after date. The party receiving such a bill, is generally charged with from $1\frac{1}{2}$ to 1 per cent as a commission to the drawer. Now, the distance between Bombay and Calcutta is 1,300 miles. The post travels this distance in about twelve days; so that the drawer will receive interest for the money for fifty-one days, and the drawee be out of his money for about thirty-nine days, exclusive of his payment of commission. Taking the average commission at $\frac{3}{4}$ per cent, and reckoning the interest at 12 per cent, the whole charge of remitting money from Bombay to Calcutta will amount to nearly 2½ per cent. In remitting money through the same channel between Agra, Benares, Patna and Calcutta, the first of these a distance of 950 miles, the second of 565, and the last of 400 – respectively travelled by the letter post in nine, five and four days. The usance is equally for all these forty-one days date. This may be compared with the practice among ourselves. The usual par of exchange between London and Edinburgh, or London and Glasgow, both of which are nearly the same distance from London that Patna is from Calcutta, is, at the highest, twenty-one days date, and the average may be taken at fifteen. Reckoning interest at 4 per cent, for there is no commission, this is a charge of less than ⅙ per cent. Even for a bill at sight, the charge is but ¼ per cent. The charge, then, of remitting funds in India, in the inland exchange, will be about three times as great in India, as it is in England. This, of course, corresponds to the respective rates of interest in the two countries. The truth is that it is far more expensive to remit funds from one portion of the British dominions in India to another, than to remit them between England and almost any commercial emporium in Europe. Still it must be admitted that the Indian Hoondee is, after all, one of the most perfect portions of the Indian commercial system.

The accommodation which the public receives from paper money in India is very limited. Throughout all British India, with its eighty million inhabitants, and an extreme length and breadth of not less than 1,500 miles each, there are just four banks; of which the whole capital cannot exceed £1,150,000. The largest and most important of these is the Bank of Bengal, of which the capital was originally £500,000 – now raised to £750,000. One-fifth part of the property of the bank belongs to the government, which appoints the secretary and three directors out of nine. This is a bank of deposit and of issue, and its notes circulate in all the provinces below Benares. The government receives its notes as cash; but, as security, requires a deposit equal to one-fourth of its issues, in its own treasury notes. Its half-yearly dividends were at the following rates per cent per annum, in the following years:

1830 June 30	8	1833 June 30	6
Dec. 31	9	Dec. 31	6
1831 June 30	8	1834 June 30	nil*
Dec. 31	7	Dec. 31	6
1832 June 30	8	1835 June 30	14
Dec. 31	7	Dec. 31	11½

The other bank, in Calcutta, is called the Union Bank, and may be considered as the successor of several banking establishments, held by the old lapsed firms, and which, without failing, had yet discontinued business. The capital of the Union Bank is but £75,000. Unlike the Bank of Bengal, which has a charter with limited responsibility, this bank has none, and is, in fact, in every respect a private concern, its notes not being received at the public treasury, nor circulating beyond the limits of the town of Calcutta. Its dividends have been at the following rates per annum:

1832 June 30	6	1834 June 30	6
Dec. 31	6	Dec. 31	6
1833 June 30	unknown	1835 June 30	10
Dec. 31	6	Dec. 31	10

There is also a small bank at Agra, of which the capital, we believe, is £70,000. Its transactions are, of course, very limited.

There is no bank at Bombay, either of deposit or of issue; nor has there ever been; so that a paper circulation may be said to be unknown to that part of India. In Madras there is just one bank upon a very small scale. This is entirely a government concern, and is a bank of deposit, discount and issue; its notes being received in the public treasury, but circulating in the town of Madras only. We have never seen stated, in any public document, the amount of the capital of this bank; and its profits, instead of being carried half yearly or yearly to account, are permitted to accumulate for a series of years, and then carried to the public credit. From its institution, in 1806, down to 1826–27, a period of twenty-one years, its accumulated profits

---

* There was no dividend in this half year, in consequence of the heavy losses sustained by forgeries of government securities held by the bank.

were £620,226; but, as in this estimate the pagoda is reckoned at 8s., and ought to be brought down to its real value of about 6s. 8d., the true profits will be only £516,855, or at the rate of £24,625 per annum. If we estimate the profits at 10 per cent then the capital will amount to near a quarter of a million. But, whence, it may well be asked, is the capital derived? The government of Madras has no surplus revenue; on the contrary, it never pays its own expenses; but borrows; and, at one period, within the time above reckoned, borrowed at as high a rate of interest as it made profit by its banking. But, supposing the Madras government to borrow the capital of its bank, at so low a rate of interest as 5 per cent, then its rate of profit will be reduced to 5 per cent also; and instead of a yearly profit of £24,000, we should have one of only £12,000. It is surely not worth the while of a government, with fifteen million subjects, and a revenue exceeding five millions sterling, to dabble in deposits and discounts, for a revenue that would not pay the salaries of a couple of its counsellors. The whole affair reminds one of what Adam Smith says of some small European governments, who derived a profit from mercantile projects. 'The republic of Hamburgh', he observes, 'is said to do so, from the profits of a public wine cellar and apothecary's shop. The state cannot be very great, of which the sovereign has leisure to carry on the trade of a wine merchant or apothecary.' Every part of this is applicable to the Madras proceeding, except the last sentence; for, surely, the sovereign that has fifteen millions to rule, and which requires an army of 50,000 men to maintain its authority, ought not to have leisure to attend to the concerns of a small money shop.

From the statement now made, it will appear that the whole of the paid up banking capital of India does not exceed £1,150,000; of which, if we suppose the notes issued by them to be equal to two-thirds of their capital, the amount will be £760,000 worth of notes, for eighty million people. If we compare this very meagre allowance with the banking establishments of America, and of our own country, the disparity will appear immense. In 1835, there were in the United States of America 558 banking establishments, with 146 branches, and an aggregate paid up capital of 231,250,337 dollars, or upwards of £48,000,000. They had notes in circulation to the amount of above £21,500,000. Thus, the amount of the American banking capital is forty-two times as great as that of British India; and its circulation of notes more than twenty-eight times as great; and perhaps, indeed, in a much larger proportion. In Scotland, there are thirty-two banks, and the paid up capital of the three chartered ones amounts to four millions sterling. The capital one of these, the Royal Bank, is one third more than that of all the banking capital of British India put together. The Bank of Ireland has a paid up capital of three millions, or approaching to three times as much as the banking capital of India; and its circulation of notes is probably eight times as great. Sixty-two out of the ninety-eight joint-stock banks of England and Wales have a nominal capital of £38,750,000 and a paid up one of £5,792,527,* or more than five times the banking capital of India. The whole circulation of bank notes throughout the United Kingdom has been estimated at about forty millions sterling,† which will certainly be about forty times the amount of notes circulated in India.

It has been said, however, that it is absurd to compare the monetary system of India with the monetary system of such countries as England and America. No doubt, it would be absurd enough to compare a poor, sluggish and misgoverned country with rich, active and enterprising ones, if we were extravagant enough to calculate on the same exact proportion in their wants. No rational person would do so. But it must not be forgotten, at the same time, that the general principles which conduct to the wealth of nations are not affected by climate and colour, and that whatever is true, in regard to England and America is true, in a minor degree, with regard to India. Banking establishments contributed greatly to the prosperity of Scotland, 140 years ago, when it was a very poor country, and surely they may now be largely extended to India with an equal prospect of success.

It is necessary, however, to state that the paper circulation of

---

* Report of Select Committee of Commons on Joint Stock Banks, 1836.
† On Joint Stock Banks; by Wm. Clay, Esq., M.P., 1836.

India is not confined to bank notes; the promissory and treasury notes of the government are largely availed of, by the European and native merchants, in the transaction of business, as exchequer bills and bank certificates are in this country. The first of these correspond to our bank certificates, being, in fact, obligations on the treasury, for the payment of the interest of the public debt. The second are of exactly the same nature as our exchequer bills, bearing a certain rate of interest per diem, which has fluctuated from $3\frac{3}{4}$ to $5\frac{3}{4}$ per cent per annum. The amount of the latter in circulation, on 30 April 1834, was 5,998,300 sicca rupees, or about £600,000. The debts of the Indian government, at the same date, amounted to £35,463,483 bearing an interest of £1,754,545. This, however, includes besides the treasury notes, the Carnatic fund exceeding £2,700,000, and various civil, military and miscellaneous claims. In fact, the whole funded, or, as it is called in India, the registered debt did not much exceed thirty millions sterling; at the respective interests of 6, 5, and 4 per cent, giving an aggregate interest of £1,534,418.

The promissory as well as the treasury notes of the government go a considerable length towards increasing the accommodation by paper circulation. But none of the notes in question being smaller than £50, their prices being of course variable, and it being unsafe to transmit them by post, as a remittance, their use is necessarily accompanied with considerable inconvenience. Whatever be the nature of the accommodation afforded by them, and it is chiefly confined to the seat of government, it is certainly not to be put in comparison with that afforded in England and America by the public stocks, canal, rail-road, and other shares of these countries.

One of the greatest gainers by the free trade of India, we may take this opportunity of observing, has been the East India Company, in its political capacity. Before the close of the last century, and while its commercial monopoly was entire, it seldom borrowed under 9 and 10 per cent; and occasionally it was compelled to give as much as 12 per cent for its loans. Even at these high rates, the Company's securities were at an enormous discount.* Down to 1810, the Company was not able to borrow for less than 8 per cent. After 1814 they borrowed at 6 per cent, and eventually at 5, and, indeed, of the whole registered debt of thirty millions sterling, upwards of £5,600,000 have been borrowed even at 4 per cent. The 6 per cent loan has now been paid off; so that the highest rate of interest paid by the Indian government is 5 per cent. Even before it was paid off, however, the average interest on the whole debt was under 5 per cent. Now, if it had been 8 per cent, as it was previous to the free trade system of 1814, the annual interest, instead of £1,754,545, would have amounted to £2,837,078; so that the government has been a gainer by the sum of £1,082,533 a year; which, added to its gain upon the exchange with England, in remitting revenue, for tribute and other purposes, makes a clear gain of £2,207,000; which is equal to one-seventh part of the entire net revenue of all India, and equal to more than the payment of the interest of the entire national debt of India in 1813. It is needless to add that the

---

* 'Have the Company any means which the private trader has not? – Yes, they have the name and authority of the Company, which carries everything before it in India. – Does it not come back to this, that the advantage of the Company is derived from the immense amount of their pecuniary means? – No, I decidedly deny it; and, in explanation, allow me to state, that the time has been when the Company had not the means of going into the market to purchase cotton, or any other article of trade; when they were obliged to apply to the merchants of Bombay for assistance to carry on their wars, instead of their commerce; and which assistance, under arrangements entered into with the Bombay government, was afforded to them in a degree, and in a spirit of disinterestedness, beyond what perhaps was ever known, under similar circumstances, in any part of the world. I allude to the period of 1803, 1804, and 1805, during the war which was carried on by Sir Arthur Wellesley, now Duke of Wellington, against Sindia and Holkar, when, in the course of little more than two years, the houses of Forbes and Co., and Bruce, Fawcett, and Co., supplied their wants, and relieved their difficulties, to the extent of nearly two millions and a half sterling; the effect of which assistance was, in one short week, to reduce the discount upon the Company's 9 per cent treasury bills from 8 and 10 per cent to 1 or 2 per cent, by undertaking, as those houses did, to receive the said paper, and to pass it current in their transactions at par, although then at so heavy a discount. At this period, so great was the distress of the government, that many lacs of rupees of the Duke of Wellington's bills were lying in the bazar, under protest for non-payment, and the exchanges for government bills on Calcutta had fallen to eighty-five Bombay rupees for 100 siccas; the relative intrinsic value of the two coins being 106 Bombays for 100 siccas. – Was not all this before the last Charter? – It was so.' Evidence of Sir Charles Forbes, before the Select Committee of the House of Commons, 1831. The discount here alluded to by Sir Charles Forbes was very nearly 20 per cent.

gain to the character of the governing body, and the advantage to the party governed, are still greater. The first, no longer distracted by the performance of incompatible functions, will have time, and liberality, and inclination to bestow on its political duties; and the latter, a far better chance than ever it had before of a fair and just administration. In truth, both results are in progress.

It would be unfair, however, to ascribe the whole improvement which has taken place in the financial circumstances of the Indian government, as now alluded to, to the influence of the free trade and the cessation of the monopoly. The greater part of it is, no doubt, to be so accounted for; but much also must be attributed to the superior political position of British India, since the subjugation of the hostile native powers, which commenced in 1799 and terminated in 1817.

The low rate of interest at which the government is enabled to borrow is, however, it must be added, scarcely less a proof of its own high credit, than it is of the defective credit of all other parties. The money rate of interest, in Calcutta, between native and native, on competent security, appears to be about 12 per cent; and among Europeans, it has for many years back been not less than 8 per cent. From the last statements that we have perused, we see that the Calcutta banks charge a discount of 7 per cent on bills, drawn at two months sight; and on bills drawn at three months sight, 8 per cent. The best security in India, next to the public stocks, is that of the chartered bank. On the average of its three last half-years' dividends, the interest paid to the stock-holder was 10½ per cent; but then the stock was at a premium of above 57 per cent; so that the real interest paid is 6 per cent. The two last half-years' dividends of the Union Bank give an interest of 10 per cent; but the stock of this bank also is at a premium of 34 per cent, which reduces the interest, on this inferior security, to something less than 7½ per cent. While such is the case, with what may be considered as the best private securities, in India, the government 5 per cent loans are at a premium of near 4 per cent, and even the 4 per cent loan, at a discount not exceeding ½ or ¾ per cent. This is clearly not a wholesome or natural state of things. There ought not to exist such a disparity between the security of the public, and good private security, as to make the first nearly double the value of the last. In this country, there is hardly any difference between the interest given by the public securities, and by unquestionable private securities; and, at all events, instead of the enormous difference which exists in India, the utmost cannot be rated at above $\frac{1}{2}$ per cent. It is the same in France, Holland, Belgium, and the United States; and, in truth, ought to be so in any country where the laws are well administered, where there is public confidence, and where the means of inventing funds in private securities are not deficient. In India, on the contrary, the laws in the provinces are imperfectly administered; and, in so far as Europeans are concerned, many of those funds for the secure investment of capital, which are so abundant elsewhere, are either wanting altogether or are very insufficient. This more especially applies to the owners of European capital. Merchants carrying on the joint business of agents, traders, bankers and exchange-brokers afford, of course, as we have already seen, no competent security; banking establishments are wholly inadequate; the security derived from property of houses is confined to a few European towns, and although Europeans be permitted to hold lands, few or none, owing to the intricacies and difficulties of the law, and the consequent insecurity of the investment, have as yet availed themselves of this means, either by purchase or mortgage. The natives, in consequence of their superior knowledge of details and localities, possess a wider field of investment, and are, therefore, in a better position – and, hence, the higher rate of interest among them. The European owners of capital, from necessity, direct their investments in India almost exclusively to the government stocks. This will appear very striking from the official statement of the public debt of Bengal, made in 1830; and which exhibits the proportion of the funds held, respectively, by Europeans, and by natives. Out of a stock of £26,529,390, the sum of £19,753,440 was held by the first, and but £6,775,950 by the latter. But, even of this last amount, a very large part appears to be accidental; and not the result of voluntary investment. Two millions of it, for example, arose out of political transactions, already mentioned, with the king of Oude; and a good deal consists in deposits of the property of native estates, under litigation in the courts of justice. It would not, perhaps, be safe to estimate the amount of stock held by natives at above three millions, of which probably the whole would be found to amount to deposits, made for mere purposes of temporary speculation. Considering the well known native wealth of Calcutta, Bombay, Benares, and other towns, which far exceeds the European; and, considering that on the part of natives, there is no want of confidence in the government this state of things can only be accounted for by our knowing that natives have more profitable means of investment than the public funds afford. With Europeans, on the contrary, there is a dead run upon them. They consider them, and justly too, as the only unquestionable security, and hence their high value, and the low rate of interest they yield.

Chapter *VII*

Suggestions for the establishment of an Indian bank. Conditions on which it ought to be formed. Objections to the scheme answered. Illustrations of the advantages which may be expected from it.

The sure mode of making a poor people a rich one is to govern them in such a way as to make life, liberty and property secure – to take from them, in the language of Mr Mill, the smallest quantity possible of their annual produce, and that quantity with the smallest possible hurt, or uneasiness. No Indian government, native or European, has ever yet acted upon this maxim; but, upon the whole, we are disposed to believe that there is, at the present moment, a far better disposition to act upon it than at any former period. When individuals of enterprise are satisfied that this is the case, the time is arrived when they may safely step forward to assist a well-disposed government, and, in doing so, to benefit themselves; for, in such cases, the advantages are reciprocal, and inseparable. The introduction to British India, by gradual and prudent means, of such a portion of the surplus capital of Britain as can be profitably and judiciously employed presents itself, at once, as one of the most useful and legitimate means, not only of promoting the welfare of the people of India, but of increasing that of the mother country, and cementing the connexion between them. Within the last twenty-three years, no doubt much British capital has found its way to India, to the great advantage of both countries. Still, a great deal remains to be done; and the main question is, how the redundant capital of England can be most prudently and judiciously invested in the open and little cultivated field of Indian enterprise.

Among the modes of introducing British capital into India, we agree with those who are of the opinion, that an extended, liberal and prudent system of banking would be one of the most obvious and beneficial.

In the foregoing details, we trust that we have satisfactorily demonstrated that India, in every department of its industry, is eminently deficient in capital; that its monetary system is rude, cumbrous, inconvenient, and expensive; that its banking establishments are wholly inadequate; that the combination of mercantile, agency and banking operations is injurious to the public, and destructive of mercantile confidence; and, finally, that there is a wide field for the introduction of British capital, by means of banking establishments.

Two projects have been agitated in this country, within the last four years, for the establishment of an Indian bank – the first, in 1833, with a capital of two millions; and the last, in 1836, with a capital of five millions. The highest of these sums cannot, we conceive, be thought an excessive amount, if we consider that Britain and India are to be the joint contributors, and that the field of employment – a field nearly unoccupied – is the whole commerce and industry of the Indies. In truth, we look upon it as but a small instalment of the fund which must, eventually, be invested in the same mode and channel of employment.

The bank which we have in view, we think might prudently conduct the following branches of business – receive deposits, giving interest on them; grant cash credits on the conditions on which they are granted on the Scottish system; issue paper money, payable in gold or silver to bearer on demand, both at its principal establishments and branches; discount good bills; and engage in bullion transactions and exchange operations, whether with the interior of India or with the United Kingdom. Such a bank ought to be bound to publish, periodically, at very short intervals, for the information of the proprietors and the public, an account, showing the whole amount of its debts and assets, at the close of each period, the amount of its notes payable on demand, and the amount of specie and other assets immediately available for the discharge of such notes: it should moreover, be liable at all times to furnish to the government in India and in England, when called for, similar accounts; and it should be debarred, by its charter, from employing its funds in loans or advances, either in the way of mortgage, or purchase, on land, or other property, not readily convertible into money.

Such are, in fact, pretty nearly the conditions on which the Board of Trade, by its minute of 16 July 1830, has recommended that charters of incorporation, with limited responsibility, should be granted throughout the Colonies, for the formation of banks; and the establishment of which, the Board expresses its opinion, 'would tend to promote the commerce and general prosperity' of the Colonies in question.

The State of Massachusetts (and most of the American States have followed its example) invariably grants banking charters, with limited responsibility, as our own government has done with its Colonial banks. We hold this principle to be equally sound, whether with respect to our Colonial banks, or to our domestic joint-stock banks. No doubt the principle has been disputed, in so far as concerns the latter; but it must not be forgotten that the question has been raised from a very suspicious quarter, the advocates of the great monetary monopoly of this country, who, while they deprecate a limited responsibility in most of the American banks, and in the longest and most firmly established of the Scottish banks, can discover nothing exceptionable in that limited responsibility and sweeping monopoly of the bank of England, which for forty years has disturbed and convulsed the currency of the kingdom.

With regard to the management; the principal direction, it is evident, ought to be where the principal body of the proprietors resides; and, this being England, from which the great mass of the capital is to be derived – the only source, indeed, from which it can be derived – the chief direction must naturally be in London.

This is the outline of our plan, and we shall proceed to reply, briefly, to the most feasible objections which have been urged against it. We beg, in the first place, to repudiate all countenance of some extravagant, absurd, and grasping projects, engrafted upon the original scheme. It has been proposed, for example, to make the new bank an instrument subservient to the Indian government, in such matters as the payment of the interest of the public debt. This would be to follow the precedent of the Bank of England, and, therefore, to follow what we consider a vicious precedent, more worthy of being avoided than imitated: it would be to imitate the old proceeding of the American government, in the creation of a national bank – a nuisance which we have just seen put down by the enlightened spirit and firmness of the executive of that country. We think the connexion would be injurious both to the bank and to the government. The interest of the Indian debt is but a trifle – perhaps not exceeding a million a year – now that the greater part of the 6 per cent loan is paid off, and the interest of the small remaining balance reduced to 5 per cent. The business of paying the interest of the public debt is performed by establishments throughout India, which cost no more than £18,000 a year; while they discharged a great number of other functions besides. By committing the payment of the interest of the public debt to the bank, it is clear, therefore, that neither the government nor the bank could be any very material gainers, even in a pecuniary point of view.

It is then stated that the bank would 'facilitate the receipt of the revenue, and its subsequent diffusion through the various channels of the public expenditure'. If by this be merely meant, that good paper money, and good bills of exchange, will give facilities to the collection and expenditure of the public revenue, there can be no question whatever but they would. Good private bank notes are received by the collectors in Ireland and Scotland, in payment of taxes; and the revenues of these two portions of the empire are remitted to the seat of government, through the Irish bank and Edinburgh banks. These are great and unquestionable facilities given by banking operations, in the collection of the public revenue. Irish and Scottish notes also are received and disbursed, by the collectors, and this is equally an unquestionable convenience. So far, the same facilities might be afforded by banks in India; but this is a matter which must be left wholly to the discretion and prudence of the government itself; and to speculate upon it, in the first instance, as a source of profit to the new bank, is a mere gratuitous impertinence. If the bank so conducts itself as to entitle it to the confidence of the government, and the public, it may be assured that the government will, as a matter of convenience and expediency, take its notes in payment. On the other hand, if its conduct be indiscreet, no bolstering on the part of the government will be able to sustain its character and credit.

Some parties, however, have construed the quotation which we have above made, into a disposition, on the part of the new bank, to take into its own hands the entire collection and disbursement of the public revenue of India. These revenues, as we already stated, are about eighteen millions sterling. There are upwards of 80,000 persons engaged in the collection and distribution of them, at a charge exceeding two millions sterling. This indeed, would be a gigantic undertaking for the projected bank, if ever the proprietors entertained so ridiculous a project. The allegation, however, is, we suppose, that of an opponent, who, for lack of good argument, has drawn largely upon his imagination.

Some of the friends of the projected bank have, we believe, advocated the making the notes of their bank a legal tender throughout India. If they have done this, they have sought a very mischievous monopoly. If private individuals find it convenient and safe to take their notes, there is not the least doubt but they will do so; but to make them a legal tender, in any description of payments, is not to be endured. The projectors, or their advocates, have proposed the incorporation of the present Bank of Bengal with their own institution. They have offered no good reason for this, if they had any; and as we consider two good banks better than one, and a mutual check on each other, we prefer the separate establishment to the union, and, indeed, hope to live to see a score of banks in India, instead of four or five.

One of the objections most urged against the establishment of an Indian bank is its proposal to meddle in the exchange operations between India and England. It is asserted that this is trafficking in foreign exchanges, and that to meddle in external exchanges, of any kind, is incompatible with the proper business of banking. It is scarcely necessary to say that British India is not a foreign country. Not only this, but the principal places in which the branches of the bank will be established are governed by the common and statute law of England, administered by professional judges appointed by the crown. All British India, for that matter, is governed, directly or indirectly, by acts of the British Parliament. Scotland and Ireland, before their respective unions with England, had banks which dealt in English exchanges; but no one, in his senses, ever thought of calling such exchanges foreign exchanges. Then, as to the matter of distance, which has been objected to: in 1695, when the bank of Scotland was established, it took nearly two months to send and get a reply to a letter between Edinburgh and London, a matter which is now done, in the usual course of business, in little more than 100 hours; and which, very soon, will be done in half the time. There was no doubt much inconvenience in a delay of two months, in conducting the exchange operations between the two places in question, but it did not prevent it. Before the establishment of steam navigation, it sometimes happened that the intercourse between Great Britain and Ireland was wholly interrupted for ten days together, by bad weather. This was no doubt very inconvenient, but it did not prevent the English and Irish banks from dealing in exchanges. The average time which it requires, at present, to send and receive an answer between England and India is about ten months, which is about half the time which was required before ships were coppered. It is not improbable, but that through steam navigation, the ten months may be reduced to five; at least, this is, at present, a very general belief. The smallest of these times is, no doubt, very inconvenient; but the inconvenience is one to which we must submit, even in matters of more importance than mere exchange operations, as in the whole commerce of India – and in the conduct of the government of India itself, carried on, as it is, at the distance of 12,000 miles from the party governed. One of the objectors proceeds to the extravagance, not only of denouncing England as a foreign country, in relation to India, but the majority of the proprietors of the projected bank, because residing in England, as strangers. These must be a new description of foreigners who conquered a country, who have exercised its whole sovereignty for seventy years, who occupy every important civil and military place in its administration, and whose traders are the most active and enterprising of its merchants!

As to the interfering in the operations of the external exchange not being compatible with legitimate banking principles, it is true enough that this is not generally done by English banks. The obvious reason is that most of the exchange operations of England are conducted in London, and by a particular class of persons – the exchange brokers, whose business constitutes what is natural enough to a great commercial country, a regular subdivision of mercantile labour. In London, therefore, if they be not conducted by bankers, neither are they conducted by establishments, at once mercantile, agency, and banking. Several of the Scottish banks do, however, engage in external exchange operations, not only colonial but foreign; and we perceive that in the Calcutta printed price currents the rates of Scottish bank bills are regularly quoted. We have one of these bills now before us, of the Royal Bank for £500; with no less than fourteen endorsements, and which had travelled over all India. Most of the banks of the United States engage in the foreign exchanges, and nothing is more common at the commercial ports of India, from Canton to Bombay, than American bank bills of exchange, especially those of the Bank of the United States. It is true that in these cases the bills are drawn on London; but this does not materially alter the case, for the

India bank would do nothing more than sell its bills on England or India, as is done by the Scottish and American banks. As to the question of advancing money on hypothecated goods, as is done by the Indian government, both in India and China, this is another matter, and the extent to which the bank may engage in such transactions will be an affair of prudence and discretion for itself. Certainly the Company has, as yet, lost nothing by such operations.

In reference to these exchange operations, the reader, from what we have already stated, will not fail to advert to their peculiar importance. The commercial transactions of India are, in fact, to an unusual extent based upon exchange operations: there are three millions of revenue to be remitted from India, and probably not less than a million and a half in the shape of private fortunes, making a total of four-and-a-half millions. Most of this consists of pure cash transactions; and it is very remarkable that one of the loudest of the present objectors to the new bank himself proposed the scheme of a bank, having these very remittances for its object. But besides the remittances just alluded to, it is to be recollected that the export and import trade of this country with India is, for the most part, in separate and distinct hands. The consignments from England to India are, in consequence, generally paid for in bills; and the exports from India also, in a great measure, through the same channel. It is very probable that the exchange operations would be better conducted if carried on as in England, by a particular class of dealers, neither bankers nor merchants; as, however, in the meanwhile, there is no probability of the establishment of such a class in India, we think there can be no question but that, without exercising any monopoly, exchange transactions may be more safely and beneficially conducted by a bank than by firms uniting, in themselves, the business of speculative merchants, indigo-manufacturers, agents, bankers, and brokers, and whose means are, as no doubt they ought to be, wholly unknown to the public.

The real objection, however, made by the opponents of the bank to its interfering in exchange operations between India and England amounts, in plain terms, to neither more nor less than this, that such interference would produce competition with the existing establishments, and, consequently, impair, in some degree, the amount of the profits which they at present derive from this source. In fact, the only objectors to the bank that we have ever heard of are themselves members of the very establishments in question. The most distinguished of them was, indeed, the projector of an Indian bank; but, in his scheme, he carefully provided for 'the existing interests of the houses of agency', by making it a condition that the bank should not interfere in the remittances – saving, however, that of the public revenue, and of the salaries of public officers. 'What the bank would gain', he observes, 'the exporter (Indian) would lose.' This seems a frank admission that nothing was apprehended but the dread of competition. Another objector is so sore on this subject, that he insists that the bare proposal of establishing a bank tends to call in question the credit and stability of the existing establishments carrying on the trade between England and India. Objectors of this description we are in candour bound to admit are following their vocation.

Without meaning any disrespect, we may safely say of them, as we should say of any other class of men similarly circumstanced, that their thoughts are more commonly exercised about their own particular branch of business than about the general interests of the public. In the words of Adam Smith,

The interest of the dealers, in any particular branch of trade or manufactures, is always, in some respects, different from, and even opposite to, that of the public. To widen the market, and to narrow the competition, is always the interest of the dealers. To widen the market, may frequently be agreeable enough to the interest of the public; but to narrow the competition must always be against it, and can only serve to enable the dealers, by raising their profits above what they naturally would be, to levy, for their own benefit, an absurd tax upon the rest of their fellow-citizens.

We leave it to the candour of these parties to consider whether they are not now levying, and seeking to continue to levy, Adam Smith's absurd tax.

One of the sweeping objections made against the proposed bank is that it would establish a monopoly as pernicious as that which has just been got rid of; that is, the commercial monopoly of the East India Company. We admit, without hesitation, that were an Indian bank established, with all the privileges and immunities, and power, which some of its indiscreet advocates have suggested; that were there men foolish enough to persevere in asking for such privileges, and other men still more foolish to grant them, that a very ugly and mischievous monopoly would unquestionably be established. But to say that any pecuniary monopoly, which a poor five millions sterling, engaged in banking, could produce, would be equally pernicious with a joint monopoly of the sovereignty and commerce of the Indies, both of them arbitrarily exercised, is a piece of polemical extravagance, which is not deserving of a serious refutation. A bank, with a capital of five millions sterling, is spoken of as if it were something fearful for its mere amount; a huge leviathan, that was to swallow up all the poor sprats that are now industriously picking up crumbs in the ocean of Indian commerce. We have no particular partiality for the number five; and, although we do not consider such an amount of millions extravagant, when we look to the magnitude of the country which is to furnish it, and of the country which is to employ it, we should have no serious objection to see a sum of three millions, or four millions named instead. All, in fact, that we desire, is to see the commencement of a laudable and legitimate undertaking.

What has lately been done for the West Indies will afford a strong corroboration of our suggestions respecting Indian banking. A charter, with limited responsibility, has been granted by the crown for a West Indian bank, with a capital of two millions. The principal direction is in London; and there are branches in every considerable West India colony, insular and continental – places much more remote, and more difficult of intercourse with each other, than almost any portions of British India. The whole population of the British West Indies, scattered over a vast and divided surface, is but 800,000 at the utmost; and, of this, fifteen parts out of sixteen are African; that is to say, consist of a race which, to say nothing of their being as yet barely emancipated from the servile state, are greatly inferior in civilization to any people of India. The total exports from the whole West Indies, in 1832, amounted to £6,257,797; and the imports to £3,694,368; making an aggregate of near ten millions.* Now this is the result of a trade which has been pampered and bolstered by a monopoly for 150 years. To say nothing of the trade of China, which is really part and parcel of that of India, this is but half the trade of India – a trade which has lain under an interdict during the same period. Surely, after these statements, we may safely argue that if a banking capital of two millions sterling be necessary for the West Indies, one of five millions cannot be considered excessive for a country having a more civilized population, and one that is a 100 times as great; a country, moreover, which instead of taking from the pockets of the British people, as the West Indies do, some £700,000 sterling a year, for civil, military, and naval expenses, and a still larger sum, as a perpetual annuity for slave emancipacipation,† pays its own civil and military charges, to the last farthing; nay furnishes a tribute of not less than a million sterling to subjects of Great Britain. But the real length of the West India voyage, it may be alleged, is less than one half that of the Indian voyage. If this be the case, we reply, that the length of the voyage to Australia, where a bank has been chartered by the crown, is at least one-fifth part more than the East Indian, and that the principal direction of that bank, of which the shares are at present at a premium, is also in London.

A bank conducted on the principles which we have laid down will, we are convinced, if duly followed up by others of the same nature, prove the commencement of a system which will tend to improve the agricultural and commercial resources of India, and the condition of its inhabitants, as well as facilitate the operations of the merchant, and the fiscal transactions of the government.

We shall conclude by a few remarks on the advantages which may be expected from the formation of banking establishments in India, upon the principles which we have attempted to lay

---

* Tables of the Revenue, etc. of the United Kingdom; Supplement: Colonies, 1835.

† Colonial expenditure, and colonial revenues; ordered by the House of Commons to be printed, 1836.

down. Bankers in India, like those in this country, will soon acquire such an insight into the operations of merchants, traders, agriculturists, and manufacturers, by means of their dealings in the money-market, as, in case of insolvency again occurring, will enable them to bring the parties to a stand in due time, and preclude the possibility of such results as astonished the public on the occasion of the recent failures in India.

To the public servants of the government, no less than to the rest of the Indian community, the establishment of banks, where bills on England may be bought and sold with equal readiness and certainty, will be of the greatest convenience. The facility which an extensive money-market would afford to exchange operations in general would create a competition between bankers, agents, and merchants, which would insure to the public the advantage of buying and selling bills, on the most reasonable terms, while it gave a stability to the exchange, which would enable speculators to calculate with more certainty the probable result of their adventures.

Instead of having, as now, only the combined banking, agency, and commercial establishments to apply to, and with whose bills, on this country, drawn at an arbitrary exchange, remitters (although aware that, in most cases, their payment depends on the result of speculations over the property of which the establishments in question are in a position to refuse a lien) must be satisfied, or have no bills at all, they will be able to stipulate for, and obtain, adequate security, as well as a fair rate of exchange. Such a state of things cannot fail to check reckless speculation at the risk of bill-holders.

In such a state of affairs, capitalists in England would see the necessity of restricting within prudent limits speculations in the hazard of which they were compelled to bear a share, and instead of employing the Indian establishments, as is now too generally done, as mere jackalls, interposed between themselves and all risk, it would be their interest to become partners in all such speculations, that they might participate in profits, as well as risks.

The commerce of India would thus be carried on by solid and

substantial capitalists, able to bear a loss should it occur, and, therefore, entitled to the full profit of their adventures; while an open competition in the bill market would ensure to the Indian public a safe and certain means of remittance to this country, which would effectually deprive agents of the too frequent excuse that no bills on England were procurable for retaining the funds of constituents, or for employing them on their own account, in speculations to this country, the risk of which is principally borne by the parties whose property is so invested. This is, surely, a risk which no one aware of the fluctuations to which colonial produce is subject in the English market can say is inconsiderable.

Such banking establishments as we have described would also induce men of enterprise, with moderate capital, to embark with spirit in agricultural and manufacturing operations. They would, then, have no difficulty in obtaining, when required, the acceptance of responsible friends to bills, which, discounted at the bank, would give what farther temporary aid might be necessary, on moderate terms; and what is of still more vital importance, unclogged by those conditions, which, at present, besides subjecting them to enormous charges, deprive them of all direct control over the disposal of their own produce.

When the produce of India can, by the means we have pointed out, be brought unreservedly forward into the markets, for open sale, those local establishments which may still continue to speculate in export products, whether as principals or agents, will have to enter into free and fair competition with speculators from abroad, and thus there will be ensured, for the best qualities of produce, the highest prices.

The agriculturist or manufacturer will then readily sell on the spot, and, abandoning all idea of speculating to foreign markets, by which he has seldom or ever benefited, will devote his whole attention and energies to improving the quality, and extending the quantity of his products. In cotton, wool, raw silk, coffee, corn, and oleaginous plants, and a variety of other productions, we may then expect to see the same improvement in quantity and quality which, in our own times, has taken place in indigo and lac dye.

In such a state of affairs, speculators from abroad would take care to come provided with such credits as would ensure the ready negotiation of their bills; and they would thus be in a condition to enter the market with cash, and in fair competition with those joint, banking, commercial, and agency establishments, into whose hands they are, in the present state of things, under the necessity of resigning themselves, although fully sensible of the undue influence such establishments have the power of exercising over the prices of produce, as well as the rates of exchange.

The relief which European banking establishments will afford, through advances, and the agency of paper money to the Indian landholder and occupant, must be so obvious, after what we have already said of their condition, that it would be quite superfluous to insist further upon it. Suffice it to say that a legitimate interest would be substituted for an usurious one; and, as far as the remedy could be applied, the party relieved from heavy interest, dependence, and extortion.

Until Europeans, possessed of capital, settle largely in the interior, as agriculturists, and interpose between the rapacity of Indian money-lenders and the unfortunate cultivators, but little improvement can be expected, either in the extension of cultivation, or in the improvement of the quality of the products of the soil; for it is in vain to expect that the cultivator will make extraordinary efforts, when aware that he can reap no advantage from the fruits of his industry, beyond a bare subsistence.

The better to explain to the merchants and manufacturers of this country, and to the Indian community, the risk they may incur as bill-holders in the present state of affairs, we shall suppose a case in illustration. A wealthy establishment in this country has advanced to its dependent establishment in India £50,000, and has since transmitted to it, through various channels, and for the purposes already mentioned, another £50,000, in all, say ten lacs of rupees, or £100,000. Of that sum, the Indian establishment lays out one lac, or £10,000, in offices, warehouses, dead stock, etc.; and, to secure the agency of indigo planters, it becomes joint proprietor in factories, to the amount of five lacs, or £50,000. The remaining four lacs, or £40,000, with, say, six lacs, or £60,000, more, which it has raised in discounts from banks, in temporary loans obtained by its native brokers from Indian bankers, and in sums received from up-country constituents, for remittance to this country, making, in all, ten lacs, or £100,000, are advanced to the indigo planters. The season happens to turn out favourable for indigo – always a most precarious crop – the drug arrives in Calcutta, and from the demands, occasioned by the high prices in Europe, it is worth fifteen lacs, or £150,000, at which price it is taken over by the Indian establishments, and shipped, on their own account, to their friends in this country, on whom they value to the amount of, say eight lacs, or £80,000, £50,000 of which go to pay the balance of the indigo, the remaining £30,000, together with the usual remittances from their friends at home, and other sums which they may be able to raise, being reserved for the necessary advances of the ensuing year.

By the time the shipments and bills reach England, however, prices have so seriously declined that the home establishment, prudently consulting its own interest, receives the consignment, but declines to accept the bills. The indigo is speedily sold, and realizes only £95,000, leaving the Indian establishment £5,000 in debt, on the previous account, besides a sum of, perhaps, £30,000, for consignments, and other funds, transmitted to them during the current year.

As soon as the non-acceptance of the bills becomes known in India, the creditors of the Indian establishment take alarm, and press upon them. To meet demands, the consignments from Europe, then on hand, are realized for cash, without reference to the state of the market: discounts at the banks are falling due, and having no hopes of obtaining a renewal, and desirous to maintain their credit, in the hope that assistance from their friends at home may be the means of enabling them to retrieve themselves, they have recourse to the shroffs, or Indian money-lenders, through their native brokers, and obtain money, at an enormous sacrifice, their outstanding obligations being already at a discount of 25 per cent in the bazar. For the money thus raised, they pledge, or mortgage, their claims on the indigo planters for advances, giving claims amounting to ten lacs as security, perhaps for four lacs, of which only three, probably, would be paid them in cash. By the time the six months' sight, at which the bills are drawn, have expired, and the protests for non-payment reach Calcutta, all the money raised at such sacrifices will have been paid away, and should the indigo season have proved a bad one, and the planters unable to repay their advances, there will be no funds left to meet the payment of the bills, and the house will be obliged to stop payment.

When the schedule is filed in the insolvent court, it may be discovered that all the fixed property of the concern, viz. warehouses, indigo factories, etc. are mortgaged to the house in England, and that all that is left to the unfortunate bill-holders will depend on the realization of some doubtful balances, due to the concern, and on whatever the fixed property, and advances to indigo planters, may realize, over and above the amount for which they were mortgaged, an amount which, under such circumstances, cannot be great. In fact, it may turn out that the bill-holders may not even get 5 per cent on their claims in five years.

If it be supposed that we have drawn an overcharged representation, all we can say is that such things have occurred, and that with the self-same elements at work, under still more disadvantageous circumstances, they are not unlikely to occur again.

In conclusion, we shall only observe that the moment for investing British capital in India is the most propitious which has ever existed in this country. British supremacy is incontestably established, from one extremity of Hindostan to another: internal peace has been established for near twenty years: peace has been established with every European nation for a still longer period: political and commercial relations have been established with all the neighbouring countries: the monopoly which had oppressed the commerce of the Indies for more than two centuries, has totally ceased: the government of India is popularized, and rendered rational, by being restrained to the legitimate functions of administration: the overgrown and pampered local commercial establishments, which sprung up under the obsolete system of restrictions, have ceased to exist; while their place has not yet been filled up by any institutions constituted on principles entitling them to enjoy the unqualified confidence of the public.*

* The American merchants seem to take a more liberal view than our Indian ones of the benefits arising from the influx of British capital. A spirited journalist speaking for them, thus expresses himself: 'We need British capital – our internal improvements demand it – our enterprise will suffer without it. Every dollar laid out upon our rivers, or in canals or railroads, is, as it were, sowing our land broad-cast with gold.'

Index

Index

Exchange: foreign, 10–11; operations, 198; rate of, 39, 41, 65, 67, 91, 92, 93, 151, 289
Exports, corrected value of, 57; production for, 3
Export of capital, 11

Fergusson & Co., 20, n. 2, 22
Finance, imperial, 91
Fiscal policy, British, 2
Forbes, Sir Charles, 297 n.
Foreign trade: fluctuation in, 24; growth of, 25
France, 76, 89, 299
Free trade, 23
Furnivall, J. S., 3 n. 3

Gibraltar, 77
Glasgow, 292
Gold, 168, 170, 174: coinage of, 92; currency, 196; export to India, 175, 177; *Mohur*, 151, 178
Goldsmiths' Library, University of London, 8, 15
Grant, Charles, 3, 28
Great Indian Peninsular Company, 172
Greenberg, M., 5 n. 1, 19

Habib, Irfan, 4 n. 2
Hindus, character of, 225
Holland, 299
Home charges, 35, 38, 282
Hoondee [Hundi], 291
Hypothecation, 38

Imports, 1, 3, 8
India, 9, 11–15, 24, 30, 34, 36
Indigo, 22–4, 26, 31–2, 70–1, 151: planters, 62; manufacture of, 248
Indonesia, 31
Industrial growth in India, 24, 231
Industrial Revolution, 19
Interest: on Indian debt, 59; rate of in India, 259, 296–8
Investments, the East India Company's, 98

Java, 15, 82–3, 148–9, 246, 248, 265
Jenks, L. H., 1 n. 3, 2 n. 3
Johnstone, J. H., 270 n.
Joint stock bank, 29

Kelly, Patrick, 257–8

Land policy, British, 1
Larpent, George, 14, 28, 38
Lima, 93
Loans, Indian, 67
London, 12, 21, 24, 29, 55

Mackenzie, Holt, 17
Mackillop & Co., 11, 40
McIntosh & Co., 22
Madeira, 77
Madras, 8, 82, 86
Maitland, James (Lord Lauderdale), 91
Malabar, 72, 82, 102
Malayan Archipelago, 38
Maldive Islands, 82
Malta, 77
Malthus, Richard, 10, 43
Multilateral trade, 36
Malwa, 32
Managing Agency System, 24
Manila, 83, 246
Mauritius, 31, 72, 149
McCulloch, J. H., 271 n.
Mexico, 80–3, 87, 92–3, 175
Military establishment: in Bengal, 61; in Bombay and Madras, 63
Mill, James, 10, 300
Mill, John Stuart, 12–13, 43–4
Money: quantity theory of, 14; quantity of, 271; paper, 292
Money market, 22, 38
Munro, Sir Thomas, 260
Mysore, 265

Nadir Shah, 265
Napoleonic wars, 12
New South Wales, 31, 85, 149

Oil seeds, 26
Opium, 16, 26, 31, 32–3, 82, 84–5, 101, 147, 152, 206–7, 208–11, 250–1

Palmer, John Horsley, 1, 6, 11–14, 29, 35, 45, 190
Palmer & Co., 7, 21, 23, 27
Patna, 292
Pegu, 83
Penang, 15, 18, 31, 63, 72, 83, 148
Pepper, 73, 208
Persian Gulf, 31, 38, 72, 81
Philippine Islands, 83, 247–8
Piece goods, cotton, 26, 34, 81, 86
Political Economy Club, 10

318

Index